# REFORMING ECONOMICS

Calvinist Studies on Methods and Institutions

Edited by
John P. Tiemstra

W. Fred Graham
Gerge N. Monsma, Jr.
Carl J. Sinke
Alan Storkey

With a Contribution by
Daniel M. Ebels

Toronto Studies in Theology
Volume 48

The Edwin Mellen Press
Lewiston/Queenston/Lampeter

**Library of Congress Cataloging-in-Publication Data**

This volume has been registered with The Library of Congress.

This is volume 48 in the continuing series
Toronto Studies in Theology
Volume 48 ISBN 0-88946-924-5
TST Series ISBN 0-88946-975-X

By the Fellows of the Calvin Center for Christian Scholarship, Calvin
College, John P. Tiemstra (editor), W. Fred Graham, George N. Monsma,
Jr., Carl J. Sinke, and Alan Storkey, with a contribution by Daniel M.
Ebels.

A CIP catalog record for this book
is available from the British Library.

The Edwin Mellen Press
Box 450
Lewiston, New York
USA  14092

The Edwin Mellen Press
Box 67
Queenston, Ontario
CANADA  L0S 1L0

Edwin Mellen Press, Ltd
Lampeter, Dyfed, Wales,
UNITED KINGDOM  SA48 7DY

Printed in the United States of America

# REFORMING ECONOMICS
Calvinist Studies on Methods and Institutions

# Table of Contents

# Preface

During the month of August in the year 1978 there was held on the campus of Calvin College in Grand Rapids, Michigan, the Second International Conference of Institutions for Christian Higher Education. The general topic of the conference was Justice in the International Economic Order. One of the resolutions adopted at this Conference asked that the Calvin Center for Christian Scholarship initiate and organize a study of economic theory and practice, based upon a proposal drafted by several of the conferees. That proposal was redrafted, submitted to the Calvin College Faculty, was approved, and subsequently became the topic of study for the Calvin Center for Christian Scholarship during the 1980-81 academic year.

The proposal called for focusing on aspects of economic theory which are important for economic practice, the utilization of talents of Christian scholars from a variety of disciplines to deal with the interdisciplinary nature of the problem, the coordination of the work of the Center fellows with that of those throughout the world who are willing and able to contribute to the project, and the provision of a starting point for future work to be taken up by other individuals and possibly by other institutions. The present volume constitutes the major part of the response of the Calvin Center to this proposal.

In the first part of this work we undertake a critical analysis of much of current academic economics. Chapter I considers the failure of economics to address many current economic problems. Chapter II takes up the internal failures of current economic theory. Chapter III is a discussion of the problems with the scientific methodology which is the foundation on which contemporary economists build their work.

The next three chapters provide the methodological foundation for our own view of economics. Chapter IV is devoted to the application of a Christian scientific methodology to economics. Biblical priorities for economic science and economic life are the subject of Chapter V. Chapter VI concerns our view of the nature of human economic interactions.

With these critical and foundational issues in place, we turn to our own approach to economic analysis and policy. The institutions of human society are our units of analysis, so in Chapters VII through XIV we take up in turn families, firms, unions, governments, and voluntary organizations. Chapter XV explores international economic relations, particularly between rich and poor countries. Chapter XVI offers a conclusion and a challenge. Readers who seek an elaborate, mathematically developed alternative theory will be dis- appointed, as will those who expect the discussion to be confined to the questions that economists have traditionally considered to be their terrain. What we propose instead is a new approach to economics, one that is explicitly normative and based on the concept of stewardship. We will raise questions that are new to the discipline, and we will suggest novel ways of researching the answers to them. We will also continually contrast our approach to the traditional one.

It should be clear that this book presumes that the reader has a familiarity with conventional economic thought. A traditional two semester, college sophomore introductory course should be sufficient background for most of the book. It might be a useful exercise to read this book alongside a conventional college level introductory textbook, particularly if one's economics training seems to be quite distant. The lay reader with a skimpy economics background can omit Chapters II and III and still profit from reading the rest of the work.

Some exposure of the major elements of our work to others has already occurred in a series of seminars for the faculty at Calvin College, and in a two day conference at the Institute for Christian Studies at Toronto. We acknowledge with gratitude the many helpful and insightful comments made by our colleagues at these sessions. These have shaped and improved our work in significant ways. At least some discussion of the work at an international level has occurred not only with the conferees at the Toronto conference but also in a more intensive way with Professor Bob Goudzwaard and Professor J. G. Knol, both of the Vrije Universiteit at Amsterdam. We are particularly grateful for their detailed reviews of our work and the many suggestions, both general and detailed, which they made.

We note with thanks the work of our two student fellows, Albertus Pereboom and Dean Rietberg, both seniors in economics at Calvin College, who participated in the project through attendance at many of our discussion sessions and by pursuit of independent study projects. Our colleague Daniel Ebels, then a member of the Calvin College Economics faculty, was a part-time participant in the project, and contributed the chapter on macroeconomics and government, and we thank him for his work. Likewise we appreciated the helpful comments of Eugene Dykema and the other members of the Economics faculty at Calvin. Max De Pree, Thomas Kamp, and Wendell Primus, from the worlds of business and government, stimulated our thinking with helpful comments and criticisms. Prof. Arnold McKee directed our attention to important areas of Catholic Social thought, and Prof. Steve Van Der Weele made helpful editorial suggestions. We acknowledge also the faithful and diligent work of our secretaries, Nelle Tjapkes, Connie Lehr, Bess Exoo, and Katie Miller who so ably transformed rough, often handwritten materials into crisp, clean typewritten copy.

Finally, we express our thanks to the Governing Board of the Calvin Center for giving us the opportunity of doing the work and to the Board of Trustees of Calvin College and Seminary for providing the support, financial and otherwise, which the project required. Especially we thank those members of the constituency of the college whose significant financial contributions make the continued work of the Calvin Center possible. We hope the results of our work serve to initiate a continuing and fruitful research effort within the Christian academic community, and encourage all of us to consider more carefully how we ought to live. Praise God from whom all blessings flow!

W. Fred Graham, Religion, Michigan State University
George Monsma, Economics, Calvin College
Carl Sinke, Mathematics, Calvin College (Coordinator)
Alan Storkey, Economics, Oak Hill College, England
John P.Tiemstra, Economics, Calvin College

# Chapter I
# Taking Stock

*Life is a toil, and love is a trouble,*
*Beauty will fade, and riches will flee.*
*Pleasures they dwindle, and prices they double,*
*And nothing is as I would wish it to be.*
*American folk song (19th c.)*

## Introduction

During the 1950's and 1960's economic progress seemed secure: the mixed free enterprise economy worked, and material success was the normal lot of a high proportion of families. Economists were primarily concerned with a form of macroeconomic manipulation like that needed to keep an automobile in good shape. The machine was pleasantly erratic and grew in complexity, but there seemed no problem which a competent mechanic could not handle, and on the whole the population accepted the expertise of the professionals.

However, in the 1970's and early 1980's weaknesses became evident in the normal pattern of economic advance. Deep-seated problems like inflation, unemployment, and trade deficits did not respond to the regular tinkering. There were even years when the standard of living fell. Various social groups became economically disaffected, and the economic supremacy of the United States, taken for granted throughout the century, was strongly challenged by Europe and Japan. In this situation, jokes about economists began to appear. To blame economists for a period of recession is, of course, simplistic. Nevertheless, a far more searching examination of economic theory is taking place in this post-euphoric age.

Is this perception of "malaise" in economic theory misplaced? Many economists would argue that inflation, recession, unemployment, and other problems involve the kind of technical adjustments and constraints which are all well charted by economic science. In the rest of this chapter we shall suggest that a wide range of important issues have outrun the scope of conventional economic analysis, a development which makes this conclusion unduly optimistic. Moreover, there is now a variety of distinct positions in the discipline, so that in the early 1980's, both in Britain and the United States, the official economic policies of monetarism and supply-side economics were at odds with mainstream economic theory; the profession is now engaged in a process of reflection which goes deeper than technical adjustment.

It is not only economists who need to reflect. The issues that are now emerging relate closely to the meaning of people's economic lives. Some experience results which are destructive—personally, socially and ecologically—in ways that the decision-makers and theorists do not take into account. Some know areas of economic defeat, emptiness, impotence, compromise, and degeneration in their lives. Many of us live comfortably partly by passing on the unpleasant consequences of the way we live to others; but grave poverty, among our fellow citizens and abroad, is pushed beyond the perimeters of our minds. People over-consume and bemoan the fact that they are overweight and short of cash. Many feel like economic pawns who, nevertheless, are pushing other people around. The very pressures of the economic system prevent us from stopping to consider our economic direction. We hope that this book will challenge many with practical and immediate tasks to stop and analyze the significance of what we all do for a living.

In this chapter we shall look at some of the issues and developments which do not fit neatly in conventional theory. All of them are important and provide a context for the later theoretical debate. They will move from global to personal considerations.

## Global Issues

### Natural Resources

Assessments of the energy crisis vary. One view is that it was an unusual market hiccup created by a sudden appropriation of monopoly power by the OPEC countries. However, the rate of use of energy and other resources, although sometimes slowing in growth, is still rising to levels which bring the life expectancy of known resources within the century or even down to a few decades. During the last quarter century world energy use has roughly quadrupled. Obviously, the energy being used up is that with lowest extractive costs, so that later resources will tend to be more expensive and require more energy to extract. Growing populations, patterns of urbanization and mechanization, and the post-1973 significance of monopolized energy reserves make another oil crisis quite likely before the end of the century.

Nor is the operation of the oil market straightforward. Since many of the giant oil companies are integrated producers, refiners, and retailers of the commodity, most of the market processes take place *within* these companies and involve a particular corporate strategy. Few economists have been able to untangle this situation. Further, major owners of oil supplies now supply not just on the basis of current prices, but also on the estimation of *future* price levels, creating a long-term extractive scenario considerably more complex than standard market theory. Finally we are forced to recognize that oil is defended (or is it?) by $20 billion or more of arms which do not enter the normal patterns of costing. [Stockhom International Peace Research Institute, 1974] This situation is thus much more complex than standard economic analysis would allow.

Nations have also developed long-term energy policies which have a unique direction. Some, like France, have become heavily committed to nuclear energy, with policies involving research and development programmes, possible accidents, radioactive waste disposal, and the selling of plants to other countries. The United States has a consumer-centered approach whereby for as long as possible, the lifestyle of the average American will be protected from world shortages. This policy has dangers. The statement by former President Carter that the United States would go to war to defend its economic interests in the Middle East was a political extension of this policy. Other supplies, like chromium from Southern Africa, tin from the Far East, and cobalt from Central Africa, could also presumably arouse military interest. [Mikdashi, 1976, p. 84] The assertion of national economic power, started by Nasser in 1956, is still working its way through the world, and this development, combined with expanding national consumption requirements, is likely to be one of the sources of war in the coming decades.

The ethos of appropriating and egocentrically using resources is in the end related to consumer gratification. The scale and nature of the appropriation of resources has sometimes led to worldwide ecological deterioration. The Sahara may be moving South for natural reasons, but it may be man-induced. Climatic changes, radiation, air pollution and sea pollution have all become normal unpriced exports. Fishing for whales or for krill, sea mining and using the upper atmosphere have all been avidly pursued. It is clear that these effects on the environment need to be brought within the scope of economic responsibility, and yet, because most of them are unpriced, economic science is at present not well-equipped to do so. [Friends of the Earth, 1977, Wilkinson, 1980]

**The Rich-Poor Divide**

The most dramatic division in the world lies between the rich nations, the populations of which have largely stabilized, to the extent that many countries in Europe have fallen below the replacement level, and the poor ones. In Asia, Africa, and Central and South America, population growth rates of 1-2% per annum are common, giving heavy momentum to the population increase well into the 21st century. Employment is required for about a billion people within the next twenty-five years, and Third World cities approaching 20 million persons are likely this century. Many of these countries can scarcely keep much of this extra population in subsistence.

This contrast is highlighted by the relationship between the United States and Mexico. Mexico has a population only one-third that of the States, but in the late 70's Mexican mothers were having two-thirds as many children. Its present population of 64 million will double in a little over 20 years. The contrast is between a rich relatively empty country and a poor teeming one. A symptom is illegal immigration; a high proportion of the estimated six to ten million illegal immigrants to the United States are Mexican and they provide an alternative tier labour force which is readily assimilated into the American work force on these non-citizen and low-overhead terms. [Bouvies, 1977, 28-29] A similar pattern has existed in Europe where Greece, Italy, Spain, Portugal, Yugoslavia, and Algeria have provided millions of workers for Northern Europe. Thus, a permanent lower tier of second class citizens seems to be normal in the West.

The drama of this division, and the West's response to it, demand attention. As the proportion of world population found in North America, East and West Europe, Russia, Japan, Australia, and New Zealand falls from just over one-fourth in 1975 to under one-fifth by the year 2000, tensions will grow. [U. S. Census, 1977] The emptiness of the Russian side of the Sino-Russian border will become more obvious. The economic pressure on other developing countries will become more acute. Some, not necessarily the poorest, will find it difficult not to default on their debts as the interest burden grows to half or more of their exports. Brazil, Pakistan, Turkey, Poland, Nigeria, Zaire, Mexico, and Peru are among the countries which are in a precarious position, and whose position is closely bound up with Western banks.

The response of the West has already been too late and perhaps very shortsighted. The Third World has needed investment, trade, and commitment, and has been the demographically dynamic part of the world economy. Help has, however, been limited, has been centered on Western strategies, and has often been in the form of arms. Already, instead of being the exporter of capital, which should have been the normal role of the West, it has become the importer of Third World debt service—not a happy role. The depth of the Third World problems is evident from their energy position. A World Bank study forecasts a rise in energy demand of 6% a year for less developed countries, where already two billion people depend on wood, dung, and charcoal to cook their meals in the face of shrinking supplies. [World Bank, 1980] The import of expensive fuels will therefore help push many more countries into a state of chronic debt. As the Brandt Report made clear, a choice needs to be made which is far more significant than the provision of Marshall Aid after World War II, but which has the same character. Is the rich North going to give substantial, unrequited aid for world development based on an integrated assessment of global needs? Again, the vision which this question requires goes far beyond the scope of much conventional study.

## The Transnational Economy

Although economic textbooks still contain chapters on international trade, this is only part of the modern transnational economy. It is not only goods and services which are transmitted but also finance, capital, economic culture, technology, plants, and managerial skills. Multinationals not only manufacture *in* a variety of countries but also *across* countries. They number over forty of the world's largest one-hundred economic entities, and the largest match the G.N.P. of Sweden, South Africa or Belgium in their sales. [Zenoff, 1978, p. 45] These companies now have world strategies, and what goes on inside them is more significant than many national policies. Yet, again, conventional economics, because of the categories it uses, is unable to face many of the issues raised by these giants.

Consider their role in relation to developing countries. Although many of them operate in Third World countries, the transfer of capital has been relatively limited; much multinational capital is raised in the host country. A United Nations study of Latin America showed that from 1960 to 1968 American corporations contributed only 17% of their total capital expenditure while they took 79% of their net profits out of the area. Often six or even ten dollars have been flowing out of the Third World country for every dollar coming in. [Heneres, 1978, pp. 112-118] It is also commonly the case that transfer prices (on goods traded from one country to another within a corporation) have been low for Third World exports and high for imports; thus profits have often been located wherever the multinational wants to put them. Clearly, a key issue here is whether the multinationals are being fair to their host countries. Often the answer will be sadly, and even sordidly, no, and yet conventional economics is not able to address this issue.

The development of transnational finance has also rendered the old view of a national monetary economy partially obsolete. The home currency transactions system, where only the dollar or the pound is legal tender, is necessarily related to a large international transactions system where there is an open, but discretionary, system of acceptability among international companies and banks. The dominance of the dollar in the system since 1970 has partly been caused by the U.S. energy position, but the result has been a ten-fold expansion in world liquidity. World money has no lender of last resort, no system of fractional banking control, and the seigniorage which has accrued to the printers of the dollar and the creators of Eurodollar credit has been considerable. [Howley, 1979, Grubel, 1969] Obviously this situation has contributed considerably to world inflation, but economists are unable to document this world of electronic transfers and hidden accounts in anything but an impressionistic way, and the precise effects are not clear.

However, despite the size and power of multinational corporations and banks, they are also vulnerable to basic changes in the status of their products and to the increasing lumpiness of competition. Moreover, in this situation, loss of national employment and production is so great and has such a severe impact that national governments will do all they can to support not just ailing giants, but also thriving ones. Thus government/multinational mutual support patterns are likely to grow. The corporate state of the Fascist thirties was roundly condemned, but it is firmly with us again. [Miller, 1976, Hannah, 1976, Griffioen, 1981]

## National Issues

### Government Economic Power

In the quarter century after 1950 economists tended to assume that the government could always put the economy right. In the face of repeated failures by governments to deliver their promises, economists have appreciated more fully the severe constraints under which governments operate. Although various forms of economic magic and utopianism still tend to recur, especially during election time, the era of faith in government to solve economic problems is over, at least until the next generation has to learn the same lesson. The current orthodoxy both in Britain and the U.S. is that only business can generate the dynamic of the economy and that the role of the government is a permissive and enabling one only.

At the same time a second crisis has occurred in the government sector. In many Western countries government economic expenditure has escalated to half or more of Gross Domestic Product. In many areas no way of effective accounting control has been developed. At the same time government finds many of the hidden costs of private economic activity dumped in its lap. In other cases the cost of supporting industry, whether nationalized or private, has been great. Again economics finds itself impotent to face the issue: What is the legitimate scope of government economic activity? In fiscal, welfare, redistributive, monetary, and other ways the subject is agnostically treated by economic science.

### The New Unemployed Class

In Europe, during the late 19th century, the success of the new industrial classes was set against the background of the dwindling and impoverished agricultural classes. Many transferred to the cities and began a new life, and many of them emigrated to the States, Canada, or Australia in search of economic success. Within the industrial sector, the skilled workers and managers who were able to use capital, even if they did not own it, stood apart from the group which had nothing to sell but its unskilled labor. The proletarian masses of Marx were divided and dwindling even while he wrote, and increasingly in Europe and the U.S. the large majority of the population found ways of establishing themselves economically. However, every generation faces the issue anew, and it now seems that a sizeable minority, often of certain ethnic groups, will find themselves evicted from the rewarding market economy for the next generation, unless there are changes.

The result is a two-tier labor force consisting of secure, well-paid, and well-trained workers on the one hand, and low-paid, precarious, and often part-time workers on the other. The power of unions and professions to exclude potential workers is considerable. Further, the development of company loyalty, emphasized by the Japanese, precludes mobility in labor markets. [Richardson and Ueda, 1981] What exists, therefore, is a set of various established economic communities to which workers belong, while others are excluded. The key elements are now education, technical and communication skills, knowledge of organizational structure, and various other personal and locational factors. Learning to be members of these communities usually involves patterns of socialization stretching over twenty years or more. Although they constitute a majority of the workforce, they are a *privileged* majority.

The minority, augmented by the electronic revolution and competing with illegal immigrants, thus represent an unemployment problem that is deeper than a failure of markets to adjust, for it is related to the way the rest of us work and are trained. Involuntary unemployment can no longer be seen as a merely residual category, but is linked to the character of our overall economic structure. Contemporary theory lacks a coherent grasp on this issue.

**The Economics of the Short Term**

World-wide variations in the value of money have become normal and quite erratic, as have exchange rate fluctuations. This has created a paradox. While economic science has become obsessed with precision in prediction, it actually seems that the economy has become less predictable. Indeed, monetarism can be seen as a cry to make the economy more predictable again. Planning for the future, the longer term, loses precision. Economists, therefore, shorten time horizons so the future gets neglected; because the horizons are fogged, we live with our eyes focused downward on the immediate. Meanwhile, in the economy people divide into fools and experts; the experts profit by changes in the value of money, and the fools lose. Moreover, when the level of inflation is of the order of 10%, holding assets which retain their value in inflation tend to become more significant than the productivity of the assets. Imperceptibly the economy begins to lose a productive dynamic and to develop a survival of wealth technique. Financial institutions housed in clinical inner city buildings begin to stab the skyline in abundance as productive units decay. Assets which financial institutions can handle, like land, property, precious metals, and currencies, experience speculative booms. Prices, responding to all kinds of specific inflationary pressures, become impoverished measures of relative value and reflect built-in rigidities and power struggles.

How do economists view this drama? It could be argued that they respond rather poorly. They insist that the price system is most accurately described through marginal analysis, and they are not able to analyze what the response to these distortions should be because of their anormative approach. There are, clearly, important gaps in the pattern of explanation.

**Economic Rigidities**

Another acute issue which is scarcely yet impinging on the public consciousness concerns the ways in which we are now historically precommitted. Modern industrial economies are burdened with the artifacts of past investment decisions which constrain our present economic choices. For example, the scale on which our cities have become *fixed* into the complexity of modern urban economic integration makes them very difficult to change, and makes any change which needs to take place more and more costly. We have largely moved from the plastic to the concrete. The same is true of our transport systems, location of resources, and patterns of supply. It may be that a city without roads, cars, garages, parking lots, driveways, gas stations, road accidents, traffic, police, and noise would be more efficient, compact, and better, but the physical commitment to roads rule out the possibility. The road system now laid down is not likely to change much in the foreseeable future. Yet often decision-making about *things* is necessarily based on earlier things and leads to a pattern of domino like development. Thus in many ways the modern economy is being presented with a *fait accompli*; paths are chosen that will never cross again. The existence of this transport system or that, of this city plan or that, is definitive for a lot of economic decisions which have not yet been thought of. The growing rate of fixed capital formation makes these situations constantly more rigid; the transfer of agricultural land to urban use is one such largely irreversible process, but there are many more. To take account of these fixed, specific parameters requires approaches which do not accord well with the universal, unconstrained analysis of much economics.

Nor is it just things that create economic rigidities. The post-industrial era is one in which organizational mores have become culturally established. Patterns of filing information within a firm embody certain decision-making processes and automatically rule out many other potential decisions. Can firms which are organized for expansion organize contraction? Can institutions which are autocratically structured become more consultative? Are there decisions which companies cannot make until it is too late, because of their internal cultural patterns? The significance of deeper cultural rationales like the belief in progress has scarcely been faced by economists, yet may probably channel decisions more decisively than many other variables.

### Economic Externalities

It has now become evident that the implications of economic activity extend far beyond the intended consequences of actions. Patterns of consumption, like other economic activities, necessarily involve many other consequences. Thus, to drive a car involves in varying degrees, (1) pollution of the atmosphere, (2) more noise for property adjoining the road (which may involve remedial expenditure or change in property prices), (3) slowing of other traffic (which may lead to changes in traffic systems), (4) wear on the roads, (5) increased danger for other drivers and pedestrians, (6) changes in the air temperature, (7) contribution to the demand for gasoline, and (8) not getting exercise. Only gasoline demand is reflected in price to consumer, and even then the marginal impact of the consumer will not change the price to him. This means that price, the overriding concern of orthodox economics, actually maps only in a very crude and limited way the significance of most economic activities. The exchange price system is merely the tip of the economic iceberg, and moreover, what we see in the price system gives us only a poor idea of what lies under the water.

In large public decisions attempts are made to take this fact into account through cost-benefit analysis, but we are all involved in many unpriced consequences every day of our lives. The necessary conclusion seems to be that, important though the price system is, and better though it can be, the making of correct economic decisions depends on far more than price calculations.

The preoccupation of economics with price theory is thus a serious constraint on the discipline. There are many attempts to extend price analysis to cover a wider set of issues, but it is not yet clear what the correct approach is. There seems to be a whole variety of distinct values in the economic arena which cannot be reduced to one common denominator, price.

## Institutional Issues

### Adversarial firms

After at least half a century of automatic economic success, Americans have been shocked by the fact that they cannot compete successfully with the Japanese, despite the fact that the latter have relatively few natural resources on which to base their industry. Obviously, Japanese culture allows a mutuality and harmony between workers and management which is creative and efficient. Trust and cooperation are normal. The contrast with the adversarial pattern that exists in Britain, the United States, Canada and many other Western countries is obvious. Here the interests of capital and labour often face one another across a negotiated truce, which easily breaks down into noncooperation and strikes. Clearly, the Japanese pattern cannot be transferred to the West because it infringes on many of the freedoms taken for granted here and because the cultural background is so different. This contract raises a challenge to economic theory because the Japanese culture implies a different organizational logic from that of the West; as commentators wrestle with the Japanese mind, they recognize that there is not one ubiquitous logic of economic science, but distinct national solutions. *Economic* cultures are not just of primitive significance but have a deep impact in modern economics.

The place of unions in this adversarial pattern can also be questioned. Are they best understood as maximizing units? Have union-management bargaining patterns contributed to unemployment? Are workers still subject to the use of economic power in an unfair way? The questions which fail to lie down are those of community and justice in industrial relations; yet again economic analysis does not have the categories with which to consider these issues.

### Creeping Economism

Many people feel, with some alarm, that various areas of their lives are becoming dominated by economics. The football game they are watching is primarily a commercial business, they are an economic pawn at work, salesmanship seems to have become mixed up with the Christian faith, and even pornography is driven by the profit motive. Elections, also, seem to mirror the selling of automobiles or toothpaste. Whatever the specific form, the trend is towards the *economizing* of life, as little bits here and there are drawn into the circle of marketed commodities.

Obviously, the decision as to whether a particular activity should or should not be economic cannot be an *economic* decision; it must involve a fuller view of life and of the place of economics within life. Nevertheless, the discipline of economics, because it has established its "autonomy" as a science, is largely unable to address the issue of what should or should not be marketed. Indeed, on the contrary, many economists are happy to endlessly extend their pattern of analysis into other areas. Yet in day-to-day life the encroachments of economism seem unavoidable; they are "happening" incrementally as a result of passivity, greed, and cultural persuasion.

**The Stifling of Economic Enterprise**
At the same time there is a perception that the level of political interference with the private economy has grown to the extent that it is seriously distorting both efficient and fair development. Many companies nestle down within government contracts or patterns of public funding which give them distinct commercial advantages. How can that square with fair competition? Similarly, if environmental regulations surround United States enterprise at every turn, and the real and bureaucratic costs are considerable, then how can American industry compete with unfettered foreign firms? How can fair competition exist when raw material costs vary widely? The underlying question of whether and for what reason there should be interference with enterprises, and if it should occur, in what form, remains unresolved.

But this process is not accidental. If firms seek to maximize their profits, as the normal goal of capitalism requires them to, then they will seek to minimize private costs and transmit as many costs as possible to the wider public. In the face of escalating social costs—congestion, disposal, pollution, and the appropriation of low-cost resources from the community—the obvious government reaction is to regulate. Thus, if we stand back and look at the logic of capitalism, we can see how regulation is the necessary end result. The discipline of economics can try to slide around this problem; its commitments to private costs make it bothersome to consider the wider issues.

## Personal Issues

**Consumption**
At a more personal level many people experience deep disappointment and dissatisfaction with what they purchase and consume. For some it grows out of the feeling of being pushed about by other people's possessions. For others it is repeated dissatisfaction at the unfulfilled promise of various goods and services, the experience of what one economist has called "The Joyless Economy." [Scitovsky, 1976] Others have the problem of getting all of the components together into a lifestyle that makes coherent sense. Many have a sense of emptiness when the picture fades from the colour television or the cigar is stubbed out. Others experience the garishness of the process of selling. It is at least evident that the automatic assumption made by economists that all goods are *good* is problematic.

**Work**
The work that a person does, whether paid or unpaid, is an important component in the meaning of his life. Often one spends a decade or more in prepa-

ration for it. Many experience the frustration of not having any work, others of having too much. Some find that they cannot do the job properly, or that their contribution is not really valuable. Weaknesses of job definition leave many less than fullhearted about the system of work in which they participate; there is tight prepackaging of jobs, defective views of responsibility, dissatisfaction with pay, and excessive demands. At the same time, many are very happy with their work and find in it values which do not normally find expression in textbooks.

**Lifestyle**

A lot of those issues are focused in people's unease with their lifestyle. Some live very comfortably, but wonder if the daily hour-long journey to and from work year after year is really worth it, in the face of the uneasy equilibrium they maintain in their personal and family lives. Some face the oppression of being perpetually surrounded by industrial garbage, but can do no more than kick the empty can further along the street. Some find the economic constraints of the daily routine too tight. Others face frustration from the breakdown of other parts of the economic system, and some just hope that the next programme or the next holiday will be enjoyable. What does it all mean for the discipline of economics?

## Economic Faith

When we stop and think about these problems and about where we are going economically, the issues crowd upon us. One way out is to leave it to the experts, and merely fit in with their conclusions. This, however, is an unsatisfactory response. Most of the experts in this century are walking backwards, observing what we have been and are doing, having repudiated any judgements about what we should be doing. Another reason is that it will eventually lead to either a political or a managerial dictatorship. There is no alternative than for all of us to turn and examine the economic faith by which we live. And here we face a curious vacuum.

Many people do not have a conscious economic faith. They may have some commitment to what they regard as their own self-interest and self-fulfillment, and after that the kind of blind faith that some invisible hand will make everything work out. Very few in the United States are committed to any kind of collective vision like that formed, at least officially, in Russia, Eastern Europe, and China. Yet most people must and do have some wider economic vision, however shadowy: perhaps a belief in economic nationalism, in success through initiative, in the efficacy of competition, in technological progress, in conquering problems, in economic rights, in the fulfillment of pleasure, in the value of hard work and other values. These ideas are important, but they may also have a deeper dimension, a *faith in humanity*—self-fulfillment, self-gratification, human success and human pride—values which deny dependence on and responsibility before God. We may be experiencing the consequences of this humanist faith in some of the problems and frustrations we have just sketched. Those who would like to face this Christian challenge are invited to read on.

However, this concern is not just a matter of economic practice, for theory and practice are closely interwoven. The form of economic life is powerfully shaped by the categories of theoreticians, and most people in business or employment use tools given to them by economists. Furthermore, economists need to be able to absorb issues of economic life if their study is not to become academic in the sterile sense. Thus, the issues covered in this introduction pose a challenge to the discipline of economics. Although there is a great deal of good work being done which faces those challenges with integrity and concern, the discipline is also constrained by its traditional paradigms of analysis which actually prevent many of these issues from being addressed. Even economists who feel they have broken away from these restrictions also have a problem, in that they have lost the coherence of the neoclassical paradigm. Indeed, one of the conclusions drawn from the earlier presentation of issues is that a coherent pattern of analysis is needed, simply because so many of the problems are related. *We suggest that a paradigm shift is needed, to give a different basis of coherence for the discipline.* Economic science has its roots in the secular Enlightenment ideas of individualism, autonomy, and rationalism. Even perspectives which have reacted against this foundation, like the Marxist one, have still perpetuated many of the same patterns of analysis; in many ways Marx was quite an orthodox classical economist. Those roots still shape the development of the science even in reactions to the dominant orthodoxy. A different Christian perspective on econmics has yet to be tried. Such an attempt is the task of this book. Before this, however, we shall discuss problems that occur within the discipline of economics at two levels. The first level concerns contradictions which have accumulated in economic theory. The second involves disagreements among economists about the kind of knowledge they are seeking. Until these problems are explicitly faced, the acute need for different approaches can be ignored as the discipline advances under its own momentum.

# Resources

Bonvier, L. F. 1977. International Migration: Yesterday, Today, and Tomorrow. *Population Bulletin.* 32: 3-42.

Clark, D. , and B. A. Schriever. 1978. *U.S. Arms Sales Abroad: A Policy of Restraint:* Washington: American Enterprise Institute.

*Energy in the Developing Countries.* 1980. Washington: World Bank.

Friends of the Earth. 1977. *Progress as if Survival Mattered.* San Francisco: Friends of the Earth.

Griffioen, S. 1981. *Facing the New Corporatism.* Toronto: Christian Labor Association of Canada.

Grubel, H. G. 1969. The Distribution of Seigniorage from International Liquidity Creation. in Mundell and Swoboda, eds., *Monetary Problems of the International Economy.* Chicago: Univ. of Chicago Press.

Hannah, L. 1976. *The Rise of the Corporate Economy.* Baltimore: Johns Hopkins Univ. Press.

Hawley, J. 1979. The Internationalization of Capital: Banks, Eurocurrency, and the Instability of the World Monetary System, *Review of Radical Political Economy* 11: 78-90.

Henares, H. M. 1978. Multinational Corporations: Bane or Boon? in Skully, ed., *A Multinational Look at the Transnational Corporation.* Sydney: Dryden Press. pp. 112-118.

Mikdashi, A. 1976. *The International Politics of Natural Resources.* Ithaca: Cornell Univ. Press.

Miller, A. S. 1976. *The Modern Corporate State.* Westport, CT: Greenwood Press.

Richardson, B. M., and T. Ueda, eds. 1981. *Business and Society in Japan.* New York: Praeger.

Scitovsky, T. 1976. *The Joyless Economy.* New York: Oxford Univ. Press.

Stockholm International Peace Research Institute. 1971. *The Arms Trade with the Third World.* New York: Humanities Press.

Stockholm International Peace Research Institute. 1974. *Oil and Security.* New York: Humanities Press.

Zenoff, D. 1978. The Future of the Multinational Corporations: The Views of an American Consultant, in Skully, ed., *A Multinational Look at the Transnational Corporation.* Sydney. Dryden Press.

# Chapter II
# Theoretical Disequilibrium

*So how can you tell me that you're lonely,*
*And say for you that the sun don't shine?*
*Let me take you by the hand and lead you*
  *through the streets of London,*
*I can show you something that may make you*
  *change your mind.*
          Ralph McTell (c. 1965)


## Introduction

In recent decades economic theory has burgeoned into a great productive industry. It has grown from a manageable body of knowledge to a size where one branch of the discipline produces more literature than the whole did thirty years earlier. Moreover, the sophistication of analysis has vastly increased, as have the available tools of computation. It seems that economics has reached maturity. Yet there is unease in the profession, the kind of unease a motorist on a highway feels when his destination slips by and he cannot turn off; the theory does not drive up to the situation. At other times it is unease at the contradictions between theorists, or from the fact that the contradictions cannot be resolved. It is not just that the reflected glory of growth and prosperity in the 1950's and 1960's has given way to a reflected professional pallor in the 1980's; there are some deep problems in the discipline. In this chapter we shall set out some of the key ones.

The perception of what is wrong varies. Economists in the neoclassical tradition see the situation as merely requiring modification of existing theoretical tools. Others are looking for new theoretical paradigms, and yet others want a change in the kind of knowledge which economists should seek. (This latter issue we shall examine in the third chapter.) In this chapter, in an attempt to assess the problems, we shall probe a range of major theoretical issues which divide the discipline. As the title of the chapter suggests, we think that those who see the discipline as floating out into ever calmer water are ignoring developments which signal rough weather ahead.

Although the vantage point from which these theoretical issues are analyzed and dissected cannot be neutral, we are surveying problems which have been widely recognized and discussed throughout the discipline. In this chapter we begin our diagnosis partly to give the reader some inklings of where the subsequent analysis will go.

## Macro and Microeconomics

Hundreds of economics texts are neatly divided into sections on macroeconomics and microeconomics; one part deals with the whole and the other with bits of the economy. If we ask whether those two sections of the discipline are complementary, we often face the problem that both are *alternative* explanations of the same behaviour, and that if the conclusions are different, they cannot both be right. The founder of modern macroeconomics recognized this. John Maynard Keynes knew when he wrote *The General Theory of Employment, Interest and Money* in the early 1930's that he was leading a revolution. Classical economics assumed that the analysis developed for specific markets could be generalized into a model of the whole economy. Keynes, however, repudiated merely sewing together the old bits into a "general" analysis, but created an *alternative* general theoretical framework to the classical, with different views of economic motives, behaviour, relationships, and categories. He saw the old classical theory as concentrating on a rather artificial case in which full employment was automatic, an unusual special case in his general theory. The alternative theoretical approaches were *exclusive*, although Keynes' microeconomics and classical macroeconomics were relatively undeveloped.

Let us therefore stop for a while to consider how the different vantage points both address the same economic activities and come to divergent conclusions. Contrary to the classical assumption that "rational" decisions lead to rational results, Keynes posited situations where the aggregate results could confound the initial logic of the decisions; people can actually save less than they intend. Another basic classical assumption was of the *independence* of supply and demand; indeed without this independence it is no longer possible to deduce the particular type of equilibrium which is fundamental to the classical tradition. However, *The General Theory* and subsequent macro analysis imply that the two are closely *interdependent*. Thus, Keynes argues that in all but the shortest term, higher levels of demand stimulate confidence, business expectations, and output. Conversely, that higher levels of supply, requiring expenditure on stocks, work in progress, equipment and labour stimulate income and demand, albeit only indirectly, for that commodity. Nevertheless, since the time of Keynes those contradictions have sat happily side by side in hundreds of textbooks, insulated by the macro/micro distinction. Let us briefly consider the possibilities that exist for solving this dilemma. The first is that the classical microeconomic perspective could be elaborated into a neoclassical macro perspective; indeed, this is what has happened, beginning with Hicks' 1937 article "Mr. Keynes and the Classics: A Suggested Reinterpretation." This elaboration, which for more than two decades was disguised under the label "Keynesian," was in reality an alternative neoclassical macroeconomic framework which allowed the classical microeconomic analysis to be incorporated without change. It was achieved by positing equilibria in the money market and the level of income determination, and ignoring the glaring inconsistencies already noted. From the late 60's onwards, this position began to collapse under two developments, one practical and one theoretical. The practical one was that many economies of the West faced obvious and serious depressions which belied the optimistic neoclassical assumptions; the theoretical one was a series of inconsistencies that came to light within these formulations. [See Hicks, 1980] In recent years the collapse of neoclassical "Keynesian" macro theory has been rapid. Here is Weintraub's assessment:

> With Hicks' admission of the theoretical inadequacy of the IS-LM model, and with the shortcomings of Keynesian inflation policy, it is an understatement to describe Hicksian Keynesianism as being in a state of disrepair; its inflation slip is showing. We have traced the several strands. In each stance new straws were grasped, each creating a new brand of Keynesians. Within a 15 year span, the parade marched first to the 45 degree banner, then to the IS-LM flag; it stepped to Phillips curve tunes, waltzed to shifting Phillips curve notes, sang 'Ignore inflation' songs and murmured Indexation chants. Still an illusion exists in textbooks that all is coherent; 'scientific' and successful. Nonetheless only few believe that Keynesianism is the assured, unassailable, formidable system that dominated the 1950's. [S. Weintraub, 1977]

Thus we have witnessed the substantial collapse of this attempt at integrating classical micro and macroeconomic theory.

However, this is not just a tale told merely for the telling; we note that the position has had important policy consequences. In the 50's and 60's the IS-LM analysis led to the money supply being taken as *given*, so that the rate of interest was deemed to be determined by the money supply and aggregate demand factors. The relationship between the government's fiscal policy and its monetary responses were sublimated in this particular equilibrium formulation. The resultant policies contributed to inflation and led to the monetarist reaction.

A second possible response is to reinterpret microeconomic theory in the light of Keynes' perspective. This has been done with increasing momentum during the last two decades by Clower, Leijonhufvud, Phelps, and others. These models fed back assumptions from Keynes-based macroeconomics, like sticky wages and prices, various forms of search and involuntary employment, quantity fluctuations, uncertainty, and trading at false prices, into microeconomic theory. Undoubtedly this has been the source of some obviously more realistic views of employment, the firm, and consumption, but this approach, too, has potential weaknesses.

One arises from the dependence of macrobehaviour on micromotives. Although the process of aggregating the motives of individuals is one which uncovers a lot of interesting phenomena, the uniformity of the process tends to ignore some important elements of that behaviour. [Schelling, 1978] The first is that various levels of institutional behaviour have their own rationales, systems of economic rules, and coherence of meanings which the pattern of aggregating identical unit behaviour tends to miss. The second is that groups and institutions are much more heterogeneous in their goals and values than the aggregative macroeconomic approach suggests. The third, which we cannot develop fully until the next chapter, is that Keynes-based macroeconomics does not easily take into account the possibility of conscious reflection of economic agents on their situation in the larger economic arena. When economic information abounds and conscious national steering is normal, micromotives are a peculiarly blind level of analysis. If neither of these attempts to resolve the contradiction is working, it suggests that a third alternative framework is needed which avoids the rational generalizations of neoclassical micro theory, and the implicit aggregation of Keynes-based macro theory. Our focus will be on an intermediate institutional framework as the one which picks up many decisive economic activities which at present slip between the macro-micro division.

## The Meaning of Equilibrium

One of the central organizing concepts of economic theory, *equilibrium*, has also experienced a crisis of identity in recent years. In the classical tradition *market* has played a central role. The stability or otherwise of particular markets was analyzed by Marshall and his followers and of general market equilibrium by Walras and his. Over the years the equilibrium of markets, and implicitly of market prices, became sacred. Walras focused on a determinate general equilibrium and its stability conditions. The former was achieved when the number of market equations and variables was the same, and the latter by his theory of tatonnement or trial and error bidding. The stability conditions were further specified in a dynamic framework by Samuelson [1947] and others. However, despite its popularity, serious problems remained with this particular approach to equilibrium analysis.

The first was that the system of equations *ex ante* assumed the success of the tatonnement or stabilization process. Walras developed an atemporal logic of the tatonnement process and ignored the actual market transactions which would normally be involved. Since, however, the adjustment process involved *inequalities* and not equations, it was impossible to argue that there was a determinate general equilibrium without assuming the conclusion.

Since the existence of significant elements of excess demand and supply have independent effects on economic decision-makers, the process is not determinate.

A far wider problem is the realization that the general post-Walrasian *market* (price) equilibrium analysis selects only one aspect of the economy for consideration. For years the Keynesian emphasis on *income* equilibrium sat uneasily alongside the market analysis. But the two were not equivalent; the same income equilibrium is consistent with many different equilibria in the allocation of resources to different ends (goods). Moreover, there were other concepts of equilibrium, like that of the *real resources* of the economy developed by Leontief [1936, 1941] and others, and that of the stability of *stocks* within the economy. The price framework, which claimed to be the ultimate one, was only one among many and could not presume the monopoly it claimed.

We also note that the Keynesian models positing an equilibrium of income and expenditure were trapped in their own form of circular argument. Again, although the specific weakness varies with the particular formulation, the underlying problem occurs in assuming from the beginning the equality of income and expenditure, for it inevitably introduced a circularity of argument. Thus in the Hansen-Samuelson approach it was necessary to already know the level of income to determine the rate of interest and vice versa! At a more significant level, the *inequalities* of government expenditure and taxes, exports and imports, investment and savings were not taken seriously; they represented patterns of indebtedness and transfers among sectors which were qualitatively different and needed to be recognized as such. Moreover, the *ex ante* postulation of the equality of income and expenditure within "Keynesianism" led to the separation of monetary theory from income analysis.

There is a yet deeper criticism of equilibrium analysis. More and more economists have tended towards a natural scientific view of equilibrium as a mechanical or numerical equality, and have ignored its deeper social scientific meaning. By constructing a system with parameters and exogenous variables, little room was left for the development of institutions and markets. The equilibrium solution was a way of freezing history. However, if equilibrium analysis is seen in terms of the stability of people's economic lives and institutions, a different approach is possible. It could be argued that the optimizing and profit-maximizing criteria used in much equilibrium analysis do not begin to do justice to the multifaceted stability of the large corporation, whose managers are normally concerned about the long-term stable employment of thousands of workers, security and order in supply and production patterns, preparing for market instability, and forming a long-term vision for the company. [Galbraith, 1967] Institutional sustainability should be an important focus of equilibrium analysis, so that a much greater level of awareness of the need for stability in people's economic lives is developed in the discipline. We also note that in the majority of situations it is the stability of people's *normative* responses, what they feel things should be like, which leads to equilibrium, not mathematical properties of an abstract system.

## Monetarists, nonmonetarists and inflation

Inflation has had to be a central concern of economists during the 1970's and 1980's, as we saw in chapter one. What is disturbing is the degree of quite fundamental theoretical disagreement which monetarism has generated for more than a quarter of a century. Economists are not just at odds about the definition of money. As Hahn says in his essay "Monetarism and Economic Theory," (1980)

> What is at stake is the underlying description of the economy. The Walrasian description adopted by the Monetarists essentially removes the need for systematic government policy even if in some sense such a policy has real effects . . . .. It seems very doubtful that empirical evidence will at present be decisive in deciding between the usefulness of the two theories. (p. 7)

Here again, we see underlying disagreements about the nature of the economy surfacing in a specific issue. The Walrasian model necessarily tends to present money as a veil and has evoked various forms of Quantity Theory, even if these, like Friedman's, take into account a wide range of variables affecting the demand for money. However, the monetarist conclusions can be and often were infuriating to economists concerned to analyze the processes in financial and other markets in detail. To them Friedman merely posited a "monistic macro solution" and did not face the specific problems. [Mason, 1980] However, there was no single alternative, but a number of non-monetarist positions on inflation. Most of these were not merely emphasizing different aspects of the problem, but implied distinct kinds of analysis. There were views which attributed inflation to excess aggregate demand. The theoretical statement of these in the Hanson-Samuelson versions was, however, expressed in non-monetary terms, which was a serious limitation. They also divided into those emphasizing excess demand for the real G.N.P. and those focussing on the labor market. [S. Weintraub, 1960] A second tradition, associated most strongly with Hicks and Patinkin [1965], recognized the significance of money, the discretionary use of interest rates, and the difference between real and nominal cash balances. All of those positions convey the impression that they are chasing a long way the developments in the economics of money and that they cannot easily be articulated to one another.

Other economists have reacted to this perspective and have sought to return to Keynes' dynamic and activist views of money, as presented both in the *Treatise on Money* and *The General Theory of Employment, Interest and Money*, [Minsky, 1977] and others have emphasized a whole variety of supply side inflationary pressures. [Wiles, 1973, Brown, 1979] Still others have concentrated on intersectoral analysis, "crowding in and out," and reinterpretations of the Phillips curve. [Cambridge Econ. Policy Group, 1975, Godley & Cripps, 1974, 1976] More recently, however, there has been a different level of intellectual commitment in papers in this area. The concern is no longer primarily with understanding the sources and working to eliminate inflation, but merely with policies which have an expedient effect on the overall process. Many economists have accepted defeat in principle and merely have some useful practical ideas.

What emerges again is a disturbing lack of congruence among the different theoretical approaches to this issue; they have become species hostile and even mutually predatory. Again, the paradigm for healthy theoretical development seems to be lost.

## The Cul-de-sac of Welfare Theory

The sad tale of welfare theory has often been told, and yet it bears retelling, because it identifies some of the more serious problems of contemporary economics. The main concern of welfare theory has been to develop criteria which have a societal rather than a private reference to evaluate whether policies are good from this wider viewpoint. Although there is a more practical tradition associated with Pigou and the emergence of cost-benefit analysis, the main roots of modern welfare theory are to be found in utilitarianism and in the work of Pareto. The criterion of Pareto optimality which became the central theoretical tool in the subsequent development, involved assumptions that the individual be free to choose among alternatives, that he value or rank those alternatives in a logically consistent way, and that his judgment of his welfare was essentially self-referential and maximizing. This established an optimal situation where nobody could be made better off without making somebody else worse off. This criterion was found to have few practical implications, and attempts were made to strengthen it.

Some economists, especially Bergson, Samuelson and Tinbergen, tried to construct Social Welfare Functions which corresponded to *socially* optimal rather than individually optimal positions. However, Arrow, in 1950, showed that, given the impossibility of interpersonal utility comparisons (which follows from the assumptions of individual sovereignty, ordinal ranking and the maximization of utility) and a commitment to non-imposed (dictated) solutions, a Social Welfare Function was normally impossible to construct.

Another move by Kaldor, (1939) Hicks, (1940) Scitovsky, (1951) and Samuelson (1950) was to develop hypothetical compensation criteria. The application of these criteria, which involved pretending to compensate those suffering from policies, offended the rule of avoiding interpersonal comparisons of well-being. Later more explicit distributional value-judgments were made by Little (1957) and others. However, this in turn implied a theory of justice, and some attempts were made to use the content of, for example, Rawls' (1971) theory in welfare judgments. This approach, therefore, moved to the edge of economics and into political theory, and the relationship to private economic activity became rather tenuous. [Suzumura, 1980]

Another direction in welfare has been to look more thoroughly at *altruistic behaviour* as a denial of the egocentricity assumption. This has been done by considering the satisfaction of others part of the individual's own utility function [Hockman & Rogers, 1969] and by looking at various forms of charity and altruism, like the provision of grants and the giving of blood. [Collard, 1978] Although this kind of analysis shows the limitations of conventional analysis, it has tended to concentrate on altruistic, selfless behaviour and ignored the most ubiquitous form of behaviour which welfare analysis has largely excluded, namely, group and personal decisions which take into account and respond to the need of others, *as well as* the subject(s). "You shall love your neighbour as yourself" is actually a more realistic starting point than either hedonism or altruism. Welfare theory is still locked in on the problems of Enlightenment rational individualism, which must leave it largely bankrupt of conclusions about wider human welfare. It also suffers from the dominance of optimization solutions. In a lot of situations the welfare of others is merely a question of whether we care or not, a straight moral choice. Optimization is a tendentious obfuscation of the issue. Indeed, many economists give the impression that they regard welfare theory as a kind of disembodied ectoplasm which they would much rather just have disappear altogether to avoid embarrassment. However, the problem is not just welfare theory per se, but the wider attempt within the main body of economics to create a value-free area of analysis.

## Micro-micro Theory

### Automated Firms

Much of economics aims to develop a *self-contained* body of theory. Only if theory is self-referential can the autonomy of the discipline be guaranteed. Over the years dogmas have been developed to create the illusion that there are no leakages in the theoretical system. One such is that the firm maximizes profit. The construction of these economic robots doing these economic things hermetically sealed the discipline from all outside disturbances. However, these robots have become defective theoretical tools, so that it has become the habit of many economists to give these poor creatures a kick for poor performance. Because it sheds light on the discipline's problems, we are going to examine this unkind behaviour a little more closely.

Two aspects of the theory of the firm are its overall goals and its internal organization. What of the overall goals? At first there was one: a rational coordinating entrepreneur had the single-minded goal of profit maximization on the basis of price information. That the firm might be prepared to use non-price information and to respond to non-pecuniary values and inputs was scarcely allowed. Given this goal and various costs, then output, prices charged, and the level of market penetration necessarily followed. The economic behaviour of the firm was charted. However, there were a number of different responses to this definitive approach.

The first said that *if* these implications are followed through, some disturbing and sub-optimal results will appear: not only could firms develop monopolies, restrict output and charge higher prices, but they would have every incentive to do so. What is evident from almost all this literature is that there is no necessary connection between profitability and the welfare of society generally; the invisible hand has disappeared. Thus profitability does not necessarily lead to the best product for the consumer; it tends to lead to all the destructive aspects of a firm's activity being treated as externalities, so that the lives of workers and consumers suffer from the firm's exported problems. It was also evident that the market *mechanism* in which the classical economists put their faith was being, and in many cases had been, destroyed by the logic of profit maximization. Thus there was a deep-seated incompatibility between the operation of capitalism and the maintenance of a free market economy, a deeply disturbing conclusion.

However, there is another approach to the theory of the firm. Rather than being a part of an ordered body of theory which describes (and implicitly prescribes) optimal positions, it looks at the way things actually are. Thus, from the 1930's onwards, many economists have argued that the profit maximizing theory of the firm is inaccurate and misleading. Some have followed through the argument of Berle and Means (1932) that the separation of ownership and control affected the operation of the firm. The models of Marris (1964) emphasized growth maximization. Baumol (1962) focusing on sales maximization and Williamson (1964), looking at the trade-off between slack and profitability, elaborated some alternative assumptions. Behavioural approaches, like those of March and Simon (1958) and the Carnegie School, looked at constraints on motivation, bounded rationality, search processes, standard operating procedures, differentiation of goals, resistance to change, and many other strategies which quite fundamentally modify the formal economic goals. Merely satisficing (seeking a satisfactory level of performance) or engaging in various forms of search does not accord well with profit maximization. Thus this perspective questions whether the formal goals can actually be said to be operative within a modern complex corporation, and whether therefore the standard neoclassical theory of the firm is much more than a myth dished up for the consumption of shareholders and students.

Another development in the theory focuses on the organizational community. Leibenstein (1976) argued that a firm's performance often varied by very considerable amounts as a result of "X-efficiency." This factor was not related to specific inputs but to the level of communal effort and cooperation; i.e., it was a largely social phenomenon. This emphasis tallies with another argument, namely, that a lot of union-management relationships in the West are adversarial, and that union wage bargaining power is related to the level of profits. Since this makes profit-maximization indeterminate, the standard theory is in a yet weaker position.

The prescribed tool of allocation has been *marginal analysis*; it has two fundamental weaknesses. The first is that production decisions are very often made in large and relatively inflexible lumps and with necessarily fixed factor inputs, so that the continuity of marginal analysis becomes a largely other-worldly assumption, present merely to allow calculus to be used. The second is that the output which is the result of the joint contributions of all the factors cannot be differentiated into the specific contribution of each. No disjunction of the contribution of factors is possible on the basis of marginality. When it is also accepted that one of the allocated factors, labour, is normally to be seen as an active, responsible participant in the process, and that the organizational integration of labour and capital takes time and incurs its own costs, it is evident that isoquants are largely ethereal, and that partial derivatives of output with respect to different factors are a myth. The standard theory leads to contradictions, is inaccurate, and ignores the significance of the organizational community. We shall argue later that what is needed is a larger normative framework which recognizes the full significance of the firm, and in this context the weaknesses and strengths of the norm of profit maximization will become readily apparent.

### Consumption

Consumption theory has been used to construct a boundary to keep economics self-contained. The consumer, it is assumed, adopting in principle a modified utilitarian framework, will consume to maximize his satisfaction, which is seen to be greater with larger amounts of goods and services, and which is essentially subjective. Whether the formulation is in terms of Utility Theory, Indifference Analysis, or Revealed Preference, the aim is to *close* Price Theory, for only if there is a "natural" process which yields determinate solutions can the discipline be held to be value-free and neutral. When the marginal rate of substitution between goods equals their relative prices, the system can be solved with a full set of demand equations, and everybody is happy.

But is this what is actually going on? Consider the range of goods and services, (like soap, toothbrushes, socks, electric light bulbs, toilet paper, doormats, knives and forks, and underclothes) which are normally regarded by consumers as automatically needed in limited quantities and which impose no serious constraints on their budget. It will be evident that little constraint is imposed on consumers by prices in this kind of situation. The marginal rate of substitution and price have little significance when there are no serious income constraints and satiety is well within reach. In this situation the search for determinate price solutions is just inappropriate.

The standard theory has also broken down in the *self-referential* orientation it assumes. The significance of *social reference groups* for consumption has long been established, as has the *social* significance of status goods. Concern for other members of the community and their welfare is so important that the individualism of the normal analysis is necessarily weak. Furthermore, a wide variety of goods is bought conjointly by groups, or by larger public bodies, and the standard subjective calculus just does not apply to these situations. Another range of *positional* goods can only be acquired by some consumers to the exclusion of other consumers enjoying those goods. [Hirsch, 1976] Much other consumption has extensive external effects on others, from noise and air pollution to the requirement of unsociable working hours. These examples show that standard consumption theory has ignored and suppressed the interpersonal, institutional, and collective aspects of consumer choice. In part this results from the attempt to make economics an autonomous self-contained science, and it is worth briefly discussing why. One concept of the relationship between disciplines is that of the *interface*—the place where two black boxes meet. Consumption theory is normally seen in terms of the interface between economics and psychology, and it therefore becomes important, if economic science is to be autonomous, for the interface to be sealed off. This is "achieved" by making the psychological component subjective and inaccessible, while the economic theory focuses on the logic of choice. However, the actual behaviour which economists, sociologists, psychologists, and political scientists analyze is not divided into discrete compartments but is composite activity, aspects of which are analyzed by different social scientists. The relation between these various forms of study has an important bearing on how theory is formulated.

## The Theory of Distribution

Another slightly embarrassing area for economists is the theory of distribution. During the late 19th century, the early unions, the Marxists, and other groups were saying that the distribution of income and wealth was unfair. Therefore, in reaction, bourgeois economists sought a justification for the existing distribution, and marginal productivity theory became the standard "rationalization" for the inequalities. Another interpretation sees economists as part of a value-free, neutral science wanting to develop a *determinate* theory of distribution. John Bates Clark, in *The Distribution of Wealth: A Theory of Wages, Interest and Profits*, [1956] details the thrust of this approach and its relation to the former interpretation:

There is, in short, a deep acting natural law at work amid the confusing struggles of the labour market. The function of this natural law is to separate the gross earnings of society into three generic shares that are unlike in kind. It causes the whole annual gains of society to distribute themselves into three great sums—general wages, general interest and aggregate profits... We may now advance the more general thesis—later to be proved— that, *where natural laws have their way, the share of income that attaches to any productive function is gauged by the actual product of it* ..... To each agent a distinguishable share in production, and to each a corresponding reward—such is the natural law of distribution. This thesis we have to prove, and more hinges on the truth of it than any introductory words can state. The right of society to exist in its present form, and the

> probability that it will continue so to exist, are at stake. Those facts lend to this problem of distribution its measureless importance. (p. 2)

Establishing what *is* (naturally) the case determines what *ought to be* the distribution.

This approach has been dealt a fatal blow academically by the "Sraffian Revolution." In his book *Production of Commodities by Means of Commodities* [1960] Sraffa avoided the arbitrary assumption of identifying a certain set of prices with a certain level of profits *or* wages, a strategy which is normal in neoclassical theory. He did this by constructing a composite standard commodity which allowed profits and wages to vary in inverse relationship without the commodity price being affected. Thus the assumption that distribution *followed from* production, was fundamentally challenged. Indeed, once the point had been made, it was obvious; it was possible to construct models where production followed from distribution. The old monopoly of natural law production models which determined distribution was broken.

Nevertheless, the arguments have moved beyond the marginal productivity approach. What of monopsony and monopoly power in the labor market? If this exists, what is its effect on distribution? What of the power conferred on some workers by educational investment? What of the situation discussed in the previous section, where the contribution of different factors and different units of the factor cannot be discriminated? What of the argument that the value of the average product of a group of workers is the fair reward rather than the value of the marginal product of the last production worker? In the face of even these criticisms it is clear that no natural law of distribution exists, and that the idea of *the* theory of distribution is in shreds.

However, there is a more fundamental criticism of the standard neoclassical approach. Since it is the combination and cooperation of groups and resources which produces the wealth which is being distributed, an approach which makes distributional relations merely consequent on other technical factors is invalid. The relations among people which produce goods and services are a matter of decision, organization, and prescription. Any approach which does not from the beginning consider what the relations of wealth and income among various groups and contributors should be—that is, a normative approach—misconceives what actually happens. Moreover, it is not difficult to show the various views of what is fair do, in fact, structure particular distributional arrangements, so that it is only with a normative distributional framework that the actual situation in a modern economy can be properly addressed. This is where much of the best work is now being done (e.g., Thurow, 1975), and in a later chapter we shall develop a more explicit Christian theory.

## Value and Price Theory

The status of price theory within conventional economic theory is very high; in fact, many economists would regard it as the ordering principle in the discipline. It is described as "the basic language of economics," and the normal neoclassical assumption is that prices to a considerable extent reflect value. The classical economists, of course, pointed out a range of anomalies, like that between the value and price of water and diamonds, but when the theory of consumers surplus was developed to cover anomalies like those, the rule of price as *the* theory of value became more and more complete, so that many texts did not even discuss value in relation to price theory. Thus, one of the messy preoccupations, even obsessions, of most of the classical economists has been eliminated from the subject. Value and price are the same thing in modern economics, because value is identified with maximum efficiency and optimization.

However, at the same time a considerable number of economists, the less tidy kind that like to sniff around, have found malfunctioning parts of the well-oiled system of price curves. The oldest is, of course the case of monopoly pricing, where the relationship between price and the cost of inputs is separated by monopoly profits. This was designated as "wrong" or "abnormal," and was treated as a problem. Nevertheless, the development by Robinson and Chamberlin of theories of imperfect competition, and the knowledge that various forms of monopoly might be common, made the optimal relation between value and price less easy to accept, especially when it was known that many firms employed an automatic mark-up of 30% and even 50% over average costs as their pricing policy. Another anomaly occurred in the area of companies which experienced very low marginal costs, so-called "natural monopolies"; it became evident that the criteria of efficiency and profitability diverged considerably in these situations, and that the significance of price was fuzzy.

Nor is it only in the area of the firm that problems occurred. From Ricardo onwards the theory of rent has sat disconcertingly on the edge of price theory. Ricardo, Malthus, West, and Torrens developed the theory of differential rent, which Ricardo defined as "payment for the original and indestructible powers of the soil," but this theory depended on the concept of marginal land and on the givenness of other payments—wages, for example. Increasingly in our era a wide range of resources is always scarce; there is no margin, and the fixity of other payments cannot be assumed, so the givenness of this price disappears. It is not only that here is a reward which is not related to productive activity, but the price of that input is only established if other inputs are given, which, it can be argued, generally they are not. [Sraffa, 1960] Thus, in an argument parallel to that used in the discussion of distribution, it is clear that the givenness of any prices in the overall system cannot be assumed to determine the rest, for the givenness of each price is dependent on ascribed values of others. (This is clear in Sraffa's work partly because the same kind of commodities appear both among the means of production and among the products, displaying more clearly the interdependence of the system.) Thus it becomes evident that all the neoclassical attempts to establish an "objective" price system prejudge the *ascribed* values of all of the members of that community. They may not be inaccurate in so doing, but not to recognize explicitly the necessary priority of a theory of value is to subvert their analysis.

There are many other areas where the incompleteness of price theory has been more fully analyzed. The significance of consumer's and producer's surpluses has been explored; it is not unusual for someone to be prepared to pay 50% more or charge 50% less than the actual price. The recognition of non-priced external costs and benefits, and the scale of their significance, has suddenly dawned on economists. The recognition, too, that more than a quarter of the work force contribute unpriced labor, and that many of the most important commodities and services in people's lives are unpriced has also shown the limitations of price theory. [Goudzwaard, 1970] Moreover, the transferability of value which is a necessary assumption of price theory (you can buy it if you can pay for it), is not always what happens; many forms of discriminatory pricing and purchasing exist. When all of these considerations are taken into account, price theory is painfully inadequate, partly because it has cut itself off from all the deeper issues of economic life and value.

## Growth Theory

R. Harrod's article, "An Essay in Dynamic Theory" [1939], began the development of another major branch of economic theory. To some extent the success of growth theory merely mirrored the rapid expansion of Western national economics after the Second World War, and when periods of recession and even contraction occurred in the 1970's, it became a less absorbing branch of theory. However, its significance is not thus to be dismissed, for insofar as it expressed where many leading economists saw the economy as going, it reflected some of the orientations and contradictions of the discipline.

First, to state the obvious, the growth theory of the period was largely macroeconomic and predicated of the Gross National Product. Relatively little concern was directed to the growth of institutions, communities, cities, and markets, but only of quantities. Moreover, most of the early neoclassical models established patterns of steady state growth, thus reenforcing the unquestioned optimism of the period. The work of Joan Robinson [1956, 1962] satirically questioned these golden age patterns of growth and showed that they were less stable than often assumed. "Limping," "restrained," and "bastard" golden age paths were introduced to show defective forms. Gradually, under the pressure of economic events and perhaps theoretical debate, the optimistic neoclassical models disappeared.

However, something deeper was also taking place. The ecological revolution meant that growth was suddenly equated with pollution and environmental destruction. From being an automatic good thing, it was questioned, and even automatically, a bad thing. The previously suppressed question—What kind of growth? was now in the open, along with the question, To what purpose? [Ellul, 1964] Economic growth theory faced its own counterculture.

More recently the arguments associated with growth theory have been more instrumental. Growth is needed to obviate serious unemployment, or to help the poorer nations, or to give the economy flexibility. But still the question lingers, for even in our economic theory we know that the materialist faith in which so much of our economic development and theory is bedded, is open to question. [Goudzwaard, 1979]

## Supply-Side Economics

Another sign of the theoretical problems of the times has been the growth of *supply-side economics* as a revolt against academic Keynesian economics. The difference has been stated thus:

There is certainly a difference in perspective here. Supply-side economists look at the economy from ground level, as it were— i.e., from the point of view of the entrepreneurs and investors who are identified as the prime movers. Keynesian economists look at the economy from above—from the standpoint of a government that is a *deus ex machina,* and which in its omniscience, intervenes discreetly to preserve a harmonious economic universe. [Kristol, 1981, p. 48]

The revolt is against the other-worldly conclusions of the academics, against the blandness of the mathematical models of the economy. The revolt is *for* decision-makers, uncertainty, risk, commitment and organization, and it highlights the tenuous relationship between theory and activity in the discipline. In a rather blanket form this vote of no confidence is querying the relevance of the academic paradigms.

At the same time it is expressing a faith. [Gilder, 1981, pp. 235-269] This faith is chiefly vested in the entrepreneur; give him the correct conditions, and he will create the necessary wealth and prosperity. We argue elsewhere that the faith of entrepreneurs in themselves is especially likely to close their eyes to all the ills that they can, and have, contributed to the economic community. Nevertheless, this explicit faith, although it can be criticized, is not to be dismissed. For it is economic faith which has been excluded from the discipline in the name of automatic economic calculations, and now the automatons are striking back. They are more than pawns in the models. The supply-side economists' revolt signals a new awareness of the importance of economic faith and commitment, which were thoroughly excluded from the neoclassical framework. When the significance of faith is recognized throughout the discipline, it will allow new approaches to tired issues.

## The Underlying Dilemma in Economic Theory

We have looked, albeit briefly and inadequately, at some of the problems in contemporary theory which are gathering momentum in the literature. It is possible to argue that each of these problems is discrete, and will have its own independent solution. However, we suggest that this is not the case. The problems have to do with the underlying paradigms of economics which are proving to be fundamentally defective, and it is the weaknesses of these which keep surfacing in specific areas.

One paradigm is the Enlightenment faith in Natural Order. Throughout the development of economic theory, from the first appearance of the invisible hand, through general equilibrium analysis, to steady state growth, there has been a strong faith in a natural economic order which can be theoretically elaborated by rational and mathematical analysis. Part of the attraction of this perspective is related to the success of the natural sciences, and the outcome is economic theory which claims to have a technical map of the economic order not dissimilar to the mechanistic picture of the universe in much 18th century thinking. The economy is a self-sustaining natural system. This approach has had several major defects. It has tended to isolate economic theory from the broader contexts of life which necessarily enter deeply into normal economic activity. It has also focused on one unifying motivating theme, namely, rational self-interest, which will integrate the whole body of economic theory. It seeks out a framework of natural order or equilibrium which is mechanical or mathematical, rather than fully human. The net effect is to foreclose the full meaning of people's economic lives in a certain kind of quasi-mechanical straightjacket which devalues the economic responsibility of humanity as steward of God's creation by picturing us all as merely pawns within the system. It is noteworthy that when serious problems of depression or economic distortion have occurred, this neoclassical natural order tradition has shown itself largely impotent to deal with the problems. Thus, as theory draws its breath, in a variety of different forms, from this underlying faith, so it partakes of these weaknesses, and the preceeding pages give some evidence to that effect.

An alternative, and to some extent a reactive perspective roots itself in the validity of human experience and behavior independent of any natural order. As we noted earlier, Keynes built more *ad hoc* statements about human behavior into his analysis and claimed that this gave a more reliable understanding of economic activity. However, this tradition, which picks up the diverse variety of human behavior, has a problem of lack of coherence. It needs a framework, for the modern complex economy cannot be regarded as just an anarchic complex of intermeshing behavior. If the natural economic order of the neoclassical tradition is cracking open, the alternative tradition has not yet gained coherence. If the economy is merely a chaos of free behavioral agents, a greater than Keynes will be needed to give coherence to the whole.

Perhaps the terms of the debate, as presently contructed, are wrong. It may be that the implicit basic categories and underlying ways of thinking lead theory into paradigms which create their own problems. Perhaps the abandonment of a theory of value, the uneasy status of welfare theory, the disjunction between macro and micro theory, monetary theory problems, and the issues that have been sketched in this chapter point to serious difficulties with the dominant paradigms in the discipline. There are certainly grounds for asking whether another vantage point could offer different perspectives which might present these tired issues in a new way.

# Resources

Arrow, K. 1950. A Difficulty in the Concept of Social Welfare. *Journal of Political Economy*. 58: 328-46.

Baumol, W. 1962. The Theory of Expansion of the Firm. *Amer. Econ. Rev.*52: 1078-87.

Berle, A. A., and G. C. Means. 1932. *The Modern Corporation and Private Property*. N.Y.: Commerce Clearing House.

Brown, A. J. 1979. Inflation and the British Sickness. *Econ. J.* 89: 1-12.

Cambridge Economic Policy Group. 1975. *Economic Policy Review*, nos. 1 & 2.

Clark, J. B. 1956. *The Distribution of Wealth*, N.Y.: Kelley & Millinan.

Clower, R., and A. Leijonhufvud. 1975. The Coordination of Economic Activities: A Keynesian Perspective. *Amer. Econ. Rev.* 65: 182-88.

Cyert, R., and J. March. 1963. *A Behavioral Theory of the Firm*. Englewood Cliffs: Prentice-Hall.

Davidson, P. 1978. Why Money Matters: Lesson from a Half-century of Monetary Theory. *J. of Post-Keynesian Econ.* 1: 16-70.

Galbraith, J. K. 1967. *The New Industrial State*. Boston: Houghton-Mifflin.

Gilder, G. 1981. *Wealth and Poverty*. N.Y.: Basic Book.

Godley, W., and T. Cripps. 1974a. Demand, Inflation, and Economic Policy. *London and Cambridge Economic Bulletin*. 8.

Godley, W., and T. Cripps. 1974b. A Formal Analysis of the Cambridge Economic Policy Group Model. *Economica*. 43: 335-48.

Goudzwaard, B. 1970. *Non-priced Scarcity*. The Hague: Van Stockum.

Goudzwaard, B. 1979. *Capitalism and Progress*. Grand Rapids: Eerdmans.

Hahn, F. H. 1980. Monetarism and Economic Theory. *Economica* 47.

Harrod, R, 1939. An Essay in Dynamic Theory. *Econ. J.* 49: 14-33.

Hicks, J. 1937. Mr. Keynes and the Classics. *Economica* 5: 147-59.

Hicks, J. 1940. The Valuation of the Social Income. *Economica* 7: 105-24.

Hicks, J. 1980. IS-LM: An Explanation. *J. Post-Keynesian Econ.* 3: 139-53.

Hirsch, F. 1976. *The Social Limits to Growth*. Cambridge: Harvard U. Press.

Hockman, H. M., and J. D. Rogers. 1969. Pareto Optimal Redistribution. *Amer. Econ. Rev.* 59: 542 52.

Kristol, I. 1981. Ideology and Supply-side Economics. *Commentary*.

Leibenstein, H. 1976. *Beyond Economic Man.* Cambridge: Harvard U. Press.

Leontief, W. W. 1936. Quantitative Input and Output Relation in the Economic System of the U.S. *Rev. Econ. Stat.* pp. 105-125.

Leontief, W. W. 1940. *The Structure of the American Economy.* Cambridge: Harvard University Press.

Little, I. 1957. *A Critique of Welfare Economics.* N.Y.: Oxford U. Press.

March, J., and H. Simon. 1958. *Organizations.* N.Y.: John Wiley.

Mason, W. E. 1980. Some Negative Thoughts on Friedmans' Positive Economics. *J. of Post-Keynesian Econ.* 3: 235-55.

Marris, R. 1964. *Economic Theory of Managerial Capitalism.* N.Y.: Macmillan.

Minsky, H. P. 1977. An Economics of Keynes' Perspective on Money. in S. Weintraub, ed., *Modern Economic Thought.* Philadelphia: U. of Pennsylvania Press.

Patinkin, D. 1965. *Money, Interest and Prices.* 2nd Ed., N.Y.: Harper & Row.

Phelps, E., ed. 1970. *Microeconomic Foundations of Employment and Inflation Theory.* N.Y.: Norton.

Rawls, J. 1971. *A Theory of Justice.* Cambridge: Harvard U. Press.

Robinson, J. 1956. *The Accumulation of Capital.* N.Y.: Macmillan.

Robinson, J. 1962. *Essays in the Theory of Economic Growth.* N.Y.: Macmillan.

Robinson, J. 1972. The Second Crisis in Economic Theory. *Amer. Econ. Rev.* 62; 1-10.

Samuelson, P. 1947. *The Foundations of Economic Analysis.* Cambridge: Harvard U. Press.

Samuelson, P. 1950. Evaluation of Real National Income. *Oxford Econ. Papers* 2: 1-29.

Schelling, T. C. 1978. *Micromotives and Macrobehaviour.* N.Y.: Norton.

Scitovsky, T. 1951. A Note on Welfare Propositions in Economics. *Rev. of Econ. Stud.* pp. 77-88.

Sen, A. 1979. Personal Utilities and Public Judgements. *Econ. J.* 89: 53758.

Sraffa, P. 1960. *The Production of Commodities by Means of Commodities.* Cambridge: Cambridge U. Press.

Suzumura, I. 1980. On Distributional Value Judgements and Piecemeal Welfare Criteria. *Economica.* 47: 125-39.

Thurow, L. 1975. *Generating Inequality.* N.Y.: Basic Books.

Walras, L. 1954. *Elements of Pure Economics.* (trans. Jaffe), Homewood: Richard D. Irwin.

Weintraub, E. R. 1979. *Microfoundations.* N.Y.: Cambridge U. Press.

Weintraub, S. 1960. The Keynesian Theory of Inflation. *International Econ. Rev.* 1: 143-55.

Weintraub, S. 1977. Hicksian Keynesianism: Dominance and Decline. in S. Weintraub, ed., *Modern Economic Thought.* Philadelphia: U. of Pennsylvania Press.

Wiles, P. 1973. Cost Inflation and the State of Economic Theory. *Econ. J.* 83: 377-98.

Williamson, O. 1964. *The Economics of Discretionary Behavior.* Englewood Cliffs: Prentice-Hall.

# Chapter III
# The Science of Economics

*Often I wonder why I must journey*
*Over a road so rugged and steep,*
*While there are others living in comfort,*
*While with the lost I labor and weep.*

*Farther along we'll know all about it;*
*Farther along we'll understand why.*
*Cheer up my brothers, live in the sunshine;*
*We'll understand it all by and by.*
    *Southern Folk Hymn (19th c.)*

## Introduction

In the last chapter we looked at some of the fissures in economic theory and suggested that they are evidence of a tension between viewing the economy as Natural Order and seeing it merely as the outcome of autonomous economic behavior. In this chapter we shall look at the basis of theory, the status of economic science. The previous chapter showed some of the fragmentation and incoherence in the way the economy was seen. *We now face the fact that economists disagree profoundly as to the kind of knowledge which constitutes theory.* Many economists are not aware of the problem; they merely pick up the theoretical blueprints that happen to lie around, but since these plans are already shaped by disparate epistemological craftsmen like Walras, Marshall, Keynes, Samuelson, Friedman or Galbraith, it is not surprising that the results are incompatible. Moreover, since few economists have any training in the philosophy of knowledge in the social sciences, the problems occurring in this area tend to be uncorrected. Long after the weakness of a certain view of knowledge is accepted in philosophy, economists still happily espouse it. The consequence is that economists are unable to discourse in a compatible language or to agree on criteria by which their theory should be evaluated. At this epistemological level also, economics is involved in a long-term crisis of scientific identity.

The status of economics as a science is more precarious than many assume. This was especially so when the first academic economists evolved out of the mire of the industrial revolution, and when there was doubt about whether the species would survive as a profession. The problem was that there were relatively few areas where economists agreed. The liberals advocating the universal efficacy of free trade were met by strong protectionist arguments. Those in favor of laissez-faire were opposed by those concerned with "the social problem." The position of Trades Unions was attacked by those believing in an unorganized market for workers. A labor theory of value was held against the more classical theory. The utilitarianism of Benthan and James Mill had been largely rejected by John Stuart Mill, and the assumed basis of political economy, the sanctity of private property, was being assailed by the idea that land should be nationalized. Economics was in danger of becoming mere opinion, and its practitioners were acutely aware of the problem. In 1876 Stanley Jevons commented thus:

> In short it comes to this—that one hundred years after the first publication of *The Wealth of Nations*, we find the state of the science to be almost chaotic. There is certainly less agreement now about what political economy is than there was thirty or fifty years ago.

Indeed, in the following year Francis Galton proposed the abolition of section F (Economic Science and Statistics) of the British Association for the Advancement of Science on the grounds that the scientific content of the papers was so weak. The President of that Section is reported to have commented as follows:

> Mr. Ingram points out that in many quarters the science of political economy, as taught and understood in England, has fallen much in public estimation. There is a general opinion, he says, among those who still profess to think highly of the science, that it has seen its best days—that, after exercising an immense influence over legislation and deciding the fate of cabinets and of parties, it is losing its hold as a study and its position as a science. [Lowe, 1978, p. 858]

Clearly a subject in this plight was not fit or able to become a respectable profession.

The response to this situation, evidenced in a lot of different countries, was to move the emphasis from trying to achieve a common body of knowledge about the economy to having *a correct method of obtaining knowledge.* Science was not a matter of *what* you know, but of *how* you know. If the correct foundation for obtaining knowledge could be established, then the knowledge acquired would necessarily be scientific and well-formed. The depth of this transition needs to be carefully savored. Faith in epistemological method became the foundation of the scientific status of economic knowledge. Thus economists became more formally concerned with the scientific form of their theory and fed on the various epistemological traditions which were around at the time to establish a scientific approach. However, although it seemed at some stages in the development of 20th century economics that there is *one* scientific approach to the subject matter, there have turned out to be a number of divergent ones which have now emerged into the open as different languages of economic theory. The internationalizing of academic economics has made this crisis more acute. Until the genesis and development of these different views of theory is understood, and the process by which they generate divisions is uncovered, the language barriers will continue to grow and the discipline will become less coherent.

Two very recent trends have served both to make this crisis worse and open the possibility for new solutions. One trend is the collapse of any consensus among philosophers about scientific method and theory evaluations. Though prompted by problems that arose much earlier in theoretical physics, this trend reached its height in the late 1960's and early 1970's. Since *all* scientific methodologies were seen to suffer from severe philosophical problems, a kind of relativistic pluralism arose. In its most extreme form this view became the position of the "sociology of knowledge" movement, which asserted that a good theory is simply one that commands the assent of most practitioners of the relevant discipline.

The second trend was the product of student demonstrations over the Vietnam War. In the face of an academic establishment that claimed that truth was value-free and could be discovered by a process of open rational discourse to which the university was irrevocably committed, the students asserted that truth was inescapably normative and could only be discovered if the university was honest and clear about its value commitments. The students won this debate, and we see today the fruits of their victory. The necessity for explicitly value-laden education is widely accepted and discussed, and much literature has been written about exactly how this is to be done. Furthermore, universities have recognized that their role in society goes beyond providing a forum for rational discourse to serving as the bearer of society's deepest beliefs and concerns. That in the 1980's these values have turned out to be conservative ones does not negate the depth of the student revolution's achievement.

In what follows, various views of scientific knowledge used in economics will be presented. First we shall examine how they are divisive. Second, we shall show that each of these epistemological positions has fundamental weaknesses which have led to frequent but unsuccessful reformulations. Third, it will be shown that since all of these positions prescribe what theory should be, they engender a form of tunnel vision which has narrowed and monotonized much theory produced during the 20th century. Last, we shall suggest that in its attempt to establish its own absolute status as knowledge, scientific economics has cut its relationship to economic life and activity and has diminished its ability to be useful as knowledge. What, then, of the various views of economic knowledge?

## The Rational Science of Economics

When the economics of Adam Smith was taking shape, the rationalist faith of the Enlightenment was dominant; reason, it was hoped, could shed light on all aspects of mankind's situation. Especially, it was assumed, science was the creation of human reason. This emphasis became an assumed part of the classical economic tradition, but there was an important difference between, say, Ricardo at the beginning of the 19th century and Walras at the end; the latter was self-conscious in his rationalism and made it *the* method of economic science, as the following quotation shows.

> Similarly, given the *pure theory of economics*, it must precede *applied economics;* and this pure theory of economics is a science which resembles the physio-mathematical sciences in every respect. This assertion is new and will seem strange; but I have just proved it to be true, and I shall elaborate the proof in what follows.
> If the pure theory of economics or the theory of exchange and value in exchange, that is, the theory of social wealth considered by itself, is a physio-mathematical science like mechanics or hydrodynamics, then economists should not be afraid to use the methods and language of mathematics.
> The mathematical method is not an *experimental* method; it is a *rational* method.... From real type concepts, these sciences abstract ideal-type concepts which they define, and then on the basis of these definitions they construct *a priori* the whole framework of their theorems and proofs.... Following this same procedure the pure theory of economics ought to take over from experience certain type-concepts, like those of exchange, supply, demand, market, capital, income, productive services and products. From these real-type concepts the pure science of economics should then abstract and define ideal-type concepts in terms of which it carries on its reasoning. The return to reality should not take place until the science is completed and then only with a view to practical applications. [Walras, 1954, p. 71]

We can see that this approach involves strong methodological prescription, and that the correct method is theorem and proof. Since from the time of Menger, Jevons, and Walras, rationalism has been the backbone of much classical and neoclassical theory, we need to follow through the implications and problems of this approach, for they are replicated throughout the discipline.

The rational science of economics has not, however, retained one coherent form, and it will be helpful at this stage to identify discrete positions. The first vests rationality in the subject and assumes that *a priori* reasoning is the normal necessary pattern of economic science. The second identifies rationality with logic and sees scientific economics as developing a logic of choice. A third tradition, which has its roots in post-Hegelian German thought, for example, that of Weber, received its most famous statement in the definition of Robbins [1952] that

> Economics is the science which studies human behavior as a relationship between ends and scarce means which have alternative uses. [p. 16]

This definition when formulated in 1932 was already a recognition that "ends" could never be designated "rational" or "irrational" without a prior value judgment, and it therefore recognized implicitly the untenability of the first position. It saw *instrumental rationality* as the domain of economics. [Weber, 1947, p. 115] Finally, there is a quasi-agnostic form of rationalism which merely asserts the need for theory to be self-consistent; although many theorists avow this form, it is incomplete, for the theory must be consistent with its own assumptions, procedures, and processes of validation. This means that economists must always hold this view in conjunction with another implicit position. We will therefore look at the implications for economics of each of the three earlier positions.

## A Priori Rationalism

The belief in the rationality of economic man gave a very strong theory of the uniformity of economic behavior; because he thought thus, so he acted. This was the central assumption of a tradition growing out of Kantian thought comprising Menger, the Austrian school, and many other economists. Self evident rational calculations gave the order to their economic universe. However, if people did not both carry out the ratiocinative processes and act on them, this approach became otherworldly, a mere metaphysical creation of the armchair economist. In fact, the universal economic *a priori* has run into just such problems. Far from each person rationally pursuing their self-interest, in a necessary *a priori* fashion, it became obvious that what people perceived as their self-interest depended on prior values and processes of validation, and that contradictory conclusions could and often did follow from their value premises. Gradually the self-evident nature of the position has broken down. It is no longer clear *a priori* what rational self-interest might be.

Apart from the problem of the *a priori*, the cogito of economic man, there were other obvious weaknesses. Many human motives were seen to be subconscious or preconscious, to be socially and culturally defined, to draw from different roots, to be contradictory, and to have different forms of justification.. The rudimentary development of the social sciences quickly weakened the model of the consistent rational individual calculator maximizing his self-interest. Another problem was that what was "rational" for the individual may well not be for the group and vice versa; hence problems like the Prisoners' Dilemma. Finally, at least since Marx and Freud, it has been evident that the justifications for action may be far removed from why they take place, that rationalizations often take place after the event, rather than reason operating to shape it.

Nevertheless, the momentum of this tradition and its influence in neoclassical economics has been great, and we therefore need to consider some of the forms of blinkered vision that it has created and perpetuated. One of the most important implicit assumptions is of the infallibility of rational man; because man rationally worked out his own economic self-interest it was impossible that he could be mistaken or wrong in the outcome. The enormity of this assumption, which has precommitted neoclassical economics to eliminating mistakes from human economic activity, can scarcely be overestimated. If everybody is rationally following her own self-interest, then all that remains for the economist is to tinker with and oil the mechanism. Nothing can be wrong, it can only be blandly sub-optimal. The "rational expectations" debate is in part merely an attempt to keep this utopian approach alive.

A second view concerns the assumption that all economic agents are free rational decision makers. It effectively excludes the possibility that people are *constrained* to economic action. Yet often they *have* to find a job, any job, to look after their parents or to get food to eat. The choices that this epistemological model assumes as normal are for most people a goal on the horizon.

The pattern of calculation is also essentially non-relational. As each rational unit calculates outward from his self-interest, other persons and groups must become mere instruments in that process. Thus we have the creation of this gigantic stage set where all the actors walk about in their own personal fog, calculating to the audience, but never meeting or interacting. Yet this fiction has become the normal theoretical script.

Another corollary of the position could be called "tunnel surprise." If economic theory has to mirror the rational processes of economic agents, it cannot take into account the unintended or unformulated consequences of these processes. As it comes blinking out into the blinding light of reality, it may well be surprised by all that is not comprehended by the simplistic *a priori* starting point of the theory. Keynes took great delight in showing how the irrational policy of filling old bottles with bank notes and burying them might be better than the classical "rational" policy. [1936, p. 129] More recently the ecological revolution has hit economics under the belt precisely because it was the incidental aspects of decisions on which ecology focused. Now the useful catch-all category of externalities is growing like a cuckoo in the economic nest, eating up garbage, pollution, public costs, vandalism, social dislocation, personal breakdown, aesthetic decay, and a host of other effects which were outside the rational intentions of standard theory.

Where does this leave the standard *a priori* approach? Although it is less explicitly used, many economists still espouse it. They argue that the underlying central economic order is uncovered by the rationality assumption, and subsequent elaborations can take account of variations. Thus *a priori* becomes the model. Samuelson suggests this kind of approach in some of his writing.

> I have assumed, throughout, perfect certainty as an analytic device. I fully recognize that it is philosophically impossible to deduce behavior on the part of perfectly rational individuals which will guarantee that his condition be fulfilled, since the behavior of each individual forms the obstacle or *liaison* under which all other individuals act, and reciprocally. It is an admittedly singular case when all people do behave in a manner which fulfills the hypothetical expectations in terms of which they have behaved. But there is no contradiction involved in the assumption; such cases need not exist, but they *could* exist. It has long been customary in economic science to consider such singular cases, and it is my belief that the clear working out of this one may prove to be a useful and illuminating introduction to more complex reality. [1939, p. 200]

This approach is based on a trust in the *a priori* rational core of man to provide useful parables from which more realistic theory can be elaborated, although the core does not exist, and the realism cannot be tacked on as an afterthought.

## Logically Scientific Economics

The weaknesses of the *a priori* view of knowledge were evident to many 19th century economists, and another more compelling scientific framework moved to the center of the discipline at the end of the century in the work of Jevons, Pareto, Slutsky, Barone, Hicks and Allen. All of these had a commitment to logic as an irrefutable basis for economic argument and saw the discipline basically as elaborating a logic of choice. What is the significance of this position? The commitment to logic aims to achieve an irrefutable methodological basis for the discipline. Nobody can disagree with logic. But what kind of logic does this position entail? It does not imply the old premise-conclusion form, because if the premises do not agree, then there is no basis for cohesion in the discipline. Rather, it implies an empty logic. This framework accorded well with the position developed by Carnap. He saw logic as the universal language of science. In the first edition of *Erkenntnis* he describes his vision thus:

> The new series of this journal which begins with this volume, will be devoted to the development of *a new, scientific method of philosophizing*. Perhaps this method can be briefly characterized as consisting *in the logical analysis of the statements and concepts of empirical science...* Since all the sentences of logic are tautological and devoid of content, we

cannot draw inferences from them about what is necessary or impossible in reality... Thus, with the aid of the new logic, logical analysis leads to a unified science. There are not different sciences with fundamentally different methods or different sources of knowledge, but only one science. All knowledge finds its place in this science and, indeed, is knowledge of basically the same kind. [1959]

However, this position has a central problem. Its faith is in logical necessity, or analytical statements which are true whatever the state of affairs in the world. This approach could claim to be totally undogmatic, in that it is not making statements about the actual state of affairs, but merely what might necessarily be the case in any possible world. Yet this scientific security was also a commitment to a pattern of otherworldliness. Logical possibilities are endless.

This kind of logical otherworldliness is widespread in economics. Its seeming neutrality is appealing, since it seems not to rule out any possibility *a priori*. Thus Green, working within this framework, claims:

The definition of rationality given in the last section is so general that it is not possible for a consumer's observed choices to be inconsistent with it. [1971, p. 25]

Yet it is this commitment to logical possibility which results in economic otherworldliness. Its prevalence is exemplified by Hicks' comment with respect to much Growth Theory, including his own.

It has been fertile in the generation of class-room exercises; but so far as we can yet see they are exercises, not real problems. They are not even hypothetical real problems, of the type 'what would happen if' where the 'if' is something that could conceivably happen. They are shadows of real problems, dressed up in such a way that by pure logic we can find solutions to them. [1965, p. 183]

This drive towards logical otherworldliness is one of the greatest influences on the development of modern theory. One area where the drama can be played through is in classical and neoclassical macroeconomic theory. In the *General Theory* Keynes states the logically necessary premise from which he is trying to escape.

From the time of Say and Ricardo the classical economists have taught that supply creates its own demand;—meaning by this in some significant, but not clearly defined, sense that the whole of the costs of production must necessarily be spent in the aggregate, directly or indirectly on purchasing the product. [1936, p. 18]

And in his subsequent definitions of the Aggregate Demand and Supply functions, which are not based on logical necessity, he does, in fact, escape, and enjoys it.

> Now, since these parts of experience do not follow from logical necessity, one must suppose . . .. [1936, p. 25]

However, the neoclassical economists were quick to reestablish the old position. Samuelson argued that

> Until the appearance of the mathematical models of Meade, Lange, Hicks, and Harrod, there is reason to believe that Keynes himself did not truly understand his own analysis... We thus reach the conclusion that, as far as the *logical* content of Keynes' theory goes, ... no revolution has taken place. [1948]

Thus reformulated, neoclassical Keynesian economics established necessary identities like Y = C + I + G which became the logical basis of many subsequent analyses. As Mini comments,

> Keynes was an imaginative artist. [But] Keynesian economics is a more or less involved tautology. [1976, p. 277]

Nor is this the only field in which logical necessity is seen as having the core role. The tortured history of the identity, MV = PT, in monetary theory evidences a similar pattern; what is necessarily the case and what is empirically the case have faced one another across an unbridgeable epistemological gulf.

What are the criticisms of this epistemological position? First, it is logically reductionist; the full complexity of economic behavior is emaciated to these otherworldly tautologies. Second, it remains essentially extratheoretical, for theory which actually relates to economic life must have a different epistemological basis. Thus, somewhere there must be an absolute (although usually masked) discontinuity. Third, the search for ultimate theoretical certainty is misconceived; by trying to erect some absolute logical necessities, economic infallibilia, on which the more precarious theory can be hung, the economist is both committing himself to *necessary* frustrating failure, because the tautologies have no hooks on which to hang theory, and is failing to understand the limited status of theoretical knowledge.

At the same time, the claim to be non-dogmatic is misleadingly false. The use of an either/or exclusive logic means that in many situations where a both/and pattern might exist, aspects of the situation are likely to be misconceived. Other possibilities are dogmatically excluded. Similarly, the assumption that equilibrium follows logically excludes all kinds of dynamic disequilibria which are normal in the real world, purely because it does not suit this method. This framework also means that the future is seen in terms of what is logically possible. Finally, we have to recognize that the very construction of much economic theory is geared solely to the *logical* solution of the problem under consideration.

## Means-ends Rationality

The modified rationalism represented by Robbins has also become part of neoclassical orthodoxy. Ends, it is acknowledged, are subjective, multidirectional, value-laden, and outside the scope of economics as a science. The discipline therefore becomes concerned with the rationality of *means*. [Robbins, 1952] The status of this rationality is very different from the previous kinds; it is not *a priori*, or logical but a rationality of process. However, as Robbins shows, the concern is still with the scientific nature of the discipline; the ends, about which we cannot pass judgment, can be analyzed through means which can be objectively and rationally judged; they can be optimal or suboptimal, efficient or inefficient. Indeed, it is clear that Robbins rather reluctantly reacted against the welfare principles of, for example, Pigou, in order to retain his "scientific" definition of the discipline. Since interpersonal value judgments could not be rational, they had to be expelled from the corpus of economics. In looking at this tradition we note both its internal weaknesses and also the way it constricts what is to be considered.

The weaknesses occur in a variety of forms. The rationalism of this system assumes that if a person prefers A to B and B to C, then he will also prefer A to C. Consistency or transitivity is the principle which follows from using a simple basis of comparison. Thus if A tastes better than B, and B than C, then A will taste better than C. However, if persons have multiple ends and use multiple criteria for ranking goods and services, transitivity rapidly breaks down. Yet multiple criteria are ubiquitous, normal, and an unavoidable part of the human condition. Do we drink water to quench thirst or wine for taste? Do we go buy a car for comfort or walk for exercise? Do we hold a particular job for its content, status, pay, location, or from inertia? There is scarcely any area where different ends and criteria are not weighed and the simplicity of instrumental rationalism breaks down.

Second, the idea that only the ends have value and the means are merely instrumental is a peculiarly teleological idea. The absolute goal, always in the future, is the only point of meaning. In fact, of course, the means are also of human value. The Japanese do not think that the only point of the tea ceremony is drinking tea, nor does the worker assume that the only point of work is pay. The falseness of the perspective which has to chase all values out of the domain of economics in order to create a neutral, scientific, instrumental area for the discipline is palpably clear. Since we all have to live in the present, and since what we are engaged in as means has to be existentially meaningful, we cannot ignore the present significance of the means. Thus there is no justification for creating this scientific value-free area. Both ends and means are subject to deep values which are interrelated at many levels, and the crude separation of the two cannot but be false.

Yet this antiseptically defined zone has prescribed what theory should be like. Theory is solving problems of technical means; it does that by chasing all the values out of the domain. The effect of this on the presentation of economic issues has been devastating, for only when the "scientific neutral technical" analysis has been carried out can the values be brought in from the periphery. Thus, work is for pay but *then* we consider job enrichment.

The fact is that the means-ends schema is a methodological lie. The means—whether our jobs, our mobility, our purchasing habits, or our economic environment—matter a great deal to us and are loaded with values. Similarly, a lot of the so-called consumption ends are themselves largely instrumental (see chapter VIII). Yet again, the rationalist assumption that it is possible to coordinate ends within a single system ignores and downplays the important fact that many economic ends of different groups and of single persons are mutually inconsistent or involve establishing priorities. At another level the means-ends schema consigns ends to the subjective area of life, and yet many people are concerned about the consistency of the ends they pursue. The whole precarious value-rational dichotomization is as leaky as a sieve, and only the power of myth keeps it afloat on the sea of human values.

Rationalism in modern theory is therefore still going through the realization that these three epistemological assumptions of *a priori* rationality, of a logical structure for economics, and a rational means/ends distinction are invalid. Where does this leave rationalist economics? Unfortunately, with little change, for this methodological train has achieved considerable speed and momentum, and even if the fire has gone out, it will carry on for many miles with the old assumptions of theory as proof, of logical analysis as method, of a technical means framework, of non-relational calculations, of maximization, and of value-freedom. Often those patterns are just habit, carried on from teacher to student. If good work is being done within this tradition, it is usually in spite of the methodological track along which these economists are travelling.

## Positivist Theory

At roughly the same time as the development of methodological rationalism, empiricism, or positivism, was also picked up, especially in the Anglo Saxon world, as *the* neutral scientific methodology. This tradition especially took shape in the treatise of John Neville Keynes on *The Scope and Method of Political Economy*. [1890, 4th ed., 1917] Keynes argued that Mill, Cairnes, and other classical economists who claimed to be deductive, were in practice more inductive. His crucial arguments depended on the methodological certitude of *facts* as a basis for economic science.

> There is a further reason why a positive science of political economy should receive distinct and independent recognition. With the advance of knowledge, it may be possible to come to a general agreement in regard to what is or what may be in the economic

world, sooner than any similar agreement is attainable in regard to the rules by which the economic activities of individuals and communities should be guided. The former requires only that there should be unanimity as to facts.... However necessary it may be to face these questions at a later stage, there is no reason why we should not have a positive science of economics which is independent of them. [1917, pp. 52-3]

During the interwar period this tradition remained strong, and in the 50's and 60's it became the most 'visible' economic epistemology and has to some extent been taken as orthodoxy. [Hutchinson, 1938; Friedman, 1953] A typical statement of the position in a recent text is as follows:

Economics, like other sciences, is concerned with questions, statements and hypotheses that could conceivably be shown to be wrong (that is, false) by actual observations of the world. It is not necessary to show them to be either consistent or inconsistent with the facts tomorrow or the next day; it is only necessary to be able to imagine evidence that could show them to be wrong. *Thus an appeal to the facts is an appropriate way in which to deal with them.* [Lipsey & Steiner, 1981, p. 19]

However, this simple textbook approach glosses the different formulations of positivism that have been grafted on to the parent stem, and have grown and withered. We shall look at major themes in modern economic positivism.

**Simple Empiricism**

The search for the unequivocal, the basic building block for the discipline, has led economists to *facts*. The philosophical roots of this position can be traced to Locke and Hume, but the renewed interest in the late 19th century has other sources. One is the sociological positivism of Comte, partially adopted by J. S. Mill (and later Durkheim); another is the philosophical positivism which began in the 1880's with Mach and became influential in Berlin under the influence of Reichenbach, in Vienna through the work of Schlick, and in Britain through Russell, Wittgenstein and A. J. Ayer. Thus, the crusade for positivism became international.

The core of this position was that observational data were the undisputed building blocks from which all theoretical statements could be constructed and by which they were judged. Schlick stated the issue thus:

We shall therefore try to see whether we can arrive at a theory of all truth by starting from truths of fact.... What criterion do we have for the truths of propositions which assert something about facts in the world of sense? The answer is very easy and undoubtedly runs: none other than by *verification*: that is assuredly the first and most fundamental rule of all factual enquiry: to consider only those assumptions correct, only those laws valid, which are verified under all circumstances. Beyond this there is no other criterion; neither the opinion of the majority of those able to judge, nor the view of an authority, nor the firmest subjective conviction and seeming insight into necessity, nor any other factor, can provide the slightest support for truth, so far as it is not itself founded in turn upon verification. [1978]

This fundamental faith in the neutrality of facts, and the unassailable conclusions drawn from facts, still permeates much economic analysis, and we shall therefore examine in detail the refutations of the position and the constrictions imposed by the method.

First (see below) the facts could not take account of mathematics and logic, which appealed to necessary conclusions, not contingent ones. Second, any criterion of verification, since it could not itself be verified, was a self-refuting proposition. The third criticism, raised by Popper, [1959] showed the impossibility of deriving any universal or general law statement from particular facts, and therefore invalidated positivism as a natural science methodology. The fourth, more devastating to a social science, was the denial of a unique and neutral observation language, a simple one to one correspondence rule, shown especially by Hanson in *Patterns of Discovery* [1969] Observation reports, rather than being bedrock facts, are shaped by the conceptual scheme and expectations of the observer so that a "fact" is merely one interpretation among a range of possible ones. One has "data beliefs" and "data-background beliefs" which allow rival conceptualizations, none of which can be validated simply by an appeal to the facts. [Wolterstorff, 1976, pp. 62-3] The final point we shall mention is that observation as a method does not handle the *meaning* of human activity; Wittgenstein's great pilgrimage from the *Tractatus Logico-Philosophicus* [1961] to the *Philosophical Investigations* centered on this realization. Thus the claims of positivism to be (a) a scientific method and (b) to generate a unique and neutral pattern of analysis failed. Nevertheless, the prescriptions of the method have frog-marched the discipline in certain very constraining directions.

One has been the kind of data collected and used in economic theory. Empiricists have been attracted, like a moth to the light, to observables, to quantification, to atomized data, to that which could be easily and cheaply gathered. Consider, for example, the largely unquestioned assumption that National Income is *the* measure of aggregate national welfare. For decades, as a result of this assumption, the unquantifiable subsistence economy was ignored. Recently many less visible concepts like disamenities, pollution, instrumental expenditures, leisure, and a host of other factors have emerged from the shadows of positivist observational language, blinking nervously on the economic stage. [Nordhaus & Tobin, 1972] Now we have also recognized the significance of human "capital" over against the more easily quantifiable bricks, mortar, and machines. Seemingly hard indicators, like unemployment, have been examined in a more sophisticated way. Thus, we are in the process of realizing how biased data have been. It would, however, be inaccurate to say that the fact that a person is unhappy in his job is yet taken as seriously as the fact that he buys a new suit.

Another inbuilt assumption has been the necessary atomism of facts and the identification of theory with the creation of patterns among facts. For the positivist, facts are distinct, and there is no possibility of inherent relations existing among the objects which are perceived. As Hume says,

> There is no object which implies the existence of any other, if we consider these objects in themselves. [1888]

Wittgenstein puts it thus:

> States of affairs are independent of one another. From the existence or non-existence of one state of affairs it is impossible to infer the existence or non-existence of another. [1961, p. 13]

This atomism, which is necessary to create the supposedly neutral basic building blocks of knowledge, involves a methodological segregation into data which destroys underlying relationships. Since a variety of possible observational languages exists, there is no necessary reason why the data should be described in a way which brings out the underlying relationships. We also notice that, because all data are given the same status, they all have the same significance as explanation, and depth relationships are excluded from the analysis.

This brings us to the heart of the Friedman monetary theory controversy. For Friedman as a positivist is concerned with the association of data, and specifically with the data of inflation and those of the money supply. The association of the two, Friedman's positivist "proof," does not satisfy those who want to know what the underlying relationships are, and particularly whether money may or may not be a dependent variable. At that point the debate begins to break down, especially when the possibility that human agents can *anticipate* trends is admitted, but as long as Friedman holds to his positivist methodology, he cannot meaningfully interact with his critics. [Friedman, 1953, Crump, 1970, Mason, 1980] It is interesting that his methodological atomism also fits in with his and Mrs. Friedman's ideology of radical individualism. [Friedman & Friedman, 1980, Firm, 1979] Thus we see again that the apparent neutrality of the foundational methodology does not stand up to examination.

Positivism also excludes the human subject from its frame of reference. The reason is that persons cannot be captured as a series of perceptions. This important limitation of positivism has an effect on economics in two ways. Neither the economist as knower, nor the human economic subjects, enters the domain of economics.

The position of the knower has been succinctly put by Wittgenstein.

> The subject does not belong to the world; rather, it is the limit of the world. [1961, p. 117]

This position excludes all reflexivity by economists, qua subjects, about their religious and ideological commitments, and their own socioeconomic situation. The effect has been for positive economists to assume that they are omniscient viewers whose objectivity is beyond discussion.

It also means that persons engaged in economic activity are *not* the subject of the economists' concern, but only the economic data which they generate by their activity. It is the data which then form the basis for economic forecasting as extrapolation and the correlation of data. The "objectivity" of data has as its flip side the "unknowable subjectivity" of the person and the theoretical meaninglessness of all statements which do not relate to observables. All the nonobservables—issues of ethics, values, volition, love, fairness, needs which have no external money expression—are banished from the universe of discourse. Thus, for Samuelson, who at times opts for a form of positivism which Blaug (1980) calls *descriptivism*, the whole complex of consumer behavior is reduced to Revealed (i.e., observable) Preference. In this impersonal economics there are no obvious problems, because problems are related to persons rather than patterns. Wittgenstein again develops the implications of the position with precision.

> We feel that even when *all possible* scientific questions have been answered, the problems of life remain completely untouched. Of course there are then no questions left and this itself is the answer. The solution of the problem of life is seen in the vanishing of the problem. [1961, p. 149]

Although many economists are more caring than their methodological position, much economic analysis does implicitly say that there are no human problems.

Another fundamental consequence of the observational stance is that all normative or moral principles slip through the positivist net; the stance renders meaningless terms like choice, responsibility, duty and care. Thus for at least a century the argument that one cannot derive an "ought" statement from an "is" statement has been used to chase normativity out of economics. Although the positivist stance has proved inadequate and internally inconsistent, it is still used to declare normative issues outside the scope of normal economic theory. Since this is fundamental to our subsequent position, it is worth stopping to consider further how the is/ought distinction is false.

Although norms and values are "unobservable" by the senses, they are an integral part of all economic activity; assent and commitment to certain values, standards, and norms are a prerequisite for the activity of economic agents, and define its meaning. Moreover, normal economic language recognizes it. "This coat is cheap" is a statement of description *and* value. If, as well, "You need a coat," it is also prescriptive, and you buy it. Most economic terms contain, often implicitly, important norms and values; "equilibrium" implies stability; "profit maximization" implies a certain valuation of workers *and* consumers, and is normative for the operation of the firm. The "rate of interest" involves time-valuation, and the price system depends upon a whole complex of values which is society-wide. The suppression of all these norms, values, and standards by which we actually live is thus only achieved by abstracting to observational, and therefore biased, data, and creating an illusion of positive neutrality. Thus the statement, "Ten tons of coal were mined yesterday," appears a brute fact, but the fuller statement, "Ten tons of poor quality coal were mined grudgingly yesterday, failing to meet the target of fifteen," provides the normative context. We therefore argue that norms, understood as precepts for living, as principles for economic activity, are necessarily woven into the subject, and indeed are the precondition of meaningful economic actions. By claiming to exclude any consideration of norms, either on rationalist and positivist grounds, the discipline has lifted certain normative principles (like maximization, growth and profitability) which are a normal part of theory to the level of dogma because they are not recognized as normative. [Skillen, 1980] By contrast, much of our later analysis will adopt an explicit, reflective and Christianly committed approach to norms.

Another constriction of this methodology is that it *must* be uncritical. Since the facts are given ultimate status as knowledge, they cannot be criticized, seen as defective, evil, misguided, or unfair; there is no way of going beyond patterning that which is given as facts. The flatness of this approach to knowledge, and its inability to adopt a critical evaluation of the economy account for much of the relative impotence of the discipline in its advisory role. The prescriptions, which must be dragged in *ex post*, can only be that a certain pattern, like zero price growth, is a good thing. They must be self-evidently good or tailored to the particular politicians who are seeking economic advisors.

Finally, we also note that positivism implies an instant "blick" view of time. States of affairs are observed at a particular moment, and there is nothing in those statements which implies anything, in causal or any other terms, for any other period of time. This essentially static methodological approach has helped to create the rather artificial and often confusing distinction in economics between *statics* and *dynamics*. Partly, the confusion is verbal, if C = f(y) is a regularity drawn from comparisons of successive relations between income and consumption, then the formulation is *stable*, not static. However, the blick perspective necessarily leads to a certain homeostasis in much theory, for example, Friedman's, as the regularities in aggregations are sought out. Part of the genius of Keynes was his ability to move from this kind of static approach to a dynamic one, especially in chapters 8-10 of the *General Theory*.

Thus we see that the methodological position of positivism, which is now thoroughly discredited, has created forms of tunnel vision in the approach to theory which have substantially shaped the development of the discipline, especially the statistical and econometric branches of it. However, we have not traced all the developments, for positivism has other forms.

### Falsificationism

There has, of course, been a long and sustained criticism of positivism this century, and specific forms like operationalism, descriptivism and logical positivism have been discredited, but this has not destroyed the underlying positivist faith. [Suppe, 1977] It has merely meant that the forms of modern positivism are different. One form, developed especially by Nagel, [1961] and Hempel and Oppenheim [1948] recognized that the problem of induction meant that theory could in no sense be derived from the facts. They therefore disassociated the business of theoretical formulation from the data base and suggested that theory was by nature hypothetical and deductive; it involved asserting some covering law which then had to be tested against the facts in a specific situation. This form therefore retained the epistemological authority of facts for the process of theory testing, but not for theory formation.

A similar position had already been developed by Popper, who was one of the strongest and earliest critics of simple positivism. His way of giving a partial role to data was to see theory formation in terms of what could be disconfirmed or falsified. Theory did not have an empirical base per se; it could in practice depend on all kinds of philosophical assumptions. However, the power of the theory was to be seen in the possibilities which it ruled out; the more a theory predicted would not happen, the more it stuck its neck out, the more open it was to empirical testing and the greater its reliability. Thus again the theoretical construction was not positivist, but the process of testing a theory was largely construed by Popper in terms of some process of empirical validation. It is interesting to note within this framework that *prediction* moves much more fully to the center of the stage as the key element in theory formation.

It is into this kind of debate that Friedman [1953] walked, although he was not directly concerned with the philosophy of science, and stated that the assumptions need not be judged by any criterion of realism; it was merely the predictions that stand or fall by testability. Partly, one suspects, this position was generated by his earlier failure to find real indifference curves, [Wallis & Friedman, 1962] but also by his commitment to predictive positivism.

This, however, is a very wobbly methodology. The sole epistemological basis is again the facts, and the theoretical structure is not merely nominal, but is largely psychological with no obvious relationship to the real world. This might be justifiable if the idea of prediction was as conclusive as Friedman thought it was. However, this has turned out not to be the case.

For prediction grows out of a quasi-experimental situation which allows other conditions to be held constant; it is a criterion generated for replicable experiments. To a considerable extent these situations do not obtain in economic life, where other conditions vary substantially. Moreover, it is possible for several different theories to explain a similar outcome or for different outcomes to be posited for one generic theory. Generally the problem may be summed up by saying that falsified predictions may be derived from what are considered "local" or "global" counterexamples, and that there are interpretive issues involved which make prediction, although an important part of economic theory, no simple criterion of knowledge. [Lakatos, 1976] Thus it, too, turns out to be merely a wave on the epistemological tide, which although many economists are still surfing on it, will dissipate into the sand.

Another development has arisen from the realization that there is a tendency for theories to develop their own particular criteria of falsification and to cluster in larger paradigmatic models which are periodically overthrown as orthodoxy. [Kuhn, 1970] This has undermined further the initial Popperian idea of falsificationism, for it is possible for different groups to see the same evidence as validating their position. This ambiguity, especially because it is not acknowledged by economists who claim that their particular theory has been tested by the facts, has dogged the debate in many areas. Testing is closely related to the structure of theory, and it may be that even though a theory stands up to an "objective" test, it is missing the point. The assumed objectivity of positivist thinking is still doing damage in economics.

## Behaviorial and Institutional Economics

There is another critique of positivism which has been much more influential in sociology, and which is slowly having its impact in economics. Basically the position is that rather than a world of hard nuggets of empirical fact, there are merely trace elements embedded in a magma of human meaning. As Wittgenstein had acknowledged by the time of his *Philosophical Investigations*, there are no discrete atomic propositions which are the building blocks of knowledge. No longer could the subject's perception of activity, the meaning of the act, be ruled out of the epistemological court.

Or, to put this in economic terms, price information, the focus of much economic theory, tells us little about the meaning of people's economic lives. A person may decide not to buy a good because the price is too high, the good is shoddily made, the colors are garish, it is environmentally destructive, or because he doesn't like the look on the vendor's face. This position recognizes that there is not one simple "rational" necessary pattern of action, and that the "facts" are very incomplete and partial descriptions of reality.

### The Approach of Keynes
We have already met one economic version of this position in the work of Keynes, for he, unlike most of his contemporaries, was prepared to consider the diverse subjective reasons why people act economically. Terms like "the state of confidence," "liquidity preference," "the state of bearishness" actually feature in the analysis, although many economists dare not look at such profanities. But Keynes in *A Treatise on Probability* had early established how weak our grasp on indirect knowledge is, and had moved away from a foundational rationalist or empiricist position in his economic analysis. He took the perceptions and orientations of economic subjects seriously as substantial guides to their behavior and contribution to the economy. That it produced a more realistic and practical analysis of the situation in the 1930's few would deny, although more would do well to take note of the kind of critical position that Keynes had developed of his contemporaries in econometrics and mathematical economics. (Keynes 1973, M. G. Phelps, 1980)

Keynes's approach was not based on a foundational epistemology; he had an interesting alternative. He had a normative commitment, often a strong and explicit one, although his normativity was related to his long contact with an establishment which normally and naturally made things happen. Already as a very young civil servant he was telling the Prime Minister, Lloyd George, that he was contributing to the devastation of Europe. Thus Keynes wrote in a letter to Roy Harrod

> Economics is a science of thinking in terms of models joined to the art of choosing models which are relevant to the contemporary world....
>
> In the second place, as against Robbins, economics is essentially a moral science and not a natural science. That is to say, it employs introspection and judgments of value. [Harrod, 1951, p. 253]

Essentially Keynes had an elitist, normative view. The chaos of activity and behavior that characterized the masses was treated as given, and, as he showed, it often had undesirable consequences. Yet it was the job of the intellectual elite to create a normative order out of this chaos, with the norms of full employment, stable prices, and growth. Although there was a gigantic increase in national responsibility as a result of this approach, by assuming the anormativity and passivity of the masses, Keynes limited the significance of norms to a few macroeconomic variables. Implicitly this meant ignoring the normative content of institutions, markets, and other economic relationships. Thus we argue that Keynes only partially comprehended the truth that we are all responsible stewards before God in all of our economic roles, and it has been an abiding weakness in post-World War II economics which derives its inspiration from Keynes that only governments are supposed to have full economic responsibility.

### American Institutionalism

A similar and more systematic development had also occurred in the United States. When John Commons wrote *Institutional Economics* in 1934 he acknowledged that his epistemological basis was rooted in Peirce's pragmatism. This position also broke down the barrier between descriptive and prescriptive. Here is Peirce seen through Common's eyes:

> Peirce's pragmatism, applied to institutional economics, is the scientific investigation of these economic relations of citizens to citizens. Its subject matter is the whole concern of which the individuals are members, and the activities investigated are their transactions governed by an entirely different law, not a law of nature but a working rule, for the time being, of collective action. [1934, p. 157]

The theme of this position is knowledge as control, theory that "works." People are an explicit part of the analysis in this framework, especially in their institutional relationships. A modern institutionalist, Galbraith, states the position thus:

It holds that industrial society is in a process of continuous and organic change, that public policy must accomodate to such change, and that by such public action performance can, in fact, be improved. Its commitment is to reformist changes....
Specifically in the modern democratic context, people seek to gain greater control over their own lives. This extends to all of life's dimensions. [1978, pp. 8-9]

There are a lot of different emphases possible within this position.
One approach focuses on evolutionary and historical development. Since what *has been* the economic order need be so no longer, it is continually necessary, argues Galbraith, to respond to what is developing. But this is no mere historicism; the evolution is not inevitable, but capable of controlled direction. What kind of direction is given by the institutionalist perspective? Is it rational, public, customary, radical, behaviorial, progressive, or what? Each of these positions involves bringing in value-judgments and norms which shape the diagnosis of what is going on. Few economists have yet acknowledged the full depth of the implications of adopting an explicit normative interpretation of evolutionary development, although some now admit that it is necessary. [Samuels, 1980] Some shelve the issue by adopting a "descriptive" or positivist stance towards the institutional or valuational differences which they accept as being significant. Yet this position is no more valid than the original positivist formulations; to discuss values as "facts" is to ignore the *necessity* of analyzing them in an interpretational language even if it is the status quo language of the values themselves.

Another emphasis has been on the "holistic" nature of institutionalist economic theory. [Fusfeld, 1980] The integral, patterned, and bilateral nature of relationships is stressed in reaction to the atomism, the unilateral causality, and the unirelational aspects of much neoclassical theory. However, this, too, raises a number of largely unresolved issues. First, what is the relation between sociology, economics, politics, law, psychology? There is a tendency for these to be amalgamated in various degrees in institutionalist work without sufficient clarity about what the new relationship among these disciplines is. Second, the integral approach to theory brings up the fundamental issue of the status of human decision-making which has been largely glossed. Concepts like "public," "countervailing power," "the corporate state," preclude the prior and important issue of what the institutional order should be. For here Western economic thinking has largely been trapped in the distinction between public/private, State/capitalist, and we shall argue that it is only with a more sophisticated pluralist institutionalist approach that we can get at some of the significant directions in institutional development.

### Marxist Economic Knowledge

To label Marxist economics as institutionalist might seem unusual to those who see it as historicist or as the outworking of a materialist dialectic. It is true that much analysis still concentrates on showing the inevitability of the collapse of capitalism; "the falling rate of profit" is still the focus of many articles.

Modern Marxist theory has, however, partly cut itself free from many of the dogmatic materialist assumptions of the later Marx and has moved more firmly to the institutional category of class and an analysis of various forms of class exploitation. [Mandel, 1970] Unlike other institutionalists who have their own versions of agnosticism about economic institutions, Marxists have one main ideological commitment. The labor theory of value, which identifies all value ultimately with the workers, is the tenet which directs their search for knowledge. This makes the Marxian critique both too narrow and too radical.

It is too radical in failing to recognize and respect the value and normative structure of the various institutions and communities that help form the economic community. The family, the enterprise, and the state tend all to be equated merely as agents of exploitation. A corollary of this is that the revolutionary goals tend to be utopian and, when realized, are shown to have failed to respect a lot of the aspects of the human condition.

It is not radical enough in identifying only capitalist forces as evil and destructive. This is a limited doctrine of sin, indeed. It is not only that the forms of human error are more varied and complex than class exploitation, but also that even the workers partake of and commit themselves to damaging economic decisions. A critique of monopoly capital is also a critique of those who support and purchase from it; economics is a discipline packed with many little decisions. In the end Marx is an epistemological position for the self-righteous economist; he, too, and the group that he identifies with are under judgment.

Finally, we note that pragmatism and institutionalism, although they have escaped from some of the constraints of positivism and rationalism in economics, still contain serious epistemological problems. The emphasis is on *theory which works*, but by what criteria is the theory judged? It is easy for blind evolutionary circularity to be the basis of economic science; acceptable theory is that which is validated by academic economists or fellow Marxists. Economic truth, as Commons acknowledged much earlier, becomes a matter of social consensus, what emerges as orthodoxy, presumably largely among professional economists. [1934, p. 152] But which pattern or story is the correct one, and in what sense? The impression is often conveyed in institutionalist literature of relativism, that one presentation of theory is as good as another. We think that this, too, is the result of leaving a more fundamental epistemological issue that has cropped up continually unresolved. Why is it that independently based theory, foundational theory, whether in positivist, rationalist, or other forms, has always proved inadequate, and why has it so strongly directed theory? The answer to both questions has a common source.

## The Underlying Epistemological Fallacy

The epistemological positions that we have examined have all been concerned with establishing the autonomy of economic science, with a foundational kind of knowledge, the truth of which can be established by some procedural protocol. As we saw at the beginning of the chapter, this faith in method was seen as a way of achieving neutrality, of guaranteeing the scientific status of the discipline and of giving the economist an unbiased character. In the preceeding sections we have shown that these foundational positions do not succeed, and that, far from being neutral, they have distinctively and divergently channelled theory.

Our Christian perspective allows us to put these failures in context. If science is a response to the creation, human and non-human, then a number of things have to be recognized. One is that the respondents, the scientists, cannot claim autonomy for their knowledge; it is dependent on what is given by God, and man must acknowledge that universal condition. Second, the nature of the response that it is finite, proximate, and subject to the limitations of the scientists; to assume omniscient economists therefore seriously overstates the competence of the science. Third, rather than the economic scientist being seen as infallible, he or she constitutes an epistemological problem, because of the sinful attitudes which economists can bring to their work. Built into the modern development of the discipline is self-congratulation, status seeking, insensitivity to evil, and especially pride; attitudes which rule out the possibility of self-criticism. Because economists are not prepared to consider that they are mistaken and misdirected, they are unable in principle to consider the sources of their disagreements. Because they are elitist, male, academically and financially oriented, they produce a certain kind of analysis. Because they have vested interests in *their* analysis, promotion, academic status and intellect, their work takes a decided form. Most important, because they rest their methodological faith on an approach which will make them infallible, they necessarily distort what they study. Thus, far from the process of gathering knowledge being mechanical and even automatic, we need to take account *within* the science of economics of the waywardness of economists.

Many of the theoretical paradigms we have examined seek to establish a single flat plane to which theory and data can be pinned. If, however, economic science is a response to an aspect of the creation, including sinful humanity, then theory must recognize levels of both diversity and depth. There is an interweaving of economic, social, psychological, and political activity and a complexity of human meanings, motives, institutions which need to be recognized in the theory. Moreover, theory must aim to be true, not just in the sense of offering a description of all phenomena, but in *distinguishing* what is good, constructive, and valuable from what is evil, destructive, and empty. Whether economic activity is based on a proper or mistaken view of the situation, whether motives are careful or careless of others, whether action is fair or unfair, all need to be normatively discerned. Many in the discipline have taken the qualitative richness of the creation and the meaning of human economic activity and, like a figure in a cartoon, have flattened it against the wall of one or other foundational epistemology. The task of gaining economic insight is more difficult than is often implied. It is not guaranteed by swallowing one particular view of economic science, and it may mean recognizing that much economic practice and theory is misguided and that the effects of sin on the discipline of economics are deeper than we have ever realized.

## Conclusion

The methodological confusion and pluralism of the last twenty years have made the justification of most present economic science problematical, and have deepened the already long-standing divisions within the discipline. But they have also opened up the possibility of a Christian approach to the economics. The breakdown of consensus on methodology leaves an opening for those who want to propose a method for economics and other social sciences that recognizes the importance of pre-theoretic commitments on matters such as the nature of humankind and social life. A new climate of tolerance for those who insist on the normativity of scholarly work has leant new legitimacy to the task of Christian scholarship, and new openness to explicitly normative social science. If economists in general still seem to be wedded to outmoded methodologies, the sophistication of the profession in these matters has been gradually increasing since the appearance of a number of important new works on economic methodology in the early 1980's.

We do not propose a relativistic approach to economic methodology, however. To serve the purpose of living out our Christian commitment in our scholarly life, we need a methodology that allows biblical norms and insights to inform our understanding of social behavior. Fortunately, the recent flowering of Chritian scholarship in philosophy allows us to propose such a method, and to that task we now turn.

## Resources

Blaug, M. 1980. *The Methodology of Economics.* Cambridge: Cambridge Univ. Press.

Caldwell, B. 1982. *Beyond Positivism.* London: George Allen & Unwin.

Carnap, R. 1959. The Old and New Logic. in A. J. Ayer, ed., *Logical Positivism.* N.Y.: Free Press, pp. 133-145.

Commons, J. R. 1934. *Institutional Economics.* N.Y.: Macmillan.

Cramp, A. B. 1970. Does Money Matter? *Lloyd's Bank Review* (Oct.), pp. 23-37.

Finn, D. R. 1979. Objectivity in Economics. *Review of Social Economy.* 37: 37-61.

Friedman, M. 1953. The Methodology of Positive Economics. in *Essays in Positive Economics.* Chicago: Univer. of Chicago Press, pp. 3-43.

Friedman, M., and R. Friedman. 1980. *Free to Choose.* N.Y.: Harcourt, Brace.

Fusfeld, D. R. 1980. The Conceptual Framework of Modern Economics. *Journal of Econ. Issues.* 14: 27-52.

Galbraith, J. K. 1978. On Post-Keynesian Economics. *Journal of Post-Keynesian Econ.* 1.

Green, H. A. J. 1971. *Consumer Theory.* Harmondsworth: Penguin.

Hanson, N. R. 1965. *Patterns of Discovery.* Cambridge: Cambridge U. Press.

Harrod, R. 1951. *The Life of John Maynard Keynes.* N.Y.: Harcourt, Brace.

Hempel, C., and P. Oppenheim. 1948. Studies in the Logic of Explanation. *Philosophy of Science.* 15: 135-75.

Hicks, J. 1965. *Capital and Growth.* Oxford: Oxford Univer. Press.

Hume, D. 1888, 1896. *Treatise on Human Nature.* (original 1739), Oxford: Oxford Univer. Press.

Hutchinson, T. W. 1938. *The Significance and Basic Postulates of Economic Theory.* London: Macmillan.

Jevons, W. S. 1876. The Future of Political Economy. *Fortnightly Rev.* N.S. 20: 346-401.

Keynes, J. M. 1936. *The General Theory of Employment, Interest and Money.* London: Macmillan.

Keynes, J. N. 1917. *The Scope and Method of Political Economy.* 4th ed., London: Macmillan.

Keynes, J. M. 1973. *The Collected Writings of J. M. Keynes.* Vol. 14, Cambridge: Macmillan.

Kuhn, T. 1962, 1970. *The Structure of Scientific Revolutions.* Chicago: Univer. of Chicago Press.

Lakatos, I. 1976. *Proofs and Refutations.* Cambridge: Cambridge Univ Press.

Lipsey, R. G., and P. O. Steiner. 1981. *Economics.* 6th ed., N.Y.: Harper & Row.

Lowe, R. 1978. Recent Attacks on Political Economy. *The Nineteenth Century* 4.

Mandel, E. 1970. *Marxist Economic Theory.* 2 vols., (B. Pearis, trans.), N.Y.: Monthly Review Press.

Mason, W. 1980. Some Negative Thoughts on Positive Economics. *J. Post-Keynesian Econ.* 3: 235-55.

Mini, P. V. 1976. *Philosophy and Economics.* Talahassee: Florida Univ. Press.

Nagel, E. 1961. *The Structure of Science.* N.Y.: Harcourt, Brace.

Nordhaus, W., and J. Tobin. 1972. Is Growth Obsolete? in *Economic Growth* N.Y.: Columbia Univer. Press, pp. 1-81.

Phelps, M. G. 1980. Laments, Ancient and Modern: Keynes on Mathematical and Econometric Methodology. *J. Post-Keynesian Econ.* 2: 482-93.

Popper, K. 1959. *The Logic of Scientific Discovery.* N.Y.: Harper & Row.

Robbins, L. 1952. *The Nature and Significance of Economic Science.* 2nd ed., N.Y.: Macmillan.

Samuels, W. J. 1980. Economics as a Science and its Relation to Policy. *J. Econ. Issues.* 14: 163-85.

Samuelson, P. 1939. The Rate of Interest Under Ideal Conditions. *Quarterly J. Econ.* 53: 286-97.

Samuelson, P. 1948. The General Theory. in S. Harris, ed., *The New Economics.* N.Y.: Alfred Knopf, pp. 146-176.

Schlick, M. 1978. The Nature of Truth in Modern Logic. in Mulder and Schlick, eds., *Philosophical Papers, Vol. I,* Boston: D. R. Lidel.

Skillen, A. J. 1980. The Ethical Neutrality of Science and the Method of Abstraction: The Case of Political Economy. *Philosophical Forum.* 11: 215-33.

Suppe, F. 1977. *The Structure of Scientific Theories.* 2nd ed., Champaign: Univ. of Illinois Press.

Wallis, W. A., and M. Friedman. 1962. The Empirical Derivation of Indifference Functions. in *Studies in Mathematical Economics and Econometrics.* Chicago: Univ. of Chicago Press.

Walras, L. 1954. *Elements of Pure Economics.* (W. Jaffe, trans.), Homewood: Richard D. Irwin.

Weber, M. 1947. *The Theory of Social and Economic Organization.* Oxford: Oxford Univ. Press.

Wittgenstein, L. 1953. *Philosophical Investigations.* (G. Anscombe, trans.), Oxford: Oxford Univ. Press.

Wittgenstein, L. 1961. *Tractatus Logico-Philosophicus.* London: Roultedge and Kegan Paul.

Wolterstorff, N. 1976. *Reason Within the Bounds of Religion.* Grand Rapids: Eerdmans.

# Chapter IV
# Christian Perspective in
# Economic Theory and
# Methodology

*Once I built a railroad, I made it run,*
*Made it race against time.*
*Once I built a railroad, and now it's done,*
*Brother, can you spare a dime?*
        E. Y. Harburg (1932)

## Introduction

In the first three chapters of this book we presented an analysis of current economic problems in western society. We have looked in detail at some of the major shortcomings exhibited by current economic theory in dealing with these problems. We have seen that during the time the foundations for much of current theory were being laid, life from an economic point of view was running quite smoothly, and that it is some of the economic disruptions of the last two decades which are producing significant challenges to existing theory.

We noted that many problems are appearing at various levels in our economic life. On a personal level people are discovering that the materialist life-style is often not really satisfying, and that one's work no longer seems significant. On an institutional level things are so often purposeless and out of control. At a national level there seems to be a growing realization that economic reality is rigid and not subject to easy change, and that neither business nor government are economically all-powerful or all-wise. The world itself is beset with economic problems such as the careless use of resources and the increasing disparity between rich and poor countries. Our concern in these beginning chapters was largely with the way in which current economic theory deals with these problems, and we took note of major shortcomings in that theory. Some of these shortcomings are rooted in what may be called *faith in method*, that is, in the identification of truth in economics with the results produced by a particular methodological approach to the subject. Surely this is true, for example, of so-called neo-classical economic theory, with its single-minded emphasis on the deductive method and on the unquestioned validity of mathematical models. Such views have tended to lead to a much too restrictive view of the subject, with many important problem areas simply being ignored.

About a half century or more ago, debate concerning questions of method in economic science was much more lively than it has been, say, in the last decade. Annual presidential addresses to professional societies in economics and social science were often concerned with the significance of methodology. Certain methodological approaches to the subject matter were recommended as being most effective for the pursuit of economic truth. Consider, by way of example, the shape that a research program would have if we accepted the advice of R. F. Harrod, given in a presidential address to a section of the British Association at Cambridge in August of 1938:

> To some minds it may seem that in the field of the social studies, workers who treat of human values in direct, simple, and intelligible terms are the most useful members of the fraternity. But not to minds well-informed of the progress of the sciences. To reach general laws it is usually necessary to abandon the straightforward terms of common sense, to become immersed for a time in mysterious symbols and computations, in technical and abstruse demonstrations, far removed from the common light of day, in order to emerge finally with a generalization which may then be re-translated into the language of the work-a-day world. [1938, p. 411]

Clearly, Harrod is here advocating a certain approach to the subject, and it may be well to look at his recommendation in more detail. It surely makes sense, at least at the beginning, to treat human values in direct, simple, and intelligible terms and to use the straightforward terms of common sense. And, as the analysis proceeds, it will no doubt involve intellectual abstraction and theorizing to a lesser or greater degree. In many cases it may be legitimate, as Harrod says, to use mysterious symbols and computations and technical and abstruse demonstrations to arrive at a deeper understanding of that which is being studied. What we must object to is any claim that such an approach is the *only* way to arrive at a true understanding of the subject.

Another example is the history of the American Economic Association. [Furner, 1975] Founded in 1885, the AEA was apparently the first professional organization for American social scientists. It began as a reformist organization, based generally on Christian principles, with the purpose of turning public policy away from laissez-faire traditionalism. Under the pressures of increasing professionalism, the advocacy role of the group was abandoned and replaced by a research role rooted in the methodology of neo-classical economics. We have here an example of the adoption of a methodological commitment changing the whole purpose and direction of a professional organization.

Our aim in this chapter is to establish what we take to be, from the perspective of Christian faith, a wider and deeper view of economic theory and practice. We think this will allow new kinds of theory to be developed and will give much of the theory that now exists a new and more fundamental meaning. We shall consider what we think the scope of the discipline should be and give some indications of the directions such a new analysis should take. We shall also pay some attention to what we consider to be characteristics of a good theory, and what kinds of methods are appropriate in the analysis of economic activity.

## The Meaning of Economic Analysis

An important aspect of any theoretical inquiry is the clear identification of the bounds or scope of the inquiry—that is, a clear specification of what is to be studied and what is to be ignored. In so far as the standard contemporary approach to the subject asserts the autonomy of the discipline, which implies the autonomy of economic considerations from the rest of life, it ignores almost totally the place which these economic considerations have in the larger context of life. It is very important at the outset of our study to recognize that no human activity can exhaustively be described in economic terms. This view stands in sharp contrast to the approach of rationalist economics, which takes economic man as its starting point and focuses on the maximization of individual utility. It also is quite different from the view of economic theorists who adopt a methodology which sees a certain kind of knowledge as foundational. Such views tend to impoverish and limit the development of a true understanding of economic activity.

A proper view of economics involves a proper view of all of life. Economic considerations form just one of the aspects of life, part of humanity's existence before God, and the significance of economic aspects of life must not and cannot be considered apart from the meaning of life itself. Too often an isolated economic meaning of a certain activity is considered, to the exclusion of any idea of coherence in the activity. Thus, for example, all may agree that the building of a factory for a certain productive purpose is primarily an economic activity, but it surely does not occur in an economic vacuum. In making an economic analysis of such a project, the economists may not arbitrarily exclude from the discussion factors such as the physical environment, levels of psychological commitment, mathematical and engineering calculations, a stable political environment, some attention to historical setting, various forms of interpersonal trust, and the economic responsibilities of the enterprise towards its workers. That is to say, at the very least, the economic analysts must be aware of the context in which the activity under study is taking place and, more importantly, must realize that a proper economic analysis must take into account this larger context.

This is not to say that we think economists must also be environmentalists, psychologists, engineers, historians, and the like, some kind of jack-of-all-trades. But it is to say that they must recognize that they in fact do deal with these areas, and that proper economic analysis must do so with respect for the other aspects of life with which it has intimate contact. The subject matter of economics is thus related to other aspects of life.

It may also be said that economic activity affects other areas of life as well, and valid economic analysis must take this fact into account. By this we mean to say that economic activity clearly may affect one's personal psychological well-being. Being laid off from work may be a personally devastating experience. Economic wealth surely has a direct effect on family life; the life-style forced on a family by poverty differs drastically from that permitted by affluence. Equally clear are the constraints which the economic condition of a country may place on political decisions or, alternatively, the political possibilities which may be considered.

Economic considerations, for example, certainly affect and in some cases dictate the directions which scientific research may take, so that even scientific understanding may well be subject to fairly rigid economic constraints.

Our point is that the full status of all of the academic disciplines needs to be respected within a coherent overall framework which recognizes the full created complexity of humanity. [Spier, 1968] In using the phrase "economic activity" we do not mean to imply that part of life is economic, part is psychological, part is physical, and so on. We emphasize the wholeness and coherence of life, and intend in this work to focus analytically on the economic aspect of life without doing damage to the idea of wholeness and coherence. Current economic theory, by making its knowledge autonomous, in large measure fails to present an adequate description and analysis of human economic activity.

## The Scope of Economic Study

Since it is necessary to view economic analysis as being one aspect of a larger whole, what then is the proper scope of economic analysis and theory? Some economists have defined the discipline as the study of all market or money transactions. Obviously this is an important part of the subject, and perhaps identifies that aspect of life which is most reasonably called economic activity by many people. But in the light of what we have said earlier, we find this description of economics to be too limited. It ignores any activity which clearly has economic implications such as the production of food in a backyard vegetable garden, which is neither a money nor a market transaction.

Others, from Adam Smith onward, have seen the discipline as being concerned with the processes by which wealth is created. We surely agree that the creation and accumulation of wealth is included under the label economic activity, but, as Alfred Marshall already recognized, man's participation in the creation of wealth makes this definition too open-ended and ambiguous. Lionel Robbins has defined economics as "the science that studies human behavior as the relationship between ends and scarce means which have alternative uses." [1932] Often some form of this definition appears in standard elementary economics textbooks. For example:

> Economics emphasizes how human actions are influenced by the fact of scarcity and the necessity of choice.
>
> In economics, scarcity means that people do not have as much of everything as they want.
>
> Economics accepts scarcity as a fact of life; but what makes life interesting, economically speaking, is not scarcity itself so much as the necessity of choosing among ways of coping with it. [Dolan, 1980, p. 4]

Or, in a somewhat alternative form:

> A great deal of the activity of a market society can be explained as the outcome of two interacting forces. One is the force of maximizing behavior—a force we have described in terms of the acquisitive behavior of men and women in a market society. The other is the constraining counterforce of nature or of social institutions—a series of obstacles that holds back channels or directs the acquisitive drive. This suggests the daring scientific task that economics sets for itself. It is to explain the events of future economic reality—by reasoning based on the fundamental hypotheses about maximizing behavior and its constraints. [Heilbroner & Thurow, 1981, p. 85]

These definitions no doubt characterize much of the work of western economists, and are accepted as entirely adequate by them. But once again we note that in our view they are too narrow and limiting. They see the relationship between means and ends as the main object of study. Thus they exclude the study and analysis of the means and ends themselves. We take this to be a serious omission, for no doubt means and ends have significant economic aspects which ought to be analyzed.

All of these specifications of the scope of economics are inadequate because they attempt to make the subject autonomous, ignoring significant aspects of the field of economic activity itself and ignoring the close relationships between economic life and the larger context of human concerns. They limit the scope of the theory too severely and thereby miss the opportunity for better explanations and deeper understanding.

We think that the defining notion of unbridled human wants in the face of scarce resources must be replaced by the idea of careful stewardship of what is entrusted to humanity by God.

We do not think the idea of scarcity is really necessary to the definition of economics, inasmuch as scarcity makes sense only in the context of the attempt to satisfy unlimited wants in the face of limited resources. This need not be the case at all. We believe, rather, that the resources of the creation are sufficient to meet all legitimate human needs, and therefore the emphasis of the analysis ought to be on what constitute responsible stewardship of the earth's resources in meeting these needs.

It must be admitted that it is no easy task to make an appropriate definition for the scope of our inquiry, and that our own definition may no doubt be subject to the same kind of criticism we have been making. However, it is important that we attempt to capture, in a few words, some of the points we have emphasized thus far.

Economics, on our view, is the study of the communal stewardship and organization of the creation to meet human needs. Or, to put it in a slightly different way, economics is the study of how people, both individually and institutionally, respond to their calling to be stewards of what God has entrusted to them in the creation.

There is, of course, a context in which this characterization of economics must be read in order to be understood. The reference to the creation is intended to recognize that the world in which we live comes to us from God, which implies that we must recognize the full meaning of economic activity before God, as well as our dependence on God's providence in the creation. The reference to being stewards and to stewardship is meant to emphasize that we do not hold absolute rights to the things we own, but rather hold these things in trust for the rightful owner, who is God. Thus our purposes in pursuing economic activity must be those of the real owner of things, namely God. This definition emphasizes that the human response to God's call for stewardship is not limited strictly to the level of individuals but occurs also in the context of human institutions. We recognize that the purpose of economic activity is to meet human needs by being "care"-ful stewards of created reality.

Responsible stewardship includes the development of the creation which insures its preservation and sustainability and which militates against waste and destruction. Thus, to take a simple example, a tree may be cared for in a way which allows the fruit to be used while the ability of the tree to produce fruit is sustained. Farmland may be cultivated in such a way so that the possibility of continuing production of food is maintained.

By human needs we mean generally all of the things required by people in order to perform this task. Minimally this includes the basic requirements of food, clothing, shelter, adequate transportation, appropriate education, and the like. We recognize that needs tend to be somewhat subjective, in that one person's need may easily become another person's want or luxury. The legitimate needs we have in mind may well be dependent on the calling of a person or the purpose of an institution. What needs are in a given situation depends on proper consideration of possible alternatives. Often, as in the case of a family, there is a process of communal weighing of alternatives which determines needs. The way in which a particular culture develops and in which a certain style of consumption emerges is important in this regard. Is, for example, air conditioning in automobiles as we know it today a genuine need or a wanton luxury? Some years ago it surely was considered a luxury, but now many consider it to be a necessity. Our point is that human needs must be viewed within the fuller context of stewardship; they are neither just personal or institutional whims nor bare necessities, but what we need to live in the way God intends us to.

We recognize too that scarcity and escalating wants are not really necessary, although choices among alternatives will be. We allow for much important activity which takes place outside of market transactions, as our later analysis of the family, for example, will show. We are prepared, by way of further example, to recognize that tradition and training may well be the reason that a person has good work habits and enjoys his or her work, as opposed to work having disutility, as most economists assume.

## Pluralist Economics

We also address the important question of individualist versus collectivist economics. There is no doubt that neoclassical economic theory views economic man as being individualistic. Its central assumption sees independent, economic man pursuing the maximization of his own utility, without knowledge of or concern for the activities of others. The result is to arrive at an equilibrium point called a Pareto optimal point. Such a point is characterized by saying that if an economic system is at such a point, no individual's utility can be increased without decreasing the utility of at least one other person. The theory ignores such important questions as whether or not such a point is characterized by justice and equity, or whether it in fact is an optimal point in any significant (from our point of view) way. We wish to avoid this highly individualistic point.

The opposite pole of this individualistic position is the emphasis on macroeconomics. The regularities among macro variables are observed and charted, and a system of equations is created which ignores and even destroys the significance of individual and institutional responsibility, resulting in a great gulf between the individual and the system. This extreme must likewise be avoided.

The Christian alternative, we think, is a more relational and pluralist view of economic activity, avoiding both extremes of rank individualism and total collectivism. We recognize a certain economic normativity and meaningfulness for both individual and institutional life. People do respond to God's call either responsibly or irresponsibly. Thus individuals and institutions are not necessarily egocentric and self-serving but often do take into account the interests and concerns of others with whom they are institutionally linked. We recognize that in their economic activity people are subject to economic norms which presuppose nonegocentric behavior.

Much of the rest of our work in this book is concerned with making this idea explicit in many ordinary situations in human life, and with looking at the unique economic character of different institutions which have often been analyzed in a reductionist manner.

There is an analogy here with the biblical teaching of salvation through Jesus Christ. There are both individual and collective aspects of salvation, and both aspects must be given proper recogition in understanding salvation. It makes sense to speak of "accepting Jesus Christ as personal Savior," that is, of making a personal, individual decision to believe the gospel message. Some church groups place almost all of their emphasis and concentrate all of their efforts on this aspect of salvation. At the same time it is also profoundly true that Jesus Christ redeems his Church, his chosen people, in which view there may be more concern for the institution than for the individual. Some denominations may place a major emphasis on this aspect. We are saying that just as a proper understanding of salvation must take both aspects into account, so too a proper understanding of economics involves both individual and institutional norms.

A final remark on the scope of economic analysis is that although most of current economic theory, at least on the American scene, emphasizes the egocentric self-centered calculus criticized above, more and more voices are being raised today which call for a total reassessment of the situation. Institutionalism in particular is calling for less analysis in individualist terms, with more emphasis on the characteristics of various institutions. A central problem raised by that approach is that of relating the attitudes and behavior of a group to the attitudes and behavior of the individual members of the group. For example, it may be asked whether a group or a society can be concerned with that goal. We see the problem as being an important one, needing a great deal of continuing research, with real promise for fruitful results. It is partly for this reason that our own work in later chapters includes analysis of such institutions as the family, the firm or enterprise, and voluntary organization.

## The Normativity of Economics

In the preceding section we gave some indication of the aspects of human life which we think should be included within the scope of economic analysis. There is another important point, that of whether or not economic analysis can be value-free, whether or not it can be a totally objective science, uninfluenced in any way by the personal values of the analyst. It should be clear by now that we do not think this is possible. All of life, including its economic aspects, is necessarily normative, since it is human and therefore involves views of how we should live and work and consume, and economic analysis must take this into account. The economic aspects of the activity of a firm or enterprise, for example, are not accurately analyzed, on our view, simply in terms of profit maximization. There must be the recognition that there are certain economic norms to which firms are subject, and that economic analysis must be concerned with the fact that the firm's behavior either goes against or is obedient to these norms. Thus an appropriate analysis must explicitly state what the analyst believes to be the right normative structure of the firm. Only when an explicit view of the healthy organism is presented is diagnosis of what is wrong possible.

The idea that economics can be value-free and uncritical is, we believe, simply untenable. Even simple descriptive analysis cannot be value free, since the choice of what is to be studied, the kinds of data which are to be allowed, and the sources of knowledge which are accepted as legitimate are all subject to the purposes and beliefs of the analyst. All economists have some implicit view of how an economy should run, and the subject is thus necessarily diagnostic. We believe that the normative basis to which we have been referring must be an explicit part of the subject and included within the scope of economics. It is on this basis that we think a distinctively Christian perspective in economics can be fashioned. This basis relates to the way God has made us and intends us to live. The content of this basis is surely not exhausted by actual, observed human behavior, but rather constitutes the ground for development, growth, and right relationships in human life, particularly in its economic aspects. We are concerned that our criticism of existing theory be constructive in that it is based on this explicitly normative approach, involving an analysis of what has gone wrong and pointing in new directions.

Specifically, this means that we believe that the human economic response cannot be categorized by a single class of so-called economic "facts," but that these need to be treated with discernment, with recognition that there are deep differences in the character of various "facts" which make them categorically different. Human responses can, in varying degrees, be good, true, appropriate, fair, and helpful or, alternatively, evil, false, exploitative, selfish and destructive. The economic health of a nation is not necessarily measured accurately by GNP, and the economic significance of being out of work is not necessarily characterized by a narrowly and somewhat artificially defined percentage of unemployment. Because attempts at developing value-free economic theory ignore these considerations, such normative diagnosis as is included in current theory is often, on our view, naive and simplistic. We think a more complex analysis, in the directions we have sketched, is necessary.

Any attempt to make economic analysis value-free and uncritical also is confronted by the fact that many motives, ideologies, and faiths shape economic development in a formative way. Many people exhibit an almost blind and consuming faith in growth and progress, a faith that declares that the way to economic peace and stability is unquestioned and almost undirected growth and expansion in the economic sphere. Others may show a faith in an economic system such as capitalism or socialism, a faith which neither encourages nor even allows the asking of basic questions. For some a deeply held commitment to nationalism and the pursuit of national interests with an indifference to the interests of other nations constitutes real faith. Even the goal of securing and preserving human rights and freedom may function in this way. We have already mentioned, for economic theorists, the dangers of faith in method. Our point is that economic analysis must take basic commitments of the sort we have described into account, and the possibility that the analysis can be totally objective and value-free is thereby diminished.

## Types of Economic Relationships

Clearly, the study of certain kinds of relationships are rightly included within the scope of economic analysis. Current economic theory tends to focus on the relationship between persons and things, to the exclusion of other relationships. Only in that context does the pursuit of individual utility by the purchase of various goods through market transactions constitute a valid paradigm for economic theory. Convinced that a broader view is necessary, we see within economic activity three basic kinds of relationships: (a) person to person, (b) person to thing, (c) thing to thing. We see the first two of these as being normatively shaped while the third may well be primarily subject to certain physical constraints.

This perspective recognizes that activity legitimately called economic does take place between persons. Persons make contracts with each other and very often these have significant economic aspects and consequences. Relationships between employers and employees are of this sort. To say that these are best analyzed in normative terms is simply to say that such relationships are not grounded in some kind of constant, deterministic natural law, but rather in a way in which God has called people to live. In responding to this call people either do so rightly and obediently or in a disobedient and irresponsible fashion. In current economic theory these person-to-person relationships have been largely excluded on the basis of the egocentric calculus mentioned earlier, because it is assumed that a person's rational behavior is essentially non-relational; that is, it is not prepared to take responsibilities toward other people into account in its calculations. A wide range of issues is involved here, such as the distribution of income and wealth, fairness and justice in economic relationships, the impact of actions on others, concern for the needs of others, and the like. Surely of economic importance are such things as the meaning of people's work, their economic dependence on and independence from each other, the way in which persons provide services to each other, and people's economic security and rest. The problem of inflation, among other things, is important because through inflation some people benefit while major economic burdens are quietly and unobtrusively shifted to others. We see these all as legitimate concerns for economic theory, since human life is subject to norms related to community, trust, fairness, and care, values which provide the parameters for economic development. Recognition is also needed of the economic relational norms of various organizations. Neglect of these relationships is widespread.

Relationships between persons and things are more fully recognized in current economic theory and are extensively treated in the literature. The existence of an individual ordinal preference function which guides the pursuit of individual utility maximization is treated in terms of the ability of an individual always to select a preferred commodity bundle, that is, some selection of quantities of various goods which are available from among a whole range of such bundles. But what is often not considered at all are the ways in which these choices are made. The full meaning of aspects of qualities such as permanence, uniqueness, adaptability, and the like, as these are part of a person's valuation of things, is often ignored. The economic significance of the difference between value and price is not recognized sufficiently, especially since many values are destroyed by externalities. Prices are concerned only with the articulation of alternatives and expanding choices through markets. Other means of choosing among alternatives are possible in cases where market freedom does not lead to the best alternatives, and these need to be explored.

Thing to thing relationships are subject largely to physical constraints, although they do involve human mediation. There are some things, surely, which are legitimately taken up as economic efforts. It is no doubt often necessary to own some means of transportaion, probably an automobile, in order to get to one's place of employment and to meet the needs of one's household. One must be aware, however, that things do have relationships to other things, relationships which seem to have at least the force of physical law. Ownership of an automobile entails the need for a place to keep it, as well as operating, maintenance, and replacement costs. It has significant effects on the environment. The acquisition of one thing often leads to the accumulation of a host of other things closely and necessarily related to it, and a point may soon be reached at which the thing becomes the subject and the person the object. Thus in the context of economic choices which all must make, the relationships between things and things become an important part of the analysis. These relationships must be analyzed and understood within the discipline.

We recognize that in the preceding paragraphs we are probably including within the scope of economic analysis areas which are often excluded in current theory. Thus our vision of the discipline is a wider one. And not only is our vision a wider one; it is a redirected one as well.

## Primary and Secondary Economics

We have so far been making the point that economic theory and analysis must avoid any attempt to make the subject autonomous, but rather must recognize the place of economic analysis in the larger attempt to understand all of life. Great care needs to be taken to specify the primary focus of a particular kind of human activity. To identify this focus, we discuss primary and secondary economics.

The economic aspect of a certain human activity can be a primary aspect, as with production processes, shopping, saving, investing, preserving, and the like, where the chief concern is with formulating and implementing an appropriate response to God's call for stewardship. For such activities the social, psychological, political, and other aspects will be secondary. Other human activities are clearly primarily social, psychological or political, and the economic aspect is secondary at best. Thus a family is primarily a social unit, but its organization and activities have economic implications. The State is primarily a political unit, but it also needs to be supported by taxes. It should, for example, in the levying of fines be concerned primarily with justice and not with maximizing the income which fines produce.

It is important to recognize that most of the economic activity of ordinary people may well take place within these secondary areas. Often the most significant economic decisions are made within the family. One of the most direct links people have with the State centers on taxes, including both amounts and methods. There are significant economic aspects of legal and penal systems. Church life usually includes tithes and offerings not only for maintenance of local programs and facilities but also for far-reaching programs of missions and benevolence. Medical and mental health programs these days have tremendous economic impacts on individual and institutional lives. Cultural programs sponsored by community groups often founder on economic grounds.

We see these activities as being normative, in that they involve human responses which may be either good or bad, and for the development of right Christian understanding it is important to recognize that although the norms of the primary aspect of the activity are the leading ones, this does not mean that the norms of the secondary aspects are to be ignored. Thus people's health, social respect, fair treatment, and aesthetic environment are necessary and binding concerns within an activity which is primarily economic, such as an enterprise. Economic ends never justify wrong social or psychological or political means. Likewise, though the State may be primarily political, it may not unthinkingly ignore economic norms which affect its activity. For example, in its concern for justice the State may rightly be interested in the way a firm uses its power to control a certain market and raise prices at will. Thus the coherence of creation norms within any economic activity needs to be recognized.

## Catgories and Forms of Economic Analysis

The major categories of standard, mainstream economic analysis include microeconomics, macroeconomics, consumption, firms, production, distribution, money, investment and capital, international trade, and the like. One may consult the table of contents of any standard textbook in elementary economic theory to see the pattern, and some comment on this situation is necessary. It follows from much of what we have said up to this point that the lines of analysis established by this pattern do not take into account many of the more important questions and problems posed in the early chapters of this book, particularly the fact that each of the categories of analysis has a normative quality which may not be ignored. For example, treating the family simply as a consumption unit ignores the important questions of why some families use up a lot of resources while others do not. For this reason we have not emphasized these categories of analysis, but have favored a consideration of broader categories and patterns reflected in the economic activities of various institutions such as families, firms, labor unions, and voluntary organizations, all of which are much involved in economic decision-making. This is not to say that the standard analysis is totally without merit. It is to say that there is plenty of room for analysis based on a broadened perspective, focusing more on decision-making institutions and organizations than on universalized categories like consumption, investment, and the like.

It needs also to be recognized that there are a lot of forms of analysis which can be incorporated into the study of economics, and that these throw light on some aspect of the subject. There are legitimate uses for various forms of mathematical analysis, for statistics, accounting, economic geography and spatial analysis, mobility studies, attitude surveys, and systems analysis. The study of economic philosophy, economic history, economic linguistics, of economic choices and ethics, and the like, are all important. So are the developed patterns of analysis such as price theory, study of markets, production, and fiscal or monetary policy.

What is important is that we recognize that none of these forms of analysis by itself is foundational, but that each in its own way contributes to an overall understanding of the subject. Further, each form of inquiry must be used properly, that is, within a normative framework which allows for both proper and improper responses to God's call for proper Christian living. For example, economic power may be neighborly or it may be egocentric. Accounting can be sensitive to the social dimensions of the operation or it can be narrowly concerned with just the bottom line. And, finally, there is of course a certain normativity that must be respected when we actually use these various forms of analysis. There must be a clear definition of the scope and significance of the procedure being used, with no introduction of distortion, inaccurate calculation, and the like. The correct tools are those which are appropriate to the specific area of understanding or theory involved. It may legitimately be asked whether the methods of multivariable calculus are universally appropriate even though they may well be so in analyzing market decisions which involve price/quantity trade-offs. Conscious and serious consideration must be given to the appropriateness of the forms of analysis used in each case.

## Theorizing in Economic Analysis

So far in this chapter we have been concerned with sketching what we see as legitimate boundaries for economic analysis and theorizing, and we have indicated that we believe not only that the boundaries set by current theory can fruitfully be extended, but also that the whole effort may be fruitfully redirected. We have discussed what we take legitimate theorizing to be, how such activity can be distinctively Christian, and what sorts of methods are legitimately used in such activity. As we draft the outlines of a theory of economics from a Christian perspective, it is important that we further specify what we mean by theory.

This is so because of the way in which theory in economic analysis has become the single level of analysis and explanation, which introduces a false sense of simplicity into the discipline. The subject is a complex one, and theory must take into account various levels of analysis such as the basic principles on which the theory is built, the internal consistency and logic of the theory, the various and complex relationships which exist between individuals, and the internal structure of institutions. We do not arrive at good theory by concentrating on only a single level of analysis.

The shape of one's theory depends on one's basic approach to the discipline. If one is committed to the formal, deductive approach, one's theories will reflect that, consisting of the statement of carefully formulated axioms and theorems which these axioms logically imply. If one is committed to the empirical approach one will build theories which rely heavily on the generation, collection, and analysis of data of various sorts. Our approach, with its sensitivity to viewing things in a normative framework, avoids both of these extremes. Theory, on our view, is more than discerning patterns—or imposing patterns on large amounts of chaotic data. Theory is more than simple prediction and more than simple explanation of cause and effect. *Theory is a wider and more comprehensive pattern of understanding.* A significant component of theory is description, that is, some statement of what we take to be the case. Another important component of theory is that of explanation, that is, a seeking to answer questions such as why the workers decided to strike. There is also, though perhaps less important in our view, a component of prediction, one which takes into account human responsibility and degrees of freedom of activity. When we look, then, for a theory of economic activity we are looking for a *basic understanding* of not only how things are in the economic sphere, but also why they are that way.

An important aspect of a theory is the sort of questions which motivate and are motivated by the theory. [Lakatos, 1978] Each perspective generates certain kinds of questions. The positive economists assume a neutrality in motivation which cannot possibly exist. The institutionalists will pose questions focused on the whole group more than on the individual. Likewise our approach has been motivated by significant questions which are not addressed by current theory, and leads to other questions which current theory ignores. The nature of these questions has already been suggested, and will become clearer in succeeding chapters.

Some comment must be made on the distinction which is maintained in much of economic literature today between descriptive and normative economic theory. By the former is meant any theory which purports to describe, in an objective and value-free way, the way things really are. By the latter some mean any recommendation which an economist might make, of the form, "If you do this, such and such is likely to be the result." Others may have in mind the slightly stronger notion of a recommendation which states, for various reasons, what "you ought to do."

We hope our foregoing analysis has made clear why we think this is a false distinction. As we have said, all of human life is normative in the sense that it involves views of how we should live, work, consume, and so on, and the normative basis of that activity must be an explicit part of the subject. Accurate description, we believe, is impossible if this normative basis is ignored. The sort of data that is sought in large part is directly dependent on the sort of theoretical analysis being proposed. The idea that economic theory, even simple descriptive theory, can be value-free and uncritical is untenable. All economists have an implicit view of how an economy ought to run, that is, a normative basis for their work.

Another important issue is that of verification of a theory. On what basis is a theory to be accepted as true or rejected as false? Or how would one decide whether a certain theory is better than another? The response of Karl Popper to the question of verification is his well-known falsifiability criterion, which says that every genuine empirical theory ought to have associated with it a so-called "crucial experiment," the failure of which will lead us to reject the theory. The problem is not that simple. Theories are complex and subject to various levels of evaluation. Even if we accept the criterion, it is not at all clear in what sense an economic theory is subject to experimentation. It surely would be most difficult to devise an experiment which analyzes some economic aspect of human life in which the many and complex variables could be sufficiently controlled in order to make the results meaningful. Whatever else it may be, economic analysis can hardly be characterized as an experimental science.

Milton Friedman's criterion for accepting or rejecting a theory is likewise well-known and simple: Does the theory predict accurately? This is to say, given a certain set of inputs, can we predict what the outcome will be? We have mentioned earlier that, while the element of prediction and the making of forecasts is present in our concept of a theory, it is not a central element, particularly in view of our interest in a theory constituting a deeper and wider understanding of the subject being studied. In Friedman's thinking there seems to be no interest in or necessity for studying causal relationships, and this seems to us to be a too restricted view of meaningful understanding.

Tjalling Koopmans, well-known for his work on mathematical analysis of economic aspects of life, believes that the validity of theories which are developed in this way lies in the accuracy with which the initial assumptions represent economic reality. When one becomes aware of the abstract nature of such assumptions, one also becomes aware of the difficulties involved in allowing the validity of the theory to rest on such grounds.

The work of Thomas Kuhn, with its use of the idea of paradigm, is helpful here. By paradigms Kuhn originally meant "universally recognized scientific achievements that for a time provide model problems and solutions to a community of practitioners." [1970] While in his later work he clarified what he meant in using this term, his main concern was with laying bare the reasons why one paradigm, after holding sway in a particular scientific community for many years, may rather suddenly be rejected and replaced by a new one. He recognizes the complexity of this process. To be a viable candidate for new paradigm status, Kuhn says, it must not only attract a sufficient number of adherents away from competing modes of scientific activity, but it must also be sufficiently open-ended to provide enough problems for the redefined group of practitioners to resolve. For Kuhn the problem is not so much one of confirmation or falsification of a theory, but rather one of understanding the historical process of competition between various segments of the scientific community which actually results in the rejection of a previously accepted theory or in the adoption of another.

Perhaps, then, what we are proposing is a new paradigm, in the sense of Kuhn, for economic analysis. In a later work Kuhn says:

> A paradigm is what the members of a scientific community, and they alone, share. Conversely, it is their possession of a common paradigm that constitutes a scientific community of a group of otherwise disparate men. [1977, p. 294]

We are not so much concerned with simplistically defined criteria for verifying or falsifying a theory as we are in what Wolterstorff [1976] calls the weighing of a theory. If one criterion for weighing a theory is how well it comports with the facts, clearly it is essential to have some agreement as to what the facts are. Wolterstorff rightly points out the influence which one's beliefs have on one's theoretical work, particularly on the sorts of questions which are asked, the kind of data which is accepted, and even the sort of theory which is allowed. An essential element, then, in the weighing of a theory is how well it comports with these beliefs.

It is for this reason that the following chapter on biblical principles for the economic aspects of human life holds such an important place in our work. It is the reason for our continuing emphasis on normativity. We believe that God has challenged people to live responsible lives and to function as his stewards in this world. What we must study is the way people have responded to this challenge.

## Methods in Economic Theorizing

In the preceding section we stated that for us a theory is basically a wider pattern of understanding, involving elements of description, explanation, prediction, interpretation, and evaluation. We emphasized that the development of such a theory necessarily occurs within some normative framework. It is important, especially if we hope to develop an economic theory characterized by a distinctively Christian perspective, that we comment on just how this is to occur.

Just how would one proceed in such an effort? In what ways, if any, will the research program differ from that of other economic theorists who are not so minded? Are there methods which quite legitimately may be of use in such an effort, and are there others whose use is inappropriate? In this paragraph we make some general remarks on these points, trusting that the work in the remaining chapters implicitly and sometimes even explicitly gives greater specificity to our answers to such questions.

It is evident by now that the fundamental starting point for the kind of research we contemplate is the clear specification of the fundamental commitments and beliefs which undergird the work, those beliefs which function in the sense of Wolterstorff as control beliefs. It is also important, in analyzing the work of others, to determine insofar as possible the control beliefs which were basic to that work. On that basis one must make some judgment as to the legitimacy and significance of that work. Our stance on this point becomes evident already in our definition of economics and in our discussion of the scope of the discipline.

However, even in the presence of a clear statement of a fundamental commitment, the researcher is faced with a whole host of specific methods and techniques which may be selected for use. Correct methods and analytical tools are those which are appropriate to the specific area of theory or understanding which is being developed. It is important that the methodological tail does not wag the theoretical dog. This seems to be the case in the way mathematical tools are used so extensively in economic analysis, at least in the United States.

It goes without saying that current positive economic theory relies heavily on quantitative methods and mathematical and statistical analysis. We do not reject these methods but, rather, recognize that many human economic activities have quantitative or arithmetic aspects which may legitimately be taken into account. The response to a question about average wages paid in a given sector of industry can be determined by inspection of pay records and is stated in numerical terms. The number of hours worked last week is obviously, among other things, a number. At this level, numerical data obtained by measuring and counting can be and probably is quite accurate and reliable, and analyses of such data may be helpful in adding to an understanding of the activity involved.

But great care must be exercised in taking something which is not primarily quantitative and representing it by a number. The tendency to do so generates strong pressures to limit one's analysis to the quantititive aspect of the activity and, thus, to ignore more important aspects. The use of a questionnaire, for example, may well be legitimate in getting information concerning people's attitudes toward a certain subject, but the fact that in many cases responses are limited to selection of a number on a scale unnecessarily limits the analysis to quantitative methods, and in so doing cloaks the whole effort with an unwarranted mantle of accuracy and precision.

Analysis which is restricted to quantitative methods also essentially limits the kind of data which is sought and is generated. There surely is no lack of such data in a society which requires massive amounts of reporting of quantitative data which can quickly and comprehensively be processed by electronic computing machines. But other kinds of data must be taken into account. There are, for example, qualitative data and relational data which are not easily quantified but which must nevertheless be analyzed. Other than standard quantitative methods are required.

One must also recognize the implications of the abstractness of mathematical models. Usually a mathematical model is constructed by abstracting from a given situation certain basic ideas from which the axioms for the model are developed. Mathematical methods of deduction and analysis are used to derive results, which are then assumed to apply to the given situation. In this way, supposedly, true knowledge is obtained. We do not wish to reject such procedures entirely, since in many cases such analysis does give new insight and leads to further avenues of inquiry. But of central importance to the value of such methods is exactly the way in which the abstract concepts of the model correspond to particular elements in the real world situation. It is not just that abstraction necessarily ignores certain other aspects of the situation; it is also that if all of these aspects are related as a whole, as they necessarily must be, then any single abstracted area may easily be misrepresented.

Perhaps an example will be helpful. Suppose one wished to measure the height of, say, a flagpole. One approach is to locate a point on the ground a specified distance from the base of the pole, and then from that point measure the angle of elevation of the top of the pole. One can then model the situation with a right triangle, and use methods of elementary trigonometry to determine the length of the side of the triangle which corresponds to the flagpole itself. All of us, no doubt, would expect that the result of such a computation would correspond very closely to the actual height of the pole. There are good reasons for this. There is, after all, an obvious and direct correspondence between the mathematical model and the real world situation which it represents. The right triangle of the model seems almost to be physically present. Further, the flagpole, being an inanimate object, cannot at will change its height or in some conscious way interfere with the measurement of process. The flagpole cannot be aware of the fact that it is under observation, and therefore cannot mislead or misdirect the observer.

The point being made here is an important one. The fairly simple and direct use made of a mathematical model in the above example must be contrasted with the use of such models in studying and representing human activity. Such a model in economic analysis may assume, for example, that each individual, in an egocentric and rational way, makes decisions on the basis of an ordinal utility function. That is to say, consciously or unconsciously each person is able to determine, in accordance with such a function, which of two given bundles of commodities is to be preferred. The correspondence between the mathematical model and elements of the human activity being represented is not nearly so obvious and direct and, in fact, may not exist at all. In response to the ever-present demand for choices amongst various alternatives, people are seldom if ever as consistent as the mathematical model assumes. As soon as it is recognized that people can and must make such choices, and are not bound by some unchanging law, it is likewise recognized that the legitimate use of mathematicl models is quite limited.

We have said that we are seeking a wider pattern of understanding, and we must ask to what extent statistical methods such as regression analysis contribute to such an understanding. Once again, we do not reject use of such methods in ways which are legitimate and appropriate. One may legitimately question, however, the meaning which simple statistical correlation between two variables has in terms of the kind of understanding we seek. For example, according to data gathered over a period of many years, there is almost perfect correlation between teachers' salaries and the amount of liquor consumed annually in the United States. What does this mean? Is there some causal relationship, between the two? Can consumption of liquor be reduced by reducing teachers' salaries? Probably not. One must be extremely cautious about translating statistical correlation into a causal relationship. Yet this seems to be the kind of analysis monetarists make in asserting that the money supply is an important variable for predicting rates of growth and inflation. While such analyses may be helpful in some respects, it surely does not constitute a wider pattern of understanding such as we have in mind.

Another point may be made about the use of mathematical models, and that is that it is much more difficult to deal mathematically with a dynamic and constantly changing situation than with a static one. The equilibrium models presented in the elementary textbooks usually assume a static situation so that the equilibrium point of the model may have a corresponding economic reality. However, irregularity and unpredictability seem to be hallmarks of a living community, and hence such models have at best limited significance. We make the point only to emphasize once again that this limited significance must be recognized when the method is used.

A final point is that the use of mathematical models is closely related to the data that constitute input for such models. As we have remarked before, there is a veritable sea of data presently available, but the economist working within our framework will have to be very concerned that the data used are significant for the subject being studied. Numerical data on total family income may be readily available, but it in fact may not be significant for the economic aspect of family life which is being investigated. New kinds of data may well be called for. Net return on investment may not measure at all how well a firm is meeting its objectives, and entirely different data likely would be needed. The wage portion of a contract between an enterprise and its workers may in fact not have much to say about the economic impact of the contract, and so other kinds of measures need to be developed.

So far we have concentrated on mathematical methods and on the study of economic aspects of an activity which may rightly be quantified. We need to emphasize that in the search program we envision there will be many things of interest which may not be quantifiable. For example, it is clear that we think the values which motivate those who are engaged in the activity are significant and properly within the scope of economic analysis. These surely are not easily quantifiable and hence must entail some other method of investigation such as, perhaps, the personal interview in which these values can be discussed and identified. Certain aspects of a new contract between an enterprise and its workers may deal with issues such as worker input into the process by which management decisions are made, and while these are important for a proper economic analysis they are not readily quantifiable. Hence other ways of analysis must be developed. There are many aspects of family life which we believe are not easily measured, which are nonetheless very important for making the kind of analysis we want, and these need to be explored by personal contact and discussion. An appropriate analysis of the business organization surely will include in-depth study of the purposes, motivations, and goals of those who are the actual practitioners, and will not be limited to narrow consideration of total sales or profit margins. The same may be said about the State and voluntary organizations. We see, therefore, the need for a much closer connection between economic theory and actual economic practice, and new and better ways of meeting this need must be devised. The methodology (and the results) of R. Bellah et. al. [1985] are a promising advance in this direction.

In this context economic history may well be a valuable tool of investigation in seeking a better understanding of a current phenomenon. More emphasis will have to be placed on interdisciplinary analysis, with much less emphasis on an autonomous approach. It is clear, then, that we do not want to be constrained to any given method or set of methods. Rather, we recognize that every human activity exhibits a variety of aspects, and each aspect may well entail an appropriate method of investigation. In many ways, numerical data is a legitimate and helpful starting point, and quantitative methods can be illuminating. Use of a questionnaire is legitimate, so long as it is recognized that there are rather severe limits on the usefulness of the resulting information. There are many appropriate methods, as one may expect when confronted by the complexity not only of human life and activity but of the creation generally.

## The Next Step

We have, in this and in the preceding chapters, been concerned with an analysis of basic problems in current economic theorizing as well as in economic life, and with sketching the outlines of a Christian persepective in economic theory. Our emphasis has been that current theory takes too narrow and limited a view of man and of human activity, and hence fails to develop the wider and more comprehensive understanding which we seek.

We have proposed, in the languge of Kuhn, a new paradigm for economic analysis, one which takes into account the complexity and normativity of human life. The complexity of our lives rules out a narrow and limited analysis and calls for an analysis which looks for various levels of understanding, using a wide variety of methods. Normativity, as we have discussed it, emphasizes the response which people make to *God's* call for responsible and stewardly living. An analysis of economic aspects of human life based on this idea naturally demands a detailed discussion of what we take this normativity to be. Such knowledge comes to us through the Scriptures of the Old and New Testaments, and we believe that the basic scriptural principles given to us in the Scriptures must be seriously taken into account when constructing economic theory. It is to these principles and their meaning that we now turn.

# Resources

Bellah, R., et. al. 1985. *Habits of the Heart.* Berkeley: U. of California Press.

Dolan, E. G. 1980. *Basic Economics.* Hinsdale; Dryden Press.

Furner, M. O. 1975. *Advocacy and Objectivity.* Lexington: University Press of Kentucky.

Harrod, R. F. 1938. Scope and Method of Economics. *Econ. J.*

Heilbroner, R., and L. Thurow. 1981. *The Economic Problem.* 6th ed., Englewood Cliffs: Prentice-Hall.

Kuhn, T. S. 1970. *The Structure of Scientific Revolutions.* revised ed. Chicago: U. of Chicago Press.

Kuhn, T. S. 1977. *The Essential Tension.* Chicago: U. of Chicago Press.

Lakatos, I. 1978. *The Methodology of Scientific Research Programs.* Cambridge: Cambridge U. Press.

Robbins, L. 1932. *Essay on the Significance of Economic Science.* London: Macmillan.

Spier, J. 1968. *An Introduction to Christian Philosophy.* Newark: Craig Press.

Wolterstorff, N. 1976. *Reason Within the Bounds of Religion.* Grand Rapids: Eerdmans.

# Chapter V
# Biblical Principles for
# Economic Activity

*The choice is ours to share the earth*
*And all its many joys abound,*
*Or to continue as we have*
*And burn God's mansion down.*

*My Father's house has many rooms*
*With room for all of His children*
*As long as we do share His love*
*And see that all are free.*
        *Pete Seeger (1957)*

## Introduction

In the introduction to this book we promised to develop the outlines of a distinctively Christian perspective on economic theory. Clearly such theory must be rooted in the biblical witness to God's revelation of his will for human life. There is much in Scripture about economics, but it is embedded in the larger issues of human response to God. It cannot be studied in isolation. For example, in the story of creation, Adam's participation in economic life—tilling the soil and tending the garden—is simply one aspect of his dwelling in intimate communion with his Maker. The role of the original couple can be understood in economic terms, but that only captures a particle of the meaning of their union. The joy Adam expresses in greeting his wife—"at last, bone of my bone and flesh of my flesh"—conveys more than the farmer's approval that he's found a laborer. She, as gift of God, is titled "helpmate," a term used for

God as well. Their joyful union is also one of sexual desire, by which they express their love and populate the earth. Most importantly, the two are meant together to mirror back God's own image. "So God created 'the Adam' in his own image,... male and female he created them" (Gen. 1:27). Human life is meant to grow from close communion with the Creator. Economic life at its best can be taken into that communion; at its worst it expresses (with fallen sexuality, fallen personal relations, fallen art, etc.) the sad human separation from the Source of meaning.

Nevertheless, it must be said at the outset that the Bible writers deal with economic life on almost every page. A quick overview will make this plain. Genesis has as its major figure Abraham, who was most probably a donkey caravanner traveling from Mesopotamia to Egypt, before changing his profession to that of large-scale cattleman (including sheep and goats) in southern Canaan. In this occupation he was followed by his son Isaac and grandsons Jacob and Esau. In the accounts of the patriarchs we read about disputes over grazing lands and watering spots, of family ties that are partly economic which span the desert between Mesopotamia and Canaan, of migrations brought about by famine, of problems of inheritance, bride price, and cattle breeding. All these are either primarily or secondarily economic matters. And when Joseph goes to Egypt and becomes a prime minister and secretary of agriculture, the economic nature of the biblical account is underscored. All of that is in Genesis alone.

The complex of laws given at Sinai and the period of wandering are notable for their attention to economic matters. Joshua and Judges relate the struggle for land by several invading peoples, among them Hebrews, Philistines, and Midianites. In the stories of the kings, from Saul and David until the Fall of Jerusalem (586/7 B.C.), we see an agrarian people losing status and freedom under the monarchies that burdened common folk with a horde of civil and military parasites, and by building projects that required forced labor by the people.

> So Samuel told all the words of the Lord to the people who were asking a king from him. "These will be the ways of the king who will reign over you: he will take your sons and appoint them to his chariots and to be his horsemen, and to run before his chariots; and he will appoint for himself commanders of thousands and commanders of fifties, and some to plow his ground and some to reap his harvest, and to make his implements of war and the equipment of his chariots. He will take your daughters to be perfumers and cooks and bakers. He will take the best of your fields and vineyards and olive orchards and give them to his servants. He will take the tenth of your grain and of your vineyards and give it to his officers and to his servants. He will take your menservants and maidservants and the best of your cattle and your asses, and put them to his work. He will take the tenth of your flocks and you shall be his slaves. And in that day you will cry out because of your king, whom you

have chosen for yourselves; but the Lord will not answer you in
that day." [I Sam. 8:11-18.]

With the eighth-century prophets economic matters move center stage, for
the prophets' call for justice was tied to their demand for an end to the idolatry
of bad religion:

When you spread forth your hands
    I will hide my eyes from you;
even though you make many prayers,
    I will not listen;
your hands are full of blood.
    Wash yourselves; make yourselves clean;
remove the evil of your doings
    from before my eyes;
cease to do evil,
    learn to do good;
seek justice,
    correct oppression;
defend the fatherless,
    plead for the widow.    [Isaiah 1:15-17]

Woe to those who are wise in their own eyes,
    and shrewd in their own sight!
Woe to those who are heroes at drinking wine,
    and valiant men in mixing strong drink,
who acquit the guilty for a bribe,
    and deprive the innocent of his right!    [5:21-23]

The Lord enters into judgment
    with the elders and princes of his people:
It is you who have devoured the vineyard,
    the spoil of the poor is in your houses.
What do you mean by crushing my people,
    by grinding the face of the poor?'
says the Lord God of hosts.    [3:14-15]

Not to overdo the connection between economic matters and God's revelation to ancient Israel, we point to only one incident in the teaching of Jesus,
where he warns us against being captivated by our wealth. A certain rich man's
lands produced in abundance and he ran out of storage room. Basking in self-
congratulation, he decided to build bigger granaries, and said to himself:

"Soul, you have ample goods laid up for many years; take your
ease eat, drink, be merry." But God said to him, "Fool! This
night your soul is required of you; and the things you have
prepared, whose will they be?" So [concluded Jesus] is he who

lays up treasure for himself, and is not rich toward God. [Luke 12:19-21]

## Interpreting the Scriptures

Generally the scriptures interpret themselves. There may be problems associated with determining what genre of literature you are reading, but if it is clear we are reading history, we treat it as history; if legal code we understand it as legal code; if epic story, we read it as an epic. Ordinarily this causes no trouble. Even when there is doubt about genre it may make little difference. For example, should Job be understood as an epic with a theological point, or as an historical figure with three pesky friends and a complaining wife—it doesn't matter. The meaning of Job comes through clearly regardless of whether it is an epic poem or a slice of history, or both.

Most interpretive problems are centered on the Old Testament, and particularly where the New Testament revelation is at odds with the Old. Some problems are easy to solve. An example is the absence of animal sacrifice in the New Testament. For when we see that the slaughterhouse aspect of Jewish worship was for Christians summed up and finished in the perfect sacrifice of Christ (Heb. 5-10), then we are not tempted to find guidelines for Christian worship in the sacrificial regulations of Sinai. Other problems are not so easy to solve, and the church has wrestled over the centuries to find a proper understanding. A good example here is the relationship between ruler or government to that of the exercise of religion. In the New Testament, estimates of the role of the state differ, depending on how the state is acting toward the newly-born body of believers. Finding Roman citizenship helpful and Roman laws protecting his activities, Paul wrote Roman Christians to obey their rulers. John the prophet, however, wrote a few years later, when Rome had already begun persecution of the Way, and he regarded Roman civil government as "the beast" whose authority was given it, not by God, but by Satan (compare Romans 13 with Revelation 13). In the Old Testament one of the tasks of the ruler was to see to it that worship was performed correctly. This, of course, has no parallel in the New, but Christian rulers have often turned to the Old to find proper guidelines, and Christian theologians have often agreed. Few contemporary Christian thinkers would agree with that interpretation even though it has the weight of centuries of theory and practice.

Generally, where problems arise, we follow the Reformers' criterion of comparing scripture with scripture. This is sharpened even more by noting the progressive nature of revelation and particularly that the forward movement focuses on Jesus Christ. The Letter to the Hebrews makes explicit the centrality of Christ and explicitly puts that above earlier revelation:

In many and various ways God spoke of old to our fathers by the prophets; but in these last days he has spoken to us by his Son whom he appointed the heir of all things, through whom also he created the world. [Heb. 1:1-2]

It is through Christ, then, that we read the scriptures. It is true, of course, that we know nothing of Him outside those Scriptures, and yet as their Subject and their Author he controls them; the Word interprets the words. Is this subjective? Yes. But, in the final analysis, the Bible demands such an inner grappling with its message. It is not law, but gospel; not dropped upon us, but converting the soul. To take an example from economic life: because Christ said he came not to destroy, but to seek and save those who are lost, and because of the whole tenor of his redemptive life, we choose the law and the prophets rather than Joshua's conquest when searching for biblical principles for economic activity. Our ancestors sometimes made the other choice and looked to the example of the Israelites' taking the land from the Canaanites as warrant for Christians' grabbing land from peoples in Africa or North America. We think this ignores the centrality of our Lord Jesus.

Both these issues—role of government *vis-a-vis* religion, and the recognition that Jesus did not sanction violence in his name—illuminate the last point in this section on interpreting the scriptures. In each case we denied the position of our ancestors. Yet we do not accuse them of being insincere in their understanding of biblical teaching. For we believe, finally, that the Holy Spirit continues to guide Christian people in such ways that (as Pastor Robinson prayed for his Pilgrim flock bound for the new world) "more light may break forth from God's word." Our Lord said he would give his disciples the Holy Spirit who would lead them into all truth (Jn 16:13). So when we look to the Bible for guidance, we look not only at the text as it lies before us and at its historical context, but also at the interpretations made by our ancestors in faith (e.g., Reformed, Roman Catholic, Anabaptist) as they wrestled with its meaning for their lives. Then, with particular attention to Jesus Christ, whom all scripture serves, we seek to find how it applies to our own times. That, of course, is the purpose of our whole study. In this chapter we are seeking for biblical principles for economic aspects of life. The last section of this chapter will begin the hard job of applying these principles to our day, while later chapters will focus upon particular problems and issues in modern economic life from this biblical viewpoint.

## The Agrarian World of the Bible: the Old Testament

In our chapter introduction we saw by glancing at a scene or two that economic issues are found throughout the pages of scripture. Now we must take a closer look at the world of the Bible. Laws and teachings are not given in a vacuum. The context is very important. It would have done no more good to tell Bedouins to leave the edges of their fields uncut so that the poor could glean than it would to give a wheat farmer today such instruction. The Bedouin has no fields; today's poor live too far from the wheatfields to do any gleaning.

According to the Bible and corollary information gleaned from the hard labors of archaeologists of the Near and Middle East, the whole of biblical history from the Conquest of Palestine in the mid-13th century through the time of Christ in the first century of our era was wrought in an agrarian culture. Prior to that, the patriarchs were evidently semi-Bedouins, and for a time their descendants were slaves in Egypt. When those Hebrew slaves escaped from bondage they wandered with flocks and herds for a long generation before invading and settling the land of Canaan. The harshness and stigma of slavery burned itself into their ethnic memory, as is clear from occasional references like this one:

> You shall not wrong a stranger or oppress him, for you were strangers in the land of Egypt. [Ex. 22:21]

But after the conquest Israel settled down into the agrarian mold. With few exceptions the laws of Moses are rules for an agrarian society, and although we might perhaps distinguish earlier from later ones by peculiarities of one sort or another, the disagreements among the scholars warn us that such a course is hazardous. So at this point we shall briefly survey developments in Israelite society over the centuries, pausing only to note certain characteristics of that society out of which came economic legislation and exhortation.

All of the theories about the conquest that scholars have constructed to fill in the sketchy pictures in Joshua and Judges agree that there was a more or less successful penetration of much of Palestine by a highly motivated group from the desert regions to the east and south. The city-states of the Canaanites gave way to a more simple village economy, attested to by Bible and archaeology alike. A democratization of the region took place. The largely peasant society that replaced the Canaanite city-state was always threatened by external foes, the chief of those being the Philistines who invaded the country from the sea at about the same time the people of Israel came from the opposite direction. The threat of servitude to the Philistines finally forced the tribes and clans of Israel to establish a monarchy, first under Saul, then under David and his descendants. Economically and politically the establishment of monarchy probably meant some impoverishment of the peasantry, as Samuel warned in the passage quoted earlier. For example, excavations at Tirsah disclosed that in the tenth century, just as the monarchy begins, the homes are all of equal size. But by the eighth century, the century of the first writing prophets—Amos, Hosea, Micah and Isaiah—the homes of the wealthy are bigger and better built, and the houses of the poor are huddled together in a different quarter of town. Certainly the establishment and growth of a class of officials and military leaders supported by the common people, which we see so clearly in the description of Solomon's reign, must have been hard on the small farmer (see, for example, I Kings 4, 5, 11).

From the time of David (1000 B.C.) to the Fall of Jerusalem to Babylon (587/6) a fairly standard division of the people is indicated. At the top was the military and ruling clique in the two  monarchies of Israel and Judah. (Israel, the Northern Kingdom, split from Judah in 922 at the beginning of the reign of David's grandson Rehoboam.) The origins of the ruling clique can be seen in the list of David's mighty men (II Sam. 23), followed by the list of Solomon's high officials and regional tax gatherers (I Kings 4). The tendency of rulers to self-aggrandizement at the expense of ordinary people is clearly exposed in the story of Queen Jezebel's murder of Naboth in order to attach his lands to the crown (I Kings 21).

A second class of favored persons in most agrarian societies—and the twin kingdoms appear to be no exception—was that of the religious leaders, which included   priests, scribes, and a few other members of the cultured elite. Throughout the period of Israelite history prior to the fall of Jerusalem, there was tension between the priests of that city and the Levites, who performed priestly worship in the countryside, as well as conflict with the royal temples built by the rulers of the Northern Kingdom. There are two curiosities of economic interest for us. The first one is that evidently King David at first enrolled some of his sons as priests, quite contrary to law and practice, and this probably underscores the temptation of monarchs to subsume the role and revenues of religion into the royal hands. (In most ancient nations of the Near East, the king was also the high priest.) The author of II Samuel simply mentions this in passing, without commenting on its importance. But I think we are safe in guessing that the fierce devotion to law that we find in later Jewish practice was strong enough even then to cause him to back off (II Sam. 8:18). The second curiosity has to do with the Levites. It is well known that of all the tribes only the Levites owned no land for the purposes of crop farming, although they seem to have pastured animals on lands they held in common (Lev. 25:32-34). After the exile only the descendants of Aaron served as priests at the only shrine, the one in Jerusalem. But earlier all the Levites seem to have offered sacrifices for the people at various hill shrines. The fact that they were to own no land, either as a clan or by families, indicates that the revenues from religious practice (mainly food) were sufficient for their needs.

The third group or class of people was a small mixed group made up of artisans and merchants. Some artisans were not Israelites, we suspect, because of the great preponderance of foreigners who worked on Solomon's temple. Some villages seem to have been made up almost entirely of people engaged in one craft (I Chr. 4), and certain quarters in Jerusalem were given over to different craftsmen. Trade was a royal monopoly evidently begun by Solomon (I Kings 9:26-28, 10:11,15,22,28-29). Probably most traders were foreigners, since we know that Phoenicians, with their excellent ports on the Mediterranean and their traditions of trade and travel, were the merchants of the whole Middle East. The term "Canaanite," meaning Phoenician, is used several times simply to mean "merchant" in the Old Testament (Prov. 31:24; Zech. 14:21). However, most early trade was probably market trade without middlemen, where the peasant and the artisan sold their wares directly to the buyers on the open market.

The fourth and largest group were the peasants, small farmers. That the land was divided up according to rather carefully worked out schemes is clear in Joshua, with the allotments made according to clans (tribes) and families. The people lived in small villages of perhaps 400-650 persons, and it is likely that so persistent was their occupation of the land that in Galilee the peasantry of Jesus' day was probably directly descended from that of the period of the monarchies. Farming was the economic basis for whatever wealth and income the people of Israel had, and most of the legislation as well as prophetic fulmination was aimed at maintaining the common people on the land of their inheritance. When we arrive at the next section of this chapter the reader should remember that almost all the principles we find are based upon laws that deal with the farmer and farming.

The last significant group were the slaves. There were two classes. First were foreigners, many of them captives of war (cf. Dt. 21:10-14; Num. 31:26-47; Dt. 20:10-15). We know that David's wars supplied slaves (II Sam. 8:2, 12:31), and most likely Solomon's Exion-Geber foundries, ships crews, and certainly his large construction crews were made up of such captive slaves (I Kings 9:27; II Chr. 8:18, 9:10). In addition, the people of the land who had been dispossessed by the Hebrews could fall into slavery (Lev. 25:44-46), and Solomon certainly enslaved many of them (I Kings 9:20-21; II Chr. 2:17-18). But even those two sources for slaves to serve the needs of state were not sufficient for the massive programs of Solomon. Native Israelites were also pressed into seasonal labor (I Kings 11:28; 12:18), and the unpopularity of this royal policy erupted into violence and rebellion when King Rehoboam's director of forced labor was stoned to death by the people of the north as the signal for the secession of the Ten Tribes from the confederacy that David and Solomon had been able to hold together. The proverbial wisdom of Solomon seems not to have impressed Israelites who were forced to build royal cities by their unfree labor!

In the census a century after the return from exile (Ezra 2:64; Neh. 7:66), about one in six of the people were slaves (7,337:42,360), most likely descendants of the captive-slaves prior to the exile. Some of them may have been descended from the ancient Gibeonites who hewed wood and drew water for the temple (Josh. 9, esp. verses 23,27; cf. Ezra 2:43-58).

The laws of Israel did not apply to captive-slaves or Canaanites slaves, but only to the second kind of slave, the native Israelite. For the native could be sold, and hence was a slave. But he could not be permanently in the ownership of another Israelite, unless he so desired (Ex. 21:1-6; Dt. 15:16-17). Indeed, any slave was a human being and had to be treated like one, so a slave who was injured by his master had to be set free (Ex. 21:26-27), and an escaped slave was not returned (Dt. 23:15-16). Both Jeremiah (34) and Nehemiah (5) were outraged by the holding of Jewish slaves by Jewish people. This may not seem noteworthy today, but for the ancient near East this protest was a radical view in favor of human freedom.

About a hundred years after some of the Jews returned from Babylonian Captivity to their land, we catch a clear glimpse of their economic conditions from Nehemiah, chapter 5. Their ruling family had vanished with the mysterious disappearance of Zerubbabel, heir to the Davidic throne. No descendant of David will rule in Israel till One reigns from a cross several centuries later. While monarchy and military power were missing—or, more correctly, were in the hands of Persia—the priests and temple workers were in considerable abundance, and the reforming work of Ezra enhanced their power and importance. The common people were divided between rich and poor, and it appears that the distinction between the two had probably returned to Judah with the exiles themselves. We read how the poor complained to Governor Nehemiah that because of the famine some of them have had to sell their children into slavery in order to pay their taxes, for others had taken away their only means of support, their fields and vineyards. Borrowing money at interest from fellow Jews, they have fallen farther and farther behind and see no hope for the future. Nehemiah, although a Jew, was Artaxerxes' governor over the land and was either able to shame or frighten the wealthy into returning the mortgaged lands and to stop their lending money at interest. Presumably the enslaved sons and daughters were also released, although this is not mentioned in the text.

By the time of Jesus' ministry some four hundred years later, the agrarian society had maintained itself through a number of political changes. Persian rule abruptly ceased with the conquest of Alexander in 331 B.C., and by the year 300 Palestine was firmly in the hands of the Egyptian Ptolemies. The Syrian Seleucids under Antiochus III took the land from Egypt in 198, only to lose it to native Jewish leadership (the Hasmonean family) in the Maccabean revolt of the 160's. This ineffective rule was terminated by the Roman general Pompey in 63 B.C., and in the adulthood of Jesus, Roman control was maintained directly in Judah through Senate-appointed procurators, and in Galilee through the delegated kingship of Herod Antipa, son of Herod the Great.

## The Agrarian World of the Bible: The New Testament

In the main, Jesus' parables disclosed two groups of people, wealthy landowners and debt-ridden peasants. In addition, we see a rural proleteriat of day laborers (Mt.20:1f), as well as powerful rulers, a judiciary (the parable of the unjust judge), and a gang of tax collectors. That gospel scenery is attested to by closer study. The general picture in Galilee was many large estates owned by absentee landlords, or by the government. Village life continued. The common people were generally free but dependent. Under Herod the Great more lands were given to his favorites, and the high taxes necessary to pay for his building operations probably cost more and more poor farmers the ownership of their land, although many of them no doubt continued to till ancestral lands as tenant farmers. The government monopoly on trade meant that peasants could not take advantage of good market conditions, because they could not enter into bargaining with their surpluses. Money lending was controlled by a license granted by the government, and probably poor peasants who got behind on taxes or rent or who needed money to buy seed for planting after a bad season were at the mercy of the usurers, despite Jewish laws against lending money at interest.

There were two tax systems, religious and Roman, and both weighed upon the poorer people without either system taking the other into account. State taxes were levies by traveling tax gatherers upon the produce as it was harvested. Then, when surplus goods were transported, they were taxed again by publicans strategically located at toll stations along the main roads. Tax collectors like Levi and Zacchaeus were probably of the latter variety. As was true in ancient Israel, there were village leaders or local magistrates who tried to mediate between the peasantry and the government or between tenants and absentee landowners, represented by their stewards—*oikonomois*, economists!—so prevalent in Jesus' parables. Many of these mediators were probably also synagogue rulers. It must have been difficult for them to keep in good confidence with either side in quarrels that were a matter of land and life for the poor.

There is no direct evidence about fishermen, but they were probably little better off than farmers. From Hellenic times on (after 300 B.C.), the salting and shipping of fish from the Sea of Galilee through the port cities of Tyre and Ptolemais was thriving business. But from what we know of the controls exercised on the fishing industry elsewhere, and the farming out of fishing rights to middlemen at high rates, we can assume no great benefit to the fishers themselves. Evidence from the gospels is inconclusive. On the one hand, men like Zebedee with several sons and servants may have done rather well in the trade (Mk. 1:16-20). On the other hand, the preponderance of fisherfolk among the disciples of Jesus may show a restlessness among that trade, a yearning for change that might have been partly occasioned by economic hardship. But this is sheer conjecture; Jesus's call to them is not based on their economic circumstances or employment group.

In summary then, the persistence of agrarian order throughout almost the whole biblical period—from the Conquest on—simplifies our task, but complicates it as well. It simplifies it becuse we do not need to look for radically different teachings to fit seriously changed circumstances. Once the monarchy is in place, by 1000 B.C., we find a general consistency in living conditions, social stratification, and biblical teaching on economic matters. However, it also means that we have no biblical teaching aimed at any other culture, so when we apply it to the modern industrial or post-industrial societies of our world, we are always in need of translation.

## Biblical Principles for Economic Activity

The reader should be warned that of enumerating biblical principles for economic activity there is no end. All any reader need do is glance at the teachings of Jesus, particularly in Matthew and Luke, or scan the legal codes of Exodus, Leviticus and Deuteronomy, or hear the breathless impatience with injustice of any of the pre-exilic prophets, and the economic nature of paragraph after paragraph will leap out. We have mentioned elsewhere the almost embarrassing amount of economic guidance the people of Israel had. Yet it should be said again that economics itself is never the focus of the Bible. Right knowledge of God is the center of biblical teaching. But right knowledge is never an abstraction:

> But let him who glories glory in this, that he understands and knows me, that I am the Lord who practice kindness, justice and righteousness in the earth; for in these things I delight, says the Lord. [Jer. 9:24]

And religious practice without regard for the poor is without validity in the eyes of God:

Behold, in the day of your fast you seek your own pleasure and oppress all your workers. Behold, you fast only to quarrel and to fight and to hit with wicked fist.... Is this not the fast that I choose: to loose the bonds of wickedness, to undo the thongs of the yoke, to let the oppressed go free, and to break every yoke? Is it not to share your bread with the hungry, and bring the homeless poor into your house; when you see the naked, to cover him, and not to hide yourself from your own flesh? Then shall your light break forth like the dawn, and your healing shall spring up speedily.... Then you shall call, and the Lord will answer. [Is. 58:3,4,6-8]

If, then, there is an intimate connection between right religion and proper economics, is it possible to find a key? We think there is, and we state it as follows:
*The Great Biblical Principle for Economic Life is that
Humans are Stewards of God's Good Earth.*

The earth is the Lord's and the fulness thereof, the world and those who dwell therein. [Ps. 24:1]

The land shall not be sold in perpetuity, for the land is mine (says the Lord). [Lev. 25:23]

The Lord God took the man and put him in the garden of Eden to till and keep it. [Gen. 2:15]

In biblical thought all things belong to God—all worlds, all peoples, all the earth. God is creator and sustainer. Humans are "strangers and sojourners" upon the lands he has entrusted to their care. We are stewards of God's fair world, accountable to God for what we do with the world put to our keeping:

The heavens are the Lord's heavens, but the earth he has given to the sons of men. [Ps. 115:16]

This is the key principle that is the impenetrable stratum upon which all the layers of biblical law and prophecy lie. It is a dominion or rule that is also a care and a keeping. And it extends beyond those things of the earth that are for human use, even to the things which we are to care for, though we make no use of them. The original pair were given dominion and care for it all—the fish of the sea and the birds of the air. The California condor and the Seaside sparrow are to be cared for in the apparent twilight of their species life, as are the strange, flowing fish that we have not yet discovered in their pitch-black environment miles below the surface. Humans are entrusted with the keeping of them all.

It is because God owns the land that the Israelites could not permanently sell the family lands (Lev. 25). It had been entrusted to a particular family for their sustenance. It is because God owns earth's increase that the firstborn of all mothers, human and animal, belong to God and were either sacrificed or brought back from God (Ex. 13:2). So Mary and Joseph traveled to the temple and presented the infant Jesus to God, offering the sacrifice of the poor (a pair of turtledoves or two young pigeons) to purchase back the child (Lev. 12:8; Lk. 2:24). While neoclassical economics operates with the concept of *scarcity* as its basic motif, Christian economics must substitute for scarcity the concept of *entrustedness*. We are only stewards (*oikonomois*), not owners, of what God has entrusted to us, whether of land or children, wealth or talent, authority or service. Under the umbrella of stewardship there is *shalom*, peace. Outside it lies false economy—wealth ill-gained and ill-used, work that is unremitting toil; in a word, injustice. We shall look in turn at wealth, work, and justice.

*Wealth is God's Creation Placed in Human Hands*

Isaac, heir of the promises to his father Abraham, became very wealthy by the blessing of the Lord (Gen. 26:12-14), and while Israel is warned that it does not live by bread alone (Dt. 8:3), yet God promises them a land so rich that they will lack nothing, and they shall bless the Lord their God for the good land he has given them (vs. 7-10). Job's great wealth is tied to his dependence upon God (1:1-5, 42:10-17), although that doesn't protect him from losing it when Satan, with God's permission, puts him to the test. The good wife of Proverbs 31 is obviously wealthy (her husband will have no lack of grain), but her hand is open to the poor and she reaches out to the needy. In the New Testament believers are warned not to trust in their wealth and to be content with enough food and clothing (I Tim. 6). But the parable of the waiting father (Lk. 15) is told without any suggestion by Jesus that the farm family pictured there should be ashamed of its wealth. There are plenty of warnings in both testaments about the snare of riches, and Jesus warns that one cannot serve both God and money. But even in Luke's gospel, which more than any underscores the rewards of poverty and pronounces woes upon the rich and full (Lk. 6:2-21,24-25), one finds wealth blessed, and even more wealth is promised in the context of giving it away (6:38).

Christians have been ambivalent about wealth. On the one hand, people occasionally trot out platitudes from the "gospel of wealth" preachings of the early twentieth century, which piously and easily equate fortune with goodness. On the other hand, socially conscious Christians sometimes wonder if it is possible to be rich and Christian. Certainly Jesus' remarks on the difficulty of the rich entering the kingdom (easier for a camel to go through the eye of a needle—Mt. 19:24) make us wary of ever equating wealth with piety. It is no wonder his disciples, astonished—for they too equated wealth with salvation—cried, "Who then can be saved?"

Nevertheless, wealth is a sign of God's blessing. That is a biblical principle. But it is an *effective* sign only when it symbolizes dependence upon God and is used to minister to the needs of the poor. That is also a biblical principle. Let us attend to Calvin on the subject. Negatively, he wrote about pseudo-Christians who, if they could, would have even the sun all to themselves:

> If they were able, indeed, it is certain that they would change the whole order of God and nature so they could swallow everything. And yet what Christians! Yes, if one wants to believe them! [*Sermon* on Mt. 3:3-10]

But positively he preaches:

> Let those, then, that have riches, whether they have been left by inheritance, or procured by industry and efforts, consider that their abundance was not intended to be laid out in an intemperance or excess, but in relieving the necessities of the brethren. [*Commentary* on II Cor. 8:15]

Dependence upon God bids the believer bless God for God's blessing and see herself as a conduit of God's bounty to those in need, or as a deacon ministering by means of God's goodness to the hurts of a poor, hungry world.

In the Bible the primary wealth was in land, just as the primary way to earn income was by working the land. There are artisans mentioned in the Old Testament—millers, bakers, weavers, barbers, potters, fullers, locksmiths, jewelers, perfumers—but most of the legislation deals with farming. As declared in our metaprinciple, property is entrusted to people, but final ownership of the land belongs to God, who gives its increase:

> Thou waterest its furrows abundantly, settling its ridges,
> softening it with showers, and blessing its growth.
> Thou crownest the year with thy bounty;
> the tracks of thy chariot drip with fatness.
> The pastures of the wilderness drip,
> the hills gird themselves with joy,
> The meadows clothe themselves with flocks,
> the valleys deck themselves with grain,
> they shout and sing together with joy. [Ps. 65:10-13]

But the land is given into the hands of specific people for their use. The Old Testament certainly knows nothing of communal ownership, except that the ownership is tied to the family, not the individual. (But there are no solitary individuals in the Old Testament, save poor old Jeremiah, who redeemed family lands near Jerusalem, even as the Babylonian army surrounded the city.) In the New Testament it is clear that the faithful are meant to use their goods for the sake of helping others. But it is still theirs. Even in the one isolated vignette of Christian socialism (Acts 4:32-5:11), there is no suggestion that Ananias and his wife Sapphira should not, as Christians, own the property they had sold. Their punishment is carried out solely because they have lied about their activities: they pretended to give all the proceeds from the sale to the early church, but in fact held part of it back. Peter James Klassen [1964] shows that it was only among a small minority of the Anabaptists of the sixteenth century that this passage was generalized in such a way as to interpret the whole Bible as a Christian Communist Manifesto. Socialism is not a biblical principle.

Because land is the primary form of wealth, the Hebrew was required to treat it with care. This is a general principle scattered throughout the Scriptures. Adam was to till and keep the garden. "Keep" has here the idea of caring for. The land was to lie fallow in Israel every seventh year. Later we shall find that the heart of this command was that the earth, like the people, keep a sabbath unto the Lord. The sabbath was a sign of rest, of *shalom*, meaning peace and wholeness. But the rest was also a way of allowing the earth to renew itself. Nothing was to be done to harm the land or to hinder its productivity. Israel was even urged to make war in such a way that trees were not destroyed (Dt. 20:19-20), and to gather eggs and chicks for food among wild fowl without harming the hen (Dt. 23:6-7).

Unfortunately, we so commonly misunderstand the source of our wealth that God's bounty is misappropriated and misused, and thus becomes a source of injustice. We believe not that the earth is the Lord's, but that it is ours. From our Renaissance legacy we speak of "property rights," and because property has been valued more than people, Marxism has appeared as the avenger. Our wealth is used not to help our sisters and brothers, but simply (as in the parable) to build bigger barns in order to enlarge our collections. For this reason the Hebrew prophets often stress the injustice people have used to gain wealth, and they angrily excoriate the way the poor are enslaved and abused. Thus Isaiah pronounces a curse upon land belonging to those who have joined house to house and field to field, when land was meant to belong to its original owners. Jeremiah calls upon the king to deliver the poor from the oppressors, to protect the alien, the widow and the orphan. King Jehoiakim is denounced for building his palace by unrighteousness, making his people serve him without pay (22:13-19). Amos, the first of the eighth-century prophets, has almost no other theme than the way wealth has found its way into the hands of a few:

> Thus says the Lord:
> For three transgressions of Israel, and for four,
> I will not revoke the punishment;
> because they sell the righteous for silver
> and the needy for a pair of shoes,
> they that trample the head of the poor into the dust of the earth,
> and turn aside the way of the afflicted;
> a man and his father go in to the same maiden,
> so that my holy name is profaned;
> they lay themselves down beside every altar
> upon garments taken in pledge;

and in the house of their god they drink the wine of those
who have been fined. [2:6-8]

In Israel, he says, wealth will be punished.  God will smite the houses of
those who are well-off enough to live in one dwelling in the summer and another in the winter (3:15); the rich women (cows of Bashan!) who oppress the
poor and crush the needy will be taken into exile (4:1-3); the cities will be de-
populated (5:3); those who can afford to make great religious offerings will not
be accepted (5:21-24); and all who live off the labor of the poor, stretching upon
ivory couches, eating, drinking, and singing, will lose all that they have (6:4-7).
Indeed, so well known is the prophetic condemnation of most forms of wealth
in Israel because it was gotten and kept at the expense of the needy, and the system of justice which worked only for the rich and powerful (5:20-22), that we
shall not belabor it here, nor call  other prophetic witnesses to the attack (cf. Jer.
5:26-28, Micah 2 and 6 for typical passages).  For the early Christian teaching,
consider only the parable of the rich fool (Lk. 12:16-21), the story of the rich man
and Lazarus (Lk. 16:19-31), and James' diatribe against the abusive power of the
rich (James 2:1-7 and 5:1-6).  In short, whenever we find wealth in the hands of
a few only, there biblical principles have been rejected.

Wealth, misappropriated and misused, becomes the strangler of faith in Jesus' parable of the sower.  It breeds anxiety.  It becomes the ruler of our lives,
says Jesus, who warns, "You cannot serve God and money."  In his letter to
Timothy, Paul puts wealth into perspective:

There is great gain in godliness with contentment; for we
brought nothing into the world and we cannot take anything out
of the world; but if we have food and clothing, with these we
shall be content.  But those who desire to be rich fall into
temptation, into a snare, into many senseless and hurtful desires
that plunge men into ruin and destruction.  For the love of
money is the root of all evils; it is through this craving that some
have wandered away from the faith and pierced their hearts with
many pangs.... As for the rich in this world, charge them not to
be haughty, nor to set their hopes on uncertain riches but on God
who richly furnishes us with everything to enjoy.  They are to do
good, to be rich in good deeds, liberal and generous, thus laying
up for themselves a good foundation for the future, so that they
may take hold of the life which is life indeed. [I Tim. 6:6-10, 17-19]

The modern picture of human life as one of unremitting consumption is
contrary to Bible economics.

We must say two more things about wealth.  The first is that the Bible
wants all to have wealth.  This is the reason for the radical legislation found in
Leviticus 25, where every fifty years at the jubilee the land is to be re-allocated
to the family of its original owners.  This remarkable legislation assumes that
stewardship cannot adequately be undertaken unless one has something to be
steward with.  Of course, ownership of land means freedom, and it is not sur-

prising that the Jubilee legislation should be found in the context of freeing of slaves at the end of six years of servitude, and is intended to be observed by free people (Dt. 15, Lev. 25). Other goods useful for production or simply for living cannot be taken away either. A millstone cannot be taken as pledge or pawned for a loan. Nor can a man's clothing be similarly attached (Dt. 24:6, 10:13). Stray animals must be returned (Ex. 23:4-5, Lev. 22:1-4). The point of all this scattered legislation seems to be to maintain people as productive persons, to allow them to be stewards of God's fair world. That is a restatement of the key biblical principle.

Failing that or in the meanwhile, before justice can be fully accomplished, the people with wealth are commanded to aid those without. We need do no more than iterate what has already been said in various ways, for scripture often repeats this injunction. Whether we are reading about allowing the landless to glean the fields and harvest the leftover grapes (Lev. 19:9-10), or providing released slaves enough to live on (Dt. 15:12-18), or simply helping the poor, it is incumbent upon the haves to help those who have not. Indeed, Jesus in his picture of the Great Assize (Mt. 25:31-47) makes ministering to the needs of the hungry, thirsty, the alien, the sick and imprisoned the evidences of salvation, and Zacchaeus's vow to give to the poor causes our Lord to exclaim, "Today salvation has come to his house!" (Lk. 19:9)

### Since Humans are Made in the Image of the Creator God, Human Work is Meant to Image Back to God His Creativity

When we first spot Adam in the Genesis story he is already at work taking care of the garden and naming the animals. After the Fall, work, like sexuality and human relationships, is distorted (Gen 3;16-19), but it never loses its proper meaning. The kind of work seems not to matter: tilling the ground, tending flocks, artisanry, homemaking, buying and selling—all are regarded as normal and good. Even the author of Ecclesiastes, that most pessimistic book of scripture, when he can find nothing good in sensual pleasures, empire-building, or philosophy, can still find pleasure in his work (2:24, 3:13, 5:12, 9:10).

Indeed, were one to search for a simple biblical definition of what it is to be human, one might find that first and foremost we are creative beings. That is the first fact we discover when we look to the Bible for a definition of good work. Like the other animals in origin ("The Lord God formed 'the adam' of dust from the ground'), only "the adam," male and female, is made in the image of God. (In Gen. 1:26-27 and 2:7 "man" in Hebrew is "the Adam"; in chapter 1 "The Adam" is male and female.) The definition of humans as toolmakers (*homo faber*) is a clumsy recognition of our creativity as we take what is at hand and work it into something new.

It is curious that the only work one finds condemned in scripture is the making of idols (Ex. 20:4). When Isaiah laughs at the person who makes a god out of a tree and then falls down in worship before that block of wood, he concludes that the deluded mind of the idolater keeps him from saying, "Is there not a lie in my right hand ?"(44:9-20) The fact is that we are made in the image of God. So it is a lie for us to make gods in *our* image. As stewards of the Creator we use our creativity to work mightily in His world. We do not flee our place of stewardship to make the Maker, or usurp God's rule (Gen. 11:1-9). We impress upon our work the very stamp of our personality, as God created the world to express His being. In the New Testament the only work we see undone is work connected with idolatry, as, for example, the de-demonizing of the soothsayer of Apollos or the impoverishment of the shrine-makers of Artemis (Acts 16:16-20, 19:23-41).

So the first biblical principle about work is that that work is good which allows us to be stewards of the creativity with which we were endowed. All the New Testament language about talents and gifts fits in here. Obviously, anything which detracts from God's gifts to us—work of no human value, work that permits of no creativity, work that makes idols—such are lies; they do not tell us what it is to work humanly. Now we must ask if modern society provides many opportunities for creative work today. Many people find value only in some secondary work—a hobby. The talent is not buried, but it isn't developed in the workplace either.

A second fact in the biblical understanding of work is that people do not work in isolation. Indeed, the sort of egocentric competition that allows one person to increase his holdings of land and another to lose his possessions is declared to be only temporary (Lev. 25). The larger family, though not the whole tribe, is the economic unit, and when a discrete family loses its hold upon the land, it is incumbent upon the relatives to re-purchase it and deliver it again into the hands of its original possessors. The need for cooperation is underscored within the early Christian community by Paul's likening the members of the church to members of the same body who need each other for the body to be in health.

Our work, then, must serve our fellows. Our Lord said he was among his friends as one who serves. His example of leadership and authority in the upper room at the Supper, when he washed his disciples' feet and commanded them, leaders in the church, to do the same, underscores the connection between work and service. As Calvin said:

> It is not enough when one can say, 'Oh, I work, I have my trade,I set the pace.' This is not enough; for one must be concerned whether it is good and profitable to the community and if it can serve our neighbors.... It is certain that no occupation will be approved by Him which is not useful and that does not serve the common good and that also redounds to the profit of everyone. [*Sermon* on Eph. 4:26-28]

Of course, this also means that people cannot give up working to live off the labor of others. It is to prevent some of the members of that body being parasitic upon the others that Paul commands the Thessalonian Christians who have quit work in order to await the return of the Lord to get back to work. If they won't work, then don't feed them, is Paul's admonition (II Thess. 3:10). The Protestant Reformers, who were insistent upon introducing biblical standards into the ordinary affairs of sixteenth-century mortals, were therefore very concerned about the commonweal, the health of society. Calvin spoke angrily from his pulpit in St. Pierre's Church about those who would deny work to strangers in the refugee-swollen city of Geneva. In contrast to Luther, Calvin approved of commerce, not just of farming and artisanry. For him trade was the natural way for people to commune with each other, and he saw the exchange of goods as necessary for the spread of God's bounty throughout society. A rather long quotation from his *Commentary* on Matthew 25:20, the Parable of the Talents, will highlight this:

> Those who use to advantage what God deposits with them are said to trade (*negotiari*). For the life of the godly is aptly compared to business, since they should deal among themselves to maintain fellowship; and the industry with which each man prosecutes the task laid on him, and his very vocation, the ability to act aright, and the rest of the gifts, are reckoned as merchandise, since their purpose and use is the mutual communication among men. And the fruit of which Christ speaks is the common profit which lightens up the glory of God.

Perhaps we can see now how the creative use of God's gifts to individuals (fact one) and the need to work cooperatively (fact two) fit together. The gifts are there within society; no one person has them all, for we are meant *together* to reflect back to God's image. Together people pool the gifts for the sake of the whole. No one is excluded:

> The eye cannot say to the hand, 'I have no need for you,' now again the head to the feet, 'I have no need of you.' [I Cor. 12:21]

Our stewardship is in common; secular individualism is not biblical; that is our second biblical principle about work.

The third fact about good work in the Bible is that work and rest go together, and when they join properly, people and land have peace.

> Six days you shall labor, and do all your work; but the seventh day is sabbath to the Lord your God; in it you shall not do any work, you, or your son, or your daughter, your manservant, or your maidservant, or your cattle, or the sojourner who is within your gates; for in six days the Lord made heaven and earth, the sea, and all that is in them, and rested the seventh day; therefore the Lord blessed the sabbath day and hallowed it. [Ex. 20:11]

In the Deuteronomic account the reason given is that the people might remember that they were slaves in the land of Egypt, and that God brought them out and commanded them to observe the sabbath (Dt. 5:12-15). Both of these explanations for the sabbath are to the point. In the Exodus version rest, like work, is rooted in God's being. It is not wasted time or `killing time' when we remove ourselves from plot or shop and commune alone, with each other, and with God. In the later version we are reminded of how false and foreign to true human existence it is to be enslaved to do someone else's work; so the slaves were to keep the sabbath too.

> In it you shall not do any work, you or your son, or your daughter, or your manservant, or your maidservant, or your ox, or your ass, or any of your cattle, or the sojourner who is within your gates, that your manservant and your maidservant may rest as well as you. You shall remember that you were a servant in the land of Egypt, and the Lord your God brought you out thence.... [Dt. 5:14-15]

It is possible, of course, to work without cessation, to turn ourselves into working machines. People in the modern world who work anxiously, sure that everything depends upon their efforts, should attend to the Psalmist:

> Unless the Lord builds the house,
>    those who build it labor in vain....
> It is in vain that you rise up early,
>    to go late to rest.
> eating the bread of anxious toil;
>    or he gives to his beloved sleep. [Ps. 127:1-2]

Elie Wiesel, novelist and survivor of the Holocaust, writes movingly of the loss of the faith and of the Sabbath of his youth:

> I would give much to be able to relive a Sabbath in my small town, somewhere in the Carpathian Mountains. The whiteness of the tablecloths, the blinking candle flames, the beaming faces around me, the melodious voice of my grandfather, the *Hasid* of Vizhnitz, inviting the angels of the Sabbath to accompany him to our home.... That is what I miss most: a certain peace ... that the Sabbath, at Sighet, offered its children, big and small, young or old, rich or poor. It is this Sabbath that I miss. Its absence recalls to me all else that is gone. It reminds me that things have changed in the world, that the world itself has changed. [1981, p. 612]

Indeed, the world has changed. While it is not the task of this chapter to decide how biblical principles shall be applied in the modern marketplace, it is passing strange that the sabbath rest is seldom kept today. Business goes on as usual, stores and those who work in them are constantly employed. When the workweek of the majority is over—the Monday through Friday crowd— there is a large minority who must continue to work to supply the inflated needs of those who use their rest for purposes of consumption. In some industries where machinery works more efficiently if it never stops, the people who serve the machines are organized into revolving shifts, so that one may work a morning shift for a period of five days, take a day or two off, then go to the afternoon shift for a period, then the evening shift. In this manner both days and hours of work are in constant cyclic flux. No regular rest is possible; because the machine does not rest, neither can the man, and so he is enslaved.

In the Old Testament the sabbath rest is a sign of God's peace, *shalom*. According to Genesis 2:3, God observed the sabbath prior to any human rest, and according to the law given at Sinai, the land itself should rest. After all, it belongs to the Lord:

> For six years you shall sow your land and gather in its yield;
> but the seventh year you shall let it rest and lie fallow that
> the poor of your people may eat; and what they leave the wild
> beasts may eat. You shall do likewise with your vineyard, and
> with your olive orchard. [Ex. 23:10-11]

In Leviticus 25 the fallow year is called "The sabbath of the Lord."

So the regular cycle of work and rest is preceded by the rest of God. Within this regular cycle both the land and the people of the land can find peace, *shalom*. That this did not always sit well even with ancient Israel is indicated in Amos, where impatience with the sabbath is linked with rapacious economics:

> Hear this, you who trample upon the needy,
>     and bring the poor of the land to an end,
> saying, 'When will the new moon be over,
>     that we may sell grain?
> And the sabbath,
>     that we may offer wheat for sale,
> that we may make the ephah small and the shekel great,
>     and deal deceitfully with false balances,
> that we may buy the poor for silver
>     and the needy for a pair of sandals,
> and sell the refuse of the wheat?" [8:4-6]

It is not surprising that such a people will have no rest. Indeed, the very land will tremble, rise, and be tossed about (8:8), for it has neither rest nor peace. Isaiah, at about the same time, said to Judah that in returning and rest—not in frenetic activity—would the people be saved (30:15).

Later, the Lord tells Jeremiah not to mourn for the people, for He has taken away His peace from them. But after they went into exile in Babylon Jeremiah wrote to them that for them "God plans for welfare (*shalom*) and not evil, to give you a future and hope." (29:11) From the translation of *shalom* as "welfare" we can see that the word has many nuances. Its root meaning is "well-being," and in the Old Testament that is usually meant in the material sense of regular rains, good crops, absence of warfare. In this sense it is an earthly "salvation," and is sometimes translated that way.

Isaiah ties *shalom* to righteousness, that is, to do the doing of justice (*mishpat*). He says that if the people had listened to God's commandments, their *shalom* would have been like a river and their righteousness (*zedaqah*) like the waves of the sea (Is 48:18). Again he says that when a righteous king comes and God's Spirit is poured out, then the land will have justice (*mishpat*) and righteousness (*zedaqah*); the effect of right doing will be *shalom*, and the result will be quietness and trust forever (32:15-17). Finally, Isaiah promises the city of Jerusalem that in the great restoration there will be an end of violence, and God will make the city's overseers peace (*shalom*) and its taskmasters righteousness (*zedaqah*).

Thus, it is clear that in scripture work, rest, peace, and righteousness are bound tightly together. Work and rest are commanded by God, and when people work and rest they are following the example of the Creator, in whose image they are made. Righteousness, or doing justice, will be discussed below, but generally it means equity, the proper balance between wealth and work. When these are, in fact, present, when God's plan for us is followed, then there is peace, *shalom*.

Perhaps, to finish this section, we might look at the homey account of Jesus' visit in Bethany with Martha and Mary. Mary sat at the Lord's feet and listened to his teaching. She was at rest. But Martha, as the account goes, "was distracted with much serving." She went to Jesus in exasperation and tried to enlist his help in getting Mary to help her. His response is well known:

> Martha, Martha, you are anxious and troubled about many things; one thing [i.e., probably one dish] is needful. Mary has chosen the good portion, which shall not be taken away from her. [Lk. 10:41]

Since our Lord was always concerned for justice, we can assume that Martha's overwork was caused by anxiety, not because her sister was lazy. She knew how to work, but not how to rest; so she had no peace.

Our third principle, then, is that work brings no peace, unless it is done justly and with due regard for rest, of which the Sabbath is the symbol.

### The proper balance between wealth and work is called justice or righteousness (mishpat and zedaqah)

The reader will have noticed that whether talking about wealth or work, the Bible keeps coming back to these words. (In the New Testament, they have become one word, *dikaiosune*, which can be translated either way.) Wealth is God's world entrusted to our stewardly use and care. Work is what we do to use it and take care of it. The proper relationship between the two is justice. Because a number of facets of justice have been treated in passing already, let us confine ourselves to three closely related biblical concerns: the prohibition of usury, concern for the landless poor, and the institution of slavery.

Lending money at interest is specifically prohibited in the Old Testament. There are a number of quotable passages, but the following encompasses them all.

> You shall not lend upon interest to your brother, interest on
> money, interest on victuals, interest on anything that is lent for
> interest. To a foreigner you may lend upon interest, but to your
> brother you shall not lend upon interest; that the Lord your God
> may bless you.... [Dt. 23:19-20] (See also Ex. 22:25-27, Lev. 25:35-37,
> Dt. 15:1-8, Ezek. 22:12 among others.)

The point of this prohibition is that lending to the farmer at interest means
(1) living off the labor of another, when each person is a steward of gifts and
energy, and (2) pushing the poor into an indebtedness that may drive a family
from its land. To charge interest upon grain for seed or upon loans that tided
the farmer from seedtime to harvest meant that a crop failure left the farmer
with nothing left to barter but the land. But to give up the land was to give up
the wealth God had given each family that was its sustenance and its place of
stewardship. So the usury edicts are of a kind with the other laws that kept the
poor from being displaced by the rich. Among them were laws pertaining to
just balances, weights, measures (e.g., Dt. 25:13-16) and standard currency (Ezek.
45:10-12), as well as laws for judges, prohibiting their taking bribes and pervert-
ing justice (Dt. 16:19-20, Is. 1:23). It is clear that as Israel grew older it became
more and more like its neighboring countries, where the simple agrarian society was being harrassed by the dispossession of the farmer through the means
prohibited above. The result of such economic and social upheaval was to produce a landless people, either rootless or enslaved to the rulers and the powerful. The prophets took up the cause of the peasantry, the backward people, the
masses who had been deprived of their land and rights. The biblical principles
attached to the usury prohibition are that (1) we should not live without
working because others are working for us; (2) that our economic activities
must not deprive others of the ability to produce or to be stewards.

So we move quickly from the usury prohibition to attend to the poor, who
receive such attention in scripture. Ideally, there were to be no poor in the land
(Dt. 15:4), but in fact there would always be some (15:11).

> You shall not oppress a hired servant who is poor and needy,
> whether he is one of your brethren or one of the sojourners who
> are in your land within your towns; you shall give him his hire
> on the day he earns it, before the sun goes down (for he is poor
> and sets his heart upon it); lest he cry against you to the Lord, and
> it be sin in you. [Dt. 24:14-15]

The two most extensive passages are Deuteronomy 15, the Sabbath year of
release, and Leviticus 25, the seven-times-seven year of jubilee, when the land
was to return to its original owners. Let us look very briefly at each, since they
legislate so much of what the prophets took to be just dealing.

The Deuteronomy passage has two commandments. First, when the seventh or sabbatical year comes around, every debt shall be forgiven, and yet
loans shall be made to the poor even though the seventh year is approaching.
(We know from rabbinic teaching much later that this command was followed

among the Jews, although exceptions and fine print were added so that lending would be done even though the sabbatical year drew nigh.) Next, Hebrew slaves had to be released in the seventh year; and not only released, but

> you shall furnish him liberally out of your flock, out of your threshing floor, and out of your wine press; as the Lord your God has blessed you, you shall give to him. You shall remember that you were a slave in the land of Egypt, and the Lord your God redeemed you.

There is, in addition, a provision whereby if a slave wanted to remain attached to the household "because he loves you and your household," then a ceremony was to be performed to make that man or woman a bonded person for life. No doubt such a person became what a few generations ago was common in this country, permanent status as a hired hand. Perusal of literature written by farming people earlier in this century shows that such an existence was not always onerous, for hired hands worked with the farmers who employed them, not for absentee landlords who ruled through managers, as was true, for example, in Ireland or Scotland.

The Leviticus passage is much longer and more complex. It bears reading, but its main provisions are these: (1) On the seventh year the land shall keep a sabbath, neither being sown nor harvested, so that the poor can benefit from its natural increase. (2) Property that has been sold must be returned to the original owners at the end of fifty years, the year of jubilee. In effect, this meant that property could be rented out, but could not be alienated permanently. (3) Relatives have the obligation to redeem land before the fiftieth year if they have the means. (4) This prohibition of selling farmland does not apply to homes within walled cities. If a house is not redeemed in the first year after its sale, then its sale is permanent. The idea behind this may be that land is the wealth the Lord gave to all the families of the Hebrews, but houses are people-made and do not produce a living. (5) The poor Hebrew should be supported either in a charitable way or as a hired servant; if he sells himself to a foreigner, the next of kin should purchase his release before the jubilee year, but if this is not possible, he must be released then. (6) Foreigners can be enslaved in perpetuity.

This chapter raises many issues that cannot be settled for certain. Was the jubilee year ever carried out or was it "ideal" legislation? Was there meant to be one jubilee for all Israel, or did the counting of years differ from place to place (so Robert North)? Was it an early piece of legislation for Hebrew farmers, but not applicable to cities because many of them were still inhabited by Canaanites, as several scholars believe?

For our purposes, however, there are three key provisions in these two pieces of legislation: cancelling debts, freeing slaves, redeeming land. All of this is "poor" legislation, in that it is meant to be a cure for poverty. Had it been followed exactly in an agrarian society, then there would have been no poor in the land, but those in hard circumstances would have returned to the land, to productive existence, their debts wiped out, able to make a fresh start. To use contemporary terminology, this is legislation based upon a liberation theology. As God liberated the people from Egypt, so shall God's people be free. But note, not free in a humanistic sense—free for self alone—but free to take up the weight and glory of stewardship again.

The New Testament teaching complements that of the Old, with Jesus sharpening his hearers' ears to the cry of the poor. The story of the rich man and Lazarus (Lk. 16:19-31) portrays a wealthy man who is damned because he was not even aware of the existence of the beggar at his door. Even the dogs licked poor Lazarus' sores, but the man of property took no notice. Paul also stresses the way Christians should aid each other in need, especially in his delight at the offerings people were making for the poor of Jerusalem. In his joy he underlines a note that we find on Jesus's lips, namely, that our care for others should flow, not from command, but from our recognition of the love God has showered upon us:

> ... see that you excel in this gracious work also. I say this not as a command, but to prove by the earnestness of others that your love also is genuine. For you know the grace of our Lord Jesus Christ, that though he was rich, yet for your sake he became poor, so that by his poverty you might become rich. [II Cor. 8:7-9]

But, although we have stressed the rule of law, when quoting from Mosaic legislation especially, yet even in the Old Testament the bedrock reason for obedience was as a response to the beneficence of God:

> You shall not oppress a stranger; you know the heart of a stranger, for you were strangers in the land of Egypt. [Ex. 23:9]

At the end of the jubilee legislation the reason for freeing the slave is given:

> For to me the people of Israel are servants, they are my servants whom I brought forth out of the land of Egypt. [Lev. 25:55]

### Doing Justice for the Poor and Powerless is the Special Concern of Government

The poor are the special concern of rulers—at least the prophets hold them to that charge. Kings are also defenders of the realm. And, oddly for modern western Christians, they must ensure that true religion is maintained. This teaching, which is the theme of much of the historical material in Samuel and Kings, is not relevant in today's world, though it does present some problems of biblical interpretation. More important to us, kings are to do justice. Indeed, in a world of totalitarian or omnicompetent states today, where all things pertain to the government, it is rather refreshing to find defense and justice the only two biblical roles that carry over to us. As for the role of religious reformer, the work of the Holy Spirit in our history has shown that religion is not the business of the state.

Under this general theme of justice—the right balance between wealth and work—we said we would look at three items. We have seen that usury impoverished the people and thus was forbidden as unjust. Now we have observed how the law provides for the poor by cancelling debts, freeing Hebrew slaves, and returning people to the land, while the prophets place on government the role of enforcing that law. Next, we turn to the hardest subject for the modern mind: the institution of slavery.

The reader will remember that Israelite society had made permanent slaves out of conquered people. In the jubilee legislation and elsewhere it is permissible to have permanent slaves "from among the nations that are round about you" or "the strangers... who have been born in your land." So although we have strong provisions against the enslavement of Hebrews, and we see that as a continuing concern even after the return from exile (Neh. 5), yet slavery of aliens is permitted. (But Ezekiel during the exile in Babylon promised upon return that aliens upon the land would become inheritors. (Ezek. 47:21-23) ). Even in the New Testament there is no command for Christian slaveholders to release their bondsmen and women. Although Paul strongly suggests that Philemon release his slave Onesimus (esp. Philemon 1:17), he does not command it. In the Ephesian and Colossian letters, masters are bidden to treat slaves well, but are not told to release them. And slaves are urged to be obedient, even when those masters are overbearing (see Eph. 6:5-8, Col. 3:22-25, I Tim. 6:1-2, I Peter 2:18-21). It is true, as Walter Eichrodt declares, that the human being is central to God's concern in all biblical legislation. He even points to the alien slave as the instance that proves this, since unlike other lands of the time, among the Hebrews if one injured a slave then one had to release the slave (Ex. 21:26f). For in the final analysis the slave is not property, but a person. Nor was the escaped slave returned to its master (Dt. 23:15-16). Nevertheless, the fact that slavery was part of the economy and was condoned in ancient Israel and the fact that it was not forbidden in the early church, pose for us one last problem in this quest for principles we need to understand the economics of the Bible.

As we move to this last section, however, we must keep firmly in mind what we have found so far. All economic facts and all economic principles lie under the general heading of stewardship. The earth is the Lord's; the Lord entrusts it to His people to till and keep—to use and care for. To balance that great wealth and that great work is to do justice. How shall we understand this last issue: that on the institution of slavery the Bible does not advance as far as we would like?

## The Holy Spirit and the Kingdom of God

The historical fact is, we know, that slavery did not long survive the ascendancy of Christianity in the Mediterranean world. We also know that from the earliest times Christians regarded slavery as wrong and worked to rid the world of the curse. (That it came back much later in the fifteenth century as an ugly by-product of the exploration of Africa and emulation of Muslims is to the church's shame.) Why, if the early church in its gospels and letters did not outlaw slaveholding, did early Christians so quickly end the practice? The answer is two-fold: on the one hand, it was clear to them that Christian principles did not condone bondage; on the other hand, we must say theologically that the Holy Spirit led them to that conclusion. The Holy Spirit or Counselor, as Jesus describes the Spirit in John 15 and 16, is promised to be Christ's on-going witness in the world. That Spirit "will guide you into all the truth," (16:12); the Spirit will take things of Christ and declare them to his followers (16:14-15); the Spirit will convince the world of sin, of righteousness and judgment (16:8-11); and the Spirit will declare the things that are to come (16:13). In other words, the Holy Spirit vivifies the written word and leads the church in a continuing encounter with her risen Lord. So, it is the Spirit of Christ, speaking through the Bible, that convinces us that it is a principle that people should be free.

Now, when we follow this a little further we are aware that there is a kind of reciprocal relationship between Bible and the Spirit of Christ. On the one hand, the church continues to be informed by the Holy Spirit, to grow in understanding of what God's will is for us. For example, in the early centuries the church wrote creeds which go some ways beyond simple scripture in exploring, say, the doctrine of the Trinity or the hypostatic union of the two natures of Christ. Yet these, we believe, are implicit in Scripture. On the other hand, the church has not always listened to the Bible and has taught or acted in ways contrary to Christ. This is why theologians of all churches point out that the church is always in need of reforming. In the latter cases we can say that the church has not listened to Christ's Spirit, for it taught or did things contrary to Him.

To put this in another way, the church always lives in hope. It believes that God, to quote Pastor Robinson again, has yet more light to break forth from His word. Now, as soon as we talk about hope we find ourselves asking about the future. Is there hope for the future? Is this world, the arena of human stewardship, doomed to destruction? When we return to the Bible for a word about that we are impressed by the multiplicity of scriptures that tell us that this world also lives in hope, that it "waits with eager longing" to be "set free from its bondage to decay and obtain the glorious liberty of the children of God" (Rom. 8:18-25). It might be possible to regard that whole marvelous passage as a pointer to heaven, not earth, were it not that our Lord taught that God's Kingdom will come on earth; indeed, we are bidden to pray:

Thy kingdom come, Thy will be done on earth as it is in heaven.

And both Old and New Testaments are full of imagery about a renewed earth, with metaphorical language about God's Holy Mountain (Is. 2:1-5, 11:1-9, 65:17-25, Micah 4:104) and the New Jerusalem (Rev. 21-22:5). Unfortunately, since the time of St. Augustine in the fourth century, there has been a tradition of interpreting these passages in a "spiritual" fashion. That is, the glorious economic images of peace, plenty, good work—the reversal of bad earthly stewardship—are understood as metaphors for heaven. Redemption is mysticized and put off to the next world. This has meant that when Christians work for justice and peace—which we do—it is done with resigned obedience, a sort of teeth-gritting resolve, not because of any expectation that it will really make much difference in this vale of toil and sin.

What this means is that it is always up to some heterodox or frankly anti-Christian ideology to recall for us the Bible's hope for earthly redemption, as well as heavenly. So we saw Shakers and the Oneida Community in the last century working out some squirrelly sexual ideas as harbingers of the Kingdom of God, because (as Jesus said) in the kingdom there is neither marriage nor giving in marriage (Lk. 20:25). Or we have Mormons proclaiming that Jesus will return and make Independence, Missouri, the headquarters of his kingdom, or people buy Hal Lindsey's blueprints of the approaching end of the world as we know it. In addition, there are Moonies and Marxists—all with scenarios for the future earthly kingdom, all filling the vacuum of hope left by classical Christianity.

A complete biblical "theology of economic life" cannot be drawn by toning down the pictures of earthy redemption or restoration or consummation. Without the lure of Christ the Omega, we fail to incarnate the Spirit's urging, and great swatches of scripture lose their relevance. To use old language, it is not a case of pre-millennialism or post-millennialism, but pro-millennialism: we must be in favor of and work for God's rule. It is integral to our stewardship of God's fair world.

## Summary

In conclusion, let us simply summarize by listing economic principles we have found in scripture:

1. The great principle is that we are stewards of God's good earth; we must use it and take good care of all of it, even what is not for our use.

2. Entrustedness, not scarcity, describes the wealth God has given us in giving us the earth.

3. Wealth is a sign of God's blessing and a means of stewardship. Everyone should have opportunity to be stewards.

4. Wealth is an effective sign only when it is received with thankfulness, and used to help those who do not have enough.

5. Whenever and wherever we find that many people are kept from ownership (wealth and means of production), or are unable to be productive for lack of work, we know that biblical principles are not being followed.

6. Wealth misappropriated or misused is a curse. It breeds anxiety, strangles faith, and becomes idolatrous. "You cannot serve God and money."

. 7. Good work permits the worker to be creative, to express the worker's gifts and energy and personality; thus we "image back" to God the image of God we bear. Good work is not a "disutility."

8. Any work, then, that dulls the image of God within, or that creates gods (idol-making) for worship, is forbidden. Only careful analysis can show when this is true.

9. Since our stewardship is in common with others, our work should serve and benefit others and be done in cooperation with others. (The radical individualism of modern Western society runs counter to this biblical principle.)

10. We may not disdain or avoid work, in order to live off the labors of others. This does not, of course, apply to those who cannot work or who are resting from a lifetime of work.

11. Good work should be preceded and followed by rest; the Sabbath Day is a symbol of this rest. Without the two there is no peace, shalom.

12. In any society the proper balance between its wealth and the work people do is called justice, mishpat. To do justice is called righteousness, zedaqah.

13. To ensure that justice be done for the poor and powerless is the special role of the government.

14. It is a principle that our economic activities must not deprive others of the right to be stewards of God's wealth, or to deprive them of work.

15. It is a biblical principle that people should be economically free; only if they are free can they be stewards of God's earth.

16. Finally, the Christian should work for economic justice with hope, believing that God has made us stewards of this world and we should expect God's promises for the earth to come true:

Thy Kingdom come, Thy will be done,
on earth as it is in heaven.

# Resources

Albright, W. F. 1957. *From the Stone Age to Christianity.* 2nd ed. Baltimore: Johns Hopkins U. Press.

Bieler, A. 1961. *La Pensee Economiquie et Sociale de Calvin.* Geneve: Georg.

Davies, W. D. 1974. *The Gospel and the Land.* Berkeley: U. of California Press.

de Vaux, R. 1961. *Ancient Israel, Its Life and Institutions.* N.Y.: McGraw-Hill.

Eichrodt, W. 1951. The Question of Property in the Light of the Old Testament. in Richardson and Schweitzer, eds., *Biblical Authority for Today.* Philadelphia: Westminster Press.

Freyne, S. 1980. *Galilee from Alexander the Great to Hadrian.* Notre Dame: U. of Notre Dame Press.

Graham, W. F. 1971. *The Constructive Revolutionary.* Atlanta: John Knox Press.

Jeremias, J. 1969. *Jerusalem in the Time of Jesus.* Philadelphia: Fortress Press.

Klassen, P. J. 1964. *The Economics of Anabaptism, 1525-1560.* The Hague: Mouton.

Kraybill, D. B. 1978. *The Upside-down Kingdom.* Scottdale: The Herald Press.

North, R. 1954. *Sociology of the Biblical Jubilee.* Rome: Pontifical Biblical Institute.

Noth, M. 1965. *Leviticus.* Philadelphia: Westminster Press.

Porter, Jr., R. 1976. *Leviticus.* Cambridge: Cambridge U. Press.

Rohrbaugh, R. L. 1978. *The Biblical Interpreter: An Agrarian Bible in an Industrial Age.* Philadelphia: Fortress Press.

Sider, R. L. 1977. *Rich Christians in an Age of Hunger.* Downers Grove: Inter-Varsity Press.

Storkey, A. 1979. *A Christian Social Perspective.* Leicester: InterVarsity Press.

Taylor, R. K. 1973. *Economics and the Gospel.* Philadelphia: United Church Press.

Tiemstra, J. P. 1978. The Bible and Economics in the Christian Schools. *Christian Educators Journal.* 18: 6-7.

Wiesel, E. 1981. Recalling Swallowed-up Worlds. *Christian Century.*

# Chapter VI
# The Economic
# Community

*I'm leaving like a thief in the night.*
*I'll try to write to you, I'll maybe phone.*
*I'll send you back the money, but not the love you lent,*
*I could never pay the interest on that loan.*
   Ralph McTell (1979)

## Ideological Polarization in Economic Thought

Superficially the main ideological economic division in the world is between laissez-faire capitalism and state control of economic activity. This is the divide which separates East and West, but it is also the main line of contention, the fault which produces earthquakes within countries, both of the East and West. Thus both the Reagan and Thatcher administrations came to office around the issue of retrenchment on state economic activity, reversals of the movements which occurred during the New Deal era and the Labour Government of 1945-51. This powerful polarization operates often under the law of the excluded middle; criticism of capitalism involves being a socialist and vice versa. It is a mind set into which even much sophisticated economic analysis automatically drops.

On the basis of the Scriptural perspective presented in the last chapter, we suggest that this law of the excluded middle, this economic iron curtain, is a fallacy, and that there is a third way. However, it is not a middle way, a mere option tossed into the arena. It is rather that many aspects of capitalist and socialist economics represent a declension from the true normative principles of economic life. Since the two common options are in many ways defective, they need to be explained by a deeper dimension of reality, namely, whether we are good or bad stewards of God's creation.

Let us begin, therefore, by looking at the way in which one defective option, communism or socialism, has been a response to another defective one, namely the one of self-directed, laissez-faire capitalism. The root faith of this latter movement has been in the assignment of freedom to economic agents to pursue their own economic ends and self-interest allied to an absolute right to private capital while others were in a state of acute dependence. The 18th and 19th century evidence for this is overwhelming, and there is no need to rehearse it further. Clearly socialism and communism in various forms were a reaction to this kind of situation. In Russia the deprivation was largely pre-industrial, while in northwestern Europe it was post-industrial, taking the form of democratic socialism. The point is that the reaction is integrally related to the original laissez-faire ideal. Because the ideal of economic autonomy produced the unemployment, the exploitation, the monopoly power, and the degradation of work, these socialist reactions occurred. In the United States, partly because of the unlimited frontiers and vast resources, the reactions have never cohered in a socialist form, but the problems have existed nevertheless. Those who uncritically champion capitalism should reflect on the close relationship between the failures of capitalism and the ideology they abhor.

However, that is not to say that the reaction is good. Often it has been motivated by a desire to eliminate economic wrongs, but a lot more is involved in changed economic structures than good motives, and even these have been mixed. When the state encompasses a wide range of economic relationships, their character is changed. It is not just that the mode of state activity is that of involuntary enforcement, although that alone fundamentally changes the form of economic life in a way against which people both in West and East react. It is also that the state becomes committed to meeting the vast plurality of needs which exist in the population, and must therefore pretend to economic omniscience when the actual system of centralized control will always tend to myopia. Further, there is the problem that the state itself becomes a substantial economic interest group, a judge in its own economic cause, with the result, among others, that it is a source of economic parasitism, for who is to tell the state that its demands are not fair? Last, there is a fundamental difference between the state being obedient to norms of justice, which is its calling, and the state assuming *a priori* that it is the source of justice. The latter claim that the state embodies the correct direction of society and the economy has been the origin of countless major injustices, and must be, because faith vested in a particular human institution must render it weak in self-criticism and in an awareness of the principles to which it must submit. Thus, although this book will not address the problems of socialism in detail, it should be clear, both now and throughout the book, how fundamentally distinct our perspective is from one which vests extensive economic control in the state.

## The New Direction

The earlier analysis suggests that much economic theory is deliberately narrow-minded in that economic agents are expected to respond, almost like Skinner's pigeons, to economic stimuli, according to simple criteria like profit and utility maximization. Both in theory and in practice, this blinkered outlook is a fundamental denial of humanity's full stewardship over the creation. In this chapter we want to break with these narrow carrot-and-stick conceptions of economic life and move into some understanding of the full economic responsibility of mankind before God to one another and the creation. We shall begin to explore the full normativity of economic life before we undertake more detailed economic analysis. Unless this is done first, the criteria of evaluation used will be applied blindly and dogmatically without any clear idea of their basis.

This then is our third way, a belief that everyone can consider more fully how he should live economically with clear principial guidance from the scriptures as to the norms of economic life. This extra-economic light is needed to put economic life in a fuller human context; economics is not autonomous. The priority of this third way is expressed in Christ's words in the Sermon on the Mount, "Seek first his kingdom and his righteousness, and all these things will be given you as well." This fundamental normativity is not elitist in the Keynesian sense of requiring some central organization of the chaos of self-interested behavior which exists within the nation, but addresses the responsibilities of all economic agents at all levels. Nor is it also not just a question of "private" ethics, but involves a principial understanding of the economic structure of our society. Let us therefore begin to explore this perspective.

## Economic Community

There has been a tendency within economic analysis to adopt as the dominant paradigm the idea of the struggle for survival of the fittest that comes out of 19th century evolutionary thinking. Competition is the organizing idea of much economics and is the route to efficiency within the price system. This idea, although significant, is a limited and local view of economic relationships which needs to be put in a far wider context. The wider perspective focuses on economic interdependence, mutuality and care, the main concern of the Mosaic Law and also of the New Testament. Although the following passage is addressed to the Church as the body of Christ, it has *implications* for all economic relationships.

> The eye cannot say to the hand, 'I don't need you!' And the head cannot say to the feet, 'I don't need you!' On the contrary, those parts of the body that seem to be weaker are indispensable, and the parts that we think are less honorable, we treat with special honor. And the parts that are unpresentable are treated with special modesty, while our special parts need no special treatment. But God has combined the members of the body and has given

greater honor to the parts that lacked it, so that there should be no division in the body, but that its parts should have equal concern for each other. If one part is honored, every part rejoices with it (I Cor. 12:21-26).

This theme is emphasized by Calvin in a similar way.

> We must recognize that God has wanted to make us like members of a body. When we regard each other in this way, each will then conclude: 'I see my neighbor who has need of me and if I were in such extremity, I would wish to be helped; I must therefore do just that.' In short this communication of which St. Paul speaks here is the fraternal affection which proceeds from the regard that we have when God has joined us together and united us in one body, because he wants each to employ himself for his neighbors, so that no one is addicted to his own person, but that we serve all in common. [Graham 1971, p. 70]

The significance of this perspective in the development of Western economic life has, we suggest, been suppressed by the Enlightenment interpretation of economic life rooted in Mandeville, Smith and Bentham. It can be argued that this communal perspective, expressed in Calvinism, Puritanism, and Evangelicalism, was the source of many of the aspects of development which became known as the Industrial Revolution. The tradition which includes Calvin, Latimer, Baxter and others provided the basis of cooperation, trust, fairness and economic responsibility which nourished that development, and we are going to reopen it.

For the dominant development of the modern economy, missed by capitalists and socialists alike, is the degree of interdependence which we have developed, and the extent of cooperation, trust, and service which are necessary to the day to day operation of the economy. Each day each of us appropriates the services of hundreds of thousands of workers, and since we are thus members one of another, it is arguable that our economic perspective should linger at this point.

To talk of the importance of economic community in no way implies involuntary or state-directed or communist relationships. Some communal issues which concern matters of justice do involve the state, but our main emphasis is on the interwoven set of free economic relationships which characterize the modern economy. These must involve the effects that economic agents have on the needs of others, and also the degree of care for those others, but they are all fundamentally voluntary; it is "merely" that care and service are the right way of economic living, not that there is compulsion so to live. Indeed, it will be part of our argument in later chapters that there are often pressures, if not compulsion, not to care and be responsible in economic activity.

## Economic Community and Institutions

It is easy for economic care to be seen in interpersonal terms, but, although care and service must be personal, they also occur in institutions. The *qualitative* differences in institutions decisively affect the pattern of communal economic relationships. As opposed to a social philosophy which has as its ultimate reference point the individual or the collectivity, recognition of the sovereignty of God over humanity, including the plurality of institutions which structure human life provokes the question: What are God's purposes for mankind in these different institutions? Family, enterprise, church, state, school are all uniquely instituted to develop their own structures within their own norms, and it is only when the character of these institutions is given respect within economic analysis, that the full richness of human life is treated with integrity. Nor is this richness limited to major institutions; as people respond to norms, like that of care, so organizations like hospitals, hotels, and old people's homes are generated. This pluralism, recognized especially within the Kuyperian tradition [Kuyper 1880, Spykman 1981], is needed if we are to escape from the false monotonization of economic life in much theory. What are the consequences of this approach?

First, we note that a major part of economic activity has an extra-economic direction to it. It supports the state, the family, churches, educational institutions, and other communal organizations which are primarily political, social, pedagogic, or ecclesiastical. This means that the primary character of the institution qualifies and affects the kind of economic activity which takes place within that institution. These qualitative differences need to be recognized. That the family is characterized by gift relationships and the state by laws deeply affects the economic processes within them. Thus the kind of accounting used in running a judicial system or in running a family is different from that used in running a firm.

It follows from this that economic activity is far more embedded, subject to extra-economic ends, than is usually acknowledged, especially if the nonexchange subsistence economy is taken into account. Using a labor standard of value, we might conclude that roughly 25% of economic activity takes place within the family, 20% within government agencies, 10% within communal organizations which are educational, artistic, charitable, and ecclesiastical, with about 45% being directly economically productive (figures are not collected in ways which allow these proportions to be accurately established). [Rudney 1977, pp. 135-141] The autonomous definition of the discipline has tended to truncate these relationships among institutions and ignore this embeddedness; this failure needs correcting. Further, the dependence of economic activity on these other institutions also needs to be more fully recognized; families, the state, churches, and schools are far more necessary for economic life than is normally allowed.

There are other implications. Poverty, for example, has normally been seen in largely economic terms, that is, as low family income. This has veiled the importance of institutional deprivation as a source of poverty; more income without family strength, schools, churches, support agencies, and access to economic facilities often cannot break poverty in an area. If institutional poverty is one of the most significant forms, it shows the need for an institutional view of many issues. [Perkins 1976, pp. 122-30]

Last, we note that in the relationships among these institutions, economic criteria and values do not have pre-eminence. It is apparent during wartime that defense of the nation-state takes precedence over many economic goals and, conversely, swords have been beaten into ploughshares. The communal priorities in the commitment of resources to different institutions involve a variety of sets of supra-economic religious values and cannot be reduced to a question of mere economic criteria. At the same time the institutional resources available depend on the pattern of economic development which has taken place together with the enabling power of the economy. Thus, through a continual plethora of voluntary decisions which reflect underlying faith commitments, economic development takes place in and through institutions. These very important themes will be picked up in later chapters.

## The Analysis of Exchange and Markets

There has been a strong tendency within economic analysis to talk of "the market mechanism" or "the market system" and to treat it as a natural automatic mechanism. This view is fundamentally defective, for the market is a normative community which people join either as buyers or sellers. In principle, community is voluntary; people and institutions should be and often are free to participate without coercion (if people are compelled through taxation to purchase public goods, we see it as an extra-market activity). If people or organizations are *compelled* to purchase through intimidation, threats, blackmail, the exclusion of choices, the use of economic power, or suppressed information, we perceive that the principle of voluntary participation has broken down. We also recognize that something is wrong when producers are prevented from entering a market by a cartel. Sometimes firms lose sight of the fact that they are voluntarily committed to a particular market, and with a weary mixture of tradition, habit, and inertia, stay there until it is too late. In recognizing the voluntary character of exchange relationships, we are saying far more than that there is free entry and exit for firms and consumers; the fundamental point is that the full freedom of persons and organizations to participate or not is a norm to be respected and upheld in the market, and if it is not, then the market is a manipulative and economically distorting force.

Other norms of market exchange are far more important than is generally acknowledged. They include care in the quality and usefulness of the good or service provided, fairness in the transaction, trust that the consumer will pay and use items properly, expectation of care for the environment in production, loyalty of customer, long-term support of the customer, and technical competence. The norms of exchange thus reach far beyond a mere nexus of exchange into mutual respect and care that is deeply personal, even though not face to face. The consumer trusts that noxious chemicals have not been used, and that the item will not break down. Indeed, one could almost say that some relationships between client and the provider of professional services are *covenantal*. The self-interested maxim *caveat emptor* is not the basis on which economic relationships work, and it reflects casualties and tragedies evidencing lack of care. Markets are premised on love and service of neighbors, not on the so-called law of the jungle.

Indeed, service, and not what is often called capitalism, must be recognized as the necessary dynamic of the free enterprise system. From the sensitivity and response to new possibilities of service comes the innovative dynamic of market enterprise. It is here, in ways that cannot be duplicated by any paternalistic centralized response, that the diversification and depth of market response becomes evident. Clearly, as well, good service often receives recompense and opens the way for growth. Some of the newer ideological defenders of capitalism have partially sighted this reality. Gilder wrote:

> The crucial rules of creative thought can be summed up as faith, love, openness, conflict and falsifiability. The crucial rules of economic innovation and progress are faith, altruism, investment, competition and bankruptcy, which are also the rules of capitalism. The reason capitalism succeeds is that it is capable of fulfilling human needs because it is founded on giving, which depends on sensitivity to the needs of others. [1981, p. 265]

Yet these fundamental Christian norms of love and service cannot be used as an ideological justification for capitalism. You cannot cheat on the norm of service and use God's standards to give *carte blanche* justifications. For capitalism also represents the perversion of the norm of service—companies which are self-serving and do not care, except in a manipulative way, for customers or workers. Some groups have found ways of living off the services of others, or of exploiting them. Thus, those who *identify* capitalism and Christian norms have fundamentally misunderstood their relationship with the sovereign God. The commands of God require obedience and cannot be pressed into a justificatory role. In every detail where the norms are contravened, the destructive results eventually come to the light, revealing how the law of God is the inescapable ground of our being.

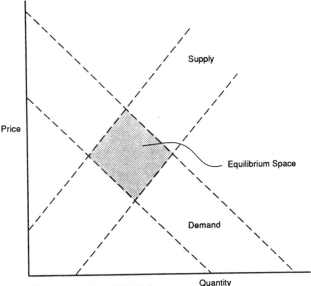

**Figure 1. Supply and Demand**

With this background we can see aspects of the theory of markets which need to be carefully respecified. One is the fallacy of precision. *This is a logical fallacy which is based on the argument that because certain quantities are sold in markets at certain prices, the outcome is a determinate price result.* This way of seeing markets removes responsibility and discretion from sellers and consumers by offering a completely mechanical explanation of what happens. Indeed, a whole range of other factors enters into the decisions people make. *Ex ante* both buyers and sellers can exercise considerable discretion in the price they accept without changing their decisions about the quantities bought and sold. Consumers often decide to purchase specific items, and *then* try to purchase at the lowest price available, so that a range of 50% in prices is not unusual. Producers on the other hand have often committed themselves irrevocably to a certain level of output and have a wide potential range on the price offered. The accurate *ex ante* theory, rather than the spurious *ex post* circular conclusion, is that there are demand and supply *bands*, yielding an indeterminate market equilibrium space (See Fig. 1).

The size of that space—namely, the amount of discretion in the market—is one of the more significant variables that differentiates one market from another; the width of the bands therefore needs careful study and implies a break with treatments of price through the calculus.

A second point is that the classical assumption of the independence of each side of the market, which yields the determinate solution (two equations in two independent variables), can be questioned. It may have been more valid when markets were dispersed and casually organized, but now a great number of markets are highly organized and institutionally controlled, and are studied by a lot of experts who develop deliberate market strategies. They are responding not to *price*, but merely to price as one element in their total market knowledge. Even without collusion it is possible for significant numbers of consumers or producers to independently decide that a certain *market strategy* is desirable, and for this to profoundly affect what happens. At a simple level during a fuel shortage it is possible for a voluntary conservation movement to eliminate the problem. At a deeper level, for decades at least, very sophisticated policies towards the market for employment have been developed and implemented. Another strategy was pursued by the Saudi Arabians in 1981 to induce a partial oil glut. The significance of these strategies for market analysis, although they merely incorporate a lot of standard supply-side analysis, is great. For we must now acknowledge that, rather than being mechanisms, markets are normative communities, shaped by policies and commitments which operate within the indeterminate market equilibrium space.

The neutrality of present analysis anesthetizes concern with the possibility that market strategies are being used by both consumers and producers to produce markedly different outcomes which may be unfair. Such strategies exist. It is possible for consumers to withdraw demand, and especially if suppliers are strongly committed, say, because of their poverty, to maintaining their income, it is possible for more to be supplied at a lower price. How widespread this practice is among Western multinationals who are the "consumers" of Third World primary products is open to more analysis than the determinate equilibrium myth allows.

Another market strategy focuses on the vulnerability of various large-scale, long-term investment decisions. It is possible for consumers to increase demand and raise the price, so that investment will take place which will then result in a long-term glut in the market with permanently low prices and rates of return for the suppliers. Because suppliers are not just reacting to price, it is possible for them to leave the equilibrium market space at one point and reenter at another. When the full dynamics of the market are taken into account, including capital and technological investment, it is evident that the market strategy can have a strong determinative influence.

There are other consumer strategies, like stockpiling with the view to threatening an expanded supply, and a whole range of supply-side strategies, which have been more fully explored, like price reduction to induce market penetration, restricting output, excluding potential suppliers, and raising prices to induce speculative scarcity (especially with positional goods). The underlying point that arises from this analysis is that the market is not a mechanism which is neutral and automatic, but is shaped by policies, motives and principles, so that its members, in making both big and small decisions, decide how the market should operate. Clearly, some have a great deal of influence and others little, but it is the job of economists to evaluate whether market strategies are fair or are based on exploiting weakness, on deception, on using capital power or on exploiting fear. It is time that the great whitewashing myth of the invisible hand over the natural order was banished from the discipline, and it is recognized that people make markets, and that they are accountable before God for the fairness and integrity of these normative communities.

Does this mean that the old idea of the "just price" has returned? Most emphatically it does. The reason why the idea of the just price disappeared from economic theory (but not from daily practice) was that there was no natural mechanism by which the just price could be justified. Eventually economics came up with its version based on the Darwinian notion of the survival of the fittest. The totem of perfect competition is raised up to rally the faithful, but it now has limited real significance, except as a mythical golden age of price theory. Really the appeal must be to a norm of fairness in exchange, in which rewards to economic agents are approximately equal for contributions of equal value. When we stop appealing to some prehistoric golden age and address this norm, it becomes clear that the price system, as well as incorporating many valuations by buyers and sellers, and reflecting the relative availability of resources, is a continual good or bad approximation to a norm of fairness. Thus valuations shape prices and wages, not some impersonal market force, and all contribute their valuations on the basis of cultural and religious priorities. Thus fairness and normativity is the framework within which markets develop, and it is time that we concede that the actual development of markets is fuller of murky motives and predatory policies than the bland textbook allows. It also consists of sound evaluations established on the basis of much market experience; for good reasons many consumers eschew cheap products and go for what they feel is a just price.

There are other ways in which the analysis of markets is weak. One is the overgeneralized model generated by a desire to mathematize. Markets have many differences which are ignored in normal analysis. Whether families, the state, or other firms are consumers makes a great difference. The intervals between purchases, whether daily or once a lifetime, and the lifetime of the good or service, also affect the market's structure. Some goods like milk have a high density of requirement, others, like trombones, do not. Some goods are almost identical; other goods and services are highly individuated and differentiated. Similarly, the extent to which consumer care can lead to conservation of an item varies widely, as does the ratio of the cost of that item to the overall cost in use. Another important element is the extent to which purchase involves other changes in lifestyle with economic consequences. In varying degrees goods and services have positional content in that purchase may or may not exclude others from access to that kind of good. All of these factors, and others, lead to the development of particular market structures and orientations which are of great economic significance. Let us focus on one. Goods can have limited or substantial impact on others for benefit or for harm, and we now nearly all recognize that it is necessary for markets to take account of these significant others where they exist. Thus in the market for cars the effects of noise, fumes, and accidents have to be carefully monitored and researched by someone, whereas the market for socks, which have only localized effects on significant others, has few of these concerns. Again it is evident that many of these differences have normative aspects.

Important differences exist among sellers. They vary with the production time required, the range of resources, the technology and experience needed to produce, the educational content of the sales process, and the pattern of communication with the market. Thus, in some markets the producer not only has to sell a good, but also to educate a consumer in its use, and doing the former without the latter would violate the norm of service. The narrowing of market analysis obsessively to the price decisions has detracted from the full pattern of economic concerns and the norms that should govern them. For markets are relational normative communities rather than just mechanisms, as many practitioners know better than economists, and it is the denial of this underlying reality which leads to their degradation and malfunctioning.

## Welfare and the Neighbor Principle

In chapter two we looked at the disembodied nature of welfare theory, resulting from the fact/value problem of positivism and egocentric rationalism. Now we are ready to look at what happens when the tyrannical dogma that all economic calculations are egocentric is dropped, and neighborly care and concern are accepted as normal. We are called to live under the principle that we should love our neighbors as ourselves, and much economic behavior in part responds to this norm. To say that all economic actions are or should be self-interested is the fundamental utilitarian lie. If this concern for the welfare of others is a normal part of economic decision-making, how does this change the pattern of economic analysis?

First, it lifts welfare theory down from the ionosphere into concrete situations. Workers do have a choice between higher wages and avoiding colleagues being unemployed. Companies can choose between high profits with built-in obsolescence and providing their customers with items which last. We now know that egocentric calculations are often socially inefficient and destructive. The blindness of utilitarian maximization makes it a cultural dinosaur which cannot survive in the modern fully populated world; calculations about the needs of our neighbors must become a normal human response.

However, this means the replacement of maximization solutions with economic criteria which relate to specified needs. In practice, of course, this has already happened in a multitude of situations. Treatment of customers, workers, and citizens are based on care rather than maximization. Standards of dining facilities, of retirement provision, of environmental care, are diverse and cannot be reduced to a simple maximization criterion. Companies must, and usually do, operate with welfare value-judgments among various criteria, and it is time that the compulsive fiction that all such decisions are quantifiable is replaced by a more mature approach. The unique shape of the company reflects its value and welfare commitments, developed through thousands of judgments, not simple maximization calculations. What is true for companies is true for all other economic agents; their exchange decisions embody transpersonal welfare judgments, and these cannot be added on as an *ex post* separate subject area which still retains non-relational self-interest as its basic premise.

Thus welfare economics is not an isolated and disembodied branch of the discipline, nor is welfare only the concern of the public sector. Indeed, it is this latter myth which is generating all kinds of economic care which is appropriately done in specific institutions, like family care of the old, the job training of the young, falling into the lap of the government. Loving our neighbor as ourselves is a ubiquitous norm for economic activity, not just the altruistic afterthought of government.

This means that care will often be related to specific needs: the availability of food, a home to live in, a means of livelihood, education, a knowledge of the Gospel, medical care, an attractive environment, water, a source of electrical energy, protection from pollution, safety, postal and media communication, old age support, and aids to the disabled. Our pricing policies should therefore reflect this neighborly care, for example, in uniform postal charges so that all, however remote, have communication access, lower transport fares for the old, and largely subsidized education. Exploring the needs of fellow citizens and how to meet them should be one of the great dynamics of all institutions and organizations in the economy.

However, there is also a need to be critically analytical, for certain groups in our socio-economic order tend to have the economic refuse dropped on them. They experience the pollution, the ugliness, the health deterioration, and the institutional deprivation of the system. They fare ill at the hands of others, though, ironically, it is often those who complain most about the ones living on welfare who contribute most to the illfare of the economically precarious. The problem of Three Mile Island pales into insignificance beside the lot of those who daily suffer the noise and fumes and physical isolation of vehicle convenience. Those who use airplanes tend to form a different population from those who live in their noise and pollution shadows. The prevailing wind theory of British urban development highlights the issue. The west end of cities is usually the smart middle class area, and the east end the poorer working class area because the prevailing wind from the west dumped the smells and the smoke of the city in the east. This is a parable of the deep patterns of illfare which compound the problems of low income and economic weakness. It could not be said that neoclassical economics has been preoccupied with identifying these phenomena; illfare theory should be one of its major concerns.

## Value and Price

Thus again we begin to see one of the underlying fallacies of modern economics. In order to be scientific, the theory of value has gradually been dropped, so that it is barely mentioned in many texts, and the price system becomes an autonomous, self-sustained, closed, solvable system. We have seen how this is only achieved by the Robbins-type exclusion of values from the means activities, and by the artificial and false closure of consumption theory. Yet this very process of making the price system analytically self-sustaining is a fatal reversal. Values, both of production and consumption, are necessarily prior to prices, and the latter merely represent—in a very limited way—the former. Moreover, the point about prices is that they should come to do justice to people's values, in as proximate a way as possible. This they often fail to do, and so there is much room for adjustment and reform in relative prices. The great lie is the supposedly neutral scientific system which tells us how to behave economically. The guide that prices provide can be, and often is, helpful, but in many ways it inadequately reflects values. Prices are therefore not themselves normative, but a response to normative valuations. Thus modern economics has walked into a basically false paradigm for understanding prices where instead of mankind being steward of his values, he hands those values over to a system which he has made, and before which the economist then bows.

The values which shape prices can themselves be misguided and destructive. They reflect priorities, commitments, faith, and economic risks which may be faulty. Market problems are often the result of these valuational instabilities. Thus a car industry which values power, speed, and individuation in its technology and production patterns faces problems in an era when consumers value fuel economy and low costs. Or in a stock market where a high proportion of the buyers and sellers value quick speculative gains, the prices become increasingly unstable. Or where consumers are concerned with status and conspicuous consumption, prices no longer reflect economic thrift. Thus the underlying criteria of value, and their normative evaluation are a significant part of economics. The meaning of thrift, attitude to time utilization, self-gratification, leisure, growth, profitability, self-fulfillment, efficiency, and other such values are important because they provide the supports for and the source of change in the price system.

We also need to recognize that economic value is only one kind of human value. Most of our values are not economic and are not given prices. We do not price freedom from violence, or peace of mind, or marital fidelity, or the salvation of human souls. This is important because most of our economic values are derivative from wider human ones; thus one may be prepared to pay $1000 for an airline ticket because of a loved one, or to support an exhaustive $1,000,000 inquiry to reinforce government probity. The valuation that takes place within the family or the state thus shapes many important economic assessments.

This all means that economic valuation, in terms of money or resources is rarely identical to exchange price. One reason is that, as we saw earlier in the chapter, the price overspecifies the valuation. Thus prices do not reflect or mirror values, and are a very poor index of even exchange value. This again underlines the fact that the price times quantity "value" of goods and services used in GNP calculations is a very approximate indicator of annually created value. The main point is that although prices have become and are becoming better indicators of exchange value, they have a dependent position in relation to human valuations.

There are a number of consequences which follow from this alternative paradigm. One is that it points to the danger of excluding unpriced values from calculations which are then used to make decisions. A second is that, as businessmen often know, prices are often poor indicators of long term future policies, and it is also necessary to consider the valuational context. A third is that prices can lag changes in valuations in the system on the demand side as stocks are taken up, and on the supply side as changes in product commitment are envisaged and planned. Much of the forecasting of markets should therefore be concerned with valuation rather than only with just prices, and these need to be considered normatively.

## Property

It is still the case that most people, including economists, polarize views of property into those which uphold private property and those which involve socialist control. This exclusive public/private property distinction has a history, and it is worth briefly exploring it. In Europe the landed gentry of the Enlightenment era developed the idea of property as an inalienable right of man at the same time as a few of them were able to amass land by enclosing commonly owned land. It was agrarian society which created propertied and propertyless classes in Europe. However, the development of industrial property, capital, led to a new concept of ownership. At first it was ownership of firms, but then later, as ownership and control became more distinct, of assets embodying various legal rights. At various periods during the 20th century, beginning with the Russian revolution, violent and democratic reactions have occurred against the concentration of property and wealth, and the power it has conferred, into socialist ownership. These polarized views dominate the political economy of the world.

Only if we get beyond the possessiveness of both these views can we have a more constructive and vigorous view of property. The insistence on the absolute right to control which the Enlightenment emphasized, ignored the full meaning of stewardship before God. Property involved the responsibility of use, and ownership is a legal definition of that responsibility which puts firm boundaries to the interference of others and creates an economic domain within which people can exercise stewardship. The meaning of property is to be found in the way it allows people to exercise stewardship, and the scriptures emphasize the fullest distribution, so that as many as possible may partake of the responsibility of stewardship.

In this area the United States knows a blessing which scarcely any other country has experienced, albeit clouded by the appropriation of property from the Indians, for land, especially after the Land Act of 1820 and the Homestead Act of 1862, was widely distributed in small parcels in a process which approximates the allotment in the Promised Land. These widely diffused responsibilities of stewardship are still one of the deepest experiences of the American nation. This private egalitarianism is slowly being modified, especially as urban immigration has continued and capital has become the dominant form of ownership. We are therefore now addressing a situation where the conventional ideology of private property must be seen with more discernment. The acquisitive, self-centered absolute right to private property is a fundamentally different perspective from the blessings and responsibilities of stewardship which so many have enjoyed. Property in the latter sense allows work and service, and is consistent with the biblical emphasis on the widest possible distribution and the most open use of it.

The Mosaic Law was characterized by an emphasis on keeping property (land) widely distributed after its initial egalitarian distribution. (Joshua 13-20) It encouraged this stewardship through the jubilee return of land, the possibility of redemption of land, the sabbatical release from credit, and setting up servants. Indeed, the hired servant (employee or wage laborer) was considered to be abnormal and defective in that he did not own his means of livelihood. These norms of independent responsibility and redistribution to prevent people from being deprived of property and of others accumulating vast economic power, although set in an agrarian context, needs to be transposed and applied to our own situation.

One obvious argument is that maintaining and creating a distributed nationwide pattern of ownership requires remedial action. Property will tend to accumulate "automatically" for a number of reasons. One is that the affluent can choose when to buy and sell, while the poorer groups are a prey to price fluctuations. Second, the rich can usually accumulate their returns on property, while the poorer groups need to consume some. Third, concentrations mean economic power which can be used to acquire greater returns. It is therefore necessary to act periodically to restore a more widespread pattern of ownership. This kind of redistribution of wealth and property has largely been ignored in the United States.

The private/public division also leads to another important lacuna in economic debate. Property is used and owned by a variety of different institutions, and the pattern of ownership of and among these corporate bodies is one of the most important determinants of the socioeconomic structure of a nation. The ownership of schools and colleges by independent groups gives a different character to education from those owned by the state. Similarly, when a high proportion of family housing is provided by public authorities, the relationship between the two institutions of family and state compromises the integrity of the family unit. The principle of plural responsibilities before God implies that the integrity of various institutions is upheld when they own the property and have the resources which it is their responsibility to use. One of the weaknesses of socialized ownership is that it removes this integral responsibility to a political center of control.

Another aspect of this theme is the complications of property relations. They involve ownership, use, the right of transfer; they also involve complete, temporary, partial and potential use; the forms of ownership can be familial, corporate, communal, proprietary, in trusteeship and partial. There can be ownership of different uses of one kind of property. As more and more possibilities for stewardship are opened up, so the sophistication of the property relations grows. (Indeed, one of the themes absent from economic analysis is the extent to which simple private property inhibits efficiency. Some of our most under-utilized resources are privately owned.) However, it is precisely in these complications that some of the deepest problems of the economy occur. Indeed, a theory of economic depressions could be constructed on the theme of the way ownership precludes the use of resources at certain periods.

In the modern economy a lot of property rights are transferred from the owners who have little effective use of them to stewards who can use them to good effect. This pattern, when it works well, is clearly of great communal benefit, for it is the use of property, not its possession, which is the key to communal health. However, there is much in the modern economy which frustrates this. Inflation and other market fluctuations mean that a lot of property is held for reasons of capital gains rather than use. Moreover, concentrations of property and of economic power often mean that owners are not willing to transfer resources to more effective users. Furthermore, there is a range of situations where the acquisitive, possessive view of property prevents its effective use. Thus it is possible that we have moved into an era when the price relationships which are posited on the possession and accumulative view of property are creating rigidities which prevent effective use. For example, companies with excess funds invest in passive property—land, real estate and fine art—rather than in capital equipment, because such property will hold its price well. Or funds channeled into financial institutions can only be invested in big lumps because of the institutional decision-making process, and fails to permeate down to the disaggregated level where it would be most useful. Indeed, this practice is one part of the explanation of current unemployment.

Thus we see some of the significance of the principle of stewardship for our understanding of property, and at least glimpse what damage the possessive ideology of property may be doing in our economy.

## Economic Freedom

A Christian perspective also implies a different view of choice and economic freedom. Neoclassical subjective choice among an infinite variety of goods and services or jobs is a myth. Economic choice has a direction. People choose to work to obtain a car. When they own a car, they have new choices which did not exist before, and other possibilities are ruled out. The new choices involve new responsibilities. Moreover, freedom is fundamentally communal; only if some others provide and many others desire services do many activities become possible. Thus our economic freedom is rooted in a process of directional development and communal growth.

Nor is this development automatically good. It is standard Christian teaching that when people serve mammon rather than God their lives become economically enslaved; they cannot say, "No," or have enough, or be content. Furthermore, respect for the freedom of others can be foreclosed by manipulative behavior, patterns of control and domination. Indeed, the goal of some enterprises is to develop a passive, receptive, automatically responsive set of customers or workers. Thus one of the neglected areas of economic analysis is where restriction of choice is a successful policy. Indeed, many who preach free enterprise most loudly make strenuous attempts to control competitors, customers, workers, and suppliers. The brewing industry has shrunk from about 750 firms in 1935 to 5 major ones now, not because of economics of scale, but largely by deliberate takeovers to foreclose free competition.

One of the major complaints today is of interference by government in the running of enterprises. This occurs when the political institution directs economic activities in ways which destroy their service potential. However, it is also possible for the failure of government to provide political justice to lead to reduced freedom. Thus firms can be given unfair advantage through poor safety and worker care standards, discriminatory charges, and fluctuations in prices. The positive task of the state is to maintain economic freedom and justice, not exercise direct control. But this may mean intervention.

Even internal direction of economic units cannot be seen as autonomous freedom, but must be recognized as normative responsibility. If righteous decisions are not made, then the structure of organizations becomes oppressive both to members and customers; thus the worker who freewheels at his job forecloses the possibilities of that company, as do bloated expense accounts; the poorly made product locks the consumer in a problem; the fixity of the pattern of industrial relations prevents new ways of organizing work; and the consumer who becomes addicted to a particular good loses freedom. All of these results occur because of the failure of organizations to do right internally.

It is time that the old liberal ideal of freedom is buried. When M. and R. Friedman write

> The heart of the liberal philosophy is a belief in the dignity of the individual, in his freedom to make the most of his capacities and opportunities according to his own lights, subject only to the proviso that we not interfere with the freedom of other individuals to do the same. [1980]

they refuse to face the inescapable facts that people live in relational and institutional bonds, and that normally their acts interfere with others. The only viable economic philosophy of freedom is one which grows from a recognition of the communal responsibility of stewardship and the slavery of sin for the corporate group as well as the individual. Slavery to jobs, patterns of consumption, and technical progress are perhaps more widespread than we normally admit. Thus, contrary to the optimistic humanist hope, new forms of bondage are continually appearing. The worship of success, income, security, economic power, consumption, and happiness has created its own structure of bondage in our society.

## Problem Displacement

Finally we acknowledge some of the difficulties that occur in analyzing problems in an economic community. One is that despite all the techniques of econometric analysis it is still very difficult to isolate the source of a particular trend or set of events. There are a number of reasons for this. One is that "causal" relationships are reflexive and complex when economic agents anticipate and predict events. A second is that where collective responses are involved, analytical isolation is a weak methodological step. A third is that much theory presumes a certain pattern of transmission of events, whereas there may be many and changing patterns. Fundamentally, however, responsibilities do not have a "natural" causal explanation, but are to be seen and analyzed as normative responses. As we look at aspects of the economy from a Christian perspective, the neat, and maybe deceptive, causal maps will lose some of their precision. Yet we shall be concentrating on the areas where the key decisions are made and where people decide how they should live economically.

However, the problems of discrete analysis (what is often called microeconomics) are not insurmountable. The origin of effects can often be traced. Nevertheless, it is possible for problems which occur in one area to receive analysis and treatment in another, especially if certain groups have power to prevent treatment at the origin. Heavy wage inflation can be met by money supply control, low productivity by fiscal policy, and long-term poverty by short-term welfare programs. Thus the symptoms can occur a long way from the original problem. Often, indeed, governments have suggested that a single strategy will cure a range of different symptoms without asking what their origin was. This both obscures economic analysis by transmitting symptoms to different parts of the system, and also prevents the real problems, whether they concern the weak or the powerful, from being faced. Thus, we shall attempt to identify the roots of problems and get beyond some of the symptoms that litter the economy and the economics journals.

# Resources

Baxter, R. 1925. *Chapters from a Christian Directory.* London: C. Bell.

Commons, J. R. 1959. *Legal Foundations of Capitalism.* (1926), Madison: U. of Wisconsin Press.

Commons, J. R. 1961. *Institutional Economics.* (1934), Madison: U. of Wisconsin Press.

Dooyeweerd, H. 1979. *Roots of Western Culture.* Toronto: Wedge.

Friedman, M., and R. Friedman. 1980. *Free to Choose.* N.Y.: Harcourt Brace.

Furubotn, E., and S. Pejovich. 1972. Property Rights and Economic Theory: A Survey of Recent Literature. *J. of Econ. Literature.* 10: 1137-62.

Gilder, G. 1981. *Wealth and Poverty.* N.Y.: Basic Books.

Gonce, R. A. 1976. The New Property Rights Approach and Commons' *Legal Foundations of Capitalism.* *J. of Econ. Issues.* 10: 765-97.

Graham, W. R. 1971. *The Constructive Revolutionary.* Atlanta: John Knox Press.

Kuyper, A. 1880. *Sovereiniteit in Eigen Kring.* Amsterdam.

Perkins, J. 1976. *Let Justice Roll Down.* G/L Publications.

Rudney, G. G. 1977. Scope of the Private Voluntary Charitable Sector. Research Papers of the Commission on Private Philanthropy and Public Needs, Washington: U.S. Dept. of Treasury.

Skillen, J. 1981. Politics, Pluralism, and the Ordinances of God,. in H. Vander Goot, ed., *Life is Religion.* Ontario: Paideia.

Spykman, G. 1981. Pluralism: Our Last Best Hope? *Christian Scholars Rev.* 10: 99-115.

Storkey, A. J. 1979. *Christian Social Perspective.* Leisester: InterVarsity Press.

Tawney, R. H. 1920. *The Acquisitive Society.* N.Y.: Harcourt Brace.

Tawney, R. H. 1926. *Religion and the Rise of Capitalism.* London: John Murray.

# Chapter VII
# Inside the Black Box

Anthony works in the grocery store,
Saving his pennies for someday.
Mama Leone left a note on the door
Said, "Sonny, move out to the country."
Working too hard can give you a heart attack,
You oughtta know by now.
Who needs a house out in Hackensack?
Is that what you get with your money?
It seems such a waste of time,
If that's what it's all about,
If that's moving up, then I'm moving out.
        Billy Joel (1977)

## Critique of Current Consumption Theory

Nowhere are the ravages of the methodological problems in economics more evident than in consumption theory. Positivists, believing only in the facts, adhere to revealed preference, and rationalists, believing in consistency, use indifference curves. Both have methodologically ruled out values and motives as extra-scientific and have declared the family a black box which economists must not look inside. When the family is one of the major economic entities in the life of a nation, this is a surprising, indeed, disastrous step. If roughly a third of the total work activity of the nation centers on the home, it seems especially shortsighted to foreclose this area of investigation.

It is perhaps worth stopping to consider why the discipline should choose to ignore what by any estimate is a third to a quarter of its subject matter. Once an swer is distressingly simple: economists are only interested in machismic material. About 90% of the members of the American Economic Association are male, and the proclivity of the discipline has been to disdainfully disregard the economic activity in which women participate most fully and to concentrate on the areas which most directly concern the male ego. This social warping of knowledge has been destructive: it has helped create the powerful myth of female economic parasitism; it has allowed the idea to flourish that only exchange relationships matter; and it has also led to a whole range of issues which are important in the lives of all of us being summarily dismissed as insignificant. It is a disgrace to the discipline that this state of affairs should exist, and these two chapters can only begin to open up this neglected area of economic life.

However, there is another reason why family economic life is foreclosed. It has to do with the methodological constraints imposed by various neutral scientific ideals in the discipline. We shall ask why such a restrictive approach has been adopted and what is needed to open the family up to a constructive economic investigation. Let us therefore look at the main characteristics of consumption theory.

*Homogenization.* Standard theory homogenizes consumer behavior. In order to have the self-contained, value-free discipline that economists have mistakenly sought, the approach has been to assume the universal human calculator who will come up with the answers, especially those relevant to the price system. All families, in all their complexity, become uniform. The standard model was described in Veblen's incomparable words as follows:

> The hedonistic calculator of man is that of a lightning calculator of pleasures and pains, who oscillates like a homogeneous globule of desire of happiness under the impulse of stimuli that shift him about the area, but leave him intact. He has neither antecedent nor consequence. He is an isolated, definitive human datum in stable equilibrium except for the buffets of the impinging forces that displace him in one direction or another. Self-imposed in elemental space, he spins symmetrically about his own spiritual axis until the parallelogram of forces bears down upon him, whereupon he follows the line of the resultant. When the force is spent, he comes to rest, a self-contained globule of desire as before. [1969, pp. 73-74]

But, respond the neoclassical theorists, since no value judgments are made about the subject, how can this charge be leveled at us? The answer is that the method which remains standard for families which are big, small, rich, poor, unemployed, urban, rural, traditional or avante garde, must misrepresent the situation when the values of the subjects affect the judgments made in purchasing. For some extravagance is a virtue, for others a vice; for some saving is the priority, for others it is residual; for some purchase must be instant, while for others it is planned. Since these differences are of great economic significance to all families (they occupy much time and thought and affect purchases), it is scarcely excusable that this diversity has been suppressed by a uniform paradigm of ordinal preferences. It should, for example, be extremely important to economists that some people are trying to buy enough to live, and the quantities matter a great deal, while others are merely considering various purchasing options. The reason for this suppression lies, as we saw in chapter three, in the hope of scientific autonomy.

*Egocentricity.* Another basic assumption of most neoclassical theory is egocentricity. From the Enlightenment onwards, consumer choice has largely been formalized as a self-serving calculus. Whether people actually make decisions on the basis of self-interest, or with care and concern and reference to others, is an important issue which we shall discuss later, but the reason for the tenacity of this assumption has again to do with the scientific status of economics. Assuming egocentricity answers all value questions at one fell swoop, the "neutral" economist is then free to be concerned with the mere technical aspects of choice. It therefore artificially keeps value and ethical issues out of the domain of economics. Unfortunately, life is not like that, and, as we shall see, consumption choices are comprehensively normative.

Secondly, with the Robbins definition of scientific economics, relational choices, which treat other people rather than just oneself as ends, are ruled out. Ends-in-themselves individuals can be kept outside the boundaries of economics. Once, however, economic agents regard other people as ends who need to be taken into account, values have invaded economic science and destroyed its neutrality. Some economists have considered altruistic and other nonegocentric kinds of behavior recently [Boulding 1973, Phelps 1975, Collard 1978], but most neoclassical work remains choked in egocentricity.

*Maximization.* Another crucial assumption is that consumers maximize satisfaction, which usually means that there are always preferred positions. This corresponds well with a materialist ethos, and it also allows economists to solve their problems with maximization techniques, but it is a restrictive view of consumption behavior. It effectively ignores the possibility that people have enough. In most areas of consumption most people do operate with a concept of enough. Often there are obvious limits; for example, in countries where medical treatment has a marginal cost to the person of zero, use is obviously limited by what customers feel they need. Most of us have firm ideas of what we need, whether of shoes, heat, or toothpaste. We also observe limits on the basis of other people's needs; consumption and giving are related. Many of us also have forms or times of consumption which we regard as wrong. All of these very significant approaches to consumption are squeezed out of the conventional stance, purely on the grounds of the methods adopted, and insofar as economic theory informs economic practice, lead to false patterns of living, where maximization of gratification plus scarcity are normal, rather than enough and contentment.

*Comparability.* Consumer theory is also inherently simplistic, in that it assumes that all goods and services and other forms of payment can be compared, and that a single criterion of comparison is used. Although the old criterion of utility has been dropped, the assumption of transitivity (that if A is preferred to B and B to C, then A will be preferred to C) requires that only a single criterion of preference be used in all cases. This simplistic approach again rules out many important aspects of consumption.

First, the things we buy and gifts we make have intrinsic or moral justification, and are not comparable to each other. Since the life-style rationale for consumption is shaped outside economics, it is wrong, especially given the scale of this phenomenon, to explain it within the discipline with this myth. If taxes, health care, tithes, education costs, family travel needs, provisions for the family, and various personal commitments all have an extra-economic motivation, their relation to economics must be considered rather than ignored. For a variety of reasons, most people only make localized comparisons among goods, and this leads to substantively different views of consumer behavior from the normal completeness axiom.

Second, the single criterion implied by transitivity is also a denial of the fact that all of us have many competing value-based criteria for evaluating consumption, and since other things never are equal, different criteria operate at different times, at the least depending on whether we are tired, hungry, generous, short of time, or whatever. Recognition of this necessarily raises the issue of what the normative framework for ordering the criteria is, and once again the leaky sieve of technical rational economics is required to recognize that it sits on a normative ocean.

Thus we see the way in which the standard assumptions in consumption theory in the name of a "scientific" and "self-contained" approach lead to a process of immunization against reality. Yet none of the epistemological attempts to create self-contained knowledge succeed. Samuelson has commented:

> Thus, the consumer's market behavior is explained in terms of preferences, which are in turn defined only by behavior. The result can easily be circular, and in very many formulations undoubtedly is. Often nothing more is stated than the conclusion that people behave as they behave. [1947, p. 91]

And yet this is exactly what revealed preference "theory" does. From what *is* the case, the basis of the theory, it cannot infer anything about what might be the case without implicitly importing the assumptions it was supposed to eliminate. Similarly, the indifference analysis has a necessary logical if-then form, but this does not mean that it provides an understanding of how consumers act. The self-contained methodological positions all finish up with their own form of other-worldliness. On what basis should people behave "rationally" in their consumption decisions, especially when that "rationality" requires unrelieved egocentrism?

## The Black Box Opens

One of the aims of this attempted scientific autonomy and value-freedom has been to close off the family from economic consideration. What is the result of this?

First, it has led to a negation of the temporal significance of consumption. Egocentric maximization is an instantaneous process which collapses the complex temporal reality of life into the instant of purchase and simultaneous consumption. The goods and services disappear forever into these black holes in the economic universe. The temporal prerequisites and consequences and duration of consumption are normally not taken into account, and yet how long things last or when they can be afforded, or when they should be replaced are very significant issues. It is not just house purchase, insurance, and lifetime savings that have longer term significance. The myth of instantaneous gratification upon purchase is a lie which distorts a lot of our economic perceptions.

Second, the identification of the family with consumption, let us call it the bottomless pit model, means that other aspects of the family's economic activity tend to be ignored or downplayed. The family is also a unit of production, conservation, and investment, and provides economic support of other institutions, the employment sector, and economic preservation. It has its own economic equilibrium and decision-making criteria. A family vantage point can see enterprises as consumers of the output of families, in the form of work and savings. Thus in subsequent sections we shall be analyzing some of these other, ignored aspects.

Third, like any other economic system the family involves a complex network of relationships. "If I get the job, will you look after the children?" These relationships also exist among the various objects used in family life—car, home, garden, furniture, and other "consumer durables." Yet all of these internal relationships have great significance for family members, and when duplicated a million times or more, are major global economic variables. The ripples of second cars and second homes are already gathering into tidal waves. Many of these relationships are often summed up in the term "Lifestyle," but this implies another issue which must also be considered.

Families have various faith commitments; they see their lives as having meanings, some of which will be strongly directional. Families travel into a commitment to leisure, to work-oriented living, to child-centered lives, and these roads are economically formative. Thus it is not possible to isolate domestic economic life from the underlying religious significance that people give to their lives as, of course, has normally been done.

Finally, we note that economic activity within the family has a different character from normal exchange activity, and it is necessary to investigate the difference and respect it, rather than conflate it with exchange relationships.

## The Economic Structure of Marriage and the Family

Marriages and families are institutions which should be recognized as having their own economic integrity. We begin by distinguishing the primarily social nature of both. To marry for money, not love, is a defective basis for the institution, and to treat children as investment or economic security is a similar travesty. Thus cultures where brides primarily carry a price or a financial reward, or where marriage centers on economic strategy, are at root defective; they involve reducing the gift of one person to another, a supraeconomic act, to a business transaction. Our Christian normative understanding of marriage is of a faithful and loving lifelong union between a man and a woman. However, this full personal troth commitment has economic implications.

For marriage and the family, although primarily social, have an economic aspect. The structure of marriage involves complete economic union in principle, and almost always in practice. The family is similarly a community of love and troth based on that union, and its "goals" and "needs" are defined in that context. The needs are basically shared in person to person relationships and involve a communal disposition and ordering of resources; food, services, space, and time are jointly organized within the family. It also aims to maintain the physical, mental and social health of its members and to provide education, training and play for the children. The structure of decision-making involves parents making decisions for their children, which translates into increasing economic responsibility for the children.

The organic nature of the family means that it has its own plastic response to external changes. When a change in job, income, or prices occur, the institution reacts in a complex way, preserving especially the continuity and integrity of the love-troth relationship. Often this change involves a new disposition of resources. Thus when the wife and mother takes up a part-time job, a move of house may take place. When there is a change of job or a holiday is planned, a weighing of the family's commitments takes place to produce new "block" decisions. Redefinition of family needs takes place in a way which is at odds with the assumption of the givenness of tastes. Moreover, important dimensions of this reordering are unpriced, like time, space, and psychological and physiological well-being. In the end, of course, these extra-market dimensions come to have important effects in the marketplace.

Thus, recognition of the internal economic dynamics of the family means that the normal pattern of looking for regularities in variables like income, consumption, and prices misses the point. Usually the whole economic activity of family life is restricted to a consumption function like $C=XY + B$ (where X stands for the probable mass reactions of all families to a change in income and B stands for a factor of disturbance, indicating the possible irregularity of their reaction) or to a similar price equation. However, it is precisely the disturbance factor which, though it is treated as residual, is central to the family, a living communal choosing-and-weighing unit responding to economic changes.

The importance of the integral nature of the family is shown by the so-called savings paradox. The normal reaction is contrary to the expected "rational" outcome. If the rate of interest is rising, one "should" expect that a rational household will save more: more money can be earned. But the evidence tends to refute this: if the interest rate is higher, less is saved by families. Why? Because a family is not a money-making unit, but a troth community which needs to make provisions for future family needs through saving. However, if interest rates rise, that provision is more easily, since the future value of saving is higher. Therefore families, just because they are families, save less if the interest level goes up. That reaction can only be understood correctly if we presuppose the internal structure of the family as an economic community characterized by love and care. The main characteristic of the internal economic relationships of marriage and family is that they are gift relationships, not exchange ones. It is a great misunderstanding to see these relationships as calculative exchange ones, as many economists do. [Becker 1973, Schultz 1973] This analysis exemplifies a breakdown of the full meaning of marriage and children into a defective contract and maximization pattern. It is an important fact that the normal character of marital economic relationships consists of giving, receiving, and sharing. However, marriages also usually provide the basis, the shelter, and protection for families. These, again, are love and gift relationships, with the emphasis on the prior care, nurture and giving of the parents to the dependent children. This involves the support, security, training, and provision of resources, but the emergence of economic independence comes at different times, affected by family size, education, and other factors. One of the important economic issues for any famly is what kind of support the children should be given. Our patterns of intergenerational support reflect a great number of our values.

However, the internal health or disintegration of the family also affects economic activity. The obsessive economic concern of economics with efficiency ignores the fact that extra-economic institutions play a fundamental role in establishing or hindering that efficiency. The economic costs of various forms of familial disruption may be a decisive influence on the modern economy, ignored because it is not "economic." We also need to examine the kind of familial support that is most needed to help units maintain their integrity. Let us therefore begin to focus on issues in the internal economic structure of the family.

## Internal Family Economic Life

### Marriage and the Distribution of Wealth

The pooling of wealth, time, and talents within marriage is a very significant and necessary step. Without it, the subsequent gift relationship would be compromised. It is interesting that technically this pooling should lead to an overall equalization of wealth; the standard deviation of the population must be greater than the standard deviation of any sample of all the pairs. However, this equalization, this regression towards the mean, can be modified or even reversed by a number of factors. One is assortative mating, whereby the rich marry the rich and poor marry the poor; it is even possible that some affluent parents encourage this. Another is that more affluent parents continue to pass on their savings, while poorer ones may pass on debts and patterns of dependence. Another is that if only "surplus" wealth is transmitted, over and above what is needed by parents, the differences in surplus may be very much more stark than the original distribution. A realistic model of this process would be very complex, and in any case information on these wealth holdings has not been, and is not likely to be, forthcoming . [Meade 1976, pp. 143-182]

However, what is beyond dispute is that quite a high proportion of newlywed couples bring very little wealth to their marriages. Moreover, levels of poverty among families of this age group are very high, nearly four times as high as those in their fifties. Obviously the needs of recently married couples, who require a house and a whole range of other basic domestic equipment, and who face the probable withdrawal of one partner from the workforce when children arrive, are especially great. It seems to be the case that many middle-aged Americans are rather slow in responding to the needs of the next generation, and that the holding of wealth by older couples possibly causes a lot of hardship and depresses the economy, for their propensity to save is higher than for younger couples. Indeed, rather than having a life-time consumption profile, many older couples just accummulate.

It is worth thinking constructively of policies to encourage the economic independence of marital units. We have already discussed how the distribution of wealth is a neglected issue (chapter 6), and it seems not inappropriate that redistribution of wealth through taxes should be accompanied by a distribution of funds or vouchers to people of the age group where these heavy capital needs are felt. Especially in a society of high longevity it is possible for younger generations to be perpetually beholden to the older generations who have, and hold, familial wealth.

### Marital Income

Marriage has a profound effect on the distribution and use of income, for a number of reasons. The economic norm is the communal sharing of all income, recognizing that there are both financial and non-financial contributions which have equal status as gifts. There have been departures from this norm both in the form of the male breadwinner who dishes out his earnings to his wife as he sees fit, and more recently in the growth of a desire for husbands and wives to have independent sources of income, both as a guarantee in case of divorce and as a source of freedom from economic blackmail within the marriage. These are sad results of the breakdown of troth within many marriages, and it is likely that this kind of marital fear is adding to the potential paid labor force.

When we look at the contribution of husband and wife to family earnings, there is an interesting pattern.

TABLE 1
CONTRIBUTION OF WIVES TO FAMILY EARNINGS, 1977
[Horvath 1980, pp. 151-153]

| Age Husband-wife Families | Husband's earnings (mean) | Wife's earnings mean) | Wife/Husband |
|---|---|---|---|
| 16–24 | 9,234 | 3,075 | 33% |
| 25–34 | 14,260 | 3,728 | 26% |
| 35–44 | 17,787 | 3,514 | 20% |
| 45–54 | 17,918 | 3,703 | 21% |
| 55–64 | 15,241 | 3,121 | 20% |

First, we note how relatively low the financial contributions of wives (especially older ones) are and the heavy dependence on the husband's earnings. There seems to be a trend towards the younger, probably better educated wife, often with a smaller family, contributing a much higher proportion to the joint income. Or as husbands grow older, they are progressively better paid than their spouses. Time will tell whether the male breadwinner pattern is breaking down into a more complex division of labor.

Another issue is how the wife's earnings affect the distribution of joint incomes. Pairing of a given distribution ought to lead to some equalization, and obviously, if partners have degrees of discretion in their occupational earnings, there is also the possibility of complementary response to low earnings of a spouse, but a number of factors work against this result.

First, there is often a strong occupational relationship among married couples, and for this and other reasons relating to educational background, the earnings of husband and wife tend to be positively correlated. Thus, for example, with both husband and wife working full-time, when the husband is earning about $7,000, so is the wife, but when the husband is earning over $25,000, the median earnings of the wife are about $11,500. [U. S. Census 1980 a, p. 125] Especially because of the links between educational background and marriage there is also a growing development of dual career marriages, where after relatively advanced training both spouses are able to earn professional incomes.

Second, the level of women's earnings is much lower than men's, even when, as in the United States and Britain, equality of pay is legally required. However, some occupations, especially professional ones, have succeeded in getting higher degrees of equality of earnings for women, and this gives a considerable tail to the distribution at the higher end. Moreover, because about eight and a half million families are now maintained solely by female householders, the low level of women's earnings leaves many of these in deep poverty, even if they are able to work. [Rawlings, 1980] It is clear that the discrimination against and exploitation of many women in the labor force continues. Male power in the employment market is used to maintain male earning ascendency.

Third, there is often a multiple coincidence of low earning power, unstable job prospects, and unavailability of or inability to work among poorer couples.

This can be combined with a long and early withdrawal of one parent from the paid labor market to bring up a relatively large family. It is interesting that many countries in Europe make direct payments to families for children, as well as tax concessions, on a larger scale than exists in the United States. However, no country, as yet, through the tax and benefit system, gives discretionary payments to parents who look after their children full-time rather than working. Yet this approach would break with the parasitic and negative approach to child care that now exists and reflect a higher social valuation of this important task.

Thus, in summary, although there is a slight increase in the equality of earnings of husband and wife combined over the husband-only distribution (as measured by the standard deviation of the logarithm), the impact is relatively limited, and many couples, especially those who have not moved into the two income idiom, are jointly poor. Indeed, because educated and trained women are indirectly replacing single male breadwinners, it may be that the double co-incidence of familial unemployment is increasing.

**Marriage and the Commitment of Work Effort Inside and Outside the Home**

The commitment to paid work is also an internal marital and family decision. There are a number of strategies available, and provided the marriage is based on full trust and a lifelong commitment to union, the couple have freedom to choose among them. They depend of course on the domestic and employment skills which partners bring to their marriages, but certain types have tended to emerge: the single earner, often the husband, with a spouse working at home, the dual career family, and the fulltime husband and the wife working part-time to provide supplementary income. The variations are many and each implies a certain kind of complementarity between husband and wife. [Hill 1977, pp. 301-329] It is worth pointing out that the best division of labor at one stage of a marriage may well not be best later, and it is important for couples regularly to discuss their employment possibilities.

The rigidity of many patterns of employment creates a barrier to shared work. The division between full-time and part-time work and the growth of employee benefits which are attached only to the fully employed has tended to make employment choices very lumpy. This problem is also accentuated by the growing level of employee overheads, and the high cost of training many workers. If employers were more sensitive, as many are becoming, to the fact that the supply of workers is given in a context of marital sharing, they could perhaps adapt.

The traditional division of labor, where the husband was externally employed and the wife internally, was often grossly unfair. The man would work his forty hours and be finished, while the woman would carry on through meals and child-care to eighty or ninety hours a week. It also created, for many women, a totalitarian (it knew no boundaries) and restrictive (there was nothing else) work environment. Moreover, with the shrinking of families, the automation of homes, and the growth of the educational system at the younger end, especially in parts of Europe, the role became less meaningful. Thus there has been a movement from within marriages for the emancipation of the woman's work role. It would be sad if the earlier demeaning parasitic image of the housewife prevalent in many cultural groups were replaced by an abdication of domestic roles by both partners, and a failure to recognize their deep significance, especially in relation to the children. [Gavron 1966, Oakley 1976] Especially this depends on the recognition that self-fulfillment is not an adequate personal philosophy, not just for the unshackling female but also for the perennially indulgent, and therefore shorter-lived, male.

At a practical level families need to consider their patterns of time commitment, and Table 2 explores in a simple way some of the issues involved.

## TABLE 2
### PROPORTION OF WAKING WORK DAY ABSORBED
### BY WORK AND CHILD CARE

| Work Pattern | No children | | One child | | Two children | | Three children | |
|---|---|---|---|---|---|---|---|---|
| | Husband | Wife | Husband | Wife | Husband | Wife | Husband | Wife |
| Single parent Half-time work | | .25 | | .45 | | .65 | | .85 |
| Single parent Full-time work | | .5 | | .7 | | .9 | | 1.1 |
| Husband full-time Wife child-care | .5 | 0 | .5 | .2 | .5 | .4 | .5 | .6 |
| Husband full-time Wife half-time & child | .5 | .25 | .5 | .45 | .5 | .65 | .5 | .85 |
| Husband full-time Wife half-time Share child-care | .5 | .25 | .6 | .35 | .7 | .45 | .8 | .55 |
| Both full-time Share child-care | .5 | .5 | .6 | .6 | .7 | .7 | .8 | .8 |

This table highlights a number of points. One could surmise that the absorption of more than .7 of the waking day is going to lead in many cases to stress or to an attempt to cut down commitments, either to children or work. It would do little harm for most families to elaborate their position and those of other families that they know and can help, using this model, with elaborations which they can introduce for home care and other commitments. The vulnerability to stress of the single working parent and the dual career family is apparent.

### The Ethos of the "Ideal" Home

One of the amazing trends of the 20th century is the way the home has become an object of faith, an ultimate ideal environment for many. Some might feel that romantic love is the great shrine of worship, but it seems that couples are ready enough to forsake one another and busy themselves with employment in order to equip the ideal homes in which they live. The home is a place of ultimate well-being, of detailed self-expression; it is a citadel of freedom and a place of exclusion of all the external problems of the daily routine. Furnishing often reflects comfort, the good life, and the idea that all is right with the world. There are many houses which are the temples of our age. The care and expense lavished on them is sometimes unlimited. What in previous generations was spent on churches or palaces has in these days often been poured into the home. This ethos has been given systematic support in a variety of ways. First, politicians have found that promises of prosperity have usually attracted sufficient voters to gain office, at least for one election. Second, the strong motivation of many businesses to sell to the limit has led to a level and intensity of advocacy to the consumer which has overwhelmed the conception of the consumers' needs. Third, the banking system has pressured people to borrow, so that consumer credit outstanding runs to about $1500 per head, or $5,000 for the average family. Other factors have been at work; technological investment in selling, presentation, consumer product development, and differentiation have often yielded higher and more immediate rates of return than in other areas. The effect has been cumulative. Through demonstration, persuasion, social contact, and self-congratulation, people have been drawn into a whirlwind of consumption, which leaves much personal and material debris in its wake.

This situation shows the limitations of neoclassical and rational formulations of theory. First, the process is part of a search for personal well-being; it is a dynamic faith. Second, rather than extrinsic ends being of no concern to economic study, we have to recognize that much of the economic system encourages and furthers those ends. This faith has prevented countless families from coming to a sober assessment of their needs and even pushes them to destroy their family life in the name of their home. Gradually the elements of unreality of which this great lie is constructed are becoming evident, judging the people, the firms, and even the politicians who have been its loyal servants. Many aspects of the ideal home cities in which we live will prove more fragile than most of us imagine.

Another part of this development is the privacy generated around the modern nuclear family. Physical distance, reduced contact through metal, glass and concrete, economic time preoccupation, and passively consumed communication create innumerable intangible barriers. Objects are given greater priority and more significance than people, so that people become locked into a lack of awareness and concern for others.

It will be readily evident that this ethos can contribute both in terms of time and finance available to the emaciation of other institutions—churches, schools, communal facilities and care, and wider family care. It also affects the effort that people are able to put into their paid employment.

However, we also need to be aware that the activities that are undertaken domestically also often include work, preservation, education, production, and organization, and it is possible for a home, as well as being bloated with self-satisfaction, to be an efficient center for other activities. Thus, when families consider the norms for household use, they are complex, and if homes are not merely seen as passive receptacles, there are many other valuable uses to which the facilities can be put. With the development of micro-electronics, the home may become an increasing locus of employment.

## Leisure

The idea of leisure has a peculiarly modern ring to it. Older generations tended to be concerned with work and rest, but now we have a distribution of time in which leisure exceeds any other waking activity, including work, for the population as a whole. Table 3 conveys the patterns and the trends.

TABLE 3
AVERAGE HOURS PER WEEK SPENT IN MAJOR ACTIVITIES BY THE URBAN
POPULATION, BY SELECTED CHARACTERISTICS: 1965 and 1975
[Robinson 1976]

| Activity | Total | EMPLOYED MEN Married | EMPLOYED MEN Single | EMPLOYED WOMEN Married | EMPLOYED WOMEN Single | Married Housewives |
|---|---|---|---|---|---|---|
| **1965** | | | | | | |
| Size of urban sample(number) | 1218 | 448 | 73 | 190 | 152 | 341 |
| Total Time(hrs) | 168 | 168 | 168 | 168 | 168 | 168 |
| Sleep. | 53.3 | 53.1 | 50.6 | 53.8 | 52.6 | 53.9 |
| Work for pay | 33.0 | 51.3 | 51.4 | 38.4 | 39.8 | 0.5 |
| Family care | 25.4 | 9.0 | 7.7 | 28.8 | 20.6 | 50.0 |
| Personal care | 21.5 | 20.9 | 22.2 | 20.3 | 21.7 | 22.6 |
| Leisure Time | 34.8 | 33.7 | 36.1 | 26.7 | 33.3 | 41.0 |
| **1975** | | | | | | |
| Size of urban sample(number) | 726 | 245 | 87 | 117 | 08 | 141 |
| Total time(hrs)! | 168 | 168 | 168 | 168 | 168 | 168 |
| Sleep | 54.7 | 3.4 | 54.1 | 55.1 | 54.3 | 56.8 |
| Work for pay | 32.5 | 47.4 | 40.0 | 30.1 | 38.8 | 1.1 |
| Family care | 20.5 | 9.7 | 9.0 | 24.9 | 6.6 | 44.3 |
| Personal care | 21.8 | 21.4 | 20.0 | 26.2 | 21.9 · | 21.4 |
| Leisure time | 8.5 | 36.1 | 44.9 | 31.7 | 36.4 | 44.4 |

The amount of leisure and its growth over against family time obviously says much about what is happening in American homes. And yet, we must not be beguiled by the word "leisure", for a quarter of the population who have so much leisure always feel rushed. [U.S. Census 1980b, p.552] Moreover, nearly seven percent of all personal consumption expenditure is now spent on leisure and cultural activities, and many of the fastest growing outdoor activities like skiing, sailing, snowmobiling, and waterskiing normally require travel and expensive equipment. It is organized gratuitous activity that is quite demanding in resources. Indoors, the dominant activity is watching television which, even though people enjoy watching it less (and how could they do otherwise?), still holds viewers for a substantial proportion of their lives. In mid-winter it holds women on the average of over five hours a day, and it is a massive domestic child tranquilizer dished out to little children to help keep them quiet and stupid.

An interesting picture in this area, which is also a symptom, is the inability of many families to promote regular regeneration. Sleep is often seriously impaired and artificially induced. Overeating and dieting introduces another set of stress patterns. Alcohol and drugs are a part of this domestic culture. Moreover, many of the leisure activities which people undertake cause much more stress than work; when work is used as a period of emotional recovery from leisure, there are bound to be hidden costs. Yet, the deepest hidden cost is the faith investment of the individual ego in the fulfilment of leisure and the inevitable disillusion that must follow.

There is also evidence that family consumption activities are becoming more and more particularized; cars, televisions, records, and entertainment are carved up into various hard-selling markets which actually prohibit the family meeting on common ground. The items—television, record player, car—carve up the social space into various alien territories occupied by individuals. To varying degrees, family social intercourse is being squeezed by these configurations. The ethos of egocentric satisfaction, rather than just being an assumption of neoclassical economists, has actually wrought destructive havoc in many families. However, the hollow joke is that economic victory is also economic defeat and destruction, for the breakdown of the social unit, the family, is one of the big, but unnoticed causes of economic decline. In the end familial nurture is the key to long-term economic development.

### Family Needs

It is worth reflecting for a while on the way so much economic consumption is family-divergent; it creates barriers. If, as we have argued, a marriage and family is a community of love, then the guiding norms for family purchasing should be social ones, and relationships should not be hindered. The norms articulating family needs will be cohesive, allow family time, not create barriers, and not lead to isolation and withdrawal. A family can have enough; more is indulgent living and encourages egocentricity. Moreover, since the members of the family are not just recipients, as in the neoclassical model, but all *give* to the family, it is continually possible to meet needs of members of the family through internal giving. It is also a dynamic economic micro-system in itself in which children learn how to contribute, help, be useful, and cooperate. Indeed, although external factors are important, the willingness of parents and children to give to one another in love is one of the keys to economic integrity, as many who are poor will testify, and many who are rich do not understand.

Thus, the dynamic of love in the subsistence economy of the family allows needs to be met through giving and receiving. It is to the loss of our culture that we have come to rely more heavily on resources bought from the extra familial economy, for in this area, as others, there are many blessings in giving.

## The Economic Consequences of Family Breakdown

Although families can be and are destroyed for economic reasons, as we have suggested, there are also intrinsically social sources of their decay which are more important. These reasons have had a devastating effect on American life. In the mid-70's the divorce level rose consistently over one million a year, and by the late 70's there were over 10 million children maintained only by their mothers. Primarily, of course, this is a social failure, but it is also secondarily an economic one in its causes and effects, the scale of which has scarcely been to the forefront of neoclassical economics.

It is not possible to give a monetary figure to the costs, since many of them are deprivational, and the most important will only be evident in the future. However, the list of economic costs is alarming. It includes the poor utilization of homes and domestic assets in split families, the costs of litigation, the failure of spouses to participate effectively in paid employment because of domestic problems, and effects like alcoholism, misuse of drugs, ill-health, and mental breakdown, all of which are related to marital instability. However, it also includes direct family costs like child care, child support, and aid to dependent children, which in part fall to state and federal agencies to meet. If we remember that in 1981 child day care cost about $1000 M, foster care about $250 M, and child protective services about $340 M, we can see how large the total care cost might be. When the costs of domestic violence—marital and family, delinquency, vandalism, policing, penal institutions, etc., are also added, the total is merely growing. It is only when the costs of educating children with difficult family backgrounds and of subsequent job failure are estimated and added that we get some idea of what a devastating economic burden family failure is already and will become. When the first generation of television and broken-home-bred children are in the work force, the full impact of this complex effect will be felt.

## Conclusion

Thus we see the way in which economic theory, by treating the family as residual, has reinforced a pattern of breakdown which will also have very serious, although not easily quantifiable, consequences for the economy. This massive leeching of resources many economists ignore, because it is external to their system; yet, while they peer down their microscopes and macroscopes, the problems are running around their feet.

The necessary alternative involves taking the integrity of the family seriously, as a social and economic unit. It is only when this unique troth and gift-based institution has both regained its own internal strength and is respected economically and politically that this tragedy will be partly averted.

## Resources

Becker, G. S. 1973. A Theory of Marriage, Part I. *J. Political Econ.* 81: 813-46.

Boulding, K. 1973. *The Economy of Love and Fear.* Belmont: Wadsworth.

Collard, D. 1978. *Altruism and Economy.* NY: Oxford U. Press.

Gavron, H. 1966. *The Captive Wife.* London: Routledge & Kegan Paul.

Hill, D. 1977. Labor Force Participation Decisions of Wives. in *Five Thousand American Families.* Ann Arbor: Institute for Social Research of the University of Michigan.

Horvath, F. W. 1980. Working Wives Reduce Inequality in Distribution of Family Earnings. *Monthly Labor Review.*

Longacre, D. J. 1980. *Living More With Less.* Philadelphia: Herald Press.

May, J. T. 1974. *Family Health Indicators: Annotated Bibliography.* Bethesda: National Institute of Mental Health

Meade, J. E. 1976. *The Just Economy.* London: George Allen and Unwin.

Oakley, A. 1976. *Housewife.* Harmondsworth: Penguin.

Phelps, E. S., ed. 1975. *Altruism, Morality, and Economic Theory.* NY: Russell Sage Foundation.

Rawlings, S. W. 1980. *Families Maintained by Female Households 1970-79.* Washington: U.S. Bureau of Census.

Robinson, J. F. 1976. Changes in America's Use of Time, 1965-75. in *Report of Communication Research Center.* Cleveland: Cleveland State University.

Samuelson, P. A. 1947. *The Foundations of Economic Analysis.* Cambridge: Harvard University Press.

Schultz, T. W. 1973. The Value of Children: An Economic Perspective. *J. Political Econ.* 81: 2-13.

U.S. Bureau of Census. 1980a. *Money Income of Families and Persons in the United States, 1978.* Washington.

U.S. Bureau of Census. 1980b. *Social Indicators.* Washington.

Veblen, T. 1969. *The Place of Science in Modern Civilization and Other Essays.* 1915, NY: Caprice Books.

# Chapter VIII
# The External Economic
# Relationships of the Family

*I went to America, working for Molly,*
*I worked all the day, and I slept all alone.*
*I saved in my pockct those sweet silver dollars*
*To clothe her in satin and make her my own.*

*"Your love has grown tired of keeping her kisses,*
*Of singing a song that can never by sung.*
*This morning your true love has married another,*
*A penniless wise man with a heart that is young.*
    Sidney Carter & Donald Swan (c. 1960)

As we saw in the last chapter, most theory has tended to push the family to the edge of the economic universe, where it hangs on by the thread of consumption. However, when we treat the family as an institution which has its own social and economic integrity, another paradigmatic change takes place. Instead of the family being just a fringe consumption unit, it is recognized as a significant institution in economic activity which involves a complex of economic relationships. Although consumption is an important relationship the family has with the rest of the economy, partly to emphasize that is is not the only one, we shall begin by considering some others.

## The Family and External Investment

The family is both an important locus of direct investment in housing, cars, consumer durables, personal development, furniture and land, and also a source of funds for other economic units. Net family worth is an important concept, but it is not just the value of initial assets plus the sum of net savings. Some families' assets are not quantifiable; they are "investing" in children, education, status, goodwill, or whatever. Moreover, the attitude to those assets affects their significance. Some have a consumer-orientation; others stress accumulation, and others emphasize the usefulness of assets. Their importance to the economy is beyond dispute. Other families have no discretionary assets and only liabilities to consider.

During the 1970's family savings were a third of gross private domestic investment. Moreover, the historical relationship between family investment and economic development has been very strong. A high proportion of the capital generated during the Industrial Revolution came from groups of worker-entrepreneurs who generated growth potential from within the family. The pattern of this dynamic has changed many times, but it would be foolish to underestimate its power. At times, much of the labor force has had little ability to generate investment funds, but recently the relative strengthening of employee incomes and weakening of internally generated profits has made family savings very important.

The ethos and values of family investment can vary widely. There was a contrast in 18th century England between the self-glorifying and self-gratifying country houses of the landed gentry and the functional investment of new capitalist families. Today, the values of families seem to be focusing on security, consumption, and avoiding inflationary losses, and, as a result, wealth has been shifted away from financial assets like corporate stock and has moved to tangible assets, such as owner-occupied houses and consumer durable goods, which act as hedges against inflation and can be used as consumer goods. Thus, between 1965-78 the ratio of net financial wealth of households to tangible wealth fell from 0.8 to 0.43 [Fellner 1979]. Furthermore, in the 1970's non-discretionary household outlays, including consumer installment debt repayments, rose substantially, signalling a partial withdrawal of the family from wider industrial investment, so that net financial investment was almost zero at the end of the 70's [Federal Reserve 1980]. Nor is this privatization of wealth away from the wider industrial scene the only trend. There is also an institutional one.

First of all, many family investors, instead of investing directly in shares, are putting their money into various financial institutions, like pension funds, banks, and insurance funds. This has created an investment market of two or more tiers in which the family becomes a largely passive agent which merely receives institutionally decided dividends. The classical assumption is that the market for credit is fairly perfect, but we suggest that this might not be so for *institutional* reasons. The institutions, especially in their handling of investment, tend to be centralized and elitist, and must therefore necessarily make big decisions; the change in locus of responsibility therefore means changed patterns of holding.

Those overall ownership figures obscure the fact that institutions and individuals tend to concentrate their holdings in different types of stocks. Institutions invest the bulk of their assets in the 500 largest NYSE stocks. They put very little of their money into over-the-counter (OTC) stocks. Almost as a mirror image, individuals are the principal investors in OTC and the smaller listed stocks [Brume & Friend,1978,p.5].

The likely result is that funds are channeled away from areas where the capital/labor ratio is lower, and that this whole tendency is reinforcing unemployment patterns. These patterns might also be maintained by upper class networks of social interaction [Ratcliffe 1980]. Thus, the overall effect is a withdrawal from the smaller dynamic investment patterns which continually fuel new developments and jobs.

In the light of these wider problems which grow from the commitments of the family, we need to consider far more deeply how it should use its resources and savings. First, it is clear that in principle the family retains responsibility for the way its funds are used by intermediaries; agnosticism is abdication of responsibility. Second, families, because of their immediacy, are often in the best position to respond to new possibilities of service; they should be generation points of enterprise. If, therefore, families lost their concern with passive financial return and regained a vision of the productive possibilities of familial investment, the national level of investment could be more healthy than it is. It is possible, for example, for ten families of stable income to put a full-time worker into business, and there are plenty of jobs needing to be done for those who look around. This constructive family vision contrasts with the passivity and defensiveness that has helped to increase the workforce in Finance, insurance, and real estate by 25% in the second half of the 70's. Having an inflation-dependent passive family sector is scarcely healthy economic development.

## The Family as Provider of Work

One of the dynamic elements ignored in standard theory is that the family organizes and develops its work contribution in a creative way. Families buy cars, undertake training, move, organize schedules, and even limit their size in order to be able to work effectively. One of the big changes, of course, has been the increased participation of mothers and wives in the labor force, which, as we have seen, may have an internal familial source. It is worth stopping to consider comparative penetration rates.

TABLE 1
PERCENTAGE FEMALE IN THE LABOR FORCE
[Semyonov 1980]

| | |
|---|---|
| Poland | 46.0 |
| Finland | 45.9 |
| Czechoslovakia | 44.6 |
| Ghana | 44.2 |
| Sweden | 42.3 |
| Hungary | 41.2 |
| United States | 39.1 |
| United Kingdom | 38.5 |
| West Germany | 35.8 |
| France | 34.9 |
| Belgium | 34.4 |
| Norway | 27.7 |
| Italy | 27.4 |
| Netherlands | 25.9 |
| Mexico | 21.6 |
| Brazil | 20.9 |
| India | 17.4 |
| Syria | 10.8 |

These reflect familial and communal values. Furthermore, the increase in women at work is a prime explanation for much of the affluence of the postwar era. The comparative ease of a small family, high-participation rate country's economic task in relation to high-fertility, poor countries like India is also evident.

We have already considered some of the internal effects of this participation, but we also need to examine the organizational factors involved in having this high level of external service. One is the fit between potential family contribution and the work available; if it is possible to have both husband and wife working 80% full-time, but only 100% or 0% is available, then 60% of availability is lost. Moreover, since husband and wife must make joint and compatible job choices, individual optimization is obviously a flawed decision-making process, although it seems that wives still make the "non-optimal" decisions [Waite 1976]. It is also important that the family be located in a space which offers jobs to both potential workers. These issues, about which couples make important economic choices, fall through the interstitial vacuities of economic science.

There is also an ethos of family work participation which may have another effect. The family commitment to high consumption, high leisure, passive entertainment, and the minimization of effort will not stay confined to the home. It points to dual career but minimal work involvement, and it is probable that this effect is slowly seeping into the workplace. The name, "the British disease," has been coined for the pattern of long weekends, long tea-breaks, and minimal effort, but it is likely that it is a transnational phenomenon. There is a break between supervisory and managerial workers and the rest; the former by the nature of their task are called to keep things working and receive rewards for doing so. They, it seems, are finding more falling on their shoulders; 19.6% of them are working at least a six-day week [Hodges 1980]. The other workers have developed a withdrawal from work, perhaps because both spouses are working; their average weekly hours have dropped from 37 to 35 in the last decade, while the overall average has stayed at 42. This divergent level of commitment is possibly behind the puzzling phenomenon of the relative stagnation of production.

The family's commitment to work is linked up with many other important decisions. Some readers will be directly aware of failures in commitment to the family through work pressures and conversely of failures in work through domestic lifestyles. Some will be aware that when the family functions cooperatively, more is often possible than when there is individualistic bargaining. Others will recognize false pride of identifying the family's external work effort with the husband's career and ignoring the wife's. The walk of faith whereby each family weighs and develops the gifts of service it has been given for internal and external use can be a source of peace and fulfillment, but it can also be source of familial and economic bitterness and frustration.

## The Family as Donor

The role of providing for older parents and the extended family is one of the more significant economic relationships which has also undergone a fundamental change. The norm is quite clear.

> If anyone does not provide for his relatives and especially for his immediate family, he has denied the faith and is worse than an unbeliever. (I Tim. 5:8)

The modern pattern of familial care has changed. Insurance, pensions, and welfare provisions have tended to individualize the concept to one of lifetime earnings. To follow through the intricacies of institutional and governmental provision would take a book in itself, but it is worth considering the implications of two models of family support. The first one is temporally lateral; it is a welfare model which involves accepting support from the stronger members of the existing economic community. The second is individualistic and anticipatory; it depends on the individual acquisition of assets which will yield a flow of income in the future, usually through intermediaries. This dependence on assets, although it has created some problems thus far, is more problematic than is usually admitted because of the strong individual requirements placed on the kind of assets needed, especially given the structural instability of the stock market and the capitalist economy [Storkey 1980]. It is possible that the former model, the communal one, will eventually turn out to be stronger. At a more immediate level the forms of care which can be given within families are far wider than can be provided by financial institution, and it is not rare for people to prey economically on the needs and infirmities of the old. Thus, again, there is a situation where individual fear and insecurity is encouraging economic conservatism and producing restricted patterns of care.

Family giving is one of the creative modes of family life. For rather than giving being residual to spending and saving, it is possible for it to be a family priority which modifies lifestyle. The priority of giving to meet the needs of others, despite all our negative rationalizations, is the norm of Christian *koinonia* and neighborly care. It is Paul, not Marx, who specified the principle that we should give voluntarily according to our abilities to meet the needs of others who require help. (I Cor. 16:2; II Cor. 8 & 9). In many areas, too, familial payments can be such as to support the provision of services for others. These inputs can have a mighty effect on the needs of others and are an integral part of our economic lives [Sider 1977].

## The Conserving Family

From this perspective, which recognizes the family as having a positive productive role, the question arises as to how well the family conserves and renews the resources committed to it. In many ways families develop patterns of care which are probably higher than those which are exercised in other sectors of the economy; they tend plants, regularly paint woodwork, and repair the structure of their houses. Yet, the issue of conservation is far wider than that. It includes the question of the design lifetime of the house, the car, and the furniture. The location of the home has significant energy implications, as the daily commuter pulse in and out of cities emphasizes. It also includes the question of the kind of upkeep required. Most important, however, are the demands made by the overall lifestyle on resources and the work efforts of others. With many, of high income especially, these demands are great. For example, those with high incomes not only travel further, but their commuting speeds are faster [Duncan & Morgan 1976, pp. 198,294]. The awareness of what we demand to sustain us as families should provoke a greater sensitivity to the norm of family conservation as a guide for a wide range of family policies and activities.

## The Family as Purchaser

We have recognized that the family is not *just* a consuming unit, but has its own economic integrity. Now we examine the significance of the family as a consuming unit. This requires us to acknowledge that firms, government, churches, schools, and communities also consume, a neglected topic, but for the moment our focus remains on family consumption.

We have already criticized consumption theory's dominant paradigm and are now in a position to look at some of the guiding principles for family expenditure.

1. In antithesis to the supposed autonomy of the consumer, it is necessary to recognize that families receive from and depend on God for all blessings. Consumption, where it is not tainted, points to the providence and care of God.

2. What we receive also normally shows our dependence on our neighbors, often many thousands of them in one day. Gratitude for the contributions they make to our needs should be a normal part of life. For families to assume that they are independent and economically self-referring is to deny the full mutuality of the economic community. They necessarily are involved in many decisions about fair or unfair recompense to all those on whose services they depend.

3. The purchase of goods and services is not an end in itself, but receives its proper meaning in the context of righteous living. Every purchase is therefore a matter of judgment in the light of various norms, and not a matter of mere maximization of family utility.

4. Purchase decisions, correctly understood, affect the needs of many others, and reduction of those decisions to an egocentric calculus involves a basic misunderstanding. The principle is starkly stated by Paul in the following terms: "Nobody should seek his own good, but the good of others" (I Cor. 10:24). Our consumption is thus meant to fully reflect and express a love of God and our neighbor, as well as our family. To give is always an alternative to purchasing.

5. What we receive depends on the commitment of effort and resources of ourselves and others; those contributions are weighed in the overall process of economic evaluation and purchase.

6. The full economic implications of purchase for the whole lifetime of the commodity or service are relevant to the purchase decision, including disposal, external and positional effect, and the kind of commitment involved.

7. Subjective pleasure is a false idiom for viewing consumption because it elevates a style of consumption needs which captivate and take away the liberty of economic choice. When the consumer is the ultimate reference point, a God-denying life is perpetrated. Humans cannot appropriate joy to themselves or be an end in themselves; they can only receive God's bounty and blessing. Thus hedonism and utilitarianism are distortions of the meaning of life, and the attempt to possess pleasure has as its inevitable long-term result the "joyless economy".

> I denied myself nothing my eyes desired;
> I refused my heart no pleasure. . . .
> Yet when I surveyed all that my hands had done
> and what I had toiled to achieve,
> Everything was meaningless, a chasing after the wind;
> Nothing was gained under the sun. [Ecc. 2:10,11]

8. A concomitant of stressing subjective pleasure is to give inordinate value to things and possessions. Such idolatry occurs when things are idolized and people become slaves to them. This attitude is both an offense to God and destructive of true humanity.

9. Many purchasing motives, like self-indulgence, family indulgence, vanity, self-glorification, greed, covetousness, and fear have degrading influence on behavior, and yet these motives may be encouraged by the psychological pressures of consumption.

10. It is possible for things and possessions to destroy and obstruct relationships. Conversely, the norm of respect for other persons and institutions is one that can be upheld in consumption decisions. (I Cor. 10:23-33).

11. Serious injustice in the familial distribution of wealth and income might make the resources available a suspect basis for making decisions. The prior issue, as Zacchaeus realized (Luke 19:1-10), is whether injustice has taken place.

12. Although prices are often an approximation to values, they might be inaccurate or even unfair in their evaluation of the effort and resources put into a potential purchase. The consumer can take into account all the information available, not just the price, in consumption decisions.

These orientating principles give us some basis for exploring the relationship between the family purchasers and the wider economy without being trapped in the blinkered vision of ordinal maximization.

## Consumption Lifestyle

The myth of consumer sovereignty under which economic theory labored so long has at last largely given way before the fact that the consumer-manufacturer relationship is a dynamic and subtle one. Galbraith's judgment opens up the issue:

> It is true that the consumer may still imagine that his actions respond to his own view of his satisfactions. But this is superficial and proximate, the result of illusions created in connection with the management of his wants. Only those wishing to evade the reality will be satisfied with such a simplistic explanation [Galbraith, 1967, p. 213].

Are consumers merely pawns in the hands of manufacturers? Obviously this is an overstatement, but we would do well to assess the weaknesses of the consumer. First, the manufacturers convey what consumers should buy. Ellul stated the point thus:

> The primary purpose of advertising technique is the creation of a way of life. And here it is much less important to convince the individual rationally than to implant in him a certain conception of life. The object offered for sale by the advertiser is naturally indispensable to the realization of this way of life. Now, objects advertised are all the result of the same technical progress and are all of identical type from a cultural point of view. Therefore, advertisements seeking to prove that these

objects are indispensable refer to the same conception of the world, man, progress, ideals—in short, life [Ellul 1964, p. 406].

Thus, in the 20th century manufacturers have transmitted culture to families on a very large scale; they have conveyed what people should look like, how they should dress, what they should play, how they should be entertained, and what kind of community they should live in. But this is not by conviction, but rather through market research, the work of the sales and research departments, and through hunches. The relationship is complex; nobody has decided against walking, but now it is difficult to walk and see a friend. When people buy a car, they do not usually also consider that they are buying a mechanic, more roadspace, a garage, and a bit of a hospital. The visions both of manufacturer and family are limited.

It is not that families are not free to purchase or refrain from purchasing, but rather that the myth of "consumption" leads to a sublimation of the truth that the family necessarily becomes a steward of the artifacts which are purchased. A lawn requires a lawnmower, weedkiller, fertilizer, and other tools. Lipstick generates eye-shadow, skin care, cleansing agents, mirrors, and tissues. Thus the family, with its own consent, is being lured into cultural patterns which have their genesis in the manufacturing process. The need to sell dominates the selling of needs. The family must, therefore, recognize that in all of its purchases, it is not buying self-satisfaction, but that it is undertaking new responsibilities of stewardship. Within this paradigm a more careful assessment of familial needs is possible.

## The Psychology of Consumption

When the simplistic nature of utilitarian economic psychology is dropped, it is possible to develop a fuller and more discerning view of the subject, one which allows the hedonism which has gripped many economic agents to be seen more critically. Consumption motives and attributes are far more complex, and are trained and developed by the subject in conjunction with a cultural system of norms of motive evaluation. "I need a new suit to look smart. But how smart do I want to look anyway? Whom am I trying to impress?" Advertisers are, of course, experts in the legitimation of motives.

So that we can get away from the simplistic standard treatment, it is worth considering some of the variety of motives that enter into purchase decisions.

| | |
|---|---|
| To meet hunger or thirst | For comfort |
| For security | For love |
| On impulse | To express love |
| For freedom | For mobility |
| To give | For information |
| For status | To learn |
| To seek acceptance | For peace of mind |
| To assert identity | For excitement |

| | |
|---|---|
| To feed an addiction | For entertainment |
| Out of health concern | To save time |
| To communicate | To care for |
| To establish social contact | To expand choice |
| To keep tidy | To undo mistakes |
| To clean | To make someone happy |
| To preserve economic value | To appear different |
| To make a profit | To avoid work |
| To preserve | To achieve privacy |
| To get something done | For safety |
| To economize effort | For exercise |
| To express creativity | To punish oneself |
| For rest | For relief of pain |
| For warmth | To be conspicuous |

These and other motives which are important to most of us are not just "subjective", they are thoroughly articulated to the external economic world. Calculations are made about safety, warmth, time-saving, and comfort. However, the motives either embody or are qualified by criteria like "How much comfort or mobility should I have?" Moreover, the motives are articulated; if I want information about a recent election, I also have a prior conception of what kind of information I want—what details, whether pictures or description, instant or digested, and so on. Thus the motives are subject to, shaped by, and critically assessed in relation to our normative identity. Autonomous motives, the staple diet of economists, belong to psychological pathology; an uncontrolled need, except in certain prescribed situations, would normally be seen as evidence of a breakdown of personal psychological stability.

Widespread manipulation and legitimation of motives leads them to become unbalanced, obsessive, and misguided, running on an emotional treadmill of work and spending. It is in this context that the standards of emotional truth provided by Christ shine across our culture.

> So do not worry, saying 'What shall we eat?' For the pagans run after these things, and your heavenly Father knows that you need them. But seek first his kingdom and his righteousness, and all these things will be given to you as well [Matt. 7:31-33]

Contentment, peace of mind, joy, and patience, are only given within a context where God is worshipped and people are forgiven; they are alien to the culture of the worship of things. From the stability of a healthy relationship with the Father, it is possible to see how many false emotions and motives have been allowed into our psyches and forced-fed so that they will grow.

The pressures to psychological dissatisfaction are very strong in current family purchasing. Many families groan each Christmas under the twin compulsions of giving and having a good time. Other consumption patterns represent an attempt to escape from failures, constricting relationships, a particular image, or inadequacy. The car, the garden, the holiday, the hobby or whatever becomes a means of getting away from it. Often, too, consumption creates a locus of legitimation for other activities, as is evident from the conventions of dating; indeed, it is astonishing how many relationships become thing-dependent in people's minds; drinking is a prerequisite for social intimacy, excitement for peer groups. It is possible for us at least to glimpse some of the forms of psycho-economic bondage that are a normal and debilitating part of our economic round and the strength of Paul's Christ-centered view of things (Phil. 3:7-11).

## Consumption and Time

The created parameters of time are highly egalitarian; each person can only live his own life, one moment at a time, and no person's life is transferable. However, as Linder [1970] and others have noticed, the economic use of time has become problematic. The problems are of two different dimensions.

One arises from the competition of people to gain time from other people. It is a view with an egocentric reference point which seeks to reduce the time spent working for others and maximize the leisure, i.e., free time available to the subject. As Veblen [1964, 1899], Bukharin [1919], and others pointed out at the beginning of the century, a small leisure class was able to sustain a position of maximal free time through absentee ownership, servants, and large scale capitalism. Where this pattern did not lead to revolution, it was normally followed by a slow democratization of the idea of leisure. Although the leisured elite has by no means disappeared, leisure is the normal assumed goal for all families, as we saw in the last chapter. However, the consumption of gratuitous time in a rewarding way often necessarily demands the time of others, and there are still major inequalities among those who can buy and those who must supply time for leisure. The relentless requirements of service make heavy demands on the time of shop-keepers, those involved in entertainment, restaurants, transport, and many other services. Since many of these are relatively unskilled, they constitute a class who are put upon by the leisured masses, and the demands on their families and persons are rarely the concern of the active leisure seekers, but they are serious.

However, the modern leisured family also tends to be panting for time. Partly this is because there is an underestimation of time commitments. If "a good night out" is accompanied by lost sleep, a hangover, and lethargy, then those need to be recognized in time accounting. Second, maintenance time for the plethora of consumer durables that the family accumulates is considerable, as are the accommodation problems: books require shelves; gadgets, plugs; and tools, a shed. The family that buys leisure-saving devices is usually also buying leisure-consuming ones, and as the latter win out, so people buy more ways of saving time. Ways to stay awake, to get to sleep, to travel fast, to eat quickly, read faster, and weed the garden are developed to economize on time, and consumers normally, but in a deeper sense pathologically, buy these time manipulators. At the same time, there is no deliberation in purchasing, and things are bought in haste, while the level of utilization later drops. The boat that cost

$20,000 is used six times a year, or the slide projector is used annually at a capital cost of 10 cents per slide. Furthermore, the process of purchase also involves extended time commitment: the sophisticated system of price variation practiced by shops produces sophisticated shopping around; the internal efficiency of shops leads to externalised time costs for shoppers; the unavoidable imposition of advertisements daily strangles one minute after another. Thus, the merry-go-round of spending money and time to save time to spend leisure time is spinning dizzily for many, and more than a few are trying to jump off. Market analysts have picked up what they call the "voluntary simplifiers". [Shama 1981] Others become adept, so they think, at doing many things at the same time. We conclude that in this area of time accounting, where we all have exactly the same income, many consumers find it very difficult not to overspend, partly because of the pressures from the market and partly because their accounting procedures are so superficial.

Each family needs to think and rethink where it commits its time, and whether it has been drawn into economic time acceleration in ways which it does not really want and will regret. It is also clear that the Sabbath day of rest has a clear message to our culture. Only when everybody and everything rests together regularly can the treadmill circles of self-centered activity in our lives be broken and peace return to normal activities. We worship our own economic activity and are judged by our slavery to it.

## Consumption and Elasticity

The use of elasticity concepts in consumption theory is standard; but what is the meaning of this kind of theory? It could be argued that it often precludes certain important kinds of analysis. Demand functions are normally written so that the demand for the good is a function of only its own and other goods' prices and income. Own price and cross elasticities involve a conceptual isolation of each variable, so that each one is represented by a partial derivative. However, these can only be handled if the other independent variables are held constant, which presupposes that we know what they are. Actually, we do not. Indeed, by adopting the *ceteris paribus* assumption, we systematically ignore the people involved. We aggregate the responses of people to establish the demand for goods, but we ignore aggregation across goods to analyze the response of persons. We are measuring the price elasticities of the goods and not the responses of the consumers. Yet the latter are highly significant. They can vary widely on the basis of different sets of valuations and judgments— how thrifty they are, their search priorities, their level of income (entirely different from income elasticity), and their religious convictions. Common wit tells us that prices rocket when there are spendthrift tourists or a lot of rich people around, and that thriftiness helps keep prices in check, but standard theory does not allow the possibility that people are significant to be formulated. The elasticity formulation is defective, because it excludes the attitudes people have to consumption, price, and inflation. To analyze prices in terms of "people elasticity" is no less valid than the current "goods elasticity" focus.

Second, the assumption that other things are held constant is not accurate for a wide range of consumption decisions. It is not merely that conditions change but, more importantly, that the family weighs a whole spectrum of prices and costs and other factors against the price of the good. The decision is integral, not differentiated. Often purchases are composite —car, tires, insurance, gas, tax, etc.; sometimes they seem inordinately so —coffee beans, grinder, filters, percolator, coffee pot, and coffee cups—by social definition. Clearly the composite price of buying into the set of purchases is different from the price elasticities of buying one. Often other costs or savings also weigh heavily in the decision to purchase into the family economy; many purchases are seen as labor saving or allow better social configurations. Further, the costs of travel, search effort, time, and uncertainty are likely to be weighed into the purchase; they are seldom constant. Finally, the costs of integrating purchases into the domestic economy are often considerable. Thus the composite nature of decisions contradicts the assumption of analytical independence built into the formulation of elasticities.

It is, of course, also the case that other things do vary. Consider the two parallel and contingent movements that often take place. As a new commodity is introduced, high initial production costs give way to lower mass-production prices. At the same time a demonstration effect takes place as the characteristics of that good, whether it be a calculator or a video cassette recorder, are passed on socially from one family to another. Other things vary, and elasticity computations, which must involve some time period for reaction to the "independent" variable, are therefore inherently dubious. Unfortunately, by a process of ex-post deterministic selectivity, economists are led to assume that they know far more about the phenomena they study than they actually do.

Does this not just mean that elasticity calculations are a little less precise than the calculation to two places of decimal in the textbook sometimes implies? It can be argued that far more than this is involved. Because consumers have been excluded from the analysis and their decisions taken as given, economists have been unable to address a number of very important issues. Are there search constraints on the consumption of certain groups like the old, the young, the poor, and the overbusy, which make them an easy prey to higher prices? How does thriftiness vary with the level of income, not merely with changes in it? How widely do vendors work to change consumers' price elasticities with respect to a good, and to what extent do they succeed? And, finally, what factors are involved, and how wide are the differences, in the price efficiency of various families?

This spurious verification of the unreal, whereby a falsely determinate linear demand relationship is created also excludes the normative aspect of the issue. If the efficiency of the price system is largely based upon the norm of thriftiness, what does this norm imply? Is it losing public efficacy under the pressures of instant gratification and shortage of time? If the price discretion that can be exercised by the vendor is considerable, is it being abused? Again, we emphasize that the normative content of economics, in this case the question of the fairness of prices and the outworking of consumer thrift, cannot be treated as an optional extra to the subject. The theory that has made it so is falsely based, for it is precisely in consistent reponses to norms like thrift and fairness that many economic regularities, such as they are, are to be found.

## The Characteristics of Goods and Services

In adopting a supposedly value-free ordinal system of consumption analysis, economists have actually imposed some very heavy constraints on the scope of their theory. The most obvious, arising from the assumption that the persons who consume are egocentrically rational and cannot be seen critically, is that goods must be good. The neoclassical non-normative stance precludes the possibility that consumers do not buy good goods. However, in fact many goods are bad. This is not merely to be dismissed as a "subjective" judgment; rather, it is based upon norms gathered from a range of different disciplines. Many goods are unhealthy, leading to addiction, insomnia, obesity, and a wide variety of fatal illnesses. Many others are psychologically destructive, leading to dependence, character disorders, and neuroses. Others are, to varying degrees, socially destructive. The evidence that people buy bad goods can easily be gathered from various sciences.

The scale of this problem needs to be recognized. If we assume that all tobacco consumption, 40% of the money spent on alcohol, drugs, and television, and 10% of the money spent on food do harm, then 6% of total consumption expenditure is directly bad. A much higher proportion has indirect bad side effects on the consumer or others, and a further batch of consumption attempts to remedy these ills. When many of these bads, like alcohol consumption and gambling, are growing, it is not surprising that national welfare is perceived to be growing. What this represents more directly is a tragic crowd of people who have been severely damaged by various forms of maximized living. The least economists could do is recognize them.

The generalized n-good model of consumption does not only have the weakness of assumed goodness. It is also founded on comparability, for the ubiquitous good, X and Y, are expected to cover the whole domain of consumption. Yet, we must acknowledge that many goods are not comparable in any significant way as alternatives. Consumers rarely compare shoes with a toothbrush, or car insurance with hamburgers, for these items occur in different domains which have already been ordered on the basis of a system of commitments to principles and priorities of consumption. Hamburgers are food and car insurance is premised on law and security, so they are obviously not directly comparable, contrary to the normal assumptions. This perspective again brings out the importance of the norms of consumption. What do people mean by security? What is the social and legal framework within which the family defines its position? It is in the analysis of the unique norms for various domains and in the extent of the *non-comparability* of goods that much of the most exciting work in consumption needs to be done.

Finally, we note that the character of consumption transactions varies widely. Many services require a personal relationship, founded on trust and extending over a long period of time. Other goods and services involve a price established after the transaction. Many goods are unique; some are positional in that their ownership is exclusive, others are creatively different, others are uniquely available, and others are aesthetically, socially, or psychologically significant. All of these prevent strict patterns of substitutability from being operative; the marginal rate of substitution does not exist for consumers in relation to those goods. The particular form of fairness that is appropriate to these transactions is usually based on indirect calculations through common factors that can be established, like appropriate rates of pay. The richness of the consumer's universe and the depth of his transactional awareness are thus generally understated within the discipline, to its cost.

## The Family and the Market

We have looked at the relative richness and complexity of the family's response to the market. Now we look again at the structure of that relationship. The family is a small and weak unit compared with most firms, although more numerous. The more dominant firms tend to have become preoccupied with the need to sell, and outsell their rivals, so that the stronger flow in the relationship has tended to be firm/family persuasion. Indeed the commitment of resources to selling has been so heavy over such a long period that people must have been profoundly affected by it. In many markets the focus is on the competing sales networks to the extent that the actual goods and services provided seem to have a secondary significance; there are some firms whose marketing technique, rather than their product, form their corporate identity. As stated earlier, Galbraith, Packard, and others have pointed out the significance of salesmanship as an independent variable in consumer demand, and the penetration of this impulse is continuing. Salesmanship has moved into the home, the highways, and even the churches; money and credit are iniquitously available. The passive and reactive roles that this implies for the average family is far from the autonomous consumer implied by theory; how far is it correct?

Perhaps the answer, and it is an intriguing one, lies in a different direction. The Galbraithian argument is in part correct, although it fails to recognize that the families which are up to their ears in credit and are heavily dependent on two incomes have in part also given up their integrity as families. Because there is a social vacuum, because the children are allowed to watch three hours of commercials a week, the family is a prey to thing and service pressure. Clearly, there is a need for families to develop immunity to pressure to buy what they do not need. Yet the argument misses something else more important, for if firms are exerting this kind of pressure, it is also a sign of their weakness. After all, if they were producing goods that were avidly needed, there would be little need to exert the intense and costly (about 40 billion dollars) pressure that is used in advertising. This signifies, therefore, a disguised crisis which has at least two dimensions. The first is that many of these products are ephemeral and extravagant, so that people do not really need to buy them. The second requires a fuller analysis.

## The Distribution of Consumption

In the early 1980's, the United States experienced a period of relative recession. In this section we shall consider the extent to which families may have been and will be responsible for it. First, we note that the decline in fertility rates beginning in the early 60's and gathering momentum since then means a heavier loss of dynamism in consumption than is normally recognized. It increases the ratio of working to non-working members of the population, and the reduced population occurs in age groups where much consumption is normally generated through home formation, transport units, education, and pre-family markets. The purchase of most consumer durables is skewed to the lower age groups. The normal dynamics of the family life cycle will, therefore, tend to depress consumption for another decade or two. (The steady decline in fertility from 126.8 to 89.3 between 1910 and 1929 is probably a more significant part of the 1930's slump than is usually recognized).

However, this effect is compounded by the relative poverty of the young who are probably slower to receive inherited and transmitted wealth from their long-lived parents and do not have the advantage of capital gains accumulated on real estate by the older generation living in an inflationary era. Thus, not only are the consumption patterns of the old relatively stagnant, but those who are in the high consumption age brackets are most heavily constrained by income and wealth. This group also experiences considerably higher levels of unemployment than middle-aged cohorts, where often both partners will be in stable jobs. The poverty of the young is therefore also hitting consumption.

Yet another factor is the distribution of income *among* families. It is a commonplace that poor families spend a higher proportion of their income than rich ones. The persons below the poverty level figure reached its nadir in 1973 at about 23 million and has risen substantially since then. Government policy in the early 1980's is likely to do little to redistribute income or wealth towards the poor; more likely it will do just the opposite. Indeed, very little thought seems to be given to the issue of the direct redistribution of wealth and income, other than through bureaucratic programs. At a time when supply-side economics is in vogue, it seems that there is a demand-side crisis which is being quietly ignored. That is sad when poor families actually need to spend more.

## Conclusion

We see that the relationship of the family with the rest of the economy is one of the most important dynamic relationships in economics. It is evident that economic analysis which fails to recognize the integrity of this unit will miss many of the more important aspects of this relationship. Moreover, we see that the norms and values which are present in the family give unique directions to the dynamics of consumption. This perspective has important implications for the way in which the discipline of economics is seen. It is, however, more important how we live as families which are also economic units. The decisions we make and the directions we follow will help determine whether the economy is shallow, unstable, and wasteful, or careful, meeting full human needs and honoring God. Families, rather than being passive economic pawns, are meant to be units of faith and economic responsibility.

## Resources

Brume, M. E., and I. Friend. 1978. *The Changing Role of the Individual Investor.*. NY: John Wiley.

Bukharin, N. 1919. *The Economic Theory of the Leisure Class.* London: M. Lawrence.

Duncan, A. J., and J. N. Morgan. *Five Thousand American Families, Vol. IV,* Ann Arbor: Institute for Social Research of the U. of Michigan.

Ellul, J. 1964. *The Technological Society.* NY: Vintage.

Federal Reserve Board. 1980a. Recent Financial Behavior of Households. *Federal Reserve Bulletin.* 66: 437-43.

Federal Reserve Board. 1980b. Perspectives on Personal Saving. *Federal Reserve Bulletin.* 66: 613-25

Fellner, W. 1979. American Household Wealth in an Inflationary Period. in Fellner, ed., *Contemporary Economic Problems 1979.* Washington: American Enterprise Institute.

Galbraith, J. K. 1967. *The New Industrial State.* Boston: Houghton Mifflin.
Hodges, J. N. 1980. The Workweek in 1979: Fewer but Longer Workdays. *Monthly Labor Review.*

Linder, S. B. 1970. *The Harried Leisure Class.* NY: Columbia U. Press.

Ratcliffe, R. E. 1980. Banks and Corporate Lending: An Analysis of the Impact of the Internal Structure of the Capitalist Class on the Lending Behavior of Banks. *American Sociological Review.* 45: 553-570.

Semyonov, M. 1980. The Social Context of Women's Labor Force Participation: A Comparative Analysis. *American Journal of Sociology.* 86: 534-50.

Shama, A. 1981. Coping with Stagflation: Voluntary Simplicity. *Journal of Marketing.* 45: 120-34.

Sider, R. 1977. *Rich Christians in an Age of Hunger.* Downers Grove, Inter-Varsity Press.

Storkey, A. 1980. Reform of the Stock Exchange. *Intl. Reformed Bul.* 77: 11-13.

Veblen, T. 1899. *The Theory of the Leisure Class.* NY: Viking.

Veblen, T. 1964. *Absentee Ownership and Business Enterprise in Recent Times.* (1923), NY: A. M. Kelley.

Waite, L. J. 1976. Working Wives: 1930-1960. *American Sociological Review.* 41: 65-80.

# Chapter IX
# The Firm:
# Prices and Products

*"Daddy, please take me back to Muilenburg County*
*Down by the Green River, where Paradise lay."*
*"Well, I'm sorry, my son, but you're too late in asking*
*Mr. Peabody's coal train has hauled it away."*
John Prine (1973)

## Responsible Behavior and the Traditional Theory of the Firm

The firm is usually depicted in economics books in the guise of a legal form, the corporation. There are the stockholders, or owners, who pool their money, elect a board of directors, and hire managers who have the day-to-day responsibility of hiring workers, buying materials, borrowing money, and selling the output. But the owners have the final say in everything, and it is their objective (usually assumed to be making as much money as possible) that guides the actions of everybody else. This picture may be a useful one for lawyers, but for Christian economists it is not adequate. A firm is a kind of community—a group of people working together with a common purpose. If all of the members of the community are to be sufficiently committed to this purpose, it can not be simply the interest of one of the constituent groups that is to be served. The purpose has to be one that all of the members can share. Since the firm is primarily an economic organization, its primary purpose must be an economic one. This economic purpose has to do with the calling of stewardship—the marshalling of the resources of creation to meet human needs.

Since firms are communities, each firm consists of a group of people with some organizational structure, with ties to other communities, and with its own set of inherited customs and traditions. No two firms are alike. The people involved have different backgrounds, personalities, and faith commitments. Although the structures are based on legal conventions, there is a great deal of latitude for each firm to determine its own structure. Ties with outsiders take a variety of forms. And, of course, each firm has its own history. In the presence of so many variables, it should come as no surprise that firms differ in their behavior from each other and over time, and differ in the quality of their commitments to the stewardship norm. Therefore, we cannot expect a theory that attributes to each firm the same motivation to do very well in explaining firm behavior, or to do very well in discovering the consequences of poor stewardship.

The arena in which firms operate, the marketplace, is often characterized as a competitive environment. Workers, firms, consumers, and lenders compete with each other, and this striving is thought to enhance performance. Hence, the more competition, the better. But communities can not long exist where competition rules all of the relationships amongst the members. Constant, unremitting, unbounded competition leads to envy, jealousy, mistrust, and stress. It may provide incentive to perform to a higher standard, but it also provides incentive to undermine a competitor's efforts. These negative consequences of competition lead many economic agents to try to avoid the competitive struggle, either by enhancing their own power and control over the situation, or by establishing relationships of covenant and trust. The power solution leads to exploitation; the trust solution leads to good stewardship. We do not expect unbridled competition to exist in most economies, nor do we think it healthy that it should exist. But we do not favor the accrual of economic power by large organizations, either.

The received wisdom in the discipline of economics tends to ignore any differences in firms' personalities and faith commitments. The paradigm case with which most textbooks begin is perfect competition. Each firm is assumed to be so small that it has no control over the price or specification of the product (and how prices are determined is a big problem for this model). The unhindered entry of new firms into the industry at the first sign of profits guarantees that in the long run every firm will just barely break even. In other words, if the firm doesn't maximize profits, it doesn't survive. The outcome of this process is the efficient or Pareto-optimal allocation of resources in the economy.

No economist would ever claim that the model of perfect competition is a completely accurate representation of how the economy works. But most of the arguments between conservatives and liberals over economic issues (especially about the regulation of business) come down to arguments about how closely the real world resembles this fable. There are a number of good reasons for believing (as we do) that firms very rarely behave the way they are depicted in the model. Firms can pursue a whole host of objectives besides profit maximization such as large size, growth, prestige, political and cultural influence, and stewardship. United Technologies does not advertise on television in order to sell helicopters to average Americans; rather, it has prestige to garner, and an ideology to promote. *Playboy* magazine does not exist wholly to make Hugh Hefner rich, but also to promote his peculiar view of male-female relationships.

ITT does not make products as diverse as telephones and bread because there is some relationship in their production and distribution, but because it is exciting, challenging, and prestigious to be involved in managing such a huge company. The traditional theory misses some important aspects of reality. One of those aspects is the limitations on competition that arise from social control over its destructive side. Most firms have more power over prices and products than the theory allows, either because they are large and have few competitors, or because their products are distinctive in some way, or because there exists some loyalty between the firm and its customers. In many cases, the investors who stand to gain from a firm's higher profits are far removed from the actual management of the company. This means either that the managers will follow their own interests and objectives, or they will respond to pressures from many groups other than the stockholders—groups that may be closer socially to the managers, such as the firm's workers, its consumers, the government, and various segments of the general public. Furthermore, the amount and kinds of information that are presumed in the received theory may not be available easily to the managers, so that they end up making decisions by trial and error or rules of thumb rather than by careful calculation.

Why, then, does the economics profession cling so stubbornly to the model of perfect competition? First, the assumption that all firms operate from the same values and motivations simplifies the analysis and gives precision to the results. A more complex approach, such as the one we are proposing, has the advantage of greater realism and richness, but the disadvantage of yielding less determinate results. On methodological grounds, economists' commitment to positivism favors the competitive model. It is the simplest model that will give empirically plausible results about prices, and as long as simplicity and not realism is the test of assumptions, the usual model has the advantage. Finally, the profession's commitment to utilitarian values is reflected in the model's welfare results. Perfect competition leads to a Pareto-optimal or economically efficient allocation of resources. Since most economists accept efficiency as the moral standard or norm for economic outcomes, the model has particular relevance to economists who are seeking to direct policy choices along utilitarian lines.

Because of this orientation toward efficiency, many problems in the economic system that are directly or indirectly attributable to the behavior of firms are ignored. It is the choices that some firms have made about consumption goods that have helped to generate pollution, congestion, and aesthetic blight, have fed our selfishness and materialism, and made the survival of the poor difficult. Some firms' decisions about production have helped lead to the depletion of resources and the waste of human talent through unemployment. Firms' decisions about prices transmit inflation. And the arm's-length style of firms in dealing with their constituencies has led to the breakdown of community in modern industrial societies. We cannot lay these problems at the feet of government and expect that, in the style of received economic theory, a benevolent efficiency-maximizing bureaucracy will deftly step in to solve them. Government is a limited social institution, not an economists' *deus ex machina*. Nor will these problems disappear if we simply ignore them, as a superficial understanding of economics has led some to believe. We must ask how firms, acting on Christian principles, can alleviate these social ills.

Christian business people often claim that if they try to act on their principles in a fallen world they will suffer a competitive disadvantage relative to their less responsible rivals. Thus they feel constrained by the market to pay attention to profits and nothing else. But this view is based on acceptance of the picture of reality painted by the perfect competition model. If that model is not true to the facts, as we have suggested, there should be room for reponsible Christian behavior by firms. If a firm does have some market power, and if its managers have some discretion, responsible behavior can be undertaken without reducing the stockholders' returns to the point where they will wish to liquidate the company. Indeed, the stockholders themselves may be willing to sacrifice some profits for the sake of responsible behavior. Consumer groups (like Nader's Project GM), churches (the Interfaith Center for Corporate Responsibility), and unions, in their roles as stockholders or groups of stockholders, have pressed for responsible behavior by firms. And if all firms are to some degree sensitive to the demands of the general public, then none will suffer by undertaking behavior that is favored by a social consensus. Such behavior might include, e.g., honoring implied warranties. We conclude that there is indeed room for Christians to behave Christianly without being driven out of business.

## The Firm and Its Constituencies

There are three basic roles people may have within the firm: investors, workers, and managers. A Christian theory of the firm must examine the way in which managers coordinate the efforts of the workers and investors, and handle the firm's relationships with customers, suppliers, and the general public.

### Managers

First we must ask: how do managers generally view their own role? Many of them feel that their authority within the firm stems from their technical expertise, either in scientific or engineering fields, or in the more newly established disciplines of finance, marketing, or management. Together with their access to information, they believe that this expertise puts them in the best position to make decisions, and that therefore these decisions should not be questioned by those, inside the firm or out, who are not in the know. They wish to relegate the members of the other constituencies, even the stockholders, to a passive role in the enterprise. Their attitude is: if you don't like my decisions, do your business with somebody else. When the other constituents take a more active role, demanding some way in decision-making, the managers become quite perplexed. The managers may feel particularly beleaguered if they perceive conflicts between the demands of different constituencies. The government may want more employment and less pollution, the stockholders will wish for high dividends and high growth, consumers expect more service and greater safety, the workers want security and high wages. Often there seems to be little room for the managers' own objectives, such as prestige or technological challenge or company-paid perquisites. It is no wonder that prominent business people often give speeches decrying the public's "anti-business attitude" and asking others to get off their backs.

The situation can be quite different if managers see themselves as stewards—servants of God and of others. Then management becomes the task of bringing together all of these various groups in the common job of serving each other while preserving the creation. If this task is to be performed properly, the relationships among the several constituencies can not be restricted to the impersonal, arm's-length channels of the market. Market prices can convey certain kinds of information quite well, but other kinds of information are also needed if responsible stewardship is to be exercised. Economists often assume that this other information (the contents of which are unspecified) is automatically available. But if the relationships among the constituencies are not properly managed, information will not be sufficient.

Managers' frequent preoccupation with size often stems from the neglect of proper stewardship. Large size often means security and stability for managers, but it brings real problems. As Christians, we know how vulnerable all people are to temptation, and having a great deal of power offers many serious temptations to most people. One such temptation is the opportunity monopolists have to restrict output and raise price, a problem that traditional economic theory treats at great length. But there are other temptations that come with size which are not necessarily related to power or concentration in particular markets. These include power to buy media time to influence the public, power over political decisions, power to make or break geographical regions or communities, power over the direction of investment and innovation, power over many peoples' lives and careers, and power over the activities of voluntary organizations. Most of these forms of power stem simply from the ability of a few people in a single organization to direct a great amount of money in one direction rather than another. If we can reduce the temptations for misuse of these powers by limiting the size of firms, the economy and the whole society will probably function better. Of course, many of the same kinds of considerations apply to governments, labor unions, and voluntary organizations as well. We take those up later.

### Consumers

The first goal of any firm must be to serve the needs of its customers and potential customers. If the firm is not turning out a product that someone finds useful, then what point is there to its activity? The managers thus must start by putting themselves in the customers' place. As a responsible consumer, what products do I need to live my life well, to fulfill my calling before God? What information about the product do I need to make a responsible decision about buying it? What price should I consider to be fair, or how much can I afford to spend fulfilling a particular need? Answering these questions should lead the managers in the direction of products that are truly useful, well-designed, durable, safe, and easy to use. It should also lead in the direction of providing advertising and documentation for the product that relate to its usefulness and the possibilities for saving resources by its use. It is too easy for the firm to shape consumer tastes by advertising and then claim that the resulting demand validates their decisions. But it is not enough to simply imagine what consumers need; the firm must also listen to consumers. If the firm is committed to making the product work, it must find out from consumers what doesn't work, and what new products or modifications to old products would be useful. This concern means talking to consumers at the point of sales and service, responding thoughtfully to their letters, and doing research into what gaps consumers find in the products that are offered to them.

This effort implies a commitment on the part of consumers also. They, too, must want to make the product work. They must follow the instructions that the firm provides, and not try to make the product do things that it wasn't intended to do. It means not indulging in useless or irresponsible consumption activity. Valid complaints or concerns must be taken to the firm with the expectation of some response. We are taught as Christians that if we have a complaint against a neighbor, we should take it to him or her first, not to some court or government agency, and not keeping it to ourselves and sulking about it. The people we buy goods from are our neighbors, too.

Unfortunately, the more common model of consumer-firm relations has the managers asking instead: What product can I somehow convince enough people to buy at a high enough price to make a profit? This approach leads to products that appeal to our vanity or our insecurity, to advertising that is mere puffery, and to the abandonment of the consumer once a sale has taken place. Consumers then become disgruntled, because the happiness they have been offered by an intentionally seductive marketing strategy is not to be found in mere goods. They then become distrustful of the whole business community, and the call goes up for tougher government regulation, and product-liability suits and malpractice cases multiply. What is perhaps even worse, our resources are depleted and our environment is choked with goods that offer no real help to us. Some firms are coming to realize the problems that this model causes, and if pressed, will respond to individual consumer problems. We often will then "reward" them by accusing them of not revealing an "implied warranty". Firms become so panicked about making money that they feel constrained to follow this hedonistic model. We need not fear that useful, well-designed products and good service will be money-losers.

### Investors

A responsible investor puts his or her money into a firm because he or she believes in what the firm is doing. This puts some obligations on the managers of the firm. The first, of course, is to be honest and forthcoming about precisely what it is that the firm is doing. Governmental disclosure requirements go part way toward meeting this requirement, but bare financial data is not enough. The question is: What is being done to make life better (or worse) for all of us? Is our capital being used in a stewardly way? A second obligation is not to use the investors' money for purposes that the investors did not envision. The best way for investors to exercise stewardship over their own resources is for them to know and consciously decide what activities they want to support, and then find firms that are doing those things and only those things. This attempt to manage resources wisely will be frustrated if the firms are very large bundles of only remotely similar pursuits. Finally, the firm has an obligation to preserve the investors' capital and offer a fair rate of return. However, this need not imply the goal of profit-maximization; as long as perfect competition does not rule in practice, a fair return can be offered even though it is less than the maximum obtainable.

What should be considered a fair return for the investors? Of course, we expect that the rate offered will include some compensation for the expected rate of inflation over the life of the loan. Otherwise, the firm would simply be appropriating the investors' capital indirectly, by repaying it in depreciated units. There should also be some reward to the investors for the risk they undertake, which will vary according to the legal form of the investment, and according to the inherent riskiness of the enterprise. (We will have some remarks later about similar rewards for undertaking risk that should be offered to workers as well). Again, a failure to provide some payment for risk will result in the appropriation by the firm of investors' capital, since some risky enterprises will, no doubt, fail and default on their obligations to investors. Some real return beyond risk and inflation is also called for. Most investors could, no doubt, find some productive use for their savings if it were not loaned out to the firm, even if that productive use simply involved giving the money away to some worthy charity. The real rate of return should thus reflect the opportunity costs of alternative productive uses of the capital. This real return would probably not be very large, however. Productive investment should not be thought of as the alternative to an opulent lifestyle, or as a means of providing a high degree of financial security for the future. Our security is supposed to come from God. If the level of real interest rates reflects a highly present-oriented, consumption-oriented, security-oriented style of living, it is not a proper response to the call for stewardship. We will have more to say about the proper level of interest rates later in this chapter.

The investors clearly have some obligations, too. If investors have any kind of commitment to the firm at all, they will stick with it for some length of time and not sell out just because of some temporary setback. The workers, managers, and customers thus should have some assurance that they are not going to be abandoned by the investors whose stake in the firm is more mobile than the others. This expectation includes the assurance that a good part of the firm's accounting profits will be reinvested in the business to provide for maintenance and normal growth, strategies which justify the stockholders' open-ended claim. Investors also have some obligation not to speculate in investments that do not contribute to the economic health of the community. Putting a lot of money into gold bars or rare stamps may look like a good inflation hedge in a modern economy, but it does not provide jobs, increase productivity, open up opportunities for consumers, or save resources. Responsible investors avoid such speculation.

This picture once again contrasts with the usual view of a firm's relationship with its investors. If the firm is held to be only a vehicle for the investors to make money, it has no obligation to restrict its activities in any way. Anything goes, as long as it is profitable. Since only financial data are relevant to the investors' interests, the firm can be fairly secretive about its more sensitive activities. This secrecy can lead to strained relations between investors and managers, and recourse to the media and the courts becomes more common.

But our view poses some problems for a dynamic economy, which we must now address. Circumstances change: New products are developed and old ones become obsolete. How is the firm to cope with a changing environment, if it feels constrained to remain within its traditional field? If we insist that a firm liquidate when its traditional product becomes obsolete, the economy will face huge costs in transferring the firm's resources to other firms with other products. This task is accomplished with less social cost if it is managed within the firm. The company continues as an entity, with much the same personnel and plant, but switches over to producing another good, related to the old one by production and marketing technique, but not obsolete. As an example, take the old meat packer, Swift & Co. As Swift's traditional business declined, the managers of the firm decided to preserve their organization by acquiring other firms in fields only loosely related by the concept of "consumer products." Though this preserved the top managers' jobs, it turned the rest of the organization upside-down, and the investors in "Esmark" had little idea what they were buying when they purchased the company's securities. The eventual failure of this strategy led to the dismemberment and sale of the company. A more desirable strategy would have been for the firm to modernize its meat-packing facilities to try to compete in the new environment; if then the investors wanted to get out of that business, they could sell their stock.

What about new ventures? At some level it seems hopeless to expect that the entrepreneur with a new idea will be able to raise the funds he needs unless he or she is part of the development arm of some large, well-established firm. Isn't research most efficiently conducted in a large laboratory anyway, and aren't investors wary of small, new, unknown firms? The evidence on the organizational basis of technological change is mixed, but much of it suggests that most important technical change comes from small organizations. [Scherer 1980, ch. 15] Think, for example, of the electronic business. The break-throughs in hand-held calculators and microprocessors came not from the big established electronics firms like RCA and GE, but from new small firms like Texas Instruments and Hewlett-Packard. However, it is still important for basic research to be subsidized by government, because fundamental discoveries hardly ever come from strictly private research, and because such basic discoveries benefit us all. It is also important for the investment community to constantly be on the lookout for the new small innovative company.

Our view of the investor stewardship places a great deal of responsibility on the individual investor. Most people do not have or do not take the time to actively participate in the management of their own assets. More and more of us rely on institutions like mutual funds, pension funds, insurance companies, and banks to manage our financial wealth for us. How can we be effective stewards under these circumstances? Most institutional investors have some kind of philosophy behind their actions. For some of them, the so-called "index funds," it is the notion that you will do best by just duplicating the market portfolio and the market performance. This is a completely passive strategy, one based on a positivist theory of how financial markets work. Most funds actively seek companies that they believe will perform well financially. In some cases this performance will be based on financial gimmicks, like pyramiding conglomerate growth, but most fund managers look for companies that have solid products with a good market outlook. A lot of these will be the kinds of responsible firms that a Christian investor should be interested in. In fact, many investment managers will avoid firms with a record of socially irresponsible behavior on the ground that the firm will eventually get into some kind of legal or public-relations trouble that will prove costly. Nestle, target of a boycott for many years, had so much bad publicity that it could hardly have been considered a good investment by most portfolio managers. In short, the idea is for the stewardly investor to find a fund that comes as close as possible to sharing his or her philosophy of responsible use of money. Since this kind of information may be hard to obtain, investors must become skilled at asking the right questions.

**The General Public**

The general public has an interest in the firm's behavior. [Ackerman 1975] Most kinds of consumption good have some kinds of "external effects"; what products we use and how we use them shape the quality of life for all of us. Just think, for example, of the contrast between older European or northeastern American cities built around public transportation and the newer cities and suburbs based on the automobile. Social decisions about the quality of life and the quality of the environment must be respected by firms, not sabotaged. Once we have come to some kind of collective decision about how much pollution we are willing to tolerate, or how much hazard, or how much crowding, or how much visual blight, the private business sector should implement these decisions. Of course, business firms should also have a role in the discussion about the costs and benefits associated with these social decisions. In the last few years, firms have become less reluctant to enter these discussions, but too often they take their role to be simply explaining the costs of social policies, not carrying on a dialogue with the other parties to the decision. Once again, this short-sightedness can lead to bad feelings and antagonism on both sides, and ultimately to bad policy decisions as well.

The firm may have particular trouble hearing the voices of the poor or voices raised on their behalf. The business sector can easily ignore those who do not have much money or political power, since they will not be perceived as either potential customers or as political adversaries. But true stewardship also involves caring for the poor, so firms must try to take account of the impact of their decisions on poor people. This concern means opening channels of communication between the firm and the poor. Moreover, concern for the poor is as important overseas as it is at home, perhaps more important if the firm has operations in a country where most of the people are poor. Most of the criticism directed at multinational corporations (such as Nestle) is based on the perception that they do not care sufficiently for the poor. If business is to be perceived more favorably by the general public, firms must take more account of the needs of the poor.

The relationships of the firm with its workers are important enough and complicated enough to warrant an entire succeeding chapter.

In summary, the relationships amongst the various constituencies of the firm are not adequately captured by the conventional economist's picture of relationships in a market. These relationships involve more than the specific, limited commitment represented by a contract for a certain quantity at a certain price. They are open-ended, multidimensional commitments, not easily specified in a once-for-all written document. Keeping these commitments alive and strong requires exchanges of information and viewpoints that must take place outside the ordinary exchanges of goods and money. Failure to maintain these commitments can lead to serious social problems such as resource waste, congestion, a hazardous environment, destitution of the poor, and aesthetic blight. What is worse, they can lead to a breakdown of social cooperation and trust, which is very costly to a complex modern economy.

## The Choices the Firm Must Make

### Choice of Product

The first choice any firm must make is to decide what it is going to produce. We have already suggested that the firm must listen to consumers' expressions of need and put itself in the place of its customers when making these decisions. Now we would like to discuss some more objective principles that firms should consider. We do not mean to suggest that these principles should have the status of law or doctrine. Nor do we think that the government should outlaw the production of everything that does not meet these standards, or that the churches should discipline business people who do not follow these principles. (However, we would not advocate repeal of the laws against such things as hazardous drugs or pornography, which are an anomaly in conventional economics anyway). We only mean to say that there are some principles that responsible business people should follow, and that it is important to have a community-wide discussion about the content of those principles.

Responsible firms should avoid products that appeal mainly to consumers' vanity or insecurity, their desire for status, or their desire to be fashionable. Single-purpose appliances, designer clothing, and gold-plated automobiles do not serve any real needs, and hence merely waste resources. Consumers only try to use these products to establish a sense of identity or to give some particular meaning to an otherwise humdrum existence. But Christianity teaches us that the meaning of life and the identity of persons is not to be found in mere goods. Trying to prove otherwise will only heighten the sense of alienation and anomie that is epidemic in modern societies. This principle does not mean, however, that all aesthetic considerations are out of place in designing products. The trend toward tasteful but classic designs in clothing reflects a growing awareness that mere fashion is unnecessary, meaningless, and wasteful. Firms must be sensitive to the role their own advertising plays in shaping consumers' perceptions of their own needs. This increases firms' responsibility for choosing carefully the things they produce.

But this does not mean that the same products will serve all consumers equally well. For instance, the transportation needs of a family of five are different from those of a single-person household. The range of products that is provided should acknowlege differences in consumers' circumstances, callings, and, to some extent, tastes. Life is no doubt boring and drab in a society where everybody wears grey Mao suits or listens to the same rock music. Things need not be expensive to be beautiful and interesting. The needs of low-income households are the ones most likely to be ignored. Firms often seem to be very reluctant to provide, say, cheap but adequate housing or inexpensive transportation. The poor are stuck with unsafe or unhealthy, dilapidated, hand-me-down houses and cars, when they would be better served by new, no-frills apartments and public transportation. The worst cases come from the Third World, where American firms try to sell soft drinks and chewing gum to people who have trouble finding enough food to stay healthy.

Sometimes consumers practice false economy. The cheapest product to buy is not always the cheapest in the long run. A house with inadequate insulation is less expensive in the beginning, but is no bargain over a longer period. Firms should offer consumers product technologies that minimize life-cycle costs, taking into account a rather long time horizon (we will say more about discounting the future later). The main pitfall here is to neglect the cost of repair or replacement of a defective product. Consumers are often frustrated by goods that are so complicated that repair is expensive or impossible. This problem is the source of much criticism of the role of technology in modern life.

Firms should also consider the ramifications of the use of their products, the effects that economists call "consumption externalities." These are so pervasive that real imagination is required to discover them. Some easy examples of products with negative consequences in use are those ubiquitous, invasive, portable stereos, or loud, destructive snowmobiles. The automobile is guilty, too, for those vast stretches of concrete and neon it has produced in our cities, making the environment ugly and the pedestrian and bicyclist extinct. Such problems are not always avoidable and require sensitivity on the part of consumers as well as firms to control. But they must surely be considered when a product is to be designed and introduced.

### Choice of Technique

So far in this chapter we have been discussing problems that economists very rarely address. We now turn to issues that are a more common part of the literature of economics. For that reason, we will have less to say that is entirely novel. Nevertheless, we believe that a Christian perspective offers some additional insights into the choice of a production technology and price and output levels.

Traditional economics assumes that firms choose a production technology by minimizing the private pecuniary cost of the desired output level. They do this, the story goes, because they want to maximize their profits. We hold that there are alternative reasons for minimizing costs, reasons which comport better with the notion that at least some firms behave responsibly. If the firm is indeed concerned about preserving the creation for its own sake, about protecting the poor, and about providing for the future of the human race, its aim will be to produce its goods with the minimum total use of resources. To a first approximation, prices provide a guide to how scarce certain resources are, and therefore how much effort should be made to conserve each particular resource. Minimizing pecuniary production costs therefore is a good starting point for the firm that is concerned about saving resources. It is only a starting point, however, because the firm can and should attempt to compensate for some systematic biases in the way certain resources are treated in the marketplace.

The interest rate is the price we put on the future. The higher the interest rates, the less value we place on economic goods that are saved now in order to be available at some time in the future. If we are very future-oriented we will save a lot, and interest rates will tend to be low. But we human beings, though we are eternal, tend to be impatient. Our vision of the future is finite, the uncertainty connected with our own deaths haunts us, and our empathy for coming generations is bounded by our own selfishness. God is not subject to these limitations, of course, and that may be one of the reasons that He forbids usury. So we expect that market interest will be too high to promote real stewardship.

One of the costs of high interest rates is the squandering of natural resources. The higher interest rates are, the more natural resource prices must increase in the future to justify not using them now. Present resource prices will tend to be depressed relative to their future levels. Besides, if we have real care for the earth as God's creation, we will want to protect it for its own sake. So real stewardship calls for economizing on natural resources more than their current prices would indicate.

A lower rate of time discount also requires a higher utilization of real capital—things like machinery and buildings. Many sensitive Christians have called for a less capital-intensive production technology, which seems to contradict this idea of being more future-oriented. In part, this concern stems from a perception that in our economy, higher use of capital has historically been connected with higher use of natural resources. This concern is based partly on the picture of the modern assembly line where workers often become the servants of the machines they work with. Also, the perception exists that greater use of capital displaces needed productive employment for people. So, if we are to urge more intensive use of capital, we must be careful about what kind of capital we are discussing. Capital can, in fact, be used to save natural resources. The best example is the use of insulation to conserve fossil fuel. Again, computers use very little in natural resources and allow people to be much more productive. While they can depersonalize economic relationships and can lead to privacy and security problems, computers can also free workers from tedious and routine tasks, giving the workers more time to think about what they are doing. There is some truth to the old IBM advertising slogan: "Machines should work; people should think." So we do need more capital, but of the right kinds.

Though education and research are not treated as capital for tax purposes, the interest rate has some influence on expenditures in these categories. Knowledge tends to be long-lived, increases productivity, and can be used to save resources and make work more fulfilling. These kinds of investment are also well-suited to smaller organizations. Lower rates of time discount will help to encourage these activities, but some government subsidy is also appropriate, because of the public nature of most knowledge and cultural activity.

The considerations that apply to natural resources also apply to the quality of the physical environment. In addition, insults to the environment often carry no price at all, and the total amount of pollution is relevant to the quality of life of all who live in its shadow. Because of these public-goods aspects, concern for the environment tends to be focused on government. Although the government does have a legitimate role in environmental protection, the number and kinds of possible environmental degradation make it impossible for the state to bear the entire responsibility. Nor should the state bear the entire burden, since it is the firms which are ultimately confronted with the decisions that cause pollution or prevent it, both in product design and production technique. The economic costs of pollution in increased health care and aesthetic maintenance have become so substantial that they cannot be ignored. As a matter of both stewardship and justice, firms may not just dump these costs on to others.

The presence of unemployment indicates that the wage rate does not function adequately as an allocator of labor time. The economic and psychological costs of unemployment are fearsome, ranging from welfare benefits to crime, malnutrition, and disease; and these costs fall either on those who can least afford them or on the society as a whole. The government bears much of the responsibility for dealing with unemployment, particularly when it is caused by macroeconomic factors or by government-mandated institutional rigidities such as minimum wages. But firms have a great deal of discretion about how much labor they will use and how they will use it. Employers tend to extract as much work as possible from as few people as possible because of the fixed costs of adding someone to the payroll. Since this makes wider sharing of the workload impossible, it is therefore undesirable. On the other hand, most firms strive for some stability in their employment patterns, not laying off or adding as many workers as would be called for by fluctuations in the volume of business. This policy increases the stability of the economy and the predictability of people's lives. Firms should always remember that the wage rate does not necessarily reflect the scarcity of labor. A better guide is the principle that both idleness and make-work are evil, so that preventing either is a good work. We will have more to say about these issues later in the book.

Since firms acting both responsibly and irresponsibly will be interested to differing degrees in minimizing production costs, we can expect that factor demand curves will indeed slope downward (a lower relative price results in higher utilization of the factor), as the conventional theory predicts. But since considerations other than price will also hold some importance for responsible firms, factor demand may be less price-elastic (less responsive to price changes) than is suggested or assumed by received theory. Since the responsible firm will focus on goods that are real necessities or that at least serve real needs for responsible consumers, the price-elasticity and especially the income-elasticity of demand will be lower than conventional theory suggests, and these facts will be reflected in the elasticities of the factor-demand functions. As a whole, we expect that the economy is less sensitive to price changes than the neoclassical faith allows. For that reason, neo-Keynesian general equilibrium theories have some appeal to us. We would not hold, as the neo-Keynesians do, that there are hardly any real possibilities for substitution of factors in the production process, but we would hold that adjustment to equilibrium is more likely to come through quantities than through prices. [Eichner 1979]

## Prices

Prices have two functions to fulfill in a properly working economy. The price has to provide the firm with the wherewithal to cover its costs, and it should provide to consumers some indication of the scarcity of the resources that the good represents. If prices do reflect scarcity, purchasers can exercise stewardship and minimize the resource demands of their lifestyles by minimizing their pecuniary costs. Since consumers do not have the facilities that firms do for processing non-price information, it is important that prices reflect scarcities accurately. Both of the functions of prices can be served if the firm sets its prices equal to long-run average costs. This is the same result that comes from long-run equilibrium in the competitive model, but we do not justify the result on the basis of technical economic efficiency, or the relationship of prices to marginal costs (which we have argued earlier is not a useful concept).

If firms are to follow this standard, they must forego the temptations presented by market power in both the short and the long-run, and the problems presented by short-run fluctuations in market-clearing prices. Short-run price fluctuations are justified in conventional theory as a way of making sure that the economic efficiency conditions always hold and that the market always clears. But efficiency in the short run seems meaningless if there are departures from standards of the cost recovery and true scarcity. These rapid price fluctuations also represent departures from equilibrium in the sense that we use the term—that is, the stability of family purchasing power, the stability of institutions, and the stability of long-term planning by all of the actors in the system. Such price flexibility can also result in increased inflation in a system where the actors strive for stability in their incomes, and where significant institutional inflexibility is present. If firms forego this kind of flexibility, the market will not clear at all times, and so there will be occasional need for non-price rationing, such as queuing, but if there are continuing, stable relationships between buyers and sellers, this informal control should not present great problems. In industrial economies, many markets function in this way.

If our picture of industrial markets is accurate, then the short-run supply-and-demand diagram of the textbooks is not a valid tool of analysis, since it assumes short-run price flexibility. In the long run, however, we do expect there to be upward-sloping industry supply curves to occur. The reason is the conventional one, that as an industry expands, the increasing scarcity of its specialized factors will be reflected in higher factor prices or greater technological demands in production, and thus in higher product prices. This is especially true if firms internalize real external costs of production, as responsible firms should. The long-run supply curve of the firm is not as close to the conventional picture. A firm that is concerned about stewardship will have the long-run objective of operating at a minimum average cost, and will welcome new firms into the industry when and if expansion is called for, so the firm's long run supply will not be a continuous curve. There is much evidence to suggest that the long-run average cost curves of most firms have a "flat bottom"—that is, an extended range of possible output levels at minimum average costs. [Scherer 1980, ch. 4] This is particularly true if firms forego the pecuniary economies of scale that result from monopsony power over suppliers. Firms thus have some choice about the size they wish to attain, even if they follow the long-run average cost pricing rule. As we remarked, bigness is a temptation because of the power and prestige it brings, but there is an opportunity for firms to opt for smallness, with the advantages of decentralization, flexibility, and more personalized style of operations that it offers. We are convinced that more firms should and will opt for smallness.

However, if firms do forego short-run price flexibility for the sake of introducing some stability into the system, the question arises of how signals will be conveyed to new potential entrants about which industries are in need of new capacity. Traditional theory has it that short-run profits attract new entry, and thus serve to allocate new resources efficiently among industries. Given the long lead time involved in getting new investment in place in an industrial economy, it seems unlikely that this process functions very well in practice. If new entrants responded only to existing price signals, expansion would come too little and too late. More likely, firms can and should (and probably do) respond to projections of demand and production quantities—in other words, to non-price information. Improving the quantity and quality of this kind of information is primarily the responsibility of the existing firms in the industry. Contemporary interest in some form of government-produced economic projections and plans, to be used for private planning purposes, is based on the failure of the private sector to provide this information and the dynamically inefficient economic response that results. The failure of productivity to grow in older industrial countries, and the inflationary pressures that result are evidence of this kind of failure.

Natural monopolies—that is, firms with monotonically downward-sloping average cost curves—present other problems. The regulators of these industries have usually opted for some form of long-run average cost pricing which does not present special problems to our theory. We think there is some place here for the use of the two-part tariff, where customers buy into the system with an initial payment to cover the fixed cost of their service, and further payments are based on variable costs. This system allows buyers of the service to make finer judgements about the scarcity of the resources they are using at any one time while preserving the cost-covering function of prices. Economists are discovering that fewer industries than we once thought fall into this category.

If prices are to reflect true, long-run resource scarcity, there will necessarily be some elements of economic rent in the system. Many sensitive Christians consider rent to be *prima facie* unjust, since it involves receiving an economic return without any work or any real investment (such as rents from land or natural resources). The response of traditional economics to the presence of rents is to suggest that justice in distribution will be served without any resulting inefficiency if the rent is taxed away and used to support programs that benefit the poor or the population generally. The same purpose is served if the rent-generating resource is appropriated by the government and managed the same way a profit-maximizing firm would. In practice, this is more difficult than the theory suggests, since the rent-generating resource is often inextricably bound to some form of real investment, such as the buildings on a piece of land or the work that goes into opening up a mine. In general, however, we side with the received wisdom on this issue, favoring some form of social appropriation of rents. Taxation of rents usually results in more just distribution of wealth and discourages unproductive speculation. As is often pointed out, there are not enough rents in a modern economy to support the government in the style to which we are accustomed, so the entire problem of public finance cannot be solved in this way. But we will have more to say about public finance in a later chapter.

## Structures for Promoting Responsible Behavior

So far we have been discussing the scope and content of the responsibilities of firms. It may seem to strain the readers' credulity to expect that we can rely simply on the goodwill of business people, even Christians, to accomplish all of these good things. Sometimes goodwill is enough, but many Christians, Americans especially, are instinctively suspicious of any agglomeration of power that can be used for good or ill depending on some private whim. We therefore proceed to consider ways of structuring business firms to make responsible behavior more likely. Each of the structural remedies we will examine has its own special problems; none is perfect. Nevertheless, we plunge ahead on the supposition that some moves in this direction are better than none at all.

Once again we must pause to make a contrast with the conventional view. Economists are not usually concerned with the internal organization of the firm. The check on abuses of economic power is supposed to be found in the external competitive environment to which the firm responds. As we remarked before, all firms, no matter how they are organized internally, are assumed to respond to this environment in the same way. Even the new economic theories of the internal operations of firms are more concerned about simple waste of the firm's resources than they are about alternative responses to the mandates of stewardship. We claim that the internal structure of the firm can make a difference in how the firm responds to its social environment, not just in how technically efficient its operations are.

We begin our discussion with ordinary capitalist firms of the sort that are most familiar here in the U.S. Every firm has a board of directors who have formal responsibility for the operation of the business. Legally, they are responsible only to the stockholders; moreover, they are responsible only for seeing that the stockholders' capital is preserved and enhanced. In practice, the board of a large firm is usually a rubber stamp for the management—chosen by management, composed largely of management personnel, with management-provided information and a management-set agenda. Alternatively, the board could be considered to be a public body charged with supervising the operations of the firm in the interest of the general public or of all of the firm's constituencies. This would involve placing on the board representatives of all the constituencies and giving the board more power and more independence from management. To some extent, this would relieve management of the task of looking out for all of the constituencies' interests and instead, place that task on the board as a deliberative body. This practice would free the firm to follow more closely the principles we have laid out. The main disadvantages to this approach are that it would require most firms to change their charters, and it puts a heavy managerial burden on what is, after all, a committee. [Stone 1975]

A somewhat less cumbersome approach would involve changing the structure or composition of the management team itself. The task of keeping up relationships with various consitutuencies could be assigned to special offices within the firm, such as the increasingly popular role of ombudsman. Or the firm could set up a special department of social concerns to serve as a kind of institutional conscience for the firm. Sometimes affirmative action programs are seen as a way of introducing into the management structure new voices with new and different points of view on issues that the firm must face, so that various officials are conceived of as being representatives of a minority point of view or a women's point of view. There are also several problems with this approach. Ombudsmen can often become mere public-relations functionaries serving merely to defend the firm's actions against hostile attacks from outsiders. An office of social concerns may be shunted away from significant decision-making points in the firm, or top management may feel that they do not have to worry about social concerns, because somebody else is being paid to do that. The dangers of tokenism in dealing with minorities and women are well known.

The social audit is a technique for bringing the attention of the firm to the demands of stewardship. The firm establishes objectives with respect to various aspects of stewardship and then periodically measures its financial performance against its financial objectives. If the objectives are not being met, a plan can then be devised for improving performance. The drawbacks to the social audit are that the audit program is only as good as the objectives the firm originally sets, and the objects themselves must be in some way measurable. If the audit shows that the firm comes up short, improvements can only be made if somebody takes responsibility for that dimension, and if the plan that is devised is a sound one.

One response to the call for greater responsibility in business has been the institution of codes of conduct for corporate managers. Typically these codes address such matters as disclosure of information to customers and, particularly in the train of recent events, the solicitation through bribes of public officials. While codes have their uses in discouraging unethical conduct, they are by their nature negative. They usually do not put much stress on the positive duties and responsibilities of business people and the others they deal with.

There is a school of thought that goes back perhaps to Galbraith's *American Capitalism* [1952] that insists that the reason that managers tend to ignore consumers and the general public is that these more diffuse constituencies are not well enough organized. If only consumers and other citizens could form organized advocacy groups, firms would have to pay more attention to their interests. This kind of thinking has been behind the formation of many such groups since the early 1960's, and proposals (now dead) to establish a consumer advocacy agency within the federal government. Such groups serve a very useful purpose, but they also have their drawbacks. The stance usually taken by such groups is that of an adversary to business, and the tactics often involve confrontation. This approach tends to polarize the various participants in the process, and therefore does not usually lead to better decisions. [Nadel, 1971] The Christian spirit is one of cooperation with our neighbors, and the style of consumer groups often does not permit such a spirit to surround the process.

The Christian spirit of cooperation is better represented in the long-standing Catholic proposal to establish industry councils. [Bowen 1953 ch.14] Each industry in each geographic region would have such a council which would be composed of representatives of all of the relevant constituencies. The councils then would be responsible for overall economic planning for their respective industries. This structure resembles our proposal for representative boards of directors, except that it cuts across firms, and it usually presumes some sort of formalized government economic planning process. Because it involves planning and inter-firm cooperation, it probably can never be accepted in the United States. It also partakes of many of the same problems as the board of directors plan. Furthermore, it leads to the centralization of economic decision-making, which, in general, we do not favor.

It will occur to the reader that if we are not completely pleased with the structure and performance of the business sector, perhaps we should advocate a more radical alternative structure—one that does away with the capitalist firm as such. Why not socialism? Socialism—that is, the ownership and control of firms by the government—at least has the advantage that the managers are less likely to be solely preoccupied with the profit motive. If the political control over them is sensitively designed, they may also have good reason to be more responsive to the needs of all of the constituencies connected with the business. In practice, however, socialist firms in most countries do not seem to be all that much different from typical capitalist firms. The same variety of motives that influence managers of private firms seem to influence managers of public firms, too. The control structure that is set over the firm by the government often emphasizes performance measures that have no more to do with real social welfare than profits do. Furthermore, a socialist system serves to centralize economic power and decisionmaking even more than a capitalist system does, and involves the government in areas where it does not have any special competence or inherent responsibility. Centralization of authority offers the temptation to abuse power and can lead ultimately to a totalitarian society. Though we believe in democratic political institutions, we do not believe that politicians or voters are any less susceptible to the lures of power than the managers of private firms are. We think that the time of government officials would be better utilized in decisions that affect all of us directly and immediately, and thus belong properly to the government's sphere.

There are alternative forms of business organizations that do offer some promise, however. The collective or cooperative form of organization has been used in the U.S. for a long time, particularly in agricultural marketing and in retailing. [Lutz & Lux 1979] We think that this form of organization, which stresses a direct role for workers and consumers in the governance of the organization, has a great many advantages that justify wider adoption. Cooperatives offer meaningful opportunities for service to their workers and higher levels of satisfaction and lower prices to their customers than do many conventional firms. The drawback of the cooperative form is that it probably works best for small organizations, so it might have limited application in industries where economies of scale are such that the efficient size for the firm is quite large. However, smallness has its own advantages. Smaller firms tend to be more responsive and flexible; there is less need in a small organization to rely on rules and written procedures to insure uniformity and efficiency in the handling of relationships. Fewer decision-makers and shorter lines of communication mean that small-scale but important decisions are not neglected. Hence there is more scope for the kinds of open-ended commitments that we have advocated in this chapter. We will have more to say about cooperatives, advantages and disadvantages of size, and other alternative forms of internal organization in the next chapter.

If firms fail to live up to their responsibilities, the problems of industrial society will only get worse. It is this failure that has led to much of the suspicion of business that is characteristic of modern economies. This suspicion leads to increased demands for government intervention in the private business sector and the increased regulation and socialization of business that results. These trends are not to be applauded, for they result in increased concentration of power and the politicization of modern life that threatens to become totalitarian. But business cannot avoid these trends by indulging in anti-government rhetoric while it continues to act irresponsibly. The culprit in the story of increased political involvement in business is the business community itself, not government. Therefore, the continuance of free society depends on the willingness of business to accept a new model of its role that is based on the givens of the Christian faith. It is this kind of model that we have attempted to present.

## Resources

Ackerman, R. W. 1975. *The Social Challenge to Business.* Cambridge: Harvard University Press.

Bowen, H. R. 1953. *Social Responsibilities of the Businessman.* NY: Harper and Row.

Eichner, A., ed. 1979. *A Guide to Post-Keynesian Economics.* N.Y: Myron E. Sharpe.

Galbraith, J. K. 1951. *American Capitalism: The Concept of Countervailing Power.* Boston: Houghton Mifflin.

Lutz, M., and K. Lux. 1979. *The Challenge of a Humanistic Economics.* Menlo Park: Benjamin/Cummings.

McKie, J., ed. 1974. *Social Responsibility and the Business Predicament.* Washington: Brookings Institution.

Nadel, M. V. 1971. *The Politics of Consumer Protection.* NY: Bobbs-Merrill.

Scherer, F. M. 1980. *Industrial Market Structure and Economic Performance* 2nd ed., Chicago: Rand-McNally.

Scitovsky, T. 1976. *The Joyless Economy.* NY: Oxford U. Press.

Silk, L., and D. Vogel. 1976. *Ethics and Profits.* NY: Simon and Schuster.

Simon, J. G., C. W. Powers, and J. P. Gunnemann. 1972. *The Ethical Investor.* New Haven: Yale U. Press

Steiner, G., and J. Steiner, eds. 1977. *Issues in Business and Society.* 2nd ed., NY: Random House.

Stone, C. D. 1975. *Where the Law Ends.* NY: Harper and Row.

# Chapter X
# Firms and Their Workers

*Now I just ramble round to see what I can see;*
*This wide, wicked world is a funny place to be.*
*The gambling man is rich, and the working man is poor,*
*And I ain't got no home in this world anymore.*
      Woody Guthrie (1961)

Current economic theories of the relationships between workers and firms ignore essential elements of these relationships, and thus fail to give adequate explanations, predictions, or evaluations of these relationships. The relationships are treated as relationships of things to things, "labor" (as an input into a production process, not as a person) in relation to other inputs and outputs. But labor cannot be separated from the persons performing that labor, and thus within a firm there are many important person to person relationships (e.g., relations with fellow workers and with customers and suppliers), and person to thing relationships (e.g., workers to machines and materials, to outputs, to the environment). Some of these personal relationships are considered in more institutional labor economic theories, but they are almost totally absent in the neoclassical approach, which has become more and more common in economic journal articles in the area of labor economics in recent decades [Ramsted, 1981] and which is the view represented in most textbooks. Since this neoclassical view of the relationships of workers and firms is held by most economists in North America today and is the basis for most of their attempts to explain, predict, and evaluate relationships in this area, we will turn to a brief examination and evaluation of this view. (Note: The term "worker" as used in this chapter refers to all who work in a firm, including managers, unless stated otherwise.)

## *The Neoclassical View*

### A Summary of the Neoclassical Theory

In this predominant neoclassical view, firms are seen as entities which are owned by some of the suppliers of capital to them (i.e., the stockholders sole proprietors, or partners). The owners' goal, and thus the goal of the firms, is assumed to be the maximization of profits. (Of course there are competing theories which view firms as maximizing something else, such as sales, perhaps subject to a profit constraint, or as not maximizing any one thing, but seeking to achieve satisfactory levels of performance with respect to multiple goals, but such theories are held by only a small minority of economists.)

Within this framework the relationship of workers to firms is seen simply as a transaction in which the workers sell a resource (their labor) to the enterprise for monetary (or similar) compensation. The enterprise is assumed to be simply buying an input to their production process (just as they may buy machines, energy, and raw materials). It is also assumed that having purchased the labor services of its employees, an enterprise has the sole right to determine how this labor is used. The workers are assumed to be simply trading some of their leisure (which they are assumed to prefer to work) for income (which is desired in order that they can buy other desired things). It is assumed that firms will always attempt to pay as little as possible for work of a given quantity and quality; otherwise they would not be maximizing their profits. It is also assumed that the work itself has disutility for the workers. They wish to work only as a means to gain income (and the consumption that it makes possible), and thus will always attempt to gain the most income possible for a given amount of time and effort devoted to work. Any non-monetary aspects of the transaction between workers and firms are lumped into the category of "compensating differentials," which is left largely undefined. When these aspects are discussed it is generally in terms of fringe benefits or "consumption benefits" of particular jobs which the workers consider along with the monetary wages and disutility of work in making their maximizing decisions. The impact of the size of the firm on its workers' roles and relationships to it and the effects of different management structures (e.g., hierarchical and cooperative) are almost totally ignored except for occasional discussions of their effects on productivity. The employment relationships are generally analyzed with short-term, static models, dealing only with explicitly contractual relationships, ignoring the longer-term covenantal relationships that are, in fact, very important to both worker and enterprise.

On this basis, the wage (which is seen as the important variable to explain or predict) is said to be determined by the marginal productivity of labor (of a given type) at the equilibrium of supply and demand for it. The supply of labor is assumed to be determined by the individual workers' trade-offs between their self-perceived disutility of work and utility of income and their alternative opportunities. The demand for labor is assumed to be determined by the additional revenue the firms can receive from using an additional unit of labor and selling the increased output it makes possible—called the marginal revenue product of labor. This marginal productivity of labor (at any given level of employment) is determined by the other inputs the firm has, the relationships between the levels of inputs and outputs (i.e., the production function), and the demand for the final product. The wage is assumed to be equal to the marginal revenue product of the workers in equilibrium, because if it is not, the firm will not be maximizing its profits if there is perfect competition in the labor market, a condition which is commonly assumed, either implicitly or explicitly.

### An Evaluation of the Neoclassical Theory

Much economic behavior concerning the relationships of firms and their workers is in part consistent with neoclassical theory, but the theory fails to adequately explain or predict behavior in this area and is not an adequate basis for evaluating such behavior. It is true that there are many firms which are basically concerned with profits, and thus with how cheaply they can hire labor (of a given quality) and produce a product. Most firms are legally controlled by owners of capital or their representatives who withhold information and decision-making power from most employees. Many decisions on the size of firms and management styles or structures are basically motivated by considerations of productivity and profitability. Many workers do view work as having disutility and evaluate jobs mainly on the basis of "what's in it for me?" Firms and those working in them often do act as if they have no obligations to each other beyond whatever is stated in their contracts (e.g., some firms arbitrarily fire workers for minor violations of rules or close plants on short notice with no aid to workers; and some workers engage in "work to rules" slow-downs, or refuse concessions when their firms are in trouble). The fact that there is a correspondence between *some* economic behavior and neoclassical theory is not surprising, since the operative faith of many Americans includes the commitments to individualism and materialism which lie at the base of neoclassical economics, and neoclassical economics is to some extent empirical. In addition, generations of people, having been taught by neoclassical economists that this is how they do (and ought to) behave, may behave this way to a greater extent than they otherwise would.

But there is much economic behavior in this area that is neither analyzed nor predicted by neoclassical economics though some is analyzed by various more institutional labor economists. Its orientation towards "efficiency," and its corresponding neglect of significant aspects of worker/firm relationships that do not fit into its efficiency-oriented framework make it an inadequate tool for explanation, prediction, or evaluation in this area. For example, its conclusion that wages are equal to the marginal revenue product of labor does not comport well with the fact that such marginal revenue products are at best very difficult to measure. The conclusion that wages for work of a particular type (adjusted for compensating differentials) will be the same everywhere in a labor market (through the utility-maximizing behavior of workers) is not consistent with the fact that rates of pay for similar jobs vary considerably within a given labor market, and that "compensating differentials" as normally measured are often higher, rather than lower, at high-wage firms. This is not predicted by the neoclassical theory and can be "explained" by it only by a widespread lack of workers' knowledge of labor market conditions or, alternatively, by the assumption that there must be some unknown compensating differentials or differences in quality of labor between firms. Since, however, these can be used to "explain" anything, the theory then becomes a tautology. These are also the only "explanations" the neoclassical economists can give for the fact that many workers enter occupations where the earnings are well below the maximum they could earn for the time and effort they devote to their jobs.

In addition, the assumption that wage rates will vary to clear labor markets is contradicted by the existence of shortages of some types of workers for significant periods of time (i.e., firms would like to hire more such workers at the existing wage rates than are available), and by surpluses of workers in other fields for significant periods of time, leading to unemployment in them and often to bitter struggles for jobs in them. It is hard for the neoclassical theory to explain the intensity of workers' struggle over anti-discrimination legislation and regulations, since it would predict that lessening discrimination in a particular occupation would only lower the equilibrium wage of those now able to obtain jobs in it, while letting others who are presently excluded share in an increased number of jobs. In fact, the struggle is so strong because the legislation and regulations often influence who will obtain some of the relatively fixed number of preferred jobs in the society for which there are more workers than jobs available for considerable periods of time.

There is also evidence that traditional wage differentials between various jobs are maintained for long periods of time in spite of significant changes in the supply of and demand for various types of labor, and that salaries for corporate executives are often dependent more on the size of the firm (or the part of it under them) than its profitability. Neither of these facts comports well with the neoclassical theory.

These things make it clear that wage rates in many cases are influenced by things other than neoclassical supply and demand for labor. Such influences include tradition, goals of enterprises and workers other than profit-maximization and narrow self interest, discrimination, and the desire to maintain hierarchical structures in enterprises. To the extent that marginal productivity plays a role, it often determines only how many workers will be hired for particular jobs at wage rates determined largely by these other forces (with markets not clearing). And it may be that sometimes jobs will be designed and workers trained to reach the level of productivity desired by the firm given pre-determined wage rates. (Some streams of institutional labor economics do consider these things, but they have not been included in mainstream neoclassical economics. Contrast, for example, the treatment of labor markets in any standard price theory text [Nicholson, 1979] with that in a fairly institutional labor economics text [Reynolds, 1978], with the model in Lester Thurow's *Generating Inequality* [1975], or with the writings of the "dual labor market" theorists [Piore, 1979].)

Besides its inability to predict or explain much of wage behavior and imbalances in supply and demand in labor markets, the neoclassical theory misses the true meaning of work. The fact that many people desire work for reasons other than the income it gives is, of course, missed by a theory which considers work to have only disutility. But evidence such as the psychological problems many people suffer when losing work (even if much of their income is replaced by social insurance programs) and the increasing desire of women to work, and not only for monetary reasons, indicate that work is something positive in itself for many people.

Nor does the fact that many firms and workers feel obligations to each other beyond the obligations of their contracts, and act on these felt obligations, comport well with neoclassical theory. Yet we see such "covenantal" relations in the actual economy (e.g., firms sometimes voluntarily retrain and relocate workers whose jobs have been eliminated, and workers sometimes voluntarily make suggestions for lower cost methods of production, and sometimes voluntarily share work or accept pay reductions when their enterprise is in trouble). The differences between such behavior and strictly contractual behavior (which is often found also) is too significant to be ignored.

Furthermore, a theory of worker/firm relationships should not ignore the fact that there are large differences in management styles and structures between firms, and that changes to more cooperative types of management have often been found to give greater worker satisfaction and higher productivity, or that some firms are owned by workers rather than by absentee capital suppliers, and that this can affect worker satisfaction and productivity. Indeed, there have been significant worker reactions to the hierarchical control structures used in most enterprises in the United States including unionism and worker alienation attitudes leading to high absenteeism and industrial sabotage, among other things, but the neoclassical theory would not lead one to expect this resistance, nor can it provide a good explanation for it.

## A Theory From a Christian Point of View

### Basic Norms and Principles

A much more adequate theory to explain and evaluate relationships between workers and firms can be developed by basing the theory (including empirical investigations) on Christian norms and the principles derived from them, rather than on the false individualistic and materialistic norms of neoclassical economics. Chief among these norms is the fact that all people are stewards of all of "their" resources, including their labor. They are not absolute owners of their labor, but are responsible to God for the use of it. This moral responsibility for the use of their labor (and other resources) *cannot* be eliminated by signing a contract giving others the right to determine its use. Thus legal and economic structures should provide all people opportunities for exercising these stewardship responsibilities; they should not make it difficult for them to do so, but should encourage them to do so. God calls people to use their labor and other resources productively in such a way that all receive justice. Economically this means at least that all families should have access at all times to the necessities of life, all families should have the opportunity to develop and use their God-given labor resources (and a share of the other resources in society) to provide for themselves in a situation that gives opportunities for responsible stewardship, and that the economic opportunities for families and other institutions in society to fulfill their callings, now and in the future, should not be impaired.

Firms are institutions in which stewards of resources join in the productive use of their resources. (Of course, because of sin they may misuse them.) All suppliers of resources continue to have stewardship responsibilities for the use of their resources by the firms, and thus should have the opportunity to exercise responsible stewardship of their resources within the context of the firm. The firm, as a community of stewards, has the responsibility to be a good steward of the resources entrusted to it.

For workers this responsibility includes the diligent, conscientious performance of their duties and the development of loving relationships with their fellow-workers, including their supervisors and those whom they supervise. But their responsibility is not limited to these relationships; it extends to the totality of how their labor is used, including what is produced with it, for whom it is produced, how it is marketed, and how it is produced (including what other resources are used and what the effects of the production are on the environment). All workers in a firm (or, more appropriately, all members of the work-community which is the firm) have some degree of responsibility for the operation of the firm as a whole. There will be differentiation of roles within most firms, both with regard to level of management responsibility and area (e.g., finance, production, marketing). Such differentiation is legitimate and results in different workers having different degrees of stewardship responsibility for different decisions of the firm within the overall responsibility that all share. For example, it is legitimate to give some workers primary responsibility for decisions about what to produce, but other workers also retain stewardship responsibilites for what is produced with their labor. It would not be responsible for them to produce pornography, even if they did it diligently, just because someone else had made the decision that this was what the firm was to produce.

Other suppliers of resources to a firm also have stewardship responsibilities concerning the use of their resources by the firm, especially if they have a continuing relationship with the firm and if the suppliers retain title to the resource (e.g., as with stockholders). In general, this responsibility is greater for stockholders than for lenders of capital and greater for both than for sellers of physical resources (e.g., suppliers of raw materials), but it is not absent for any of them, and it might be quite significant for some suppliers of physical resources (e.g., in the case of a lessor of land).

In order that they may have the opportunity to make responsible stewardly decisions about the use of their resources in the firm, it is important that all suppliers of resources, and especially all workers, have access to full information about how their resources are or will be used by the firm in the broad sense indicated above. Thus they should have access to information regarding all aspects of the functioning of the firm.

But since it is often hard for workers to change employment relations without significant loss (e.g., loss of seniority and pension benefits or the necessity of starting at a lower-level entry position in another firm), and since sometimes leaving a firm would make it difficult to fulfill other responsibilities (e.g., to provide for one's family), it is desirable to go beyond providing information to providing broad decision-making roles for all workers in the firm. It is even more important to give workers such a decision-making role than it is to give this to investors, since workers' lives are more fully bound up with their firms, and they generally have less opportunity to freely change the use of their resources from one firm to another than investors do. And giving all workers a role in making decisions would be a reflection of the biblical ideal of giving each family opportunity for decision making in the productive use of its labor and a share of its society's other resources. This was reflected in the Mosaic economic legislation in which the status of "hired servant" without decision-making power was to be only a temporary status to enable a family in dire need to support itself until it could again become a decision-making producer at the next Year of Jubilee at the latest.

It is also important for members of a firm (workers and other major contributors of resources) to have common basic commitments regarding the goals and functioning of the firm. If they do not, some will be in the position of having their resources used in ways that violate their basic commitments, and it will be hard to establish and maintain the trust which is necessary for a well-functioning firm. Then covenantal relationships will tend to degenerate into purely contractual ones.

Regarding rates of remuneration, the Bible does not provide a formula that can be used to determine just should be what the proper rate of pay for every worker in a firm, but it does contain principles which are relevant to this question. Families should have the opportunity to support themselves from the use of their resources, at least in the long run. Thus, as long as most families are primarily dependent on their labor for their support, rates of pay should, if possible, be high enough to achieve this. In cases where it is not possible for a firm to pay all workers enough for them to adequately support their families, efforts should be made to make this possible, for example, by raising the productivity of the workers or by adjusting other costs, such as other rates of pay, or by adjusting revenues by changing output or pricing decisions.

The effort and time contributed to the enterprise by a worker is a legitimate concern when determining rates of pay, and account may be taken of the time, effort, and money needed to prepare for a position in determining the rate of pay for it. "Productivity" may at times legitimately play a role in determining rates of pay, but it is very difficult to determine, and in any case should not be used in such a way that some families would be unable to support themselves. And workers should not receive higher rates of pay than others just because their productivity is high, because they have had large sums invested in their education, or because they are working with large amounts of capital. Market values of labor elsewhere (the monetary opportunity costs for the workers to work in the firm) are not necessarily proper determinants of rates of pay within a firm. Although these values may have to be taken into account in order to fill some necessary positions, they should not be used to such an extent that some families cannot adequately support themselves.

Although efforts should be made to make jobs safe and pleasant, if danger is present in some or the demands of the job are such that they limit the length of time one can perform it, or if the job is unpleasant, these conditions may be taken into account in determining the rate of pay.

Although workers and their families should have opportunities for stewardship of their earnings, and thus not all payment should be "in kind," it is appropriate for the firm to provide some of the remuneration in kind when there are significant savings in doing so, and it is a basic good which it is desirable for most, if not all, families to have (e.g., providing medical care by means of group insurance).

Rates of pay for workers affect the rate of return that can be paid the suppliers of capital and the prices that are charged for products. These effects should be considered when rates of pay are set in order to avoid injustice. As part of a general reform of the structure of firms giving more opportunities for responsible decision-making to all employees, it might also be desirable to change the method of payment of workers and suppliers of capital, so that each worker receives a basic wage determined in line with the above considerations, and suppliers of capital receive a basic return, with both sharing in any surplus the firm has after meeting its other obligations or taking a reduction, if necessary, in hard times. This policy would give the firm more flexibility when faced with changes in costs or revenues, and might in many cases allow it to maintain employment when it otherwise might have to lay off workers. The part of the risk of the firm that is now borne by the workers as a risk of losing their jobs, a crisis which, if it comes, affects some completely and usually others not at all, would be changed to a risk of fluctuating income, and would be more evenly shared. Although it is not recognized by neoclassical economics, workers do share some of the risks facing their firms under present conditions, for not only are their jobs endangered if the firm is in trouble, but also rates of pay are often influenced, at least in the long run, by the firm's "ability to pay."

The manner of setting pay rates for various positions within a firm will depend on the nature and degree of commitments shared by the members of the firm or those who control it. For example, one would expect a firm where the members shared a Christian commitment to exercise a greater concern to see that the needs of the families of all its members were taken care of, and thus usually to have more equal rates of pay than firms in general where more emphasis would be placed on such things as monetary opportunity costs and presumed productivity.

Personnel policies within a firm should always reflect the fact that all workers are people made in the image of God and are thus entitled to be treated with dignity. They should never be treated in an arbitrary manner. They should have the right to be heard with respect to decisions which affect them. Their needs as well as the needs of the firm should be taken into account when decisions are made.

When deciding on production methods and making other decisions which have a bearing on employment, firms should try to provide continuing employment for their current workers, divide the work, or help find alternative employment for those who must be laid off when it is not possible to provide all their workers with full employment in a way that is consistent with the firm's other stewardship responsibilities. (Exceptions to this general principle could occur if a firm's employees have good alternative employment opportunities.) In addition, a major goal of firms should be the creation of stewardly employment opportunities for people who would otherwise lack the opportunity to employ and develop their labor in a manner consistent with good stewardship of it, thus enabling these workers to provide for their families in a responsible manner. This goal should be a major influence on the various decisions of the firm.

Workers should consider the effects on their firm when deciding whether or not to leave it. They should not leave it if their doing so would cause serious harm to the firm's ability to fulfill its legitimate goals, unless they could do significantly more good elsewhere. While they remain members of the firm they should use their abilities and opportunities to insure, as much as possible, that their labor and the other resources of the firm are used in a manner consistent with good stewardship.

**A Descriptive Theory Based on These Norms and Principles**

A theory of relationships between workers and firms based on such norms and principles can give a more adequate explanation or understanding, as well as a more adequate evaluation of these relationships, than can theories based on other principles, such as the neoclassical theory. Such a theory examines various types of organization of firms and management structures, policies, and actions, to determine to what extent they promote good stewardship of resources. Since the aspects of stewardship having to do with prices, products, and environmental effects have been discussed in Chapter IX, in this chapter we will examine the effects firm/worker relationships have on stewardship more directly through the treatment of persons within (or potentially within) the firm. As we have seen in Chapter V, God calls on those who have control of resources to use them to promote justice; firm/worker relationships have important influences on some of the basic aspects of justice in the Biblical sense, including:

1. The distribution of opportunities for families to earn income and obtain the necessities for life in the society at any given time.

2. The distribution of opportunities for the development and use of the labor resources of the workers in the firm and of those lacking such opportunities who are not presently within the firm.

3. The distribution of opportunities for responsible decision making regarding the use of labor and other resources in the firm and in the economy in general.

Thus we shall examine the effects of various types of firm/worker relationships on these issues. We should not forget, however, that the aspects of firms' stewardship discussed in Chapter IX are also important, and that firm/worker relationships should be such as to promote acceptance of stewardship responsibilities and responsible actions by workers for these concerns as well.

We will begin by examining a number of different structures of organization and management of firms, describing them in terms of the norms and principles discussed above, and then draw some general conclusions from this examination before evaluating these structures and policies.

*Firms Controlled by Owners of Capital, Hierarchically Managed, and Not Unionized*
The first type of firm to be examined is one which is owned and controlled by its proprietors or stockholders or their representatives, has a hierarchical management style, and has no union. This type of firm is very common in North America. In such a firm the vast majority of workers have very little opportunity to exercise responsible stewardship of their labor. They have virtually no role in the decision making of the firm, and in most cases they have little access to information necessary to exercise responsible stewardship in the broadest sense. They often do not have access to information about decisions regarding the design of the product, such as trade-offs made between safety and cost, or about the effects of the production on the environment, or on the overall pay structure of the firm. In many, if not most, firms of this type, pay and benefits between the highest and lowest paid workers vary greatly. This is especially true of large firms of this type which often have policies requiring that supervisors on any level have significantly higher rates of pay than those under them. But firms in this category vary a great deal in exercising justice in their particular personnel policies. For example, some have a more equitable wage structure than others, some have more internal opportunities for workers to develop their talents than others, some have carefully developed discipline procedures with penalties proportionate to violations and provisions for appeal. Other firms, however, have no constraints on the management's disciplinary powers and engage in arbitrary discipline. Some managers are more authoritarian, and others try to lead with more cooperative styles. Some try to share work during periods of slow demand or try to help workers find other jobs when they lay them off. Others show little concern for the plight of workers laid off and may even have rather arbitrary layoff policies. These firms also vary a great deal in the degree to which they are good stewards of their resources in the areas of design of products, pricing, and environmental effects. But, in general, the other workers have to rely on the management of the firm for whatever good stewardship there is in the internal or external relations of the firm. They have no role in determining policies and actions of the company in the personnel area or other areas, and often have little information about them.

*Firms Controlled by Owners of Capital, Hierarchically Managed, but Unionized*
The other type of firm organization and management that is common in North America is similar to the first one, but some of its workers are members of a union with bargaining rights regarding conditions of employment. This type will be discussed only briefly here, since it is in most respects similar to the first type, and the special role of unions will be discussed in Chapter XI. The presence of a union gives the unionized workers a somewhat greater role in the decision making of the firm, but the role is usually limited (in the United States, in any case) to a very narrow range of issues involving wages and working conditions a policy which excludes many of the decisions of the firm which have a major bearing on the stewardship of the workers' labor. And the hierarchical control/union structure tends to create decision making through adversary relationships rather than cooperative action, although the degree of strife and

cooperation varies a great deal between enterprises in this category. As in the non-union hierarchical firm, the policies affecting stewardship of labor vary a great deal between firms in this category.

*Firms Controlled by Owners of Capital, Cooperatively Managed*

A third type of firm found in North America (but less frequently than the above types) is the firm which is owned and controlled by the suppliers of capital or their representatives, but which has adopted a formal "cooperative" management plan. These firms may be either unionized or not. A prominent example of such a cooperative management plan is the Scanlon Plan. [Lesieur, 1958] This plan, developed originally by Joseph Scanlon, a Steelworkers Union official in a steel company having trouble surviving during the Great Depression, calls for production committees in each area of the firm with elected (nonmanagement) worker members and an appointed management member. These production committees meet regularly to discuss ways of improving the work in that area, including suggestions from workers, and any other matters affecting the work in that area. The suggestions that are approved by the committees are referred to the management for implementation (management can refuse them if they wish). There is also a company-wide or plant-wide Screening Committee generally composed of equal numbers of management and non-management employees. This committee goes over the performance and bonus figures for the last month, considers any important issues affecting the company and its work in coming months, and reviews the suggestions that have been discussed in the various production committees. A bonus is paid to all workers (including management) in proportion to their other earnings on the basis of a formula stated in an agreement setting up the plan. In the traditional Scanlon Plan, the bonus is based on any reduction in the ratio of payroll costs to total value of production below the ratio in some base period preceding the plan (the "norm"). The norm is adjusted from time to time to account for changes in variables such as wages, prices of inputs and outputs, product mix, and technology. Although the original Scanlon Plans were developed for use in unionized plants along with a regular collectively-bargained labor contract, they are currently being used in non-union firms as well. The Herman Miller Company, a major producer of office furnishings in Zeeland, Michigan, is a firm with a highly developed Scanlon Plan an arrangement in which the committees serve as effective two-way channels of communication between supervisors at various levels and those they supervise, and in which cooperative management styles and personal development of workers are encouraged. Most of its plants are not unionized.

In general, within "cooperatively-managed firms," whether they have a Scanlon Plan or some other variant, the basic decision-making power still rests with a small proportion of the workers in the firm (the managers), but information is more widely shared with the other workers, and their suggestions are actively sought. Thus the workers have a greater opportunity to obtain the information necessary to decide whether working in the enterprise is a good stewardship of their labor than do workers in the more predominant types of organization discussed above, and they have some opportunity to try to influence policies they disagree with. Often there is a bonus or profit-sharing plan covering all of the workers as well. Management styles tend to be more cooperative than authoritarian. But within this category of enterprises there are significant differences in the degree of information made available to all workers and in the particular policies followed in personnel, product choice, production methods, and other areas relevant to proper stewardship of labor and other resources. The attitudes of supervisors and other workers, as well as the structure of the organization, have been found to be important determinants of the results in such plans. It is hard to accomplish much if the supervisors at any level retain authoritarian attitudes, even if the structures provide for cooperation. The non-supervisory workers must have real opportunities to participate in the operation of the firm (beyond just "doing what they are told to do"), and must accept responsibilities for such participation if the change in structure is to make a significant difference in the operation of the firm. Changes to more participatory management styles and structures including Scanlon Plans have often been found to result in both greater worker satisfaction with their jobs and greater productivity for the firm. [Stokes, 1978, pp. 33-36; Blumberg, 1969, chapter 6]

*Firms With Workers as Stockholders*

A fourth category of enterprises includes corporations where the employees are the main or sole stockholders, but otherwise are similar to firms in one of the first three categories. Some firms in this category have resulted from employee purchases of firms which the owners were planning to shut down. Other firms are moving in this direction through Employee Stock Ownership Plans (ESOP's), in which employees' pension funds or other monies are invested in the stock of the corporation which is held in trust for them by an Employee Stock Ownership Trust. Significant tax benefits accrue to corporations setting up certain types of ESOP's in the United States. The experience under this type of organization is quite mixed. Sometimes the employee stockholders have gained a real role in the decision making of the firm, although even then the role is more proportionate to their capital holdings than to the labor they contribute, but at other times, especially with ESOP's, the workers gain little or no role in decision making, and there is little change in the personnel or other policies of the enterprise. The inflexibility of policies and the lack of real participation in decision making in some firms of this type have led to disillusionment of their workers. If the shares of the corporation are freely marketable by the workers, there is no assurance that ownership and whatever control it gives will remain with the workers, and it will be expensive for new employees to gain a voice in the decision making if they can do it only through purchase of stock. Under an ESOP it takes new employees a long time to acquire a significant voice in the operation of the firm, even if they have voting rights for the shares of the firm which are assigned to them. And if an ESOP is substituted for a normal pension plan, this plan may, in effect, provide the company with a new and less expensive source of capital, increase the workers' risks (because now their pension funds are invested primarily or exclusively in stock of the corporation which employs them rather than in diversified investments), and at the same time give them little or no more opportunity to participate in the decision making in their firm than before.

## Co-determination

A fifth type of firm structure is co-determination an arrangement in which representatives of workers and capital-suppliers share authority for decision making in the firm. This is highly developed on a national level in West Germany, and aspects of it are found in most other Western European countries as well. In West Germany every firm with more than five employees must have a "works council" elected by the workers. By law the works council has the right of co-determination with management on a wide range of issues regarding conditions of employment. If the management and works council cannot agree on an issue, it is usually referred to an arbitration panel. The areas in which works councils have co-determination rights include methods for determining pay rates, changes in working conditions (including technological changes), safety regulations, work schedules (including short-time and overtime work), shop rules, guidelines for personnel selection and vocational training, and plant welfare services. The works council cannot strike but may sue management for breaches of rights. In addition, the workers in many firms are unionized, and the unions and firms engage in collective bargaining on wage levels, often on an industry wide basis. In addition to these structures, giving workers a role in determining wages, benefits, and working conditions, the law in West Germany mandates worker representation on the supervisory boards of large companies The supervisory board of a German company is responsible for setting the long-term policy of the company; there is a management board responsible to it which administers the company on a day-to-day basis. The degree of representation of workers and the method of selecting the workers' representatives varies with the industry and size of the firm, but basically workers and stockholders in firms in the iron and steel industry have equal representation on the supervisory board. In firms with 2000 or more employees, the workers and stockholders have equal numbers of representatives, but one of the workers' representatives is elected by the managerial employees, and the chairman, who is one of the stockholders' representatives, receives an extra vote if this is necessary in order to end a deadlock. In firms with 500 to 1999 employees, workers have one-third of the representatives on the supervisory board and stockholders have two-thirds. This representation on the supervisory boards gives workers some indirect voice in the general decisions of the firm, as well as the more direct voice they have in personnel decisions through their works councils and unions. Although, as in other structures, the policies of the firms which are important to stewardship vary a great deal, there tends to be more concern for the employment opportunities of current workers, with more work sharing during periods of slow demand and fewer lay-offs and terminations than in the United States.

## Worker Cooperatives

A sixth type of firm structure is the worker cooperative. There each worker becomes a member of the cooperative by buying a share of the cooperative, and each has one vote in the general management meetings, which are the final authority for the enterprise. Examples of this form include a number of plywood producing cooperatives in the Pacific Northwest region of the United States. In these cooperatives, which are in an industry in which the demand fluctuates a great deal, the work is shared among the members of the cooperative, and any annual surplus is divided on the basis of the work contributed by each member. The cooperatives have a common wage rate for the members except for a few in managerial positions. The Board of Directors is made up of owner/workers. Each worker has access to information regarding the operation of the firm, and an opportunity for sharing in the decision making, although the degree to which workers actually participate in the decision making varies from firm to firm. Some long-term difficulties in the preservation of these firms have appeared, however. Sometimes there are conflicts between a desire of the worker/owners for more current income and the need for funds for investments important for the long-term survival of the enterprise. And if the enterprise grows in value, it becomes very expensive for a new worker to purchase the shares of a worker who is leaving the enterprise, and there is pressure to allow the sale of shares to non-workers. This problem could be alleviated if the shares of workers leaving could be sold to the cooperative, which would re-sell them over a period of time to new workers. This is done in the large Mondragon group of cooperatives in the Basque region of Spain. Of course the cooperative form of organization is no guarantee that the decisions of the enterprise will reflect good stewardship, but there is a tendency for the personnel decisions, at least, to be more in conformity with the standards for justice discussed above than in North American enterprises in general.

### Communal Settlements

A seventh form of firm structure is a communal settlement, or worker community. Although there are some of these in North America, perhaps the best-known modern examples of these are the Israeli kibbutzim. In a kibbutz there is a communalism of both production and much of consumption. The general assembly of all members is the final authority. All property is held in common. In theory there should be no hired labor, and there is an equal distribution of income (with some allowances for differences in individual consumption). Each production branch regulates its own activities within policies laid down by the general assembly. Many of the standards for justice are met well in the internal relations of such a firm, although the small area allowed for individual decision-making would restrict opportunities for responsible stewardship unless the members of the community hold a common religious viewpoint and common views on its implications for their communal life. And there is no assurance that the decisions of the commune regarding their external relations (e.g., what they sell to others, how they price it, how they affect the environment), will be in line with proper stewardship.

### Commonwealth or Foundation-owned Firms

An eighth type of firm structure is a firm owned and controlled by a commonwealth or foundation in which the workers play a large, but not an exclusive, role. The Scott Bader Commonwealth Ltd., a chemical company in England, is one example of such a firm. Other examples include the John Lewis Partnership, a retailing firm in Great Britain; Rowen Engineering in Scotland; and the deHaas Shipbuilding firm in the Netherlands. Ernst Bader, the Christian owner of the Scott Bader Co. Ltd., transferred ownership of the shares of the company to the Commonwealth, a communal body whose members are the workers in the operating company. The workers have an opportunity to exercise responsible decisionmaking regarding the use of their labor through their membership in the Commonwealth, which decides, among other things, on the distribution of any surplus; through their election of a community council, which, among other things, approves the selection of the directors of the operating company, may make recommendations on any matter to the Board of Directors, and makes the final decision in disciplinary cases; and through the practice in the company of delegating much authority down the line to semiautonomous working groups. Some restrictions are built into the commonwealth charter in an attempt to keep the enterprise in the paths of proper stewardship. For example, the maximum ratio of salaries allowed is 7:1; no more than 20 percent of the net income at the end of the year can be distributed to the workers as a bonus; an equal amount must be given to charity; and the rest is to be devoted to investment in the enterprise. There are restrictions on the size of the firm and the products that can be produced. Such a structure gives the workers opportunities for responsible stewardship of their labor and puts some restrictions on the decisions of the firm so that it is less likely that those who joined the firm agreeing with the decisions it made would find after a time that the basic thrust of the decisions had changed so that they could no longer agree with them. The limits on the decisions also make it less likely that the narrowly perceived self-interests of those in control (the workers) will be followed and more likely that the just interests of others will be heeded.

### General Explanatory Conclusions Regarding Structures of Firms

From this analysis of various structures of organization and management of firms some general conclusions can be drawn. First of all, it is clear that although changes in ownership and the highest authority structures of firms are important in giving workers full opportunities to exercise stewardship over their labor, they in themselves are not sufficient. Cooperative, participatory decision making, with full information regarding the firm available to workers on all levels is important, but is not guaranteed even if employees are major owners or if they have representatives on the Board of Directors. On the other hand, if the highest authorities of the firm have no structural responsibility to the workers, the workers' ability to influence policies which have a major bearing on the stewardship of their labor will be limited to the power of suggestion, at best.

Second, in general workers have more opportunities for responsible stewardship of their labor under the less-usual structures discussed above (cooperatives, communal settlements, and "commonwealth" type enterprises) than under those most common in the United States (control by capital owners with hierarchical management), since they give workers more opportunities to influence the ways their labor is being used and to change them if they believe it is being misused or not being used as well as possible. The other alternatives examined, ("cooperatively managed" enterprises, major worker ownership of stock, and co-determination) fall in between these extremes as far as giving workers opportunities for responsible stewardship is concerned, and vary a great deal within the types.

Third, there is also a tendency toward more equity in internal personnel decisions of the enterprise where workers have a greater role in management. The distribution of income tends to be more equal with all receiving enough to support their families, work is more likely to be shared during slack periods, and greater attempts are generally made to avoid lay-offs. However, there is no assurance that individual employees always will be treated fairly in situations such as promotions or discipline. Furthermore, there is no assurance that the decisions regarding external relations of the firm (e.g., choice of product, amount of pollution) will be more in accord with proper stewardship in firms where workers have more decision-making power than it will be in other firms. Restrictions on the decision-making powers of the firm or incentives for good stewardship, either internal to the firm (e.g., in its charter), or external to it (e.g., in the legal framework) can promote more stewardly actions. Of course, if the restrictions are misguided, they may promote bad stewardship, and if they are too tightly drawn they could seriously limit the opportunities for decision-making stewardship itself.

Fourth, within any given form of firm organization, the commitments of the members of the firm and the policies they adopt in response to them will have a large influence on the nature of the stewardship of the firm. This is illustrated by the variations between firms with similar structures on such things as the equity of the distributions of income and opportunities for the development of workers' abilities within the firm, the equity of the hiring and job-creation policies, the product choice and marketing decisions, and the effects of the firm on the environment. Simply giving workers opportunity for responsible stewardship will not insure that they will always be responsible stewards.

Fifth, if members of the enterprise do not share common commitments and goals, it will be impossible for all of them to have their labor and other resources used in a way that seems proper to them. This is likely to create tensions and difficulties within the firm and break down the trust that is necessary if there are to be truly cooperative or covenantal relationships rather than purely contractual ones.

Sixth, as enterprises become larger, it becomes more difficult to have such a shared commitment from all workers, and each worker will have more difficulty knowing and influencing the various policies that have an important influence on the stewardship of his or her labor. Both the amount of material to be comprehended and the communications problems grow as enterprises become larger. Furthermore, the larger enterprises grow, the few different enterprises there will be for workers to choose from; thus workers may have more difficulty finding one whose policies reflect their basic commitments.

Seventh, there is evidence that firm structures which allow and encourage considerable participation often result in both greater worker satisfaction and higher productivity. This will not be true in every case, however. And if the management of a firm introduces the form of participation without real substance to it in an attempt to gain higher productivity and keep all the gains for itself without worker objections, the workers are likely to realize this deception quickly and will lose faith in the "participation" process, with the result that neither productivity nor worker satisfaction increases.

## A Prescriptive Theory

The above data, analysis, and norms and principles, indicate that firm structures and management policies that give workers significant roles in decision making, both in their own work areas and regarding the general decisions of the firm, are preferable to those which do not, other things being equal. Such structures are preferable because they give more workers opportunity to be responsible stewards of their labor and other resources, which is one of the requirements of justice. They are also desirable because they tend to lead to more equitable internal personnel policies and greater productivity, both of which contribute to good stewardship of resources. This analysis also indicates that relatively small firms are preferred, other things being equal, since they make a meaningful role for workers in decision making in the firm more feasible if there are good structures, and because, having more smaller firms rather than fewer large ones makes it more likely that workers in a pluralistic society can find firms which share their basic commitments. The optimum size for a given enterprise will be influenced by other factors as well, including economics of scale and competitive conditions.

We can also conclude that some internal controls on a firm's decisions and activities can be desirable, because firms' decisions will not always reflect good stewardship, whether or not workers have a major role in decision making. Such controls could be included in the charter or constitution of the firm and might include such things as restrictions on the type of output the firm will produce, limitations on the amount of any surplus that can be paid out as bonuses to workers, limitations on the range of wages in the firm, and provisions for an independent body to judge grievances. Such internal controls can help workers make a long-term commitment to a firm with less danger that the firm will change to policies they can no longer accept.

These norms and this analysis also have implications regarding government policies in this area (governmental policies will be considered in more detail in chapters XII and XIII). In line with their general task to establish justice, governments should encourage firms to give all workers a major role in decision making in their firms. It could do this by requirements in corporation law that the Boards of Directors contain representatives of workers as well as stockholders, and that workers be given rights of co-determination regarding working conditions via works councils, unless they already are given these rights in their contracts. Governments could also help in this area by encouraging small-scale and worker-managed enterprises, for example, through a more progressive corporate income tax, more rigorous anti-trust laws and enforcement of them, removal of the tax-deductibility of advertising expenses above a certain amount per enterprise, and providing or guaranteeing loans to small worker-owned and managed enterprises. Governments could also encourage firms to act justly and as good stewards in their employment relationships by providing incentives for them to hire and train those who would otherwise have difficulties obtaining employment. Of course, in all of this, the government should consider its task of promoting justice in a broad sense, and thus must consider the possible effects of its policies in this area on other areas before making a final decision. In our imperfect world it will be impossible to establish complete justice in all areas.

Although it is beyond the scope of this chapter to evaluate various personnel policies in detail, it would perhaps be helpful to state some of the implications of the norms discussed above for personnel policies. Since justice requires that all families should have the opportunity to earn income to meet their needs, firms should attempt to hire some of those whose opportunity for employment elsewhere is low, in addition to hiring some of those already most able to contribute to the achievement of the legitimate goals of the firm. Also, the firm should not discriminate against those who have difficulty obtaining employment elsewhere, such as members of racial minorities, women, handicapped persons, and older workers. In order to continue to provide families with opportunities to support themselves, work should be shared during slack times rather than keeping some workers on full time or even working overtime, while laying off others (unless other good employment is available for the workers). Allowing employees to collect partial unemployment insurance when their hours are reduced, as is done in California, would help to encourage this.

Firms should, through their training and promotion policies, give their workers opportunities to develop and use their God-given talents; they should not rely primarily on external criteria, such as degrees, when the development of talents or skills can also take place gradually on the job.

With respect to styles of supervision, cooperative styles are better than authoritarian styles. Supervisors should be "facilitators" or "coordinators" rather than "dictators", in order that workers can have real responsibility for their labor. There should be "two-way" responsibility throughout the firm (that is, supervisors should be responsible to those they supervise, as well as those supervised to the supervisors). Both the "one-way" responsibility found in the predominant hierarchical structures (those below only responsible to those above them in the hierarchy), and a possible "inverted one-way" responsibility (supervisors responsible only to those they supervise) are inadequate for a community of stewards engaged in a common task, which is what the firm should be.

In order that the dignity of workers be honored, discipline should not be arbitrary, and there should always be a right of appeal in discipline cases with some support (such as a union grievance committee or an ombudsman) available to the worker making the appeal. Discharge should only be for very serious or repeated offenses, and help should be available to workers with problems which affect their activities in the enterprise.

On the other hand, employees should carry out their tasks diligently and work to achieve the legitimate goals of the firm, even if such activity goes beyond their job description. As well as seeking responsibility for decision making in the firm, they should be willing to bear a share of the risks involved in the operation of their firm. Workers should also seek to cooperate with and behave lovingly toward all others in the firm. But even as a firm must seek a just balance between its obligations to its workers, other suppliers of resources, customers, and the general public, workers do not owe ultimate allegiance to their firm, and must balance their obligations to it with obligations to others in society, such as their families and churches.

## Summary

In summary, there is much distorted behavior in relations between firms and their workers today—much that is self-seeking, non-stewardly, nontrusting, inequitable, poverty-producing, and psychological-problem-producing; neo-classical theory tends to promote and justify many of these distortions. But there is also more positive behavior in both "traditional" and "alternative" types of firms which can serve as sign-posts toward a better way, and a theory of worker-firm relationships from a Christian perspective can help to identify and encourage more faithful stewardship.

## Resources

Antonides, H. 1980. *Industrial Democracy, Illusion and Promise.* Toronto: Christian Labor Ass'n of Canada.

Bernstein, P. 1976. Necessary Elements for Effective Worker Participation in Decision Making. *J. Econ. Issues.* 10: 490-552.

Blumberg, P. 1969. *Industrial Democracy, The Sociology of Participation.* NY, Schocken.

Goudzwaard, B. 1975. *Aid for the Overdeveloped West.* Toronto, Wedge, (Ch. 4 discusses some of the themes of this chapter).

Kuhne, R. J. 1980. *Co-determination in Business.* NY: Praeger. (European models described)

Latta, G. W. 1979. *Profit Sharing, Employee Stock Ownership, Savings, and Asset Formation Plans in the Western World.* Philadelphia, Wharton School, U. of Pennsylvania.

Lesieur, F. G., ed. 1958. *The Scanlon Plan.* NY: John Wiley.

Marshall, P., et al. 1980. *Labor of Love.* Toronto: Wedge.

Nicholson, W. 1979. *Intermediate Microeconomics and its Application.* 2nd ed. Hinsdale: Dryden.

Piore, M., ed. 1979. *Unemployment and Inflation.* NY: Myron E. Sharpe.

Ramsted, Y. 1981. Institutional Economics: How Prevalent in the Labor Literature? *J. Econ. Issues.* 15: 339-50.

Reynolds, L. G. 1978. *Labor Economics and Labor Relations.* 7th ed., Englewood Cliffs: Prentice-Hall.

Stokes, B. 1978. *Worker Participation: Productivity and the Quality of Work Life.* Washington: Worldwatch Institute.

Thurow, L. 1975. *Generating Inequality.* NY: Basic Books.

# Chapter XI
# Unions

*I've seen my brothers working*
*Throughout this mighty land,*
*I prayed we'd get together,*
*And together make a stand.*
*But the banks are made of marble*
*With a guard at every door,*
*And the vaults are stuffed with silver*
*That the workers sweated for.*
                    Les Rice, 1950

Current economic theories of unions ignore essential elements of these organizations, and thus fail to be adequate tools for either understanding and explaining union's roles and behavior or for evaluating them.   As Bob Goudzwaard has stated, "The trade union is commonly considered to be a power organization designed only to further the material interests of its members.   Generally the trade union is expected to carry out a well-organized, relentless drive for more and more." [1975, p. 697]   But this perception, as Goudzwaard goes on to point out, is a truncated view of unions, one which ignores the fact that they are made up of human beings who are creatures responsible to God, their Creator, and to their fellowmen for their actions. God has set down the norms for our behavior, and an adequate theory of unions must recognize that structures and behavior can be responsible or irresponsible in light of these norms and must help us understand to what degree a particular structure or behavior is responsible or irresponsible.

## Current Economic Theories of Unions

Just as neoclassical economists' theories of firms and consumers assume that they maximize something (profits and utility, respectively), so neoclassical economists have attempted to analyze unions with theories which assume that unions maximize something of interest to their members and/or their leaders. But in contrast to the situation with theories of the firm and consumer, the neoclassical economists studying unions have not been able to come to any agreement on what unions maximize. And none of the proposed maximands has proven to be an adequate explanation of actual union behavior.

Neoclassical economists generally assume that unions are monopolies in the sale of a particular type of labor who face a given downward sloping demand curve for this labor (i.e., the higher the wage, the lower the quantity of labor that will be hired). They assume that as a monopolist the union raises the price of the labor above the free market price and reduces the quantity which is sold below the free market quantity, and thus causes economic inefficiency. Even this result is not clear in their own analytical framework, however, unless there is perfect competition in the rest of the economy, for economists have not yet fully worked out the conditions for efficiency in one sector of the economy when there is a lack of perfect competition in one or more other sectors; this is called the second best problem. Some have suggested that in this situation unions will seek to maximize the average wage of their employed members. But if this were their goal, the standard neoclassical analysis would indicate that unions would seek to raise the wage to such a height that only one member would remain employed, for if the wage were low enough so that two or more members were employed, the neoclassical analysis would indicate that there would be some higher wage which would reduce the demand for labor from the present level to only one worker. This obviously is not the normal union behavior. Thus, others have suggested that unions seek to maximize the total amount of wages paid to their members (the "wage bill"). This would be analogous to a firm wanting to maximize its total revenues. But no convincing reasons why this would be the goal of unions have been adduced, and if this was their goal, unions would seek to *lower* wages whenever the demand for their labor was elastic and the supply of workers was sufficient that the additional job offers induced by lower wages would be accepted. But this does not seem to fit much union behavior. Others have suggested that unions seek to maximize the size of their employed membership, but this would imply even more wage cutting than the wage-bill hypothesis.

Because of the difficulties in finding a single maximand that can explain union behavior, many neoclassical economists have turned from the analogy of the profit-maximizing firm to the analogy of their theory of consumer behavior and assume the union wishes to maximize the value of some utility function which includes both higher wages and higher levels of employment as goals. But, besides the well-known (to economists), but often ignored problem of deriving a utility function for a group made up of individuals with diverse interests, any behavior can be made consistent with the maximization of some utility function. If the particular form of the utility function must be inferred from the behavior of a union in a particular situation, then that utility function cannot be used to "explain" that behavior without being involved in a circularity of argument. [Mitchell, 1980, pp. 65-66] And it seems clear from even a casual observation of union behavior that there is no one specification of a utility function in terms of wages and employment that is consistent with the variety of behavior of unions in the United States, to say nothing of the varieties of behavior internationally.

Even if we make only the seemingly innocuous assumption that unions would generally like to have both higher wages and more employment for their members, or the even weaker assumption that unions seek only the self-perceived interests of their members, we still cannot explain much of union behavior. For example, the United Auto Workers and many other unions support broad social welfare programs, many of which will not directly help their members.

Nor can the standard models of economists adequately explain the significant differences in the behavior of various unions, for example, that some have pushed for very high wages even at the expense of a substantial reduction in employment for their members, while others have accepted low wage increases or even wage reductions to preserve employment for their members. Different unions have taken considerably different political stances, and unions have differed significantly with respect to the degree of internal democracy, organizational integrity, and stands on racial issues. Economists generally try to explain such differences by pointing out to the differences in economic constraints facing the various unions. But while these are important influences on union behavior in many cases, they are by no means sufficient to provide a full explanation of the differences in behavior, as we will see below.

One of the important factors that influences union behavior is the ideology of the union—its view of society and the economy and its role in that society. This is a strong influence on the principles and goals of a union and thus on its behavior. But this is often ignored by economists when they analyze unions. In fact, some claim that American unions, in contrast to Socialist, Communist, and Christian unions in Europe, have no ideology. Rather, they say that the U.S. unions practice a non-ideological "business unionism," which accepts the capitalist system as found in the United States and merely attempts to gain more income and security and better working conditions for their members within this system. While it is true that most unions in the United States practice such a "business unionism," it is not true that this is non-ideological. "Business unionism" is itself based on an ideology. In addition, even in the United States unions have held to this ideology to varying degrees, and some unions in the United States have rejected it. As we shall see, these differences in ideology are important to understanding, explaining, and evaluating union structure and behavior.

## A Theory From a Christian Point of View

### Basic Norms and Principles

A more adequate understanding and evaluation of unions and collective bargaining structures and behavior can be obtained from a theory based on Christian norms and principles than on the individualistic and materialistic norms and principles which underlie much of the current economic analysis of unions. Such a theory is grounded in the fact discussed in chapters V and X, that workers are stewards of labor resources which God has entrusted to them and are called by God to use them in the ways that he has commanded. Among other things, this means that they are to be used by workers in such a way that their and other peoples' needs can be justly provided for and that truly useful products are produced. Workers remain responsible to God for the use of their labor, whether or not they are union members, and this responsibility goes beyond questions of wages and working conditions to matters of what is produced and how it is sold.

Unions, as organizations of workers, should help workers in the proper exercise of these stewardship responsibilities. They should be instruments for achieving more justice in the employment relationship and for enabling workers to achieve a more stewardly use of their labor in the broadest possible sense. If they do this, unions will be advancing the true interests of their members and the true interests of others in society (both of which will be advanced by proper stewardship), but these true interests may differ at times from the self-perceived interests of union members or others.

This approach means that unions should work to achieve a just wage for their members. Although no biblical formula for a just wage can be given, the principles regarding proper wages discussed in Chapter X are relevant here as well. Wages, and thus union wage demands, may be too high as well as too low. They should be high enough so that the workers' families' needs can be met, but not so high as to endanger the provision and sustainability of employment opportunities of workers. Nor should they be so high as to put an unfair burden on the poor of society who must buy products produced with the highly priced labor. Unions should help workers to achieve security in their opportunities to work and provide for their families, and should help them to obtain meaningful work, work in which they can develop their God-given talents and be a responsible part of a cooperating, decision-making work community. They should not have to be mere hired servants following, without question, the orders of others in return for their sustenance. This means that unless there are already opportunities for workers to influence the policies of their firm which have a bearing on the stewardship of their labor, unions should seek to gain these opportunities for the workers and should encourage workers to take the responsibility for their actions that goes with such opportunities.

Workers should be free to join and be represented by unions of their choice and to refrain from joining a union when their conscience forbids it, so that workers are not forced to join a union whose ideology and behavior are in conflict with their beliefs. They should not be hindered in their choice of unions by their employers, their fellow workers, or any union. Unions should treat all people as image bearers of God and deserving of respect and dignity. This means, among other things, that members should be free to express their opinions and work for changes in union policy, and that any discipline should not be arbitrary but should provide for appeals to neutral parties.

It is best for unions to use cooperative means for attaining their proper ends, as for example, joint committees with management, collective bargaining in a cooperative spirit, mediation, and arbitration. But this will not always be possible, especially if the other party (usually management) refuses to cooperate or agree on a particular just demand. In such cases non-violent confrontational methods may be used, for example, strikes and picketing, if the harm from failing to achieve the proper goal is serious, and if due regard is taken for the possible harmful effects on those who are not parties to the dispute. Thus a given strike may be a responsible or irresponsible action by a union depending on the issues involved, the possibilities for alternate ways of reaching a settlement, and the effects of the strike on third parties. Likewise, a management's action in failing to reach an agreement which would avoid or end a strike may be responsible or irresponsible.

### A Descriptive Theory of Unions based on These Norms and Principles

*The Causes of Unions.* A more adequate understanding and explanation of unions and of the structure and practice of collective bargaining can be obtained from a theory based on these norms and principles as well as empirical observation than can be obtained from a theory which presupposes unions act only out of the self-perceived materialistic desires of their members or officials. In the typical hierarchically controlled non-union firm in the United States, the vast majority of workers do not have adequate opportunities to fulfill their responsibilities for stewardship of their labor. The hierarchical control has left them without any opportunity to share in decisions about their wage rates, job tenure, or promotion, or the grounds on which these things are determined. This makes their ability to provide for their families, both in the present and in the future, insecure, because it heavily depends not only on their own actions, but also on the actions of those above them in the hierarchy of their firm over whose decisions they have no control. The hierarchical control of the enterprise also denies most workers adequate opportunities for meaningful stewardship in that it denies them opportunities for responsible decision making regarding the use of their labor within the firm. They are in much the same position as the Israelite hired servants (or temporary slaves) were, rather than in the position of the independent, responsible, decision-making farmers, and the latter was the ideal situation which the God-given law was designed to repeatedly restore.

The attitude of many managers toward their workers in the years before wide-spread unionism contributed greatly to the injustice the workers suffered. Referring to the period around the turn of the century, Philip Taft reports that many corporate leaders regarded labor as only another factor of production, not much different from a machine. In testifying against an eight-hour workday on government contracts, C. J. Harrah, president of the Midvale Steel Company, declared that `once a man passes inside the gate and gets inside the red fence, he stays there until his day's work is through'... and `we have absolutely no regard for machinery or for men.' [1964, p. 161]

Frederich Winslow Taylor, whose widely adopted system of "scientific management" utilized time and motion studies to break tasks down to their simplest components in order to find the most productive way of doing the whole job, wrote:

> In the past, the man has been first...In the future the system must be first... All possible brain work should be removed from the shop... The time during which the man stops to think is part of the time he is not productive. [Stokes, 1978, p. 11]

George F. Baer, president of the Philadelphia and Reading Railroad stated during a strike in 1902 that:

> The rights and interests of the laboring man will be protected and cared for—not by the labor agitators, but by the Christian men to whom God in His infinite wisdom has given the control of property interests in this country, and upon the successful management on which so much depends. [Taft, 1964, pp. 178-179]

Apparently Mr. Baer did not consider the possibility that the concentration of control over property might be counter to God's will as it was during so much of the history of Israel and Judah, rather than in line with it. In any case, even if Mr. Baer had more concern for his employees than Mr. Harrah did, they were clearly deprived of any opportunity to decide before God how their labor was to be used within the firm, and he wished his employees to be completely dependent upon him for their well-being. But there is certainly no biblical evidence to indicate that those who have control over property should be in control over the labor of those who do not. Although the attitudes of many managers in both union and non-union firms on these issues have changed in recent decades, such ideas are by no means totally absent even today.

Unions arose in response to the injustice of such situations which made it impossible for most workers to fulfill God's calling for them. This is not to say that all or even many workers and union organizers recognized that they were unable to fulfill God's call for them; but the unjust situation in which they were unable to provide for their families with any sense of security and in which they had no ability to influence the conditions of their work called forth a response from those suffering from these dehumanizing practices. Many of the early and often unsuccessful attempts at unionism in the United States came when employers reduced the wages of their workers and when their very jobs were at stake. The fact that unions were often formed by skilled workers rather than unskilled workers does not contradict the premise that they were formed in order to enable them to support their families adequately. The unskilled workers may have desired unions just as much, but had even less ability than the more skilled workers to call for a successful strike in face of the abundance of unskilled workers available to the employers for use as strikebreakers. Walter Galenson says of the motives of the workers during the rapid organization of the industrial unions in the late 1930's:

> What workers rebelled against was the insecurity of their employment, the arbitrary character of management decisions affecting their lives, and the speeding up of work by companies... [Estey, 1981, p. 33]

While there are other forms of firm structure and management (discussed in Chapter X) that gives workers more opportunity to exercise meaningful stewardship of their labor than the "hierarchical control with unions and collective bargaining" structure, as long as control of a firm is vested in the suppliers of capital and their representatives, as is the case for most firms in North America and many other parts of the world today, unions do provide a means for workers to exercise some measure of control over the labor resources God has entrusted to them. (This is also true for workers in enterprises controlled by some other non worker group, such as a governmental body.) The responses unions make to this general condition of hierarchical control will vary from union to union and time to time. Some responses are proper (faithful stewardship) while others are improper (unfaithful stewardship); many actions of unions will be some mixture of proper and improper response to the situation. The same is true of the actions of managements and governments in this area. Among the factors influencing a union's response to a particular situation are: 1). the legal structure for unions and collective bargaining relationships; 2). the economic constraints, for example, the demand for and supply of the labor of their members; 3). the ideology of the members and leaders of the union, including such interrelated aspects as their religous commitments, ethical principles, views of society and the economy, and immediate goals; and 4). the responses of management of the firms to the union's activities, whether active opposition to the existence of the union, grudging acceptance of the union, or cooperation with the union. Economists tend to emphasize factors 1 and 2, sometimes to the exclusion of the others. But a theory that neglects any of these factors is inadequate to explain union behavior.

*The Legal Structure for Unions and Collective Bargaining in the United States.* While there is not room in this chapter to give a complete description of the legal framework for collective bargaining in the United States, some of the important features of the legal system regarding unions will be identified and their effects discussed. The three most important laws regarding unions in the United States are the National Labor Relations Act of 1935 (Wagner Act), the Labor-Management Relations Act of 1947 (Taft-Hartley Act, a major amendment to the Wagner Act), and the Labor-Management Reporting and Disclosure Act of 1959 (Landrum-Griffin Act). The major purpose of the Wagner Act was to allow workers to form unions and bargain collectively with their employers without interference from their employers. To do this, the Act prohibited managements from engaging in a number of "unfair labor practices," including discriminating against workers for union membership, dominating or interfering with any union, or refusing to bargain collectively with duly chosen representatives of their employees. It created the National Labor Relations Board (NLRB) to administer the Act. The Act provided for representation elections in which workers could select a union to represent them or choose to have no union if they wished. The NLRB decides which workers should be included in a bargaining unit, and if a union receives the majority of votes in a representation election for a unit, it is given exclusive bargaining rights as the representative of all workers in that bargaining unit. The Taft-Hartley Act added provisions prohibiting certain union actions as unfair labor practices, including coercion of employees in the right to choose their union or choose no union, refusal to bargain with an employer, striking to force an employer to stop dealing with another firm or person (a secondary boycott, sometimes used to put pressure on the other person to sign a union contract), and striking over jurisdictional conflicts between unions.

The protections of the rights of workers to bargain collectively contained in the Wagner Act reduced greatly the number of strikes over the refusal of employers to recognize a union as the representative of their workers and bargain and sign a contract with it. Prior to its passage many strikes were called over this issue, and many employers used "on a large scale . . . the time tested-tactics of espionage, the use of armed guards, and the denial of constitutional and civic rights by local authorities to a labor organization seeking recognition [Taft 1964, p. 516], along with the use of strikebreakers as means of denying recognition" to unions. The use of such means decreased substantially after the passage of the Wagner Act. But the provisions of the Taft-Hartley Act adding unfair labor practices for unions, however much good they did in other respects, gave opportunities for employers to file unfair labor practice charges against unions as a way of delaying representation elections, and it provided that if an employer replaced workers who were striking for economic reasons with strikebreakers, the strikebreakers could call for a decertification election in which the strikers could not vote, and thus the striking workers could lose the right to have their union as bargaining representative in the plants. The Landrum-Griffin Act changed this to provide that both economic strikers and strike breakers could vote in any representation election held within a year after the strike was called. In addition the penalties which the NLRB can assess on employers who engage in unfair labor practices are not stringent enough to deter a really determined employer from illegally fighting unionization of its plants. An employer can fire employees active in the organizing campaign and refuse to bargain or sign a contract with a union even if it has won representation election, and only be forced to rehire the workers and pay back wages and be ordered to bargain in good faith after years of litigation before the NLRB and the courts, by which time the workers may have been scared or forced through lack of resources to drop their demands for unionization. An extreme case of a company recently engaging in a fight to deny its workers the right to be represented by a union of their own choosing is the J.P. Stevens Company, which has been found guilty of violating the Taft-Hartley Act in fifteen cases, eight of them upheld by courts of appeal and three by the supreme court. [Bloom and Northrup, 1981, p. 715] (Not all of them reached the appeals stage.) After many years of struggle, it finally signed contracts with the Amalgamated Clothing and Textile Workers covering some of its plants in 1980, after unions had begun to use pension funds and other means to put pressure on banks, insurance companies, and other firms with which Stevens had interlocking boards of directors, to sever their ties with it.

These Acts also do not cover agricultural workers who have no protection of rights to unionize and bargain collectively in federal legislation. This has made it more difficult for agricultural workers to organize unions and secure contracts from employers, and has sometimes resulted in employers signing contracts with a union not chosen by their workers when the contract with the workers' union expired. This happened in 1973, when some California grape growers signed contracts with the Teamsters Union, which had not been chosen by the workers when the growers' contracts with the United Farm Workers expired, because the Teamsters would give terms the employers preferred to those the UFW was asking for. California passed an Agricultural Labor Relations Act in 1975 which provides for representation elections and adjudicating of unfair labor practice charges to prevent this problem from happening again, but agricultural workers in most states are still without such protection. Thus, although the labor legislation since 1935 has gone a long way to protect the rights of workers to be represented by a union and thus gain some influence over their wages and working conditions, it has not done this completely by any means.

But although labor laws in the United States give workers considerable rights to be represented by a union in their dealings with their employers, the system of awarding exclusive bargaining rights for all of a bargaining unit to the union chosen by a majority of the workers in it limits severely workers' rights to be represented by *the union of their choice*, if their choice is different from that of the majority of workers in their bargaining unit. If the majority of workers choose a union whose ideology or practice is at variance with the views of some of the workers, the minority workers must still be represented by the union, and they must work under the contract it signs with the firm, or leave their job. The system found in some European countries (including the Netherlands) of allowing workers to join the union of their choice, with the unions together bargaining with the employers, would provide more freedom of choice for the workers in their bargaining, and would not force workers to be represented by a union they cannot accept. This would make bargaining considerably more complex, however, and might enable anti-union employers to play off various groups of workers against each other in an attempt to defeat any real representation. Some of these problems could be mitigated if, when changing to a system of non-exclusive representation rights, the legal system also provided for works councils with broad co-determination rights over conditions of employment (as in West Germany). The various unions representing workers of a firm could propose members for election to the works council and could make suggestions to it regarding policies (as could any employee). This would tend to give a representation of at least the major groups among the workers in the process of negotiating the rules of work. The unions would still negotiate with the management on rates of pay, as in West Germany.

Workers who are working under a contract with a union-shop provision must not only be represented by the union representing their bargaining unit, but must also join the union (or at least pay dues to it). Such union-shop provisions are allowed in thirty states and outlawed in the other twenty. In 1980 the Taft-Hartley Act was amended to allow workers under a union-shop contract who object to union membership on religious grounds to give an amount equivalent to union dues to a religious or charitable organization instead of joining the union and paying dues to it. (Unions may charge them a service fee for processing grievances, however.) This provides a way to relieve many of the most serious problems of workers being forced to choose between joining a union against their consciences or losing their jobs without creating the "free-rider" problem that exists if there is no provision in the contract requiring workers to join the union or pay an amount equivalent to dues. (The "free-rider" problem arises from the fact that all workers must be represented by the union and receive any benefits gained from the union contract; if there is no compulsion to join the union or pay for these benefits, some workers might decide not to join the union in order to get a "free ride", enjoying the benefits of the union's work but not paying for it.) The lack of a union shop contract probably does not weaken a strong union very much, but might severely weaken an already relatively weak union facing a strongly anti-union employer, if the employees are afraid that the employer will illegally discriminate against the union members.

The labor law in the United States limits the subjects which unions and employers must agree to bargain over to "wages, hours, and other terms and conditions of employment." While the last phrase is fairly general and has been subject to much interpretation by the NLRB and the courts over the years, it has not been held to include many issues that are important to workers' stewardship of their labor, including such things as the choice and pricing of products. Since either party may legally refuse to bargain over "non-mandatory" issues, and since most managements would refuse to do so if a union asked them to, this seriously limits the extent to which unions and collective bargaining can be used by workers in the United States to gain some influence over the broad range of decisions that have important effects on the stewardship of their labor.

Labor laws on both federal and state levels provide for mediation services which have proven to be useful at times in avoiding or settling strikes. Arbitration is also available if the parties agree to it, and government fact-finding (proposing a solution) is provided under the Railway Labor Act; fact-finding or binding arbitration is mandated in cases of impasse in some state laws dealing with public employee collective bargaining. Although fact-finding and arbitration have sometimes proven to be helpful in reaching settlements without strikes, they have often hindered the process of bargaining, since the parties are less likely to make concessions during bargaining if they think the dispute will go to a fact finder or arbitrator who is likely to propose a settlement somewhere between the final positions of each party.

The Taft-Hartley Act allows the President to seek an injunction forbidding a strike for eighty days if the strike threatens national health and safety. During the eighty days attempts are made to settle the dispute, but the strike may resume after that time, if the dispute has not been settled. The use of these provisions have reduced the harm to third parties from strikes in a number of instances without seriously weakening either party in the collective bargaining process. However, laws that prohibit strikes completely, without giving alternative means for unions to pursue their ends, severely limit the degree to which unions can achieve their legitimate goals. They have also proven ineffective in a number of instances, for if a strong union does strike anyway, it is often difficult to get work resumed without agreeing to waive the penalties for striking provided in the law. This happened in the case of New York State's law against public employee strikes, for example.

The regulations contained in the Landrum-Griffin Act with respect to internal union government, including requirements for financial reporting, restrictions on national unions taking over local unions via trusteeships, procedures for fair elections, standards for handling union finances, and a "bill of rights" for union members, have given workers more rights against the corruption and dictatorial government sometimes found in unions. Experience under the Act has shown that such problems occur in only a very small proportion of unions. Relatively few actions against unions have been brought under the Act, and most of these have been for technical failures in reporting which were then corrected. Benjamin Civiletti, then acting Deputy Attorney General, testified in 1978 that fewer than one-half of one per cent of local unions were influenced by racketeers. Philip Taft concluded that experience under the Landrum-Griffin Act showed "that for probity and integrity the labor movement compares favorably with other American institutions". [Taft, 1964, p. 706] The act has been used in several instances to redress serious wrongs by overturning fraudulent elections and removing corrupt officials from their union offices.

*The Behavior of Unions and Practice of Collective Bargaining in the United States.* When investigating the behavior of unions in the United States it is important to recognize the multiplicity of factors that influence union behavior. We have already pointed out how the legal structure influences this in a number of ways (for example, by determining representation rights, setting mandatory topics for bargaining, and regulating rights to strike and internal union behavior). But union behavior is also influenced by the economic constraints facing the union, its ideology, and the response of management to the union. We will now discuss some examples of the influence of these factors on aspects of union behavior and then look at some of the general results of union actions in the United States.

Economists have often pointed out that economic conditions play a role in unions' decisions regarding the wages they will seek. Besides the general economic conditions, such as the rates of inflation, unemployment, and other wage changes, unions are often concerned with the elasticity of demand for the labor of their members, which will influence the amount of employment available to their members at various wage rates and alternative job opportunities available to their members. But it is obvious that ideologies of unions also play a role in their wage policies. For example, the United Mine Workers "have pursued a high-wage policy in the face of shrinking employment with announced unconcern" [Rees, 1977, p. 50], in spite of the fact that alternative employment opportunities in the area of many of the mines were not plentiful. On the other hand, the International Ladies' Garment Workers' Union has been known for its concern for employment for as many of its members as possible, and has moderated wage demands when high demands would have endangered the employment of its members, as well as advocated sharing of work during slack periods. There is also some evidence that local unions are more apt to accept pay cuts when their jobs are threatened because of non-union competition, if their relationships with management have been more cooperative in the past than when management has been more confrontational. But national unions have differed in their reaction to local unions' desires to accept pay cuts, some being accepting of local unions' desires, and others resisting the locals' desires for cuts in order to maintain a more uniform national wage policy. [Rees, 1977, p. 57] For example, the two major national unions in the meat packing industry responded differently when some local unions desired to accept pay reductions in response to a move in the industry toward non-union packing plants located closer to the areas where the animals were raised.

The ideology of union members and leaders, as well as economic conditions, have also influenced unions' practices in racial matters. Economists often point out that the fact that craft unions have tended to discriminate more against blacks than industrial unions have is due to the craft unions' desire to make gains for themselves by restricting entry to their craft. Industrial unions, in contrast, seek their bargaining power by gaining the support of as many of the workers in an industry as possible. But this cannot explain why southern locals of some of the industrial unions discriminated against blacks while the policy of the national unions and of most of the locals was strongly in favor of creating equal opportunities for blacks. For example, the United Auto Workers has disciplined and even expelled locals in the south for discriminatory behavior. And it cannot explain why some craft unions (such as the bricklayers) have adopted constitutional prohibitions against racial discrimination, but others, including the Railway Trainmen and Locomotive Firemen, formally barred blacks from membership until the 1960's and many others followed informal exclusion. As in industrial unions, the degree of discrimination varies from local to local within craft unions. Union racial discrimination was outlawed by the Civil Rights Act of 1964, but that provision has not eliminated all informal discrimination.

The response of management to the union will also influence union behavior with regard to work rules and technological change. If the management does not accept the union and tries to weaken it and, if possible, displace it, the union is not likely to cooperate with it on devising more productive work rules or accepting technological changes which increase productivity. Often in such cases the union will resist any such changes. This was the stance of most managements and the reaction of many unions before the 1930's, and is still the practice of some today. But when a management accepts the presence of a union and seeks to cooperate with it, unions will sometimes (but not always) cooperate in finding production methods that are more productive and give more worker satisfaction. An early example of this is the cooperation between the International Association of Machinists and the Baltimore and Ohio Railroad in the 1920's. [Taft, 1969, pp. 381-382] More recent examples include the joint union management productivity committees in the steel industry in the 1970's and programs of the United Auto Workers with various employers which provide more worker involvement in decisions regarding the methods and organization of work. (The Scanlon Plan discussed in Chapter X is another example of this.)

Although almost any generalization that can be made about the effects of unions and collective bargaining in the United States will have some exceptions, some useful generalizations can be made. First of all, unions have increased the ability of many workers to provide adequately for their families and, in particular, have increased the security of their members in the provision for their needs. Unions, on average, have raised the wages of their members over those of similar non-union workers. Although it is very difficult to estimate just how great the difference is, H. Gregg Lewis in a widely cited study concluded it averaged about ten to fifteen per cent for strong unions in the 1950's, and Daniel J. B. Mitchell has recently estimated it to have been about twenty to thirty percent in the 1970's. [Mitchell, 1980, chapter 3] The extent to which this increase enables families to support themselves more adequately depends on the sufficiency of the non-union wage, of course. While most unionism has not taken place among the lowest-paid workers, much of it (especially industrial unionism) has included many workers whose incomes without the union differential would be considerably below the median for our society.

But more important than the increases in average pay have been the increases in security that have come for many workers with unionization. Before there was widespread unionization in the United States, it was not unusual for rates of pay to be reduced during recessions (and often by more than the cost of living fell). Indeed, many early unions were formed and strikes called in attempts to combat this practice. Now this is an infrequent occurrence under union contracts, and is considerably less frequent in non-union situations as well, except in some of the "secondary" labor markets. Perhaps even more important is the protection against arbitrary firing or lay-off that most union contracts provide. While not all non-union employers were or are arbitrary, without the protection of a seniority system and a grievance system for settling disputes with foremen or other supervisors, workers have little security of employment, and many have lost their jobs suddenly without any recourse. Some non-union employers have also adopted systems that give workers some measure of protection.

Unions have also helped to provide security for their members by securing fringe benefits which have helped them to meet sudden large bills (such as medical insurance) or provided a source of income when the worker's income from employment was stopped (such as pension benefits, life and disability insurance, and supplemental unemployment benefits). Such fringe benefits were uncommon for blue collar workers before the rise of unionism in the 1920's, except for some provided to members of craft unions, but have since become much more common. However, there is still a significant difference in degree of coverage between union and non-union workers. Daniel Mitchell presents data showing that the relative difference in cost of fringe benefits for union and non-union workers is much higher than the relative differences in wages [Mitchell, 1980, ch. 3], and a study in the mid-70's found that ninety-one percent of workers in unionized groups were in firms with retirement plans compared to only forty-eight percent in non-union groups. [Bloom and Northrup, 1981, p. 203]

Sometimes union wage and benefit gains have been achieved at the expense of others less able to bear the burden. Examples of this would include gains by excluding minority-group persons from employment opportunities or cases in which prices of necessities were raised because of increases in wages. Although unions generally do not seem to be major initiators of inflation in the United States, their response to inflation in the form of seeking higher wages, together with firms' responses of seeking to pass on the higher wages by raising prices, can help to perpetuate an inflation started by other causes (for example, excess aggregate demand or commodity price rises), long after these initiating causes have disappeared. [Mitchell, 1981, pp. 218-219] When union members (and other powerful groups) in society seek to keep their real incomes constant or rising when the per capita real income of the society is not rising (as was true of periods in the 1970's owing to slow productivity growth, commodity price increases, and recessions, among other things,) often the poor in society, who cannot protect their incomes, will bear much of the cost of the sustained real incomes of the more powerful.

The provisions in many union contracts which limit formal systems of discipline and grievance procedures with provisions for appeal with the support of the staff, and limiting the ability of foremen and other supervisors to arbitrarily discipline workers, has made the workplace a more humane place for many workers. However, sometimes grievance procedures do not lead to just outcomes because, for example, the union is too weak to have an adequate procedure written into the contract, or the union is strong relative to the firm, and it prevents the management from exercising legitimate discipline, or there is favoritism in the processing of grievances.

Many unions have gained for the workers some degree of influence over changes in working conditions so that workers' jobs cannot be changed or even eliminated without some opportunity for them to respond. Some unions have used this influence to block technological changes or insist on work rules that have seriously hindered productivity growth for long periods of time (for example, some of the railroad and building crafts unions), but others have allowed technological change and even cooperated with managements in introducing new and more productive methods, while at the same time safeguarding members from speedups or loss of income. In addition to those mentioned above, the International Longshoreman's and Warehouseman's Union agreed in 1960 to let the members of the Pacific Maritime Association make technological changes in return for a guaranteed annual wage for registered longshoremen and improved pension benefits. Such actions have forced managements to take into account some of the human costs of changes in technology and working conditions, and have led to the amelioration of the costs to the workers of such changes in many cases.

Unions and the system of collective bargaining in the United States have done little to give most workers an opportunity to exercise meaningful stewardship of their labor in aspects other than wages, benefits, and working conditions, however. This is in part due to the fact that most unions are not interested in involvement in other areas such as choice of product, pricing, marketing, and also because the laws do not require management to bargain about these things even if a union wishes to become involved in them, and most managers do not want to involve the workers in them. This has contributed to alienation of workers from their firms, and encourages an attitude among them of attempting to get the highest possible pay for the least possible work.

Strikes cause relatively little loss of working time in the United States; in most years much less than one-half of one percent of working time is lost to strikes. And although strikes sometimes significantly inconvenience third parties, they usually do not cause serious permanent damage to them.

### An Evaluation of Unions and Collective Bargaining

*The Legal Structure of Collective Bargaining.* The above norms, principles, data, and analysis indicate that legislation in the United States protecting the rights of workers to organize unions and bargain collectively with their employers is desirable as long as firms are controlled by capital owners or their representatives, since such legislation has led to greater opportunities for workers to have some influence over and security in the use of their labor, thus giving some somewhat greater opportunities for responsible stewardship of their labor. It has also lessened the degree of conflict over representation, which is desirable. But such legislation does not now cover all workers in the United States, and it would be desirable to extend rights of representation and collective bargaining to workers which presently do not have them, such as agricultural workers and some government employees, although the specific rules governing bargaining of such groups might have to be somewhat different to reflect their particular employment situations.

Prohibition of various "unfair labor practices" for both employers and unions and regulations concerning union governance have in the United States provided more opportunity for true worker representation and collective bargaining than was true without such legislation. Most of such provisions in the major acts of labor legislation in the United States can be justified on this basis, although there are problems with some of the specific provisions of these laws. Some aspects of the law have made it easier for anti-union companies to fight off weak unions, and the penalties provided for unfair labor practices are often not stringent enough to protect workers' rights to representation by unions of their own choosing.

On the other hand, the system of granting exclusive bargaining rights for a bargaining unit to a union chosen in a representation election hinders the rights of some workers to exercise stewardship of their labor in a manner they believe proper, since they must be represented by the union whether or not they agree with its principles or policies. Where this was accompanied by a union shop without exceptions the problem for dissenting workers was even greater. The union shop part of the problem has been alleviated by the provision of exceptions for those with religious conscientious objections. Attempting to solve the problem by a total prohibition of the union shop, as is done in twenty states, brings with it the "free-rider" problem. The real problem is with the system of exclusive bargaining rights. More opportunities would be given for workers to be represented by unions of their choosing if this provision were eliminated, with provisions for joint bargaining between the unions representing workers in a given bargaining unit and the employer. If this were done, it might be best to establish works councils in each firm as representatives of all the workers with co-determination rights on broad areas of conditions of work. Although the increased opportunities for representation of workers' varied views that such a system would give would be desirable, it might make it easier for anti-union firms to fight employee representation, especially if works councils were not made mandatory for all firms (union and non-union). This would not be desirable.

As discussed in Chapter X, the legal structure should enable all workers to influence all aspects of the operations of their firms which have a bearing on the stewardship of their labor. Although there are better means by which to accomplish this with respect to many of the issues than collective bargaining, if these other means are not provided, then the legal structure should not limit mandatory issues of collective bargaining to a subset of these issues, as is done in the United States; rather, both parties should be obligated to bargain on any issue regarding the operation of the firm that the other wishes to bargain about in order to give workers more opportunities to exercise meaningful stewardship of their labor.

It is desirable to provide means to lessen and help resolve conflicts between unions and managements by providing mediation and arbitration services when these can be helpful, and to put limits on strikes or lockouts that would cause serious harm to third parties. The provisions of the Taft-Hartley Act in this area are helpful, but various types of arbitration such as one which requires the arbitrator to choose between the last offers of each of the parties, (which might encourage more concessions during bargaining) and "non-stoppage strikes" (in which work would continue, at least at some partial level, but both workers and employer would have their incomes drastically reduced) should be tried in an attempt to devise new and better methods of conflict resolution in situations in which ordinary strikes would cause serious harm to third parties.

*The Actions of Unions.* While an evaluation of all of the many instances of union behavior in any country is obviously beyond the scope of this chapter, several general classes and particular instances of responsible and irresponsible union behavior in the United States need to be discussed.

Included in the classes of responsible behavior is the raising of wages of low-wage workers by union action, such as has been done by the United Farm Workers Union in California in the last decade. Many unions have also acted responsibly in obtaining more security for workers in the provision for their families' needs by negotiating and administering contracts providing protection from unreasonable firing or discipline through a formal grievance system, protection of job opportunities for workers who have contributed to the firm for a long time through seniority systems, and protection of family incomes through pension and insurance programs. Some unions have also helped to preserve employment opportunities for workers by negotiating shared-work arrangements when demand for labor is low. The International Ladies' Garment Workers' Union has been known for this policy, and it is also served by the practice of some union hiring halls (including many in the maritime unions) of referring the workers who have been without a job for the longest time to newly available jobs. Union actions in securing a role for workers in work rules changes and, together with management, finding ways to allow desirable technological change while preserving workers' abilities to support their families also represent responsible union actions.

Some unions have also acted responsibly in seeking greater decision-making roles for workers in their firms, thus giving them more opportunities for responsible stewardship. Usually this initiative has been limited to "shop-floor" level actions, but occasionally this has extended beyond that, such as the recent placement of UAW President Douglas Fraser on the Board of Directors of Chrysler Corporation.

The leaders of the major union federations (AFL, CIO), most leaders of national or international unions, and many local union officials have worked to create more opportunities for minority workers by opposing racial discrimination. Most unions and union officials have also responsibly dealt with their members and others in open and honest ways. The United Auto Workers and the Upholsterer's International Union have independent public review boards to which members can appeal if they believe they have been mistreated by the unions. Other unions could do well to follow this type of responsible action.

But although unions have often acted responsibly in the United States, there are classes and examples of irresponsible union actions as well. Some unions have raised wages of their members above a just level. A striking example of this is the Air Line Pilots Association, whose members, in 1981, received an average salary of $52,000 per year [Business Week, May 11, 1981, p. 42], but some of whose members received over $100,000 per year. [Bloom and Northrup, 1981, pp. 537-538] And while many unions have increased the security of their members and achieved more justice for them by establishing grievance procedures, others have obstructed necessary discipline by vigorously pressing unjust grievances, and a few have even conspired with managements to get rid of "troublesome" workers.

Some national unions have irresponsibly lost jobs for their members by insisting on high wages and rigid work rules, even when the local union members wished to agree to changes in pay scales and work rules in order to save their jobs. And others, including some of the railroad and building trades craft unions have resisted work-rules changes that would provide more efficiency beyond what could be needed to do justice to existing workers, rather than seeking to cooperate with employers in finding ways of introducing new methods while protecting the legitimate interests of present workers.

The racial discrimination that has been practiced (formally or informally) by some unions is obviously unjust to those discriminated against, and thus irresponsible. And the small proportion of union officials that have dealt with their members or with others in corrupt and violent ways (of which some recent national and local officials of the Teamsters Union are all too clear examples) have obviously acted irresponsibly.

Finally, most unions have not sought actively to extend the range of influence of workers to the full range of issues that have significant bearing on the stewardship of their labor, and thus have been less effective than they might have been in securing greater opportunities for workers to exercise responsible stewardship of their labor.

*The Actions of Managements.* Just as unions have acted responsibly and irresponsibly, so managements have acted responsibly in some instances and irresponsibly in other instances in their dealing with their employees and their union representatives.

Among the responsible actions are the many instances of managements accepting unions chosen by their workers as representatives of them, negotiating and cooperatively administering contracts with them providing for wages and fringe benefits, and effective discipline and seniority systems, which give workers opportunities to provide adequately for their families with security. Some managements have also responsibly agreed to work cooperatively with unions on changes in technology and work rules in order to alleviate the human costs of such changes, and some have agreed to greater worker roles in decision-making on the shop floor (for example, General Motors' quality-of-work-life programs with the UAW).

On the other hand, some managements have irresponsibly fought the establishment of unions by their workers and have attempted to weaken and, if possible, displace unions chosen by their workers. The legal and illegal activities of the J. P. Stevens Company in this regard in recent years, are all too clear an example of such behavior, but it is not alone in this. Indeed, there are a number of firms whose sole or primary purpose is to help other firms keep their workers from having union representation or to weaken or displace the unions if they are already present. And other firms, although bargaining with union representatives of their workers, have refused to agree to wages and fringe benefits and discipline and lay-off procedures that enable workers to provide adequately for their families with some measure of security (some of the actions of southern textile firms provide examples of such irresponsible behavior). And many firms have irresponsibly sought to deny most workers any role in setting work rules and influencing the many other decisions of the firm which have an important bearing on the stewardship of their labor.

*The Role of Unions in More-cooperatively-managed Firms.* As was discussed in Chapter X, structures of firm governance which give all workers in a firm an influence on policies of the firm (such as worker cooperatives and co-determination) give workers greater opportunities for meaningful stewardship of their labor than do the typical hierarchically controlled structures, even if there are unions representing the workers in the hierarchically controlled firms. But what is the role of unions in these other types of firms?

In firms with a co-determination structure there is a role for unions in developing and helping to represent the workers' views. There should be room for more than one union representing the workers in any one firm, with the workers free to join a union representing their point of view on important issues. The various unions could recommend policies and actions to the Works Council and Board of Directors. The unions could also aid workers in the processing of grievances. And the less complete is the workers' role in determining policies of the enterprise, the more role there will be for collective bargaining as well (as in West Germany, where the unions bargain with the firms regarding the level of wages).

In fully worker-controlled firms (such as worker-cooperatives) there is less role for unions, but they might be useful in aiding individual workers to process grievances if such aid is not otherwise available to them. They might also be useful as occupational organizations in which workers could investigate, discuss, and take action on issues of importance to them. They might be particularly useful in addressing issues affecting workers in more than one firm, in workers' relations to other institutions (such as governments), and in administering multi-firm pension or insurance funds, but would not be engaged in collective bargaining with the worker-controlled enterprises.

## Summary

Given the hierarchical control of most firms by owners of capital or their representatives, unions in the United States have in general been instruments for giving many workers more security in providing for their families and have in a limited way given them some opportunities for influencing the way that their labor is used. But unions have acted irresponsibly as well as responsibly in the situations in which they find themselves in, and a theory based on norms and principles for proper action is necessary for distinguishing between these types of action so that the former can be discouraged and the latter encouraged.

## Resources

A New Labor weapon to stop New York Air. 1981. *Business Week*. May 11, p.42.

Bloom, G. F., and H. R. Northrup. 1981. *Economics of Labor Relations*. 9th ed., Homewood: Richard D. Irwin.

Estey, M. 1981. *The Unions: Structure, Development, and Management*. 3rd ed. NY: Harcourt Brace.

Fairfield, R., ed. 1974. *Humanizing the Workplace*. Buffalo: Prometheus.

Goudzwaard, B. 1975. *Aid for the Overdeveloped West*. Toronto: Wedge. (Chapter 7 concerns unions).

Marshall, R. 1967. *The Negro Worker*. NY: Random House.

Marshall, R., A. M. Carter, and A.G. King. 1976. *Labor Economics*. 3rd ed., Homewood: Richard D. Irwin.

Mitchell, D. J. B. 1980. *Unions, Wages, and Inflation*. Washington: Brookings.

Rees, A. 1977. *The Economics of Trade Unions*. Revised ed., Chicago: U. of Chicago Press.

Reynolds, L. G. 1978. *Labor Economics and Labor Relations*, 7th ed., Englewood Cliffs: Prentice-Hall.

Stokes, B. 1978. *Worker Participation: Productivity and the Quality of Work Life*. Washington: Worldwatch Institute.

Taft, P. 1964. *Organized Labor In American History*. NY: Harper & Row.

# Chapter XII
# The Role of the Government—
# Microeconomic Aspects

*Only a poor man was Lazarus that begged,*
*He lay down at the rich man's gate*
*He begged for crumbs from the rich man to eat,*
*But they left him to die like a tramp on the street .*
*Grady and Hazel Cole (1940)*

Neoclassical economists view the government or state as an institution whose economic function should be to raise the economic welfare of society, where the economic welfare of society is assumed to be some positive function of the self-perceived utilities of all the individuals in society. Thus their evaluations of government actions are based upon whether or not the actions increase individuals' self-perceived utilities. This basic stance is held by economists with a wide variety of views on public policy, from conservative to liberal—though, some of course, they differ on what they think will raise individuals' utilities). It is also held by those in the newer "Public Choice" school, an approach which emphasizes the processes by which actual governments provide and finance goods and services and the outcomes of these processes, as well as by those taking the more traditional approach, which emphasizes that governments should be involved in a market economy because of the failure of private markets to produce "economic efficiency." Although most neoclassical economists would also agree that there is a role for the government in achieving the proper distribution of income and wealth in the society, they usually have less to say about this than about what they view as efficiency, since they realize that distributional questions involve difficult ethical questions that cannot be answered by the "value-free" theories they seek to use. Of course, as we have seen in chapter IV, no economic theory can be value free, but most neoclassical theorists fail to concede that point. In contrast to the neoclassical view, a theory of the economic functions of government from a Christian point of view does not see the function of the state as rooted in increasing the self-perceived utilities of its citizens. The state is an institution ordained by God, and thus subject to the norms He has set down for it. Its basic economic task is to establish economic justice, an obligation which is part of its overall task to establish justice in a broad sense. Thus a theory of government microeconomic activity from a Christian point of view should emphasize ways in which government actions help or hinder the establishment of justice, rather than emphasize to what extent they raise or lower individuals' self-perceived utilities as the neoclassical theories do. Before developing such a theory from a Christian perspective, however, we will briefly examine neoclassical welfare economics, for the acceptance of this welfare economics is the common and fatal basis for the neoclassical economists' analyses of government microeconomic actions, no matter how much they may differ in their views of the desirability of particular actions.

## A Critique of Neoclassical Welfare Economics

We are using the term "neoclassical welfare economics" to refer to the avowedly prescriptive branch of modern economic theory as practiced by the main stream of English-speaking economists, including not only highly theoretical and abstract welfare economics, but also applications of this abstract welfare economics to actual situations by which economists make evaluations of or give advice regarding particular institutions or actions. A key element in welfare economics is the acceptance of the standard of "Pareto optimality" (often called "economic efficiency") as a major, if not the only, standard for evaluating various situations and actions. A Pareto optimal or "economically efficient" situation is a position from which it is not possible to make anyone better off without making at least one person worse off. This is not a unique position for any one economy; rather there are many such positions, differing only in their distributions of welfare. This standard for an "optimum" is generally extended to changes between "non-optimal" positions by saying that a position A is better than another position B, if at least one person is better off in A than in B, and no one is worse off.

There are a number of major faults in neoclassical welfare economics from a Christian point of view. In the first place, it was developed originally in an attempt to obtain an "objective, "value-free" or "scientific" normative economics. Although some economists have realized that it is impossible to have a "value-free" prescriptive economics, many economists continue to treat Pareto optimality or "economic efficiency" as an "objective" goal for the economy or, at the very least, do not make explicit in their writings the ethical presuppositions on which their advice is based.

The goal of Pareto optimality is based, among other things, on two individualistic ethical assumptions that are not acceptable from a Christian point of view. The first such ethical assumption is that each person is *always* the proper judge of what is best for himself; in the development and application of neoclassical welfare economics it is also assumed that each person in fact does choose what is best for himself given the situation he is in (his wealth, income, knowledge, the prices he faces, etc.). Christians and some others know that this is not true. All persons are sinful, and our sin distorts both our evaluations of what is best for ourselves and our actions. A second basic individualistic assumption implicit in the Pareto Optimality criterion is that individuals' valuations of how an action affects them fully determine the *social* value of that action. For example, if an individual changes his consumption in such a way that he believes he has a higher level of welfare, and no one else's self-perceived welfare is diminished by this action, the Pareto criterion would say that society's welfare has increased. But this is not acceptable from a Christian point of view, for if individuals' perceptions of their welfare are distorted by sin, these perceptions should not be taken as determining true social welfare. This is not to say that individuals' evaluations of actions are unimportant in determining the social desirability of such actions. Often they will be important, but it cannot be accepted as an immutable principle that they always correctly determine the social desirability of actions.

In addition to these unacceptable individualistic assumptions, neoclassical welfare economics as it is normally developed makes a false materialistic assumption; this is the assumption that a person's welfare necessarily increases if he can fulfill to a greater degree his insatiable desire for goods by means of a higher level of consumption, other things being equal. This is far from the spirit of the Bible with regard to material goods—namely, that men are stewards of resources which God has entrusted to them and that they should use these resources according to God's law, a standard which involves as much concern for the needs of others as for one's own needs. While it may be true that because of sin most people perceive themselves to be better off whenever they have more goods (other things being equal, including the amount that other people have), it is clear from the Bible that one can have too many goods for one's own welfare as well as too few, and that people should attempt to restrain their desires rather than attempt to fulfill them with ever higher levels of consumption.

Neoclassical welfare economics also invalidly treats economic welfare as a completely separable part of overall welfare, and assumes that actions in the economic sphere or changes in "economic welfare" will not affect any other aspects of welfare. But man is not a mechanism of the sort that part can be changed without affecting the others, nor is society mechanistic in that sense; and thus the effects of actions in the economic sphere on other aspects of society should not be ignored.

The individualistic and materialistic ethical assumptions underlying neoclassical normative economics not only cause it to evaluate an economy on the basis of how well it satisfies individuals' preferences and desires for goods and prevent it from questioning and evaluating these preferences and desires; these assumptions also create a serious technical problem for the analysis if economic systems and economic actions within the systems can influence the people's desires and preferences (commonly called their "tastes" by economists). For if an economic action (for example, a change in market structure, a change in price, or even a change in the economic system itself) changes the standard by which the action was to be evaluated, there is no longer a consistent way of judging which situation is better. In fact it seems quite clear that tastes *are* influenced by economic actions. As Scitovsky has stated, "Even the most ardent believers in consumer sovereignty must realize that most tastes are acquired." [Scitovsky 1962, p. 265] Desires for consumption are created by the level and type of consumption of others, and by advertising and other promotion of goods. Perhaps as Veblen stated, "Invention is the mother of necessity" [Graff, 1967, p. 44] more often than the reverse.

The absence of any criteria concerning the social welfare implications of changes in the distribution of individual welfare makes it impossible in almost every instance for neoclassical welfare economics to indicate whether a particular economic action improves social welfare or not on its own grounds, because almost every action will make at least one person worse off (in his own perception), even if it makes many people better off (in their own perceptions); in such a case the new situation is not clearly better or worse than the old by the Pareto criterion. If one had a fully specified social welfare function and knew all of the effects of the action, one could evaluate it on that basis. But neoclassical economists are not generally willing to make the ethical judgments necessary to get such a fully-specified social welfare function, especially since it has become clear that it cannot be obtained from some combination of individual preferences. This limitation is often forgotten when cost/benefit studies of government projects which generally ignore the distributional implications of the projects are used to evaluate them.

Additional technical problems with neoclassical welfare economics, such as the fact that it is a static theory and thus neglects many important dynamic effects of economic institutions and actions, could be discussed. But the arguments we have made are sufficient to indicate that this theory is an inadequate basis for an evaluation of government institutions or actions as well as for the evaluation of other economic institutions or action.

## A Theory of Government Microeconomic Actions From a Christian Point of View

### Basic Norms and Principles

We must now discuss briefly a Christian view of the nature of the state and its proper role in general in order to provide a context for discussing its economic role. Christians have differed greatly over the years in their views on the state, and still do today. Our view is in basic agreement with that outlined by Nicholas Wolterstorff in sections VI and VII of his article "Contemporary Christian Views of the State: Some Major Issues" [Wolterstorff, 1974], which is in turn based on writings of Emil Brunner and Herman Dooyeweerd. [Brunner, 1945, Dooyeweerd, 1957, vol III, part II, ch. 3]

The state is a God-ordained institution which God has endowed with power to compel obedience. But the state is not autonomous. It may not do whatever it pleases with its power; whether the officials of the state are democratically chosen or not and whether the state has a constitution limiting it or not, the state's power is not absolute. For, as is true of other institutions, it is called to follow norms which God has set down for it. It should not replace these norms with either the "will of the people" (however that may be determined), or with the will of the sovereign, dictator, or other government official. God calls the state to act justly in all that it does and to promote justice in society. Although it is beyond the scope of this work to fully define justice, it includes certain measures of peace, order, and freedom in society. Economic aspects of justice have been discussed in chapter V and will be discussed further below. If a state is to act justly, it must acknowledge the God-given rights of individuals and other institutions (for example, family and church) to their existence and to whatever is necessary for them to carry out their God-given callings. Brunner calls a state which recognizes these rights a "federal" state, one which always has this essential element, "that the independence of those who unite in it is never forfeited, that the whole which is formed never absorbs all the rights of the parts." [1945, p. 275] The "parts which unite" need not be governmental units as in the "federal" government of the United States, but are the individuals and institutions which make up the state.

Since the state is the only institution that legitimately has a power of compulsion over all members of a society, it may exercise compulsion to achieve legitimate ends. But it may only act in a *just* way to achieve these ends. This means, among other things, that it must uphold the other legitimate institutions of society in the fulfilling of their God-given callings. Even though it has power of compulsion over them and may restrict them when they act unjustly, it may not abolish them and, except as a last resort, should not take over their functions.

There are a number of areas in which capitalistic market economies generally fail to give results which are in accord with God's call for proper steward ship, areas involving serious problems of economic injustice, or waste, or both. These are legitimate areas for state involvement in such economies, but the intervention must be done in a just manner. First of all, the distributions of wealth, economic opportunity, and income in capitalistic economies, unless modified by government action, historically have been such that they leave some families without the opportunity to fulfill their God-given roles in the economy and society in general. This deprivation is obviously unjust from a biblical point of view. In addition, in market economies, resources may be used to such an extent to meet the present desires of individuals and institutions that insufficient care is taken for preserving the possibilities for fulfilling the needs of people and institutions in the future.

Furthermore, some goods have what economists call "externalities," that is, some of their costs or benefits cannot be priced in the market. This can lead to both waste of resources and injustice, as, for example, when a firm pollutes a source of drinking water because there is no market mechanism which can charge a price for its pollution, and it is seeking to maximize its profits by minimizing the monetary costs of producing its output. There is also a class of goods which economists call "public goods," such as lighthouses, which have the characteristic that if they are provided for one user, others can benefit from them at no additional costs. There are often problems of waste or injustice in the provision of these goods by a private market, and sometimes they will not be provided at all without the compulsion of government, even if they are desirable. There may also be cases in which society wishes to overrule individual preferences and encourage or discourage the use of other goods. (Richard Musgrave [1959, p. 13] calls this the case of "merit wants".) Although the state must be careful in its interventions in this area, for there is an ever-present danger of taking away people's opportunites for responsible stewardship, it is true that people (and institutions) often engage in irresponsible stewardship, and when their actions involve serious danger or harm to themselves, the government may legitimately restrict their actions.

As capitalist economies have developed, so have strong tendencies towards concentrations of power within them, both within individual markets (monopoly elements) and within the economy as a whole. This grasping for power also creates injustice and waste in the economy, and is a legitimate reason for government intervention. Furthermore, such economies have shown themselves to be subject to recurring episodes of high unemployment and inflation (this will be discussed in Chapter XIII).

It should be emphasized again that although there is a legitimate role for government action in all these cases, it is important that the action be a just action, which respects the legitimate rights of the individuals and institutions involved and aiding them where possible in fulfilling their God-given callings. Here we can see a clear and important difference from the neoclassical approach. Although most neoclassical economists would see a potential role for the government in most of the above-mentioned areas, their emphasis in examining or evaluating government behavior in them is on the "efficiency" of these actions in individualistic and materialistic terms, whereas the emphasis in our approach is on the justice of these actions and on the degree to which they contribute to proper stewardship. This difference can be illustrated by the example of problems created by the existence of a monopoly. The main concern of neoclassical economists in this case is that the existence of a monopoly causes economic inefficiency, because it charges a price higher than the marginal cost of producing the good. Again, we would be more concerned with the injustices in the distributions of wealth, income, and economic power that might be caused by the existence of the monopoly, and would be concerned that any policy used to eliminate the inefficiency caused by the monopoly would not leave these problems unsolved or worse.

In addressing these problems of poor stewardship in the economy with the resulting to injustice or serious waste of resources, the government may use a variety of methods. In some cases it should restrain unjust actions of a person or institution. For example, it may prevent a public utility from setting an unjustly high price for its product, or correct an unjust action after it has taken place, such as by requiring the repayment of money which was acquired fraudulently. In other cases the government should provide persons or institutions what they need to sustain themselves and to have the opportunity to fulfill their God-given callings, such as providing a basic income to families who have no other opportunities to gain it and, going even further, providing them with opportunities to earn incomes with which to support themselves. In still other cases the government should provide a framework which enables and encourages other institutions to better fulfill their callings. For example, it ought to provide in law for a corporate structure that allows workers as well as capital suppliers to exercise some stewardship over the resources they contribute to the firm (as was discussed in chapter X), and provide a legal structure which encourages collective bargaining in a way that allows freedom for workers to be represented by unions of their own choice (as was discussed in Chapter XI). In some cases more than one of these methods may be employed together, but whatever methods are used, they should honor the legitimate rights of the people and institutions in the society. The government should not take over the functions of the other institutions unless they cannot be induced to end their unjust or wasteful behavior by any other just means. Governments should be concerned for the international effects of their actions as well as the domestic effects, and should not pursue unjust policies even though the injustice is done to those outside of their borders (international aspects of economic behavior are discussed in chapter XV).

The degree of actual government activity with respect to the economy that is needed in any state will be influenced by the degree to which the people and non governmental institutions practice proper stewardship of their resources. What Brunner says regarding the general activity of the state is true of its economic functions as well:

> The state has only to take charge of such tasks as are beyond the capacity of the other communities, and of such as arise from unwillingness and from the destructive, anarchic and antisocial tendencies existing in man . . . .
> The more forcefully state-free justice, the social *ethos*, has developed, and the more thoroughly it shapes society according to the law of justice by its own strength without state compulsion, the more state help can be dispensed with. The fundamental Christian realization is that the state has only to intervene where individuals, families, free social groups, the churches, the municipalities, cannot (or will not) perform their tasks . . . the greater the decline in the moral vigour of society, the more tasks the state must take upon itself, and the greater the expansion of the element of compulsion in justice . . . [Brunner, 1945, p. 275]

To give an economic example, if hardly any employers practice racial discrimination in hiring, legislation against discrimination in hiring will not be needed. This, of course, is the preferred situation for society. But if many firms discriminate, injustice occurs, and it would be desirable for the government to prohibit such action. If a simple prohibition causes employers to stop their unjust behavior, this act is sufficient; but if they find ways to evade the law (for example, by using seemingly fair but actually discriminatory tests), the government will have to prohibit such actions or take more stringent measures if the injustice is to be remedied. But this has its own problems, because such detailed laws or other stringent measures are apt to have their own unjust side effects.

These ambiguities remind us that perfect justice is not attainable in our imperfect world. The state can restrain some evil, but even a perfectly motivated state could not achieve perfect justice. Since action a state takes will have multiple effects, a state seeking justice must be continually weighing effects of the various actions it can take to try to find the most just set of policies possible, given the situation that faces it. It will have to consider its own limited resources and capabilities and how these can best be used to bring justice to its society.

We must recognize also that governments are not perfectly motivated, and that they do not always take the proper actions even when they do have proper motivation. Sin affects government actions as well as private actions; thus governments, as well as other institutions and individuals, will act irresponsibly as well as responsibly. The irresponsibility of governments may come from inaction in the face of injustices that they should be opposing, as well as from improper reactions to injustice or actions in areas in which they should not be involved. Since sin affects both sectors, we should not absolutize either government or private economic decision making. The best mix of government and private decision making will vary from time to time and place to place, depending upon the degree to which each is affected by sin and enlightened by common grace. The same is true regarding the level of government in which decisions should be made. Although it often may be desirable to make decisions on many matters on a local level, where there may be more knowledge of the particular facts involved and more opportunity for extensive citizen participation, a lack of concern for justice in many localities may call for action on a higher level; for example, the lack of action by many state and local governments to provide adequate opportunities for schooling for students from poor and minority families has called for federal government involvement in this area in the United States.

### Description and Evaluation of Various Areas of Government Microeconomic Policy

In the light of these principles, we will now examine various areas of government microeconomic policy and evaluate some examples of current and alternative policies in the United States.

*The Distributions of Income, Wealth, and Economic Opportunity.* As we have seen in Chapter V, in a just economic order all families would have the following: 1) access to the goods and services necessary for them to live and fulfill their God-given roles in society; 2) opportunities to develop and use their labor resources and a share of the other resources of society so that they can provide for themselves; and 3) opportunities to be responsible decision-making stewards of resources, both in production and in consumption. If these are not present for a family, it will not have an opportunity to fulfill its God-given roles as steward and producer, and if it does not have access to enough to live meaningfully in its society, it obviously cannot fulfill other God-given roles. A just society would provide these basic conditions to all its families and assure the possibilities of providing them in the future to the extent that it is possible to do this without violating other standards of justice. To achieve this, limitations will have to be placed on the degrees of concentration of wealth, income, and economic power in the society, for as these become too concentrated, those with the least of them will be deprived of the opportunities listed above. This does not mean that there must always be an equal distribution of them, however. The Mosaic economic legislation, if obeyed, would have provided these opportunities, and the prophets often called the nations of Israel and Judah to turn from their evil ways when they did not provide these opportunities for their families. If a good conceptual definition of poverty is "the lack of opportunity to fulfill God's callings," then a family would be economically poor to some degree if it does not have the opportunities listed above.

If we examine the situation in the United States, it is evident that none of the three standards are met. Many persons in the United States meet the government's own definition of poverty. By this definition (which is based only on income and in 1980 counted a non-farm family of four as poor if their income was below $8,414), about 29,000,000 persons or thirteen percent of the population were in poor households in 1980. [U.S. Bureau of the Census, 1981, p. 3] This income-based poverty line is very low in relation to the income required to provide the food, shelter, medical care, education, transportation, and other resources necessary to function in our complex, affluent society. Although many poor families also receive some "income-in-kind" which is not included in their income when the government measures poverty (such as food stamps and Medicaid benefits), even when these costs are added to the families' incomes many remain below the all-too-low official poverty line. [Hsieh, 1979, p. 524]

The government statistics also show that about half of the heads of poor households worked during the year, although many were without work part of the year (mainly due to lack of opportunities for work, family responsibilities, illness, or disability), and some worked only part-time. Of the half of the heads of poor households who didn't work during the year, most did not work because of illness or disability, family responsibilities, or retirement. Thus, even allowing for some mis-statements and lack of initiative, it appears that most of the households below the poverty line are there because they do not have access to enough income from their own earnings or other sources.

Why are so many families left with so little income in such an affluent nation? It is because the income transfer programs, both governmental and private, do not provide an adequate income for those not able to earn it for themselves. One of the causes of this defect is the fact that whereas some of the most important governmental transfer programs in the United States are federal-state programs, many states have set very low benefit levels for these programs. This is true, for example, of Aid to Families with Dependent Children (AFDC).

In addition, restrictions on the eligibility of families for aid under the programs leave many low-income families without support. For example, in many states a family is ineligible for AFDC if there are two adults in the family, and in others the family is ineligible if it has two adults one of whom is working, no matter how low the family's income is. Besides leading to inadequate income for families, these policies give disincentives for family stability in those families in which the father's labor has a low market value.

The low income of these families creates many problems for them. For example, they have higher rates of illness on average than families with higher incomes, and their children suffer from poorer nutrition, health care, and education, all of which lower the market value of their labor when they enter the labor force. This tends to perpetuate their poverty.

In addition to the many families who do not have access to enough income for functioning in our society, families lack the opportunity to develop and use their labor resources to support themselves adequately. These families include 1) many of the "working-poor" mentioned above, 2) those whose heads are working and earning more than the poverty-line income for their family but not enough to adequately support them (working "near-poor" according to the government statistics), and 3) many who do not have jobs because of a lack of demand for their labor.

Government policies which contribute to this problem include fighting inflation with policies that cause high unemployment (discussed in Chapter XIII), the lack of effective anti-discrimination policies in many areas, the inadequacy of job-training and job-creation programs, and the failure to provide adequate education, nutrition, and health care to children in poor families, deficiencies which lower their labor value when they enter the labor market. There are also disincentives to work in many income transfer programs. These include the fact that when recipients earn more income, they often lose some benefits from each of a number of programs (such as AFDC, food stamps, and housing aid) for each dollar they earn. The combined loss (the implicit tax) may come near to the value of their take-home pay. Even more serious is the fact that some programs, such as Medicaid, have an abruptly cut-off aid when a family's income exceeds a certain level. This policy creates a strong disincentive for earning just a little more than that amount. In spite of this disincentive, surveys of welfare recipients indicate that most have strong desires for work, and that there are generally more applicants for job-training and job-creation programs than there are places available. Thus, the main problem seems to be a lack of adequate job opportunities, not an unwillingness to work.

Many families who are not poor nevertheless lack the ability to exercise full stewardship over their own labor and a share of the society's physical resources, since physical and financial wealth is so unequally distributed, and since the control of most enterprises is vested in the suppliers of capital or their representatives.

Significant alternatives to the current income and wealth distribution policies of the government can also be described and evaluated in terms of the standards for justice listed above. One such alternative is a negative income tax. A negative income tax pays money to families whose income is below an amount called the break-even point, an amount which varies by size of family. The amount given to a family with no other income is called the income guarantee, and the rate at which the payments are reduced as the family's other income rises is called the "implicit tax rate."

A negative income tax, with the income guarantee at the official poverty line and a fifty percent implicit tax rate (that is, payments are reduced by fifty cents for every dollar of other income the family receives), as a replacement for the current AFDC and food stamp programs would do much toward meeting the first standard (access to necessities) and would aid many lower-middle income persons as well. In itself this provision would do little to meet the other standards, nor would it assure access to adequate education, health care, and housing, in areas where these are presently lacking. But it would provide more incentives for work and less incentive for family break-up than the present welfare system. Although it would be administratively cheaper than the present program, its overall cost would be considerably higher. On balance it would be an improvement on the present programs, if it could be funded without seriously hindering other desirable programs.

Another possible change in present welfare programs would be the addition of a work-requirement. This measure would not improve the equity of the system to any considerable degree if it were just a requirement that recipients work at dead-end jobs for the number of hours required to pay for their benefits at the minimum wage. Such a change would not raise the family's income, nor give it more stewardship responsibilities, nor give family members the satisfaction that even a subsidized but more regular job (such as a CETA job) would provide. Experience has shown that such a requirement would not be likely to reduce the welfare rolls much. The biggest reason there are welfare recipients who do not work is the lack of available jobs, not an unwillingness to work.

A somewhat related but significantly different type of change would be to classify low-income families into those who have no one able to work and those who do have someone able to work. The former should be given an adequate income, and the latter should be provided with a job or training for a job, and only a very low income if the job or training is rejected. President Carter's "Better Jobs and Income" proposal was of this type, but with an inadequate income guarantee for those not able to work, and an inadequate number of job guarantees for those able to work. If adequately funded, a proposal of this type would go a long way toward both assuring adequate income and providing opportunities for families to produce for themselves. Although such a proposal would be expensive in terms of training costs, job-placement costs, and costs to provide jobs for those who cannot be placed in other jobs, it might actually be less costly in the long run than an adequate negative income tax (though many lower-middle income and "near poor" families would receive less than under a negative income tax.) This would be a desirable approach if the problems of the division of the poor population into the able and not-able-to-work categories could be handled equitably, including allowing those judged not-able to apply for jobs if they wished, and if enough resources could be devoted to the program to provide an adequate income for those not able to work, and adequate jobs for all those able to work. The reason for classifying families into the two groups is to reduce costs for payments to the not-able-to-work group by having a high implicit tax rate on their benefits without creating disincentives to work for those able to work.

Although they are not normally thought of as income or wealth distribution programs, programs which provide more adequate education, nutrition, and health care for the poor and which reduce discrimination raise the value of the labor of many poor families, at least in the long run, and thus give them greater access to income and greater opportunities to produce for themselves. Policies which have contributed to this in the United States include the Head Start program, the Food Stamp program, Medicaid, and the various civil rights acts, but unmet needs still remain in these areas.

But even if policies to provide access to adequate income and opportunities for jobs were instituted in the United States, many workers would still be left without the opportunity to exercise full responsible stewardship of their labor, and many families would still lack the opportunity to exercise stewardship over many resources other than their labor, due to the very unequal distribution of wealth in the United States and the vesting of control of enterprises in the suppliers of capital. Laws requiring co-determination in firms would help to give workers more opportunities for stewardship. The very unequal distribution of wealth in the United States continues over time because of the lack of effective wealth taxes. Although there are taxes on transfers of wealth by gift or bequest, they have many loopholes which allow many large transfers to escape most taxation. The replacement of these taxes with a progressive lifetime accessions tax (a tax based on the amounts of the gifts and bequests one has received over a lifetime) would encourage donors to spread their wealth more widely when they give it away. There should be provisions for exemption from taxation of small or medium-sized accessions, with provisions for payment of any tax due over time when the gifts or bequests are in non-monetary form, in order to enable family farms and small businesses to be passed on to future generations. There might also be exemptions for gifts or bequests to those whose current income and wealth are very low. If such a tax were instituted, and the proceeds used to assist in the creation and development of small worker-managed cooperatives and other small business through provision of management aid and low-interest loans, more families would acquire opportunities to exercise reponsible stewardship of resources in production as well as consumption. This action would be an example of government aiding other institutions in society to fulfill their callings, rather than taking over their tasks itself.

In income and wealth distribution programs, as well as in other areas, even governments which wish to act justly are faced with serious problems of how to promote maximum justice in an imperfect world. It may often be true that because of other legitimate calls on government resources, and the unwillingness of taxpayers to support the government at an adequate level to meet all of the needs, not all programs can be funded at the level that full justice would require. Governments in such situations should weigh carefully the competing demands, and consider the broad effects (not only the economic effects) of their taxation and expenditure programs, in order to arrive at the most just policy attainable.

*Externalities.* Externalities occur when markets are unable to charge a price for some of the costs or benefits of a good or action. Pollution is an example of an external cost, and the benefit neighbors receive when a family paints the exterior of its house is an example of an external benefit. In the case of external costs, since the persons or institutions whose activities cause the external cost cannot be charged for it, others in society must bear the cost. And in the case of external benefits, if they are produced, those who benefit from them cannot be charged for the costs of producing the benefits.

Neoclassical economists recognize the problems markets which have with externalities and generally call for taxes or subsidies on activities that produce externalities. The tax should be equal to the marginal external cost of the activity, or the subsidy equal to the marginal external benefit of the activity, in order to induce production of an "efficient" level of activity. While this might indeed induce an "efficient" level of the externality and activity associated with it, if all other conditions necessary for efficiency are met (which never happens), it may result in inequitable situations, especially if those harmed by the external costs are not compensated (and normally they are not), or those receiving the benefits are not in any way charged for them (as is also often the case).

The degree of government involvement required in the case of externalities will depend on the actions of people and institutions in society. The more they act in a narrowly self-interested way, the more government action will be necessary if proper use of resources is to be achieved. For example, if all firms and other institutions would show such care for the environment that they would not cause health hazards or threaten its continued usefulness for others, there would be no need for government action to control pollution; but since many ignore the effects of their actions on others in an attempt to fulfill their own goals, the maximization of profit or utility or some other goal, the government must take action if the despoilation of the environment and serious injustice are to be averted. And if all owners of housing in an area keep their houses in good repair so that they do not harm the property values or the safety of neighbors, there will be no need for a governmental housing code. When there is a need for government action, the action should be a *just* action. In general this would include apportioning the costs of continuing external costs to those who cause them, compensating those who are harmed, apportioning fair payments for external benefits, and honoring the rights of individuals and institutions. For example, the government should not nationalize an industry just because it pollutes, nor forbid private home ownership just because some families don't keep their homes in good repair. A just policy would also involve seeking to achieve a non-wasteful level of the external costs or benefits, levels which preserve or even enhance the opportunities of institutions to fulfill their God-given roles in society.

The difference between this approach and the usual neoclassical approach can be illustrated by several examples. Suppose the production of a luxury good has negative effects on poor people living nearby, perhaps because of air pollution. And suppose, further, that the wealthy people who buy the luxuries are willing to pay a tax which is calculated to be equal to the monetary value the poor neighbors place on the harm done to them. Should production continue? Conventional economics says yes. But continued production would be inequitable if the compensation is not actually paid to those who are harmed, or if the harm done is of a life- or health-threatening nature, both of which often occur in the externality situations. Nor should a group of wealthy persons be able to force a group of low-income workers to pay a large tax, or sacrifice their jobs, because something which is necessary to the workers' production process offends them and the monetary value they assign to this offense is high because of their high income, as the efficiency criterion might suggest. Even less should the government prohibit the production processes, as some suburbanites have tried to have governments do after moving into farming areas and finding some of the sounds or smells of farming disagreeable. These are extreme cases chosen to make the point of difference clear. In many actual cases the weighing process in which the government must engage if it is to act justly might be much more difficult. When externalities have to do with life- or health-threatening situations, as is often true in cases of air and water pollution, the neoclassical efficiency calculations, usually based on costs of medical care, amount of income lost, and/or measures of people's aversion to risk of death or injury, generally underestimate the harm done. Surely life and health are worth more than the costs of medical care and lost income, and calculations of individuals' "risk premiums" (the amounts they are willing to pay to avoid risk of death or injury) may underestimate people's true valuation of death or injury if people are ignorant of the true risks of the different options, if there are some "risk-lovers" who tend to choose the riskier options, or if some people do not have real options (such as those faced with a choice between the risk of "black lung" by working in a coal mine or not being able to support their families). But even if individuals' valuations of their lives or health are correctly estimated, it is not clear that the "efficient" solution they indicate should be the one used to determine public policy. Christians would often want to place a higher value on life and health than these individual valuations, even if they cannot give a formula for calculating it. In addition to these problems, serious equity problems occur in the case of life- or health-threatening externalities even if some calculated compensation is paid. Frequently people start off with very different incomes and thus different marginal utilities of income which would affect the size of the compensation required under the standard neoclassical calculations. Of course the equity problems in life- or health-threatening externalities are especially great, and the "efficient" solution even less appropriate, when compensation is not paid to those who are harmed.

In general, governments should encourage other institutions in society to behave justly in the face of externalities. Sometimes this can be done with a system of taxes or subsidies, but at times it might have to be done via prohibitions of required actions. To avoid waste, the tax, requirement, or prohibition should be placed on the externality itself, if possible, and not on some process or activity which may or may not cause the pollution. For example, it would be better to prohibit air pollution above certain levels (if it were feasible to enforce such a prohibition) than to require any particular devices (such as "scrubbers") or prohibit the use of some inputs (such as high sulphur coal). As neoclassical economics correctly indicates, directly addressing the pollution problem gives producers an incentive to find the least-cost way of meeting the desired goal—the reduction of pollution. Persuasion and education may be desirable features of government policy in some cases of externalities.

*Public Goods and Merit Wants.* Public goods are goods which have the characteristic of non-rival or joint consumption, that is, if the good is produced and consumed by one person, it can be consumed by others without additional production cost. For example, if a road is cleared of snow so that one person can drive on it, others can benefit from the clear road without additional plowing costs. This case is in contrast to a private good where if one person consumes it no one else can consume it; for example, a hot dog which if eaten by one person is not available for others' consumption. Many public goods also have the characteristics of non-excludability, that is, the condition that people cannot be excluded from the benefits of the good by charging a market price for it. National defense is such a public good. No one could sell national defense on the private market offering to protect one family if it pays for the protection while not protecting the neighboring family if that family refuses to pay. As neoclassical economists point out, public goods will not be provided by a market in "efficient" amounts, especially if they have the characteristic of non-excludability, for then no firm can cover the costs of producing the good by charging a price for it. While some public goods might be provided by voluntary contributions, this practice becomes more difficult as the group benefiting from the goods becomes larger and less cohesive, for then the problem of the "free rider" becomes greater. The "free rider" problem recognizes that some, often many, will refuse to contribute to the costs of providing the good, thinking that whether they pay or not will have little or no influence on whether the good is provided or not, and hoping that others will contribute enough so that they can benefit from it without paying for it. But even if it is possible to exclude people from using the good by charging a price (as in the case of television signals where it is possible to encode them and charge a price for use of a decoding machine), a private market would not provide the good in an efficient manner, for once the good is produced it costs no more if additional people use it (watch the television program), but private producers to cover their costs will charge a price for the use of the good, thus excluding some people who could benefit from the good by using it. The benefits of many goods are partly private and partly public. An example is education, much of the benefit of which accrues to the person obtaining it, but which also often benefits other people. Such goods can be treated as goods with external benefits if the "public" part of the benefits has the characteristic of non-excludability.

There is another class of goods often provided or mandated by the government called "merit wants." These are goods which would not be provided by strict "consumer sovereignty" or neoclassical welfare economics criteria. That is, the people who benefit from them would not be willing to pay the marginal costs of providing them if they were given a free choice in the matter. Corresponding to this are government restrictions on the consumption of certain goods which are justified on the basis of the harm the consumption would do to the person involved rather than on the basis of the harm that the consumption does to other people. Some neoclassical economists consider this a legitimate area for government involvement (as an exception to their normal individualistic approach), but others view such actions as always harmful. In fact, many governments do take actions with respect to merit wants, such as requiring use of seat belts in automobiles, or providing all people with access to medical care, and we would not rule this out. Since people are sinful, their consumption decisions are not perfect and should not be absolutized into a norm from which no exception can be made. However, the government must be very careful in its actions in this area, recognizing that its views about what is best for people and institutions are also distorted by sin, and realizing the violence done to the rights of families to have the opportunity to be responsible stewards in their consumption decisions if the government restricts them too greatly.

Neoclassical economists generally call for the government to provide public goods (especially if they have non-excludability) and prescribe some type of marginal cost-marginal benefit calculus as the way to determine the proper "efficient" amount of the various public goods to provide, while admitting great difficulties in making these calculations in many cases. But the decision of which public goods to produce, and how much of them to produce, should not just be based on a cost/benefit analysis. Rather the implications of a project for the establishment of justice should be of first concern. Thus providing infrastructure to a poor region that would enable its people to support themselves should take priority over providing opera or ballet for middle or high-income people, even if on a cost-benefit criterion the latter was preferred. But cost-benefit measures might be useful in deciding which infrastructure programs to provide to the poor region, and it might be possible to subsidize the arts and advance justice by paying the costs of making them available to the poor. The degree to which the impacts of the projects on the distributions of wealth, income, and economic opportunities should influence the decisions on public goods will be determined by the degree to which these distributions are already just in the society, and the degree to which any adverse distributional conditions will be corrected by other more economically efficient and politically feasible measures.

Goods or services necessary for sustaining life or for the development and use of peoples' labor resources so that they can be productive members of society should be high on the list of public and merit goods provided by the government. These include food, medical care, shelter, transportation, and education and training. Of course many will be able to obtain the private goods included in this list without government help, but if there will be some who would not have adequate amounts otherwise, it is proper for the government to give them access to them. And some transfer payments to correct inequities in income distribution may be made by providing such goods rather than money, if such goods would not be easily available to the recipients of the assistance on the open market (as may be true for housing and medical care in some low-income areas), or if the recipients would not choose to spend their income on them. But families should retain some opportunities to exercise decision making regarding their consumption, so not all transfers should be "in kind."

Not every public good that individuals want and that therefore would pass a standard cost/benefit test, or everything that some (or even a majority) consider a merit want, should be provided by the government, because desires are distorted by sin, and providing them might lead to less justice and lower welfare for society. As possible examples of such public goods consider a development project that would destroy a native people's mode of life (such as the McKenzie pipeline [McCallum et al, 1977]) or pornographic programs on public TV (which could conceivably be desired by enough people to be "efficient"). As a possible example of a bad "merit want", consider abortion on demand.

It will not always be best for the government to provide desirable public or merit goods directly. Often justice will be better served by contracting with private businesses to provide the public goods, since there will be more scope for individual stewardship of resources if the resources of production stay in the hands of many private enterprises than if they are all under the direct control of government. Concerns other than cost, which relate to justice, such as size of the firm, its type of control, practices of the firm in hiring disadvantaged persons, degree of unemployment in the firm's labor market, and the justice of the firm's wage policies, are all relevant to decisions about whether to award a contract to a particular firm. It is also desirable to give users of the goods opportunities to exercise responsible stewardship by giving them choices where possible. For example, since education is basically the responsibility of the family, it would be more just to let parents and students choose between various schools, as with a voucher system, rather than continue the present system in the United States of having the government administer publicly supported schools and forcing families who wish an education from an alternative perspective to pay all the costs of such an alternative education, while also paying taxes to support the government system. But any voucher system should be carefully designed so that it does not become a source of discrimination against the poor or various minority groups who could be left in poor quality schools if a low-value voucher plan is adopted and they are excluded from many schools by high additional charges or discrimination.

National defense is a legitimate public good; indeed some defense is needed by almost every country if it is to be able to provide justice for its people in the face of external threats. But funds spent for military might to keep an unjust regime in power are wrongly spent by our principles, and nations which seek their security in military might rather than in following the Lord's call to justice should see the sinfulness and futility of this course from both biblical and general history.

*Government Regulation of Economic Activity.* There is strong pressure for deregulation in the United States which often is based on a faith that the market will always give good solutions, an attitude resulting from an incorrect understanding of the results of neoclassical welfare economics. The truth is that there are legitimate roles for government regulation. Of course it is also true that some particular government regulations will be irresponsible, either because they are instituted in areas where none are desirable, or because they regulate in a mistaken way areas where regulation is legitimate. Regulation should have as its aim a proper stewardship of resources; thus it must be concerned with promoting justice and reducing waste of resources. Just regulations must recognize the legitimate rights of institutions or people who are regulated, and should guide and enable them to better fulfill their God-given tasks.

Among the institutions which should in general be subject to regulations are public utilities (natural monopolies) such as electricity, natural gas distribution, and telephone service. Since there is the potential that unjustly high profits could be earned in such areas, especially harming the poor in the cases of goods which are necessities, it is desirable to regulate the prices and earnings of such natural monopolies unless they have clearly shown themselves to behave in a proper manner. It may be appropriate to mandate lower prices for a basic amount of the good or service for the poor, if the good is a necessity, and if the problems of poverty cannot be solved by more direct means. When "lifeline" prices can be combined with general approximations to average-cost pricing, such pricing is generally desirable. But there may be exceptions to this. For example, if it is desirable to reduce consumption for national security reasons, or to conserve resources for future generations, then a system of increasing prices as consumption rises might be appropriate, even if the average costs were constant or declining as more was supplied to each customer.

Regulation is also often warranted in situations where the health and safety of people is at stake. Often in such cases the information necessary for individuals to make proper choices is absent if there is no regulation, or people are in the situation that they have little or no option to avoiding the risk. For example, low-skilled workers in a town where the main source of employment is a textile mill, and where there is a high incidence of "brown lung" disease among the long-time workers, may be put in the position of accepting the risk of serious illness or being unable to fulfill God's call for them to provide for their families. And even if people have the proper information and real options, sin may lead them to make improper choices.

Health and safety regulation is practiced in the United States in the areas of food and drugs, consumer product safety, transportation, and occupational health and safety. Regulation in all such areas is desirable, although particular regulations might not be. There are currently calls in the United States to eliminate those regulations that are not "cost effective." While it is desirable to know the costs of regulations and to compare them with the potential benefits, the standard neoclassical calculations of benefits from prevention of injury, disease, and death, are likely to be too low to be used in determining just policies. However, it would in general be desirable to write the regulations in such a way that the least-cost methods of attaining some end could be used, rather than specifying some particular method. When government sets the stringency of ethical drug regulation, the potential harm from withholding or delaying the availability of beneficial drugs should be weighed against the potential harm of allowing some unsafe drugs on the market. It may also be desirable at times for the government to prohibit harmful actions even if people know the risks and are willing to take them. That is, it is legitimate to interfere with consumer sovereignty to protect people from themselves, for example by making use of seat belts mandatory or prohibiting the use of certain harmful drugs. This action should not be done lightly, however, or it could lead to a totalitarian state, with little freedom for responsible stewardship.

Regulation is also appropriate in situations in which there is serious ignorance or misinformation in the absence of regulation. Truth in advertising and mandatory-labelling legislation fit into this category. If consumers are to be responsible stewards, they must have truthful information concerning the products they buy. If truthful information is not provided without regulation (and there is abundant evidence that it often will not be), then it is desirable that the government require it, within limits. Similarly, it is important that information be available to investors in and employees of firms, so that they will have a base for the responsible decision making they are called to exercise. If information is not freely given, it is appropriate for the government to require it be made available.

*Regulation of Market Structures.* Because of the tendency for economic power in capitalist economies to become concentrated, both within specific markets and in the economy as a whole, unless restrained by the government, regulation in the areas of market structure and concentration of economic power is desirable. The policies in this area, as in others, should promote justice and discourage waste of resources. Thus the policies should be designed to limit concentration of control over wealth and other forms of economic power, since these tend to reduce the possibilities for responsible stewardship for others. If such concentration occurs within a particular market, the choices consumers have are decreased, and often they are presented with prices that fail to reflect the true cost of production. As the concentration increases in the economy as a whole, firms become larger and fewer in number, and there are fewer opportunities for workers and investors to exercise real stewardship of their resources. When policies are being determined in this area, these effects and the effects of concentration of the control of productive resources on the distribution of income should be considered as well as the "dead weight" efficiency losses that neoclassical welfare economics concentrates on. Looked at in this light, the present anti-trust policy in the United States is not sufficient, since it does little to break up existing concentrations of power. It is particularly ineffective against conglomerate mergers which, while not leading to inefficiency in the static, neoclassical sense, do lead to the concentration of control over resources and to the possibility of unfair competition in some markets.

Present policies regarding market structure in the United States could be improved by the adoption of an anti trust law similar to the legislation introduced in the early 1970's by the late Senator Philip Hart of Michigan, which provided for the division of large firms in concentrated industries into smaller units unless very significant economies of scale could be demonstrated. If this were done, more sharing of research and development and component design could be allowed in order for firms to take advantage of economies of scale in those areas. Stronger and clearer prohibitions on conglomerate mergers should also be enacted. In addition to such changes in anti-trust laws, concentrations of power could be discouraged by making the corporate income tax more progressive, and by limiting the tax-deductibility of advertising and lobbying expenses to some moderate amount per firm. Since international competition between giant firms is increasing, perhaps international coordination of market structure policies would be helpful in achieving more justice.

*Taxation.* Taxes are needed to pay for the various activities of governments. The basic criterion for taxes, as for other areas of government activity, is that they should be just. It is also desirable that they do not unnecessarily distort the incentives of people and institutions in society. This is not to say that that they should never affect these incentives, however.

On this basis we can say that the overall system of taxation should be progressive with respect to income; that is, it should take a higher proportion of the income of high-income families than of low-income families. Low and middle-income families should be taxed less in relation to their income than higher-income families, because the former have much less discretionary income left after meeting their basic needs for functioning in the society according to God's calling for them. No one proper degree of progressivity of the tax system can be determined from the criteria for justice for all situations; rather, the proper degree for any given situation has to be based on enlightened judgments in each particular case, weighing the effects of particular tax systems on the distributions of income and opportunities and on incentives in the particular situation.

Taxes should be horizontally equitable as well, that is, equals should be treated equally. Most economists would agree with this; the question is what factors should be considered in determining which families are equal. From our perspective, the relevant considerations include income, wealth, family size, extraordinary expenses of maintaining life or health, expenses of earning income, and uses of income and wealth (such as spending it on luxury consumption versus contributing it to a charity). A just approach to taxation would involve weighing these various considerations in arriving at an overall taxation policy. Taxes should be progressive with respect to wealth as well. Since continuous wealth taxes are difficult to administer, progressive taxes on wealth transfers may be the best options here. This would limit the concentration of ownership of wealth over time (as the Mosaic laws of the Year of Jubilee would have done for the nation of Israel had they been consistently enforced).

Special taxes on luxury consumption (even progressive ones) could be equitable as part of a taxation system, but it is hard to devise consumption taxes that would treat equally those who are equal. In addition, taxation of goods which are harmful to the individuals consuming them is a legitimate interference with "consumer sovereignty," in line with the principles discussed above in connection with "merit wants."

Benefit taxation—that is, taxation in proportion to estimates of the benefits that various families (or other tax paying units) receive from government services—should not be used as a general mechanism for financing government, for then there could be no net redistribution of benefits toward the poor. But benefit taxes might well be used in cases of public goods (or goods with externalities) that are provided mainly for middle and upper income persons. And, as noted before, taxes are appropriate as ways of charging for external costs in some instances.

In addition to the taxation of stockholders of corporations on the income they receive from their stockholdings (through dividends and capital gains), taxation of corporations is just, since the privilege of the corporate form of firm organization often gives additional power and control to the firm and limits the liability of the stockholders. But the heavier total taxation of dividends, as compared to retained earnings of corporations (taking into account the income taxes on both the corporations and stockholder), gives improper incentives for corporations to retain earnings, and thus to grow larger.

Judged on these criteria, there is considerable need for improvements in the overall system of taxation in the United States. Most studies have concluded that, taken as a whole, taxation in the United States is not very progressive. They find it may even be regressive at very low-income levels or roughly proportional there and across the vast middle range and considerably progressive for only the top five percent of families (at the most). [Okner 1980, pp. 69-84] This lack of progressivity results from the greater proportional burden of sales, property, and payroll taxes on low-income families, and the fact that income taxes are less progressive than they seem, because of loopholes in them. On the whole, federal taxation seems to be mildly progressive, while state and local taxation seems to be somewhat regressive. Horizontal equity is harmed by the existence of serious loopholes in the federal income tax, including the lack of taxation of interest on state and local government borrowing, the special treatment of capital gains, depletion allowances, the treatment of owner-occupied housing, and the lack of taxation of fringe benefits. Removing such loopholes, especially the capital gains treatment, exemption of interest on state and local government bonds, and the depletion allowances, would not only make the federal income-tax system more horizontally equitable, but would make it more progressive and would decrease the distorting incentives now present in the tax system.

Making corporate income tax more progressive and reducing taxation on profits paid out as dividends (but taxing dividends fully to their recipients) would add to equity by discouraging concentration of economic power in the economy. Corporate income taxes are subject to many of the same loopholes as personal income taxes in addition to some special ones involving international activities; these, too, should be adjusted or removed. Subsidies on investment (such as the investment tax credit and accelerated depreciation) create distortions in favor of higher capital/labor ratios in production, which result in the need for higher levels of GNP and greater resource use in order to achieve full employment, thus leaving fewer resources for future generations. If the goal of such taxes is to stimulate employment (as is often claimed), it would be better to give a direct credit for employment.

It is inappropriate to use the regressive Social Security payroll taxes to pay for the Medicare program, the benefits of which are available to all persons over 65 regardless of their work experience and payments into the system. It would be better to fund Medicare from the more progressive general federal taxation system, using the released payroll taxes to help solve the problems of funding facing the retirement portion of the Social Security system.

Wealth taxation (estate, gift, and inheritance taxes) is woefully inadequate in the United States. Because of loopholes (such as the possibility for using long-term trusts to avoid taxation) many large estates escape most taxation. A progressive accessions tax would be a more equitable way to tax transfers of wealth, as noted earlier.

It is desirable to exempt basic necessities from sales taxation in order to increase the progressivity of that tax. But there are problems of horizontal equity and creation of distorted incentives these exemptions, since it is often difficult to distinguish between necessities and luxuries. For example, some types of food, a class of items often exempted, are necessities, and some types are luxuries.

User taxes to pay for roads and other transportation facilities, or to pay for convention or recreation facilities, are legitimate ways to cover at least some of the costs of these services. Basic necessities, however, such as medical care and elementary and secondary education, should not be financed in this way. Special taxes on the consumption of items which harm the consumers of them or others, such as taxes on tobacco products and alcoholic beverages, are legitimate instruments to discourage their consumption.

## Summary

In summary, there are legitimate roles for the government in the economy. But governments may act unjustly in the economic sphere, either by failing to act to promote justice where this is necessary, by acting in cases where it should not, or by taking the wrong types of action where it should act. An economic theory from a Christian perspective which stresses that governments should act justly, respecting the rights of individuals and institutions in society and helping them to fulfill their God-given callings, can help to distinguish irresponsible government action from responsible government action.

# Resources

Aaron, H. J., and M.J. Boskin, eds. 1980. *The Economics of Taxation*. Washington: Brookings Institution.

Baumol, W.J. 1967. *Welfare Economics and The Theory of the State*. 2nd ed., Cambridge: Harvard U. Press.

Brunner, E. 1945. *Justice and The Social Order*. NY: Harper & Row.

Chiswick, B.R., and J.A. O'Neill, eds. 1977. *Human Resources and Income Distribution*. NY: Norton.

Dooyeweerd, H. 1957. *New Critique of Theoretical Thought*. Vol. 3. Philadelphia; Presbyterian and Reformed Publishing Co.

Graff, J. 1957. *Theoretical Welfare Economics*. Cambridge; Cambridge U. Press.

Hsieh, D. 1979. *Fiscal Measures for Poverty Alleviation in the U. S.* Geneva: International Labor Office.

McCullum, M., K. McCullum, and J. Olthuis. 1977. *Moratorium*. Toronto: Anglican Book Centre.

Meade, J. E. 1965. *Efficiency, Equality, and the Ownership of Property*. Cambridge: Harvard U. Press.

Meade, J. E. 1976. *The Just Economy*. London: George Allen and Unwin.

Mishan, E. J. 1969. *Welfare Economics*. NY: Random House.

Monsma, S. V. 1985. *Pursuing Justice in a Sinful World*. Grand Rapids; Eerdmans.

Musgrave, R. A. 1959. *The Theory of Public Finance*. NY: McGraw-Hill.

Musgrave, R. A. 1969. Cost-Benefit Analysis and the Theory of Public Finance. *J. Econ. Literature*. 7: 797-806.

Musgrave, R. A., and P. G. Musgrave. 1976. *Public Finance in Theory and Practice*. 2nd ed., NY: McGraw-Hill.

Okner, B. 1980. Total U.S. Taxes and Their Effect on the Distribution of Family Income in 1966 and 1970. in Aaron and Boskin 1980, pp. 69-84.

Scitovsky, T. 1962. On the Principle of Consumers' Sovereignty. *American Econ. Rev.* 52.

U.S. Bureau of the Census. 1981. *Money Income and Poverty Status of Families and Persons in the U.S.*, 1980, Washington: U.S. Government. Printing Office.

Wolterstorff, N. P. 1973. Contemporary Christian Views of the State. *Christian Scholars Rev.* 3: 322-32.

# Chapter XIII
# Macroeconomic Problems and Policies

*The banks are all broken they say,*
*And the merchants are all up a tree.*
*When the bigwigs are brought to the bankruptcy court,*
*What chance for a squatter like me?*
     *Australian Folk Song (1930's).*

The past decade has not been an easy one for macroeconomics. The pervasive faith of the late 1960's in a technical mastery of the economy which would advance us to a fine-tuned future of full employment, stable prices, and climbing productivity was shattered by events in the 1970's which made the earlier optimism a target of ridicule. The new era of limits applied not only to natural resources but also to the perception of inherent limitations in our ability to understand economic relationships. Optimism was replaced by a cynical and pessimistic scaling back of economic objectives. The apparent bankruptcy of government macroeconomic policies led to a retreat to the old time religion of balanced budgets, concern with the money supply, and a greater degree of expressed faith in private market solutions.

It is our belief that reliance on private market solutions is as fundamentally misplaced as was the reliance on elitist technical solutions of earlier policy. Both approaches ignore the fundamental issue: our present difficulties with inflation, unemployment, poverty, and an aging, energy-intensive capital stock are due to the emphasis on those human values on which neoclassical economic theory is based. These values, which are allegedly broadly, if not universally held, are frequently in opposition with more traditional notions of fairness and responsibility which are deeply rooted in our Christian heritage.

This chapter will illustrate the contrast between market and Christian perspectives on individual behavior, macroeconomic objectives, and appropriate policies. The first sections will pick up from Chapter III the notion of rational behavior as understood in economic science and show how this notion leads to alternative conceptualizations of economic problems and policies. The section on macroeconomic objectives sets the sights on our target, what we believe can and should be achieved as goals of national policy. The remaining sections then show how the perception of rational economic man prescribes a set of policies which frequently move us away from the target, while acknowledgement of the influence of moral values suggests a substantially different approach.

## Rational Economic Man—Life in One Dimension

Two ways in which conventional economic theory has led to inappropriate macroeconomic policies have to do with the so-called microeconomic foundations of macroeconomics. Standard micro doctrine proceeds from the assumption that the behavior of firms and individuals can be explained in a simple straightforward fashion. They are assumed to "maximize" something and, therefore, whether that something be utility or profits or volumes of sales, they are assumed to function in a rational, orderly, and predictable manner. Such behavior leads the economy to some sort of equilibrium point at which whatever it is that people are bent on maximizing is perceived to have been maximized so that no further changes in behavior occur. This equilibrium is typically one in which all markets clear; that is to say, the demand for anything is just equal to the supply of that item. If market clearance did not occur, some economic agent could presumably change his behavior so as to take advantage of the shortage or surplus situation in the non-clearing economy. Hence the world we observed before the changes in behavior were implemented obviously could not have been in equilibrium.

The emphasis in the development of macroeconomic models has been in part one of explaining real world phenomena. Unfortunately, macroeconomists have also frequently volunteered to constrain their efforts by operating under these twin principles: maximizing behavior and flexible, market-clearing prices. The result is a set of perspectives and models which presume that equilibrium exists and that equilibrium is a situation in which resources including labor are fully employed and all markets clear. There remain only a few sticky points involved in the determination of the speed with which the economy will return to equilibrium if knocked off course by some non-market influence. Our understanding of the way in which the macroeconomy works continues to be prejudiced by the belief that its workings must be consistent with these microfoundations.

The degree of insistence with which economists link macroeconomics to microeconomic assumptions has produced a spectrum of viewpoints on the necessity and usefulness of government intervention. The greatest degree of faith in the functioning of micro markets is exemplified by the rational expectations monetarists. This school of thought fully subscribes to the notion that a full employment equilibrium is the normal state of affairs. Any doubts to the contrary are evidence of a lack of appreciation and understanding of a competitive market system on the part of the doubter. Macro relationships are derived from individual utility or profit-maximizing decision making while ignoring constraints placed on individuals by the macroeconomy; i.e., a one-way causal relationship from individual behavior to macroeconomic results is assumed. Prices are assumed to adjust more rapidly than quantities, and Walras' Law is employed to link the markets for money, commodities, and labor. The conclusion is that full employment and an efficient allocation of the world's resources prevail, except in the case where surprises move the economy briefly away from full employment equilibrium. The rational expectations world is one in which government policy intervention is usually unnecessary, and, to the extent that policy actions are anticipated, they have no impact at all on the levels of output or employment. If, on the other hand, policy actions are a surprise, they will have an impact on output and employment, but only because they have jolted some markets away from the utility-maximizing, market-clearing state. Therefore, if government policy does produce a short-term impact, the impact is generally viewed as being detrimental. Even if unemployment is reduced, the government has done no one a favor, because the unemployed are viewed as being voluntarily and therefore optimally unemployed.

The difficulties of maintaining this position are numerous and are for the most part fought out in great detail in intermediate level economics texts. They include such issues of debate as, for example, the time span of the adjustment period from any sub-optimal disequilibrium position, and the effectiveness of policy activism in accelerating the adjustment process. However, two sources of controversy are particularly germane to the radically different perspective on individual motivations and the characteristics of equilibrium which will be presented in the next section. The first problem with this extreme market-oriented approach is that it treats all new information as atomized bits of experience which individuals can logically assimilate in determining their own optimal response. But this skips a prior step in the epistemology, as the information is meaningful within the analytical framework of the individual only if his analytical framework is identical to that ascribed to him by the predictor. If the individual's framework of thought is not based on the same economic principles as that of the predictor, he may respond in a surprising "sub-optimal" manner, even if he really is attempting to maximize whatever it is that he was assumed to maximize. At the extreme, people may be unable, because of inexperience or a lack of education, to develop a causal model at all. Or perhaps the model they develop is at odds with that developed by others, so that one set of events, a recession for example, may produce many different and conflicting behaviors. Clearly there is no guarantee here that an unfettered market will move back to an optimal full employment equilibrium, even if we continue to accept the notion that people are single-dimension maximizers who operate in flexible price markets.

But there remains an even more fundamental issue. The idea that people's behavior is a predictable response to outside forces requires that a person's entire being is focused on a single objective. This view leads to a useful understanding of the world only if, in fact, values are single dimensional, e.g., if the single purpose of life is to maximize consumption. In other words, the behavior of man is viewed as mechanical and automatic, leaving no room for human thought, plan, emotion, or responsibility. Contrast this perspective with that of people being created in the image of God and given dominion over the earth! On this issue both the liberal-activists of the 1970's and the conservative passivists of the 1980's unite in error. Both groups designed economic policies to deal with a mechanistic, single-dimensional economic man who could be manipulated by government bureaucrats in the former case and by the rigors of the marketplace in the latter.

## *More Dimensions Means Greater Complexity*

An alternative perspective with a broader view of human behavior is most frequently associated with the post-Keynesians or institutionalists. From this perspective economic activity produces an equilibrium that can best be described in terms of people being essentially satisfied with their decisions and behavior rather than dealing with the narrower issue of whether excess supplies or demands exist in the economy. The economy, in any case, is perceived as being in a continuous state of adjustment and development. This is caused by changes in population, technology, or laws, among other things. More generally, we retreat from the notion of "economic man" and behavioral changes determined solely by economic events. Individual behavior is regulated by a set of norms which change over time, which may be violated at any point in time, and which may be perceived as conflicting with the norms of others (requiring, if the conflict is serious, a change in laws or institutions), or even conflicting with other norms held by the same individual (requiring a rationalization of that individual's beliefs and further changes in behavior). In any case, human behavior in response to economic events is unlikely to be very predictable, and is certainly not governed by economic laws. It is unpredictable in that individuals operating under numerous norms will not maximize anything, and therefore will always appear irrational when their actions are evaluated by a theory which posits such maximizing behavior. We are left with a view of individuals who are faced with a situation which is always new and changing, so that the correctness of a decision is frequently impossible to evaluate until after commitments have been made. Within this uncertain environment, individuals can be expected to exhibit varying degrees of responsibility for family and community, and will operate on the basis of faith and fear, generally relying on habits or principles which seem to have worked well in the past.

Now this array of uncertainties presents us with a very messy picture of the world. Equilibrium has been downplayed both in terms of meaning (e.g. as some sort of reference point) and in terms of optimality. Empirical regularities in personal behavior may exist, but their correctness is open to question and their interpretation is surely and obviously a normative exercise. Much has been gained, however, in recognizing that human motivations and activity are complex. This approach comports well with several Biblical principles. We believe that since creation is coherent, our perspectives and explanation should also be coherent. "Economic man" can then be a misleading framework, as it excludes most of the story. We also believe that individual perceptions and motivations are influenced by the presence of sin. Therefore behavior is less likely to be consistent. Further, even if consistent behavioral regularities exist, their correctness must be evaluated. Acknowledgement of the sinfulness of persons negates any of the moral justification for consumer sovereignty. Hence any description or insight into personal motivations cannot be construed as a justification for the resulting behavior. So we've gained a broader perspective in exchange for the cost of reduced ability to rely on empirical regularities and the additional burden of having to evaluate any such regularities which we do discover.

Nevertheless we have some cause for optimism in our attempt to understand and evaluate economic relationships. We believe that God reveals Himself in the world. Since God is articulate we believe that His world is articulate and ordered as well. The order remains difficult to perceive both because our perceptions are clouded by sin and because violations of norms obscure this order. Because our perceptions are influenced by both faith and sin, what we observe and attempt to explain may be positive in the sense of being descriptive but is surely not value-free. To complicate matters, the lines of causation between reality and belief run in both directions. Not only does our faith influence our theories, but the resulting theories become a component of our culture or faith which become institutionalized in new patterns of behavior. To cite a prior example, observation of the world might lead to a theory which suggests that "employers treat labor as a substitute for other inputs in minimizing the cost of production." This theory then becomes accepted as factual knowledge, which in turn is used to justify such activity on the part of employers.

With these precautions, let us begin with some generalizations concerning the way the world works. For the reasons mentioned above, Christians should be somewhat skeptical about the usefulness of a descriptive, model-building approach. Yet such an approach is useful because any situation involves more facts than can be handled by our limited human capabilities. A model-building approach will assist us in determining what is useful information. The generalizations are obviously influenced by one's views of humankind as well as what is important for persons and society. A belief in rational autonomous consumers would stress the ability of the economy to respond to expressed demands. On the other hand, an acknowlegement of the sovereignty of the Creator and the sinfulness of man requires an analysis that distinguishes between responsible and irresponsible demands, one that establishes a priority of needs and requires that the economy be able to meet high priority needs before responding to those of lesser urgency.

## New Microfoundations

Our Christian faith should release us from the tyranny of inherited beliefs concerning rational economic man and faith in the impersonal authority of the marketplace. Perhaps an appropriate starting point in both rebuilding the microfoundations by which we understand macroeconomic events and go on to establish useful policy goals is an insight expressed by J. K. Galbraith:

> Specifically, in the modern democratic context, people seek to gain control over their own lives. This extends to all of life's dimensions. They do not neglect the most obvious of all goals, which is greater control over their income. It would be inconceivable were they to struggle for greater self-determination in all other aspects of life and leave this most vital of dimensions untouched. [1978, p. 8]

Attempts to control income are expressed in numerous ways in the modern economy. They include licensing of various occupations, the establishment of labor unions and price fixing agreements, import quotas, and crop support payments. The search for economic security is responsible for the massive development of social welfare programs in the post World War II era, programs which are designed not only to reduce the incidence of poverty but also to provide assurance to middle and upper income classes that they will never experience economic destitution. In short, the neoclassical orthodoxy with its market paradigm is becoming increasingly irrelevant as attempts to achieve greater self-determination produce economic freedom and an escape from the tyranny of markets. As this process continues, flexible wages and prices no longer operate as the equilibrating variable. The replacement of the market discipline with income protection has led to a fixed price, flexible output and employment description for a major share of economic activity.

Given the sinfulness of man and the resulting illegitimacy of consumer sovereignty, we must still determine whether this basic motivation of gaining control over one's own life by reducing economic insecurity is in fact a proper objective. To the extent that doing so constitutes an effort to act responsibly towards oneself, one's family, and one's community, it seems that this is a laudable objective. We wish to uphold families as viable economic units by promoting economic sustainability. It is particularly appropriate for individuals to seek some economic guarantees, and for government to assist, if in fact such guarantees lead to reduced preoccupation with the consumption and accumulation of economic wealth. Such guarantees should lead to greater personal and interpersonal freedom and realization of non-economic goals and norms. Lester Thurow argues that achieving a flexible and adaptable social interchange requires the wholesale replacement of the current hodgepodge of private efforts to acquire income or employment security with government provision of a guaranteed minimum income. [Thurow 1980] There is a problem, however, in that commodity fetishism could be replaced by security fetishism. As Tibor Scitovsky points out in *The Joyless Economy*, neither high levels of consumption nor strict adherence to a rule of caution prove to be particularly rewarding paths of human development. [Scitovsky 1976] The provision of economic security should be made with the explicit expectation that a society should then become more venturesome, not only in terms of willingness to accept economic risks, but in the much broader arena of human development.

There is a second possible difficulty related to the provision of minimum economic guarantees. It seems that people are acutely conscious, not only of their ability to meet basic economic needs, but also of their economic status relative to others. Perhaps this attitude exists because people still believe that their income is a reflection of their social contribution—an unfortunate carryover from neoclassical economics. This attitude may be due to the belief that high levels of consumption are associated with high levels of satisfaction. Such beliefs are likely to perpetuate themselves as relatively high incomes enable their recipients to achieve success in acquiring what Fred Hirsch calls "positional goods". [Hirsch 1978] These are goods which cannot be produced in greater numbers by the market economy and hence are available only to those who have the financial means to outbid everyone else for their use. Examples of positional goods would include the choicest locations for summer homes or the best seats at the symphony. The competition for positional or status goods would not be objectionable if all the competitors were endowed with a fair share of the world's resources, and if the competition deprived no one of the ability to meet basic economic needs. However, in a world where hunger and poverty still exist, a devotion to economic status is inappropriate. It does deprive those who are hungry and sick of assistance which is their right and which God requires the more fortunate to provide. And, fittingly enough, the attempt to achieve status or esteem by way of materialistic consumption is destined to failure. When consumption is no longer an end objective, but is used as the means by which to achieve the end of providing economic status, the economy is incapable of producing the good which is ultimately in demand. The good being sought is economic and social status. Since status is dependent on relative position, no amount of economic growth will provide satisfaction. All that is produced is consumer dissatisfaction as increased effort does no more than hold one's relative position constant over time. The economy becomes increasingly dependent on other countries to supply its growing demand for resources, increasingly susceptible to supply shocks or resource shortages with their attendant economic dislocations, and increasingly reliant on militaristic and nationalistic means to protect external resource supplies. The pursuit of an economic solution as a means of achieving higher levels of human development then becomes incompatible with the attainment of a minimal degree of economic security for everyone.

## Macroeconomic Objectives

We are dealing with a world in which efforts to escape from the market and to achieve economic security and status should be accepted as facts. Our response to these facts necessarily goes well beyond the Keynesian prescription of demand management, although it would not ignore the necessity of controlling aggregate demand and thereby influencing the levels of income and employment. But it is apparent that the objective should not be the traditional growth-oriented objective of maximizing output per person, without distinguishing among different types of output which meet different types of need among different groups of people. Rejection of the notion of consumer sovereignty allows us to attempt to distinguish between high and low priority needs. Acceptance of some notion of a minimal guarantee of economic security redirects our attention from the total volume of output to the distribution of output. Questioning the value of economic status does the same.

A proper set of government macroeconomic policies should be directed toward the attainment of a just distribution of the economy's resources. At the same time freedom of choice should be maintained in order that each of us can exercise our God-given mandate of stewardship in the use of resources and personal responsibility for others. Our policies should place less emphasis on economic growth because continued economic growth will not lead to any sort of utopia. A reduced emphasis on growth also is appropriate in our attempt to exercise stewardship by saving resources and the environment for use by future generations. Also, we should be at least skeptical of the abilities of a market economy to provide the correct level and type of output and jobs. This skepticism follows from the concern with distributional issues which the market economy makes no claim to adequately address. If the distribution of wealth and income is unfair, then market output will be skewed in the direction of the preferences of the wealthy, while the needs of the poor are ignored, because the poor do not have the financial resources to "demand" the things which they need. Skepticism is also in order because the scriptural perspective of man raises both factual and value questions about the supposed rationality, selfish preferences, and near-perfect knowledge that are required assumptions for smoothly functioning markets. What we desire is a set of policies which are designed to produce a framework for economic activity which allows and encourages people to exercise responsible economic stewardship before God.

What does this mean in terms of specific policy objectives? One objective, already dealt with, must be fair distribution of income which allows everyone to satisfy basic needs. Redistribution is not as simple as handing out money to the needy. While this straightforward response is an efficient means of meeting economic needs, it is certainly detrimental to the development of such basic non-economic needs as human dignity. While some income support payments are appropriate, the goal of distribution should be to assist people in developing their own abilities to participate in the economic community. This requires a concerted effort to redistribute productive wealth rather than just income. In the agriculture-based economy of Israel, God required a continuous redistribution of land ownership and limits on accumulation. An equivalent policy in our economy would focus on the distribution of human capital in the form of education, job training, and health care, along with limitations on the accrual of financial wealth.

Closely related to these distributional objectives is the provision of adequate employment opportunities. This is a necessary goal, because employment provides a basic means for distribution, a source of income to all who are capable of participating in the marketplace. Work fulfills God's mandate to tend His garden; that is, it is a means by which responsible stewardship can be realized. Responsible stewardship in the development of personal abilities is promoted by the learning, cooperation, and interaction that can occur in the workplace. Private markets are not generally appreciative of these benefits and treat all labor as a cost which is to be minimized, when in fact, a great deal of work entails corresponding benefits, suggesting that wages are sociologically determined, rather than being a necessary compensation for the disutility caused by work. As a result, the market price of labor may well overstate the true costs imposed upon employees, resulting in a market outcome with too little employment.

A third objective of macroeconomic management policies has also been partially justified at this point. The government should encourage conservation. A conserving economy could effectively increase the availability of resources by emphasizing greater value and durability from a unit of resources rather than insisting on increasing consumption and resource use in tandem. Christians should encourage resource conservation out of concern for future generations and out of belief that our plans and demands are shortsighted and reflect impatience when compared with God's plan. The costs of a high level of use of natural resources are likely to be greater than are reflected by market prices, for several reasons. The market does not adequately account for the needs of future generations, it does not account for the costs of military activity associated with high levels of resource demand, and it does not reflect the fact that energy use is a substitute for the use of labor with its attendant benefits to the employee.

Macroeconomic policies should encourage diversity and flexibility in the economy to reflect the diversity and resulting flexibility in the rest of God's world. A policy solution which relies on one or two large scale programs imposes a great deal of risk on the economy in the event that these solutions prove infeasible. Many smaller scale responses such as might be expected to occur in a market system are far less spectacular but also more likely to show the way to a broad set of solutions. Large, well-capitalized firms may be well suited to accepting economic risk, but concentrated and large-scale industries, whether steel or automobiles, or nuclear power generation, impose significant failure costs upon not only their own employees but on the entire economy. It is also necessary to bear in mind that in a fallen society we should be concerned with unduly large concentrations of economic power which, in turn, increase the probabilities of unjustifiable exploitative economic behavior.

Finally, the government should design policies which are compatible with a low and stable rate of inflation. High and variable rates of inflation impose several costs upon society. Inflation increases concern with one's relative and absolute level of purchasing power, and thus causes increasing concern with economic matters and increasing social divisiveness. Families feel threatened by the wage-price race and feel that they are being robbed by inflation, even when that may not be objectively the case. But so long as they feel that they are getting the short end of the stick they suspect that someone else is getting the long end. Such suspicions counteract altruism, trust in elected officials, and the spirit of cooperation which should exist between employers and employees.

Inflation also disrupts the planned responsible use of resources over time. Businesses are discouraged from making long-term durable investments in the capital stock and rely on short-lived capital investments which can quickly be monetized with a high rate of return. Inflation in conjunction with current tax laws penalizes saving and encourages present consumption. And inflation rapidly becomes more tenacious and self-perpetuating as individuals and institutions change their behavior. Escalator clauses, shorter contract periods, and higher markups to reflect the growing gap between replacement costs and actual historical costs all contribute to the wage-price spiral. The resulting inflation is largely immune to government policy. Inflation is a struggle over relative income shares, and continuing inflation will shift income from the weak to the powerful. Restrictive fiscal and monetary policy only assist and accelerate this shift in income shares by reducing the market power of these groups whose incomes remain subject to the vagaries of supply and demand. A return to expansionary policy renews the battle by shifting the balance of power back in favor of these groups.

Two currently popular objectives are notable for their absence from our list. One is the major objective of supply-side economics, which is to increase economic growth. We argued above that growth offered little benefit after basic needs have been satisfied. In particular, growth as a response in the race for economic status imposed greater costs on the economy. A closely related objective has been deregulation. Deregulation will presumably reduce costs and make the economy more responsive to changes in supply and demand. Both, it is argued, will reduce inflationary pressures. Deregulation which reduces the costs of economic activity has merit if the regulations were unnecessary or ineffective to begin with. However, non-market costs such as reductions in environmental quality or worker safety could climb rapidly with the removal of effective regulation. The second part of the deregulation argument reflects the personal faith and predilection of economists who would attempt to salvage the competitive market economy by removing subsidies, unwinding government regulations, and reducing income support programs—in short, insisting on the preservation of the market economy with its alleged benefits rather than recognizing broad social demands for economic security and something better than the impersonal tyranny of the market system.

## The Market Economics Paradigm

The conventional (monetarist) view of the way in which the economic world works is based on the utility-maximizing, flexible-price market paradigm described at the beginning of this chapter. The remaining sections will compare the dynamic adjustment process as understood by monetarists with the alternative view of individuals searching for a modicum of refuge from the narrow and rigorous life of rational economic man. This perspective provides insights into the dynamics of the price-setting and wage-setting process in a market economy—insights which retain their influence in people's minds in spite of the fact that the market economies which these insights purported to describe have largely disappeared. The continued viability of the conventional view is made possible because it encapsulates at least a germ of truth. A few goods, primarily raw materials and agricultural commodities, continue to be traded according to the impassive laws of supply and demand. Trade in finished goods and in services will, to a lesser extent, appear to observe the same economic rules, although not as neatly. At times seemingly paradoxical events require *ex post* revisions of conventional theoretical structures in order for them to maintain their claim to validity. A great deal of such revisionism within the framework of the market paradigm occurred, for example, after the early 1970's episode of rising wage inflation combined with a rising unemployment rate, a combination of events which had been ignored by previous versions of the paradigm. This constant process of revision is particularly embarrassing, because economists claim an ability to *predict* future events, a claim which is clearly at odds with the observed process in which contemporary events can only be made digestible with model adjustments which in themselves require a considerable time lapse.

While the conventional market economy view is probably better than no view at all, it does exact a cost. Based as it is on historical antecedents and, to a limited extent, on current reality, it continues to block consideration of alternative viewpoints by claiming sufficiency in explaining the supply and demand of everything from wilderness preservation to children. In fact, the very notion of supply and demand is so simple and straightforward that its continued wholesale adoption is perhaps more a matter of convenience than immediate relevance.

The market view of the world argues that labor and financial markets can be analyzed in the same fashion as the markets for goods and services. It is this argument which provides the framework for conventional macroeconomic analysis and its attendant policies. In the case of labor markets the supply of labor is a measure of the willingness of people to work at various wage rates, all of which must be positive because people don't enjoy working and therefore require compensation. Greater compensation will elicit greater effort by bribing individuals to sacrifice more of the pleasures of not working and by increasing the likelihood (or threat) of being able to find replacements if the currently employed fail to maintain peak productivity. On the demand side the willingness to offer a given money wage is determined by the value of output produced by the workers. The interplay of these considerations produces an endogenous money wage just sufficient to equate the demand for labor with its supply. Anyone who remains unemployed at this wage level has done so voluntarily by demanding a higher wage rate than the market is willing to offer. The entire process is impersonal; i.e., no "non-economic" considerations need to enter the analysis. The derived demand for labor (based on the value of additional labor-produced output) and the supply of labor are sufficient to determine the level of employment, real output, and real income. All of this works, in the general case, without any assistance from fiscal or monetary policy.

Fiscal policy, the manipulation of taxes and government expenditures, determines the division of the predetermined level of real income between the government and the private sector. But fiscal policy, at least in the short run, also allegedly has no impact on the price level. Though large government deficits are not supposed to affect prices or interest rates, experience has shown that deficits combined with monetary restraint drive interest rates to dangerously high levels, increase costs, and hence put upward pressure on prices.

The last linkage which we will examine with our conventional theory glasses is that between money and the price level (or between the growth rate of the money supply and the inflation rate). This linkage is established by the Quantity Equation, a tautology which states that the sum of the quantity of money and its velocity is identical with real income multiplied by the price level, or MV=PT. The money supply then determines the price level if velocity is constrained by existing laws and technology, if the level of real income has already been determined by other forces acting in the economy, and if the money supply is determined exogenously rather than in response to other economic events. Perhaps the large number of "ifs" in the prior sentence explains the failure of interest rates to reflect a lower level of inflationary expectations in periods such as the 1980-81 episode of dramatic reductions in the rate of money supply growth. Even if each of the individual qualifications seems reasonable, the probability of something going wrong increases with the number of qualifications. Suppose, for example, that real wage rates are not determined only by the supply and demand for labor. Then a reduction in the money supply could translate into a reduction in employment and income rather than a reduction in the price level. Casual empiricism suggests that at least one of the qualifications which we attached to the conclusion that the money supply determines the price level is wrong. Recent observations suggest that ninety percent of a given money supply contraction will appear as a reduction in employment and real incomes, and that only ten percent of the impact appears in the price-level term. [Okun 1979, pp. 1-5] This conclusion is unfortunate, because the neat dichotomy between the determination of real income and the price level disappears, foreshadowing the need for a more realistic approach which threatens to be more complex as well. It is also unfortunate, because current U.S. domestic economic policies are predicated on a quantity equation view of the world which indicates that fiscal policy activities are neutral with respect to both the full employment and stable price level objectives. A failure in any of our theoretical "ifs" under these conditions will translate into personal difficulties for thousands of families.

The purpose of this section was to briefly survey the market economy view of the way in which the economy works. According to this view, real income, employment, and output are determined in an auction-like market for labor. The price level, including money wage rates, is determined by the money supply. Fiscal policy determines the allocation of real income between the public and private sectors. In such a world the government bears no responsibility for dealing with unemployment, which is presumably voluntary. The macroeconomic responsibilities of the government are limited to two concerns. First, since the inflation rate is directly determined by the growth rate of the money supply, the simple solution to inflation is to maintain strict control of the money supply, allowing money on the left-hand side of the equation to grow at the same rate as real transactions on the right-hand side. Any other rule raises the oft-invoked specter of too much (little) money chasing too few (many) goods. Finally, the government will influence the level of private investment and therefore of productivity and growth by its activity in the capital market. The government can indirectly encourage private investment by reducing its own deficit and consequent need to borrow.

The traditional introductory course in macroeconomics develops this general theoretical framework as well as various "special cases" which deviate from it. These special cases might include private sector investment which is unresponsive to interest rates, or perhaps a money wage which fails to adjust downward in the face of excess labor supplies.

The difficulty with these special cases is that they are essentially at odds with the central theoretical structure which assumes efficient, i.e., utility-maximizing, market interchanges. Each after-the-fact revision of this theory requires another in a growing list of explanations as to why markets don't really equate supply and demand when that is presumably their only function. Conventional theorists have recently avoided admission of market failure by laying claim to perception failure: markets are operating efficiently but only in the long run, or only as becomes apparent if we revise our definition of unemployment, or the money supply, or of some other data series which fails to accurately measure its objective. In other words, if a disjuncture exists between economic theory and reality, then lay the blame on our perceptions of reality! Such an attitude at least reduces the rate at which qualifications must be added to the market paradigm.

## Employment and Prices in the Real World

### Administered Prices

There may remain in a modern industrial economy a few industries in which traditional market forces predominate in the price-setting process. An example might be agricultural commodities, though in that case the government plays a very important role. But in most product markets the sellers are price-makers. A printed price tag is attached to the goods, and the seller will tolerate a minimum of haggling. These administered prices are relatively inflexible, that is, they do not respond rapidly or sensitively to changes in market conditions, particularly changes in demand. This feature of industrial markets tends to reduce the sensitivity of the inflation rate to demand-oriented policies, and changes in demand thus are reflected in realized profit levels rather than in prices.

There are several reasons for this inflexibility of prices. The simplest to understand has to do with the costs involved in changing prices. These are often called "menu costs": if a restaurant wants to change its prices, it must undertake the cost of printing new menus (or of reprogramming its counter-top computers). All businesses that use price tags, catalogues, advertising, computerized inventory systems, and the like face such costs.

Most businesses rely on a stable, established customer base for most of their sales, whether they sell directly to consumers or to other businesses. To maintain such a customer base the firm must make an implicit commitment that its prices will always be at fair levels. Frequent or unpredictable price changes lead customers to suspect that they are being exploited, and will lead them to search for other suppliers. Since this kind of fairness norm also operates in labor markets where the bulk of costs is made predictable if not stable by means of long-term agreements, it is easy to stabilize prices by making them a fixed percentage above the usual level of average costs. As labor costs ratchet upward in predictable fashion, so do prices, but in a manner that everyone perceives as being fair. As we suggested earlier, this kind of pricing behavior has advantages for the smooth operation of the economy and for families' economic security.

The final reason for the stability of administered prices has to do with the structure of industrial markets. In most markets there are few competitors (oligopoly), so that in changing prices a firm must anticipate the reactions of a few other sellers. This guessing game is never without risks. The wrong hunch can result in a serious loss of market share which most firms would prefer to keep stable. The safer course is not to change prices frequently, and/or to tie them to some safe mark-up formula.

### The Primary Labor Market

The conventional free market view of wage setting and employment has proven inadequate in contributing to our understanding of labor market behavior for a very simple and obvious reason. Employment and organization of workers is a far more complex feat than the maximization of output with the least possible work effort. The very existence of such fields of study as industrial relations attests to the fact that a human dimension exists in the employment and production equation, a dimension which the standard theory frequently ignores. A mechanistic view of labor market transactions leaves no room for typical human concerns such as family responsibilities or human dignity. It admits only the driving force of greed and self-preservation. According to the text-book version of reality, the typical labor market transaction is one in which the employee comes to the individual bargaining table with a known and fixed set of acquired skills which determines his readily apparent productivity. The employee's productivity and his happiness with the resulting wage rate are both assumed to be individualistic; they are not influenced by the productivity or the wages received by others in the same workplace. If this story were true, wage inflation and unemployment could not coexist. Wages would be individualistically determined in response to the forces of supply and demand. But, of course, inflation and unemployment do coexist. What is wrong with the story?

Apparently almost everything!

1. The labor market parable ignores the fact that many skills are acquired on the job, whether through formal training programs or by daily experience in the work routine. In either case the labor market is not so much a market place for existing skills, but a market place for training positions. Acceptance of such a position by the employee amounts to a time commitment as well as a commitment to the activities of the firm. The offer of a position by an employer indicates a trust on the part of the employer that the new worker will exhibit such a commitment, and the offer commits the employer to a reciprocal commitment to the employment security of the worker. These commitments arise because the training period is expensive for the employer and endows the worker with skills which are frequently valuable only so long as the worker remains employed in the existing firm or industry.

2. Since no available supply of workers exists in the absence of training programs for job-specific skills, and since the willingness to hire new employees is no longer measured by the preferred money wage but also by training, promotion, and job security provisions, wages are no longer the endogenous market results of shifts in the supply or demand for labor. Neither demand nor supply curves for new workers are well defined in this long term relationship. Workers would frequently be willing to work for somewhat less than existing wage rates because they would find it difficult to market their acquired job-specific skills to employers in other industries. Employers would prefer wage increases over offering the existing wage to new workers who would have to go through an expensive training period. If wages are not uniquely determined by well-defined supply and demand curves, they must be influenced by non-market forces.

3. The argument for wage determination by market forces becomes even more problematic when we recognize that productivity is not inherent in the worker and is difficult to observe. Productivity depends not only on acquired skills but also on the amount of physical capital which is given to the worker and how well the new worker fits in and cooperates with existing employees. The productivity of the individual worker is therefore not dependent on that particular employee so much as on the entire workplace. This means that each person is dependent on all the others for his wage or standard of living. Since wages are not an accurate measure of an individual's contribution, and therefore the wage structure is substantially released from market forces, and income is as frequently allocated by the forces of market power or perceptions of fairness as it is by the alleged efficient market allocation of skills.

4. Perceptions of fairness commit the labor market to a pattern of rigid relative wages. This is because the satisfaction of workers in one job classification depends not so much on their absolute real wage rate, but on the relative wage appropriate to their occupational status. The employer who takes advantage of a relative surplus of workers in one occupation to reduce their relative wage

will do so at his peril. Worker productivity may decline, and the quit rate will increase in response to an action which takes "unfair" advantage of the market situation.

This set of alternative assumptions produces an employment and wage-setting process which is unlike that of textbook economics in several respects. The labor market is much more complex and interesting than is suggested by dealing with homogeneous labor services and market clearing wage rates, as is typically done. Some of the implications will be explored here. The impact on the inflationary process and appropriate macroeconomic policy will be dealt with in a following section.

The present analysis first of all provides a basis for two types of employer-employee relationships. Our non-market analysis suggests that both the quantity and price of labor services are impervious to general business conditions. A slowdown in the pace of economic activity leads to stockpiling of employees with specialized training because of the expense involved in training new workers when the economy recovers. Real wages do not drop, either relatively, because of the perceived fairness of the existing wage structure, or absolutely, because recently experienced rates of money wage increase also became institutionalized as fair and are independent of short-run business conditions. If wage increases of ten percent were the norm last year, then, unless the inflation rate has declined drastically in the intervening period, it would be unseemly for employers to offer a five percent wage increase this year because of slower business conditions and a rising unemployment rate. Employees would respond with reduced productivity and a greater likelihood of quitting in the next business recovery when their present employer is not in need of skilled workers but other employment opportunities are also widely available.

For the group of employees in specialized positions such as professional, managerial, and certain skilled craft positions, employment and income are insulated from business cycles. This result is beneficial for the employees and their families as economic security is assured. The risk associated with business cycles has been shifted to the employers' profitability. When the economy expands, sales can increase faster than employment because of the earlier labor stockpiling. Even though raw materials costs may be increasing in response to increases in demand in what remains a flexible-price market sector of the economy, unit costs of production for the producer may remain stable or even decline because of greater labor force productivity. For a time, as the business expansion moves the economy toward full capacity, the expansion is anti-inflationary. Profits and business investment can both increase without an increase in product prices. Inflation, in other words, is slow starting. An increase in demand creates its own supply at the existing price level.

But the results cut both ways. The institutionalized wage structure produces an inflationary bias in the economy in two ways, both of which are largely independent of the level of aggregate demand or percent of utilized capacity in the economy. First, even in the complete absence of business cycles, wages and prices would tend to increase because of the interdependence of worker preferences, in which one worker's satisfaction with his position is based on what he earns compared with what others are earning. This produced the structure of rigid relative wages which is largely independent of shortages or surpluses of various skill categories. Now suppose that a rapid increase in the price and demand for coal allows the mine worker's union to extract a substantial wage increase from the mine owners. The mine worker's settlement then spills over to influence contracts for related groups, such as the auto or steelworkers, who will demand similar increases even if demand is slack in the latter industries. The mine worker's settlement will have a lesser impact on wage settlements in unrelated occupations such as state and local government white collar workers. Nevertheless, a sectoral shift in the demand for products or services is sufficient to generate wage and price increases which ripple through related job contours producing an inflationary wage bias which is independent of the general level of unemployment. [Dunlop 1979, pp. 63-74]

A second wage setting process recently described by George Perry is directly influenced by the business cycle. [Perry 1980] As the economy moves up toward full employment the *rate* at which it expands will also influence wage inflation. Because of the length of the training process, bottlenecks occur for various labor skills and commodities. If computer programmers are in short supply, more training slots will open up for computer programmers, but this does not immediately fill the gap. The shortage will persist if the training period is long or if the expansion in demand is rapid. The result is that short-run wage increases for computer programmers accelerate as employers try to solve their shortage problem by raiding other firms. But the resulting wage inflation is more pervasive than in the previous sectoral shift situation as prices of commodities which are produced in the flexible price market sector of the economy are also rising rapidly. Again, this is due not so much to the level of demand but to the fact that demand has increased more rapidly than has producer capacity, with a resulting increase in price. The accepted norm or fair rate of wage increase is now influenced by the example set in job shortage categories as well as by the need to keep up with the increased inflation rate. Wages then push up finished goods prices which are based on a fixed markup over cost, requiring another round of wage increases. The shifting of the economy to a permanently higher inflationary trend can be avoided only if the expansion phase is brief so that temporary high rates of wage inflation do not have time to become institutionalized as the norm, or if the expansion phase is gradual, producing a situation in which increases in supply can keep up with increases in demand without necessitating a price increase. If neither of these conditions is met, the pattern of wage and price increases eventually acquires a life of its own, independent of the demand forces by which it was initiated.

The reverse case, a business slow down, is not entirely symmetrical with respect to wage and price setting procedures. True, just as inflation is slow starting during a business expansion, it is slow stopping during a contraction. The largest share of the response to a short-run reduction in demand is a reduction in the quantity of output with only a minor impact on price trends. But wage inflation is less prone to reductions than it is to escalation. The reason is that the rate of wage inflation has to change *prior* to any resulting change in the rate of price inflation. The need for reductions in the rate of wage inflation may be perfectly clear to workers and management alike. No firm can afford to stock-

pile labor forever, and if the recession is a deliberate attempt to restrain inflation on the part of policy-makers, the recession will eventually result in significant increases in unemployment in the event that wage increases fail to moderate. Therefore an immediate reduction in wage and price inflation (perhaps
even deflation) proves advantageous to everyone by ensuring job security and
firm profitability. Yet no group of workers will be willing to make the first
move! The first step in the process involves acceptance of a lower rate of wage
increase by some groups, which then results in a reduction in the rate of increase of consumer prices which, in turn, allows workers to retain their real
standard of living while at the same time agreeing to a reduction in the rate of
wage inflation. The difficulty is that the initial step in the process does not
readily occur in this downward spiral, because the first group which volunteers
for wage reductions will suffer an absolute decline in their standard of living
and a shift of relative income shares toward those groups whose wages de-esca-
late more slowly. In a market economy, recessions will reduce inflation
rapidly, because firms do not control product prices and have no reason to
maintain wages above their market-clearing level. Thus both wages and prices
drop rapidly and evenly with little description to relative wages and relative
income shares. As the economy evolves from the market structure to one of
administered prices, the market remedy of fighting inflation with recession becomes progressively less workable.

**The Secondary Labor Market**

A germ of truth remains in the recession prescription, because market
forces continue to operate in the market for unskilled labor. This section will
describe the market or textbook case as it operates in a world where most prices
and wages are controlled by sellers. In this administered price—market
economy hybrid world, inflation can be controlled with recessionary policies.
However, we will see that such policies work only with associated costs which
would not occur in either pure market economy or in a pure administered
price economy.

The previous section illustrated that various forces insulated the market for
skilled labor from the traditional forces of supply and demand, because long
term employment commitments and a wage structure based on fairness rather
than market forces was in the mutual interest of employers and employees.
However, such an employment policy is not without its costs. If employment
is to remain stable for the firm through the business cycle, profits will be highly
variable, rising when sales are high and employees are working steadily, and
declining when sales fall while labor costs remain constant. Clearly the firm's
owners will seek to minimize these fluctuations with a pattern of production
costs which is responsive to fluctuations in sales. This means that they will
willingly extend long-term employment commitments only to the number of
employees needed to maintain the level of production which can be sustained
over a long period of time. The additional volume required during periods of
high demand will be met by drawing down inventories and by additional short
term employment. This employment strategy divides the labor force into two
groups. The primary labor force, those who benefit from long-term commit-

ments and benefit from job-specific training, are assured their economic security because of the treatment extended to short-term employees. This *secondary* labor force, composed of marginal workers (marginal in the sense they are easily hired and easily fired, not in the sense of being inherently less productive) must contend with a great deal of economic insecurity. Their jobs will exist only for so long as the level of economic activity remains high. Further, the jobs which are given to secondary workers will be qualitatively different from those offered to primary workers. Because their employment is probably temporary, the employer has little incentive to assume the costs of any training costs which would boost their productivity. So, unlike the primary workers who hold positions requiring a broad range of managerial or craftsman skills, the secondary workers will be offered positions that require a minimum number of skills. They will therefore understand their work not so much in the cooperative sense of achieving some broad objective but in narrow instrumental terms. The assembly line worker with a narrow job assignment has no choice but to perceive his work as a set of routine procedures or habits which he memorizes and then repeats in appropriate order. Because understanding of the entire production process is impossible under such conditions, these employees must be constantly subject to the commands of someone who does know what is going on. From the perspective of both the employer and the secondary laborer, such a use of people makes them equivalent to machines or other raw material inputs rather than participants in a humanized work community. Little loyalty, responsibility, or concern can be expected from either side in this impersonal exchange.

The distinction between the characteristics of primary and secondary occupations has a parallel in the distinction between the characteristics of workers selected for the primary labor force training slots and those of the workers allocated to the secondary or market sector. When a person applies for a job his potential productivity is not at all evident. Even more important, the employer has no idea whether the job applicant is likely to remain with the firm after the training period. Since neither productivity nor longevity are self-evident, the employer relies on external characteristics which might indicate which job applicant is to be entrusted with a long-term skilled position. The external characteristics historically sought after have been those possessed by white males with twelve or more years of formal education. Whether or not being black or female or young actually is indicative of a higher quit rate is impossible to determine. The selection process contains an element of self-fulfilling prophecy, since these "less desirable" employees are given the less desirable jobs found in the secondary labor market. With no employment guarantees, they have little incentive to remain on the job.

## Recessions and the Two-Tier Labor Market

Reliance on recessions has proven admirably effective in the past as an antiinflationary weapon. True to textbook theories a reduction in demand would cause suppliers to reduce their asking price in order to remain competitive. In fact, from 1850 to 1940 the price level in the United States exhibited no inflationary trend. Price increases during periods of high demand, usually caused by high government spending during wartime, were offset by price decreases which occurred during periods of slack economic activity. It is not surprising that recessions have less effectiveness in reducing inflation today, because an increasing share of economic activity is taking place under conditions where the sellers can control the price, whether by quotas, licensing procedures, or, as in the case of the primary labor market, by valuing a long term buyer-seller relationship. The replacement of impersonal market transactions by economic security guarantees, and the resulting shrinkage of the flexible price sector, have made the short term behavior of prices largely impervious to changes in demand.

Like any broad generalization, the previous statement is not entirely true. Wage rates in the secondary labor market will exhibit some responsiveness to the forces of supply and demand because conditions in this market do approximate the standard textbook assumptions of homogeneous labor services which can be readily employed and just as readily disemployed. One solution to the inflation problem then becomes apparent: reduce spending demand with restrictive macroeconomic policies. The reduction in demand must be large enough so that the reduction in wage rates in the price-responsive secondary labor market is sufficient to offset the continuing wage inflation in the primary labor market. As the secondary labor market shrinks in relative size, over time recessions will have to be larger or longer to achieve a given reduction in the inflation rate.

The previous section referred to the fact that the costs associated with deliberate recessionary policies are particularly high in a world which contains both an administered-price (primary) labor market and a flexible-price (secondary) labor market. The distributional problems inherent in such a situation now become apparent. But the resulting redistribution is not limited to a redistribution of income. During periods of low unemployment employers will have little choice but to fill training positions for primary labor market positions with people who are "less desirable" as determined by such external characteristics as race or sex. Equal opportunity employment becomes an economic necessity rather than an onerous government regulation. But when the pool of job seekers increases during a recession, employers are presented with the opportunity to trade up to higher perceived labor force quality. The result is that unemployment rates for less-sought-after groups rise to multiples far beyond those of prime age white males.

Table 13-1 portrays the unemployment picture for 1984. In spite of high rates of unemployment by the standards of the 1960's and early 1970's, white middle-aged workers in white collar positions apparently had little to fear. The inflationary battle is being waged with the jobs of those who have least control over the terms of their employment, primarily the young, non-white blue collar employees. The unemployment rates among minority teenagers are five times the national average. White unemployment rates are only half those for non-white workers in every age bracket. A textbook competitive labor market that

| | | | |
|---|---|---|---|
| Civilian Labor Force | 7.5% | | |
| White Collar | 5.0% | | |
| Blue Collar | 11.5% | | |
| White Males | 6.4% | Non-White Males | 14.7% |
| 16-19 | 16.8% | 16-19 | 38.9% |
| 20-24 | 9.8% | 20-24 | 24.5% |
| 25-54 | 5.2% | 25-54 | 11.0% |
| 55-65 | 4.2% | 55-64 | 8.5% |
| 65 and over | 2.6% | 65 and over | 7.4% |
| | | | |
| White Females | 6.5% | Non-White Females | 14.0% |
| 16-19 | 15.2% | 16-19 | 38.5% |
| 20-24 | 8.8% | 20-24 | 23.5% |
| 25-54 | 5.5% | 25-54 | 10.9% |
| 55-64 | 4.0% | 55-64 | 6.1% |
| 65 and over | 3.7% | 65 and over | 4.7% |

*Table 13-1. Unemployment in 1984*

functions on the basis of variable wage rates would make such a situation impossible. Relative wages would flexibly adjust so that unemployment rates among various groups of workers would approach equality. Rather than shrinking, the disparity has grown worse in recent years even as the overall unemployment rate has increased.

In addition to suffering from substantial increases in unemployment, secondary workers who manage to retain jobs suffer a decline in real wage income relative to workers in the primary market where wage increases are not particularly sensitive to demand. The share of the wage income pie received by secondary workers is therefore declining for two reasons, both of which are redistributing a greater share of available income in the direction of already higher income primary workers. The resulting economic costs are quickly transformed into personal and family costs, which have little to do with the textbook story of declining utility directly induced by a reduction in consumption. Loss of employment imposes strain and tension on all family members due to the preoccupation of parents or spouses with debts and job-seeking. Old routines are disrupted and a person's sense of worth and responsibility is shattered by the realization that one's employment can be taken away. The loss of identity (people frequently introduce themselves by describing their occupation, not their family or the size of their bank account) and psychological anguish are frequently so great that the recently fired find it difficult to venture outside of their homes, let alone fill out employment applications and participate in interviews. [Piore 1979, p. xxi] The resulting deterioration in physical and mental health is such that according to a recent study, a one percent increase in the long-term unemployment rate ultimately causes 30,000 extra deaths each year. [Brenner 1976] One can only guess at the costs imposed on the surviving 970,000 job losers associated with that one percentage point increase. In any case the medical statistics belie the commonly held notion that the unemployed benefit by receiving unemployment compensation without the responsibilities of employment.

If recessions create such major dislocations, surely there must exist offsetting benefits in order to justify their inclusion in the government arsenal of anti-inflationary weapons. Yet it appears that the anti-inflationary influence is temporary for two reasons. From the most optimistic perspective available the inflation rate is reduced for the duration of the recession. The root cause of the inflationary trend is a battle among various groups in the economy for income shares which sum to a total greater than the economy's ability to produce. A recession resolves the battle by forcing a real income reduction upon those groups with the least amount of market power, the secondary workers. But even though the inflation rate abates, the war continues. Any resurgence of economic activity increases the demand for unskilled labor with a resulting reflation in wage rates as wage levels in the secondary or market sector catch up with those in the administered sector. The unskilled regain their market power with the resumption in demand for their services. In the case of a brief recession the inflation rate remains low only for the duration, and quickly moves back up to the longer-term trend rate when the economy recovers. The short-term responsiveness of inflation to recessionary policies thereby exaggerates the effectiveness of such policies.

From a more pessimistic perspective, it is not entirely clear that the inflation rate could be held down permanently by a permanent increase in the overall unemployment rate. Lester Thurow argues that an effective anti-inflationary policy would require a continuous rise in the unemployment rate. [1980, pp. 72-73] Because the underlying trend rate of price inflation is based on the rate of wage inflation in the primary sector, an effective recessionary policy must be severe enough to cause increases in unemployment among the group of primary workers. But employers will respond by replacing less preferred with more preferred workers in the normal process of labor market turnover. So unemployment among the preferred group gradually subsides back to the normal or "full employment" level even as the overall unemployment rate remains high. When this happens, policymakers are faced with the choice of living with the existing levels of inflation and unemployment or of creating another increase in the armies of the unemployed. This latter course requires successive upward revisions of the natural rate of unemployment, the rate of unemployment consistent with non-accelerating inflation. This unemployment target which stood at below four percent in the mid-1960's, has now reached six percent with every likelihood of further increases in the 1980's. The policy record of the early 1980's is consistent with this view. Anti-inflation policies have exacted a fearful price in unemployment, though the reduction in inflation has been aided by an artifically overvalued dollar.

## Phillips Curves

The wage-setting and inflation process dealt with in previous sections can be described with the traditional Phillips Curve diagram, which illustrates the relationship between unemployment and inflation. Both the flexible and administered price approaches suggest the existence of an inverse correlation between inflation and unemployment rates in the short run. Such a relationship is illustrated in Figure 13-2(a). An increase in economic activity will reduce the unemployment rate at the cost of a short term increase in the inflation rate. Increases in demand will raise prices in the flexible price sectors of the economy while administered prices move upward to keep up with what is perceived as a temporary increase in the inflation rate. Because the higher inflation rate is perceived as being temporarily rather than permanently higher, the notion of the normal or fair rate of wage increase remains below the current rate of inflation. Over time, if the inflation does not subside, the norm rate of wage increase will move upward to correspond approximately to increases in the cost of living. [Okun 1981, p.242]

The difference between the flexible and administered price approaches becomes apparent in the long run relationship. Figure 13-1(b) illustrates the monetarist or flexible-price view of the way the world works. The economy is operating at full employment at unemployment rate $U_1$; remaining unemployed workers at this rate are voluntarily remaining out of the employed labor force by placing a high reservation wage on their services while searching for the best offer. Any point to the right of $U_1$ indicates excess supplies of labor and output; with excess supplies available prices are bid downward, and the inflation rate declines. To the left of $U_1$, with the economy operating above full employment, the reverse process occurs, and the inflation rate will accelerate. In either disequilibrium situation, market forces automatically move the economy back to full employment at $U_1$, a position which is compatible with any fixed rate of inflation. Hence a vertical Phillips Curve represents the set of long-term equilibrium positions which are possible.

The alternative represented by Figure 13-2(c) assumes that wage inflation, and therefore price inflation as well, is essentially independent of the levels of supply and demand and therefore exogenous. The result is that any unemployment rate is consistent with a given inflation rate. Starting at point A, an increase in demand will still drive prices up more rapidly in the short run (point B) as market determined prices seek a higher equilibrium level and as capacity constraints are reached. However, the resulting investment in physical and human capital will allow a reduction in the inflation rate for the longer run (point C), although such a reduction will occur only if the higher rate of price increase has not become institutionalized as the new norm in

### Figure 13-1. Phillips Curves

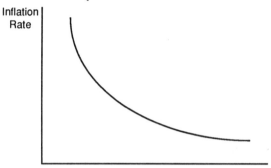

**(a) Short-Term Relationship**

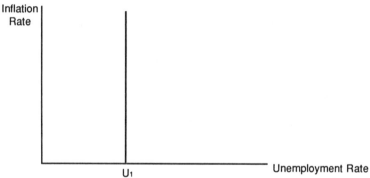

**(b) Long-Term Relationship: Flexible Price Markets**

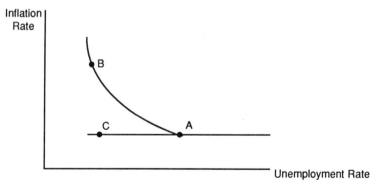

**(c) Long-Term Relationship: Administered Price Markets**

determining the rate of wage increase. Essentially then, any inflation rate is consistent with virtually any unemployment rate in the long run.

The horizontal long-run Phillips Curve exists because the underlying or inflation rate is determined in the administered price sectors of the economy. It is because wages are exogenous in this sector that fluctuations in aggregate demand have so little impact on wage and price setting behavior. The exogeneity of wages in the primary sector also operates, as we have seen, to shift the entire burden of adjustment to the workers of the secondary labor market who have not managed to achieve a similar degree of economic security. But there is a bright side to the argument that wages are exogenous. The independence of wages and prices means that they do not serve to equilibrate supply and demand and thereby produce an efficient allocation of resources. Although recessionary policies have reached an impasse in the war on inflation, the only other policy weapon, wage and price guidelines, now become more acceptable, because they do not necessarily interfere with the efficient use of labor. It is difficult to argue that the government should not be allowed to influence wage and price decisions when such decisions are already being determined outside of market mechanisms.

Wage-price guidelines may take many forms, ranging from the outright controls of the Nixon era to Carter's well-publicized guidelines with no penalties attached, to widely discussed Tax-based Incomes Policies (TIP) which would use tax penalties or incentives to encourage moderation. None of these schemes is perfect. All of them interfere with what are essentially private decisions between employers and employees and between buyers and sellers. If private agreements affected only the negotiating parties, none of this information could be justified. But we have already seen that the inflationary process which is generated by the sum of these private agreements imposes costs on non-participants, particularly those who continue to live in the market economy. Protection of those who are not represented in the negotiation process becomes a matter of justice. Wage-price guidelines are a means of allocating the existing income to competing groups. Inflation and recession will accomplish the same purpose but with the outcome tilted in favor of the economically powerful. Reliance on guidelines will require a flexible and innovative policy which responds quickly to private sector attempts at confrontation or circumvention. Arthur Okun has argued that just as keeping a lamb in a cage with a lion requires a large supply of lambs, so also society may need a large supply of guidelines policies. In spite of the administrative costs and private sector interference, guidelines policies have the potential to shine as paragons of efficiency and justice when compared with the alternatives.

## The Supply Side

The variations in employment dealt with to this point have been responses to variations in aggregate demand. Historically, demand has been the underlying source of variations in output, whether because of intentionally restrictive or expansionary government policies, or because of less planned fluctuations, such as wartime spending or fluctuations in private business investment. However, the sources of economic uncertainty during the 1970's were more frequently associated with production than demand. Unanticipated supply shocks, such as poor harvests and energy shortages, were accompanied by government programs which raised prices by raising payroll taxes, expanding regulation, and restricting imports. Each of these events has the effect of imposing new price increases on the existing output.

Assuming that the supply reduction was beyond the control of government, i.e., a bad harvest rather than a payroll tax increase, the government is limited in its immediate response to reliance on demand oriented strategies. The limitation exists because the supply of goods at any given time is determined by the available labor supply, capital stock, and inflationary expectations. None of these changes very rapidly, and none is particularly responsive to any government action.

The policy maker with an extreme market orientation would suggest doing nothing. The government should maintain the existing level of aggregate demand. In this case the increase in food prices would presumably force reduced spending on other items, causing reduced production and temporarily rising unemployment. But the unemployed would bid down their wage rate, and prices of goods in surplus would decline, causing automatic readjustment back to full employment with the original inflation rate. Such thinking led to the relative lack of concern when OPEC quadrupled the price of crude oil in 1973. The action was not regarded as inflationary, since the shift toward greater expenditures for energy would result in a decrease in expenditures and prices in other sectors. Some people went so far as to argue that the impact would be deflationary, since the higher import price would operate like a tax and reduce the demand for domestically produced goods and services.

In fact, a very different set of events took place, a set of events which was both plausible and predictable if one takes seriously people's attempts to separate their personal lives from the capricious events of the market place. The oil price increases posed a threat to both minimum and relative household economic positions. As real incomes declined, consumers responded by reducing savings rates in order to maintain accustomed lifestyles, thereby maintaining a high level of aggregate demand. Labor force participation rates moved to record levels as depleted savings forced families to seek additional sources of income. This response, in turn, increased not only the unemployment problem, but also the inflationary pressures on the economy due to the resulting decline in productivity. And the apparent and widely publicized increases in consumer prices produced a corresponding wage explosion in 1974 and 1975, even as the unemployment rate was moving upwards to a post-war record. The rapidly declining interest rates indicated that the acceleration in wage settlements was not a response to rational expectations of increasing inflation in the future, since interest rates rise when anticipated inflation rises. Rather, this was a reaction to declining levels of real income in the present.

Since wages are being established in a process which is independent of the presence or absence of slack in labor markets, fiscal and monetary restrictiveness will have little influence on the resulting wage inflation. Goods prices also tend to be independent of demand and tied closely to wage levels, so they will also be insensitive to monetary and fiscal policy. Potential output is largely independent of the price level, and expansionary fiscal and monetary policy will effectively reduce unemployment. Expansionary policy will also prevent the further redistribution of income that the adjustment process would otherwise produce. Recall that the primary labor force members are largely protected by unemployment guarantees and wages which are indexed either formally or informally by the cost of living. But these devices have served to give the inflation, once started, a life of its own. And the victims of this process, in the absence of expansionary policy responses, are the secondary workers, who can least afford it. The protection given to primary workers redistributes the decline in income from both the initial supply shock and the resulting inflationary spiral to the secondary workers, who lose in terms of increased unemployment and declining absolute and relative real wages. Any perceived tapering off of inflationary pressures owing to the business slowdown belies the case as the redistribution from the secondary workers increases their determination and need to catch up in the next expansion.

In fact, the longer-term result can be even more severe. Consider the response of firm owners and managers to an administration which espouses free market ideologies and solutions. Such an administration would not express particular concern about high or variable rates of unemployment, because these would be perceived as problems which are self-correcting through endogenous wage adjustments. Rather, the administration would tend to be more concerned over increases in the price level which are perceived to be caused by exogenous increases in the money supply or government spending. With this set of slated priorities as evidence, it would be reasonable to anticipate a future economy which is highly cyclical and characterized by high unemployment rates and high interest rates as growth in the money supply fails to keep pace with the desired growth in nominal spending. With an uncertain business climate in the offing, a reasonable business strategy would be to defer any long term investment and rely instead on expansions and contractions of employed labor as the variable input. Such a strategy would have its benefit in producing more jobs for a given level of output, since the reduction in business investment will result in a reduction of output or productivity per worker. But rather than relying on capital as the marginal input, expanding investment during good times and retiring obsolete or energy-inefficient capital during bad, people have become the variable input. According to labor market economist Michael Piore, the number of jobs in the secondary labor market has grown rapidly in the latter part of the 1970's owing to the uncertain business climate. [1979, pp. xxii-xxiii] Lester Thurow attributes the same growth to the lack of a commitment to full employment policies. [1980, p.205] In either case the net result has been to shift an increasing level of market risk from investors and entrepreneurs to employees.

## *An Alternative Macroeconomic Program*

During the 1970's West German spending on social welfare programs significantly outpaced that of the U.S. as a percentage of GNP. In Japan the government social safety net is supplemented by private employment commitments that typically last for the lifetime of the employee. Both countries notably outperformed the U.S. in terms of achieving lower rates of unemployment, higher levels of per capita investment, and increased productivity. The preceding analysis suggests that the contrast in economic performance is directly tied to U.S. reliance on conventional market-prescribed nostrums to resolve its economic difficulties.

When confronted with supply or demand shocks which threaten to move the economy from its desired level of employment, makers of monetary policy should attempt to stabilize employment and output rather than the price level. Because wage settlements are largely imposed upon the economy rather than being determined within the market process, unemployment and inflation are independent phenomena. Essentially the Phillips Curve is flat, though sometimes it may be that wage increases in shortage fields spread with comparison to related occupations even if these have a labor surplus, or an increase in secondary labor market wage rates owing to expanding aggregate demand may become institutionalized as the new norm for determining primary labor market increases if the secondary labor market wage inflation is persistent. But the primary cause of wage inflation is the *change* in employment. If unemployment can be reduced without institutionalizing the wage inflation, then the wage inflation should subside after reaching the lower level of unemployment. Wage inflation in the U.S. has been inadvertently encouraged by policies which attempted for two or three years to reduce unemployment but without reliance on wage restraint programs. When inflation reaches politically intolerable levels, a dose of recession is added. This response raises the unemployment rate, but has little impact on the higher rates of wage increase to which primary market employers have become accustomed. A return to full employment policies ratchets the inflation rate upward but, again, with only a temporary impact on the unemployment rate.

Stop-and-go policies should be replaced with a declaration of a low unemployment rate target and the resolve to maintain that target. Such a policy commitment on the part of government would reduce the need for private markets to rely on flexible market arrangements for survival in an atmosphere of economic uncertainty. Stable employment and income levels would encourage the development of long-term employment and exchange commitments which are mutually beneficial. Businesses would be better able to make long-range investment commitments with equivalent long-range guarantees to employees in terms of willingness to train and to retain during short-term periods of low production and demand. The remaining risk in the economic game would thereby be shifted to those best able to afford it as profits would vary over any remaining business cycles caused by labor stockpiling. Similarly government deficits or surpluses would display greater variability because of the greater financing needs of income support programs whenever the economy slows down. But these risks are shared by a broad class of investors in the former case and are proportionate to the distribution of the tax burden in the latter. The resulting declines in income threaten the livelihood of no one, and would leave the production of commodities and services which meet basic human needs unaffected.

The list of macroeconomic objectives presented earlier is much more extensive than the list of the extreme monetarist, which is limited to controlling the price level. Therefore the set of required policies is also more ambitious than the monetarist recommendation to control the money supply. In our model, since inflation is exogenous and based on wage behavior, the growth rate of the money supply will have its impact not on the price level but on quantity, specifically the quantity of employment. Monetary policy should attempt to maintain the target unemployment rate. The Federal Reserve should also attempt to achieve as low an interest rate as is possible without causing overemployment. Low real interest rates encourage long-term investment decisions rather than deliberate rapid obsolescence of the capital stock. They also encourage a more rapid transition to resource conserving-echnologies, thereby reducing one source of inflationary pressure. And a policy of credit availability promotes diversity and flexibility in the general economy by increasing the ability of small businesses to borrow. During periods of restrictive monetary policy small businesses suffer disproportionately. The prevalence of small businesses in the competitive flexible price sector limits their ability to pass on higher borrowing costs in the form of higher prices. And, unlike major corporations, small businesses have no access to such channels of credit as the Eurodollar or corporate bond markets.

Achievement of low interest rates requires either a limiting of consumer loan demand or additional cooperation in the management of fiscal policy. If, as was argued earlier, the jobs created by business investment are more valuable than wages or product prices indicate, then there is reason to shift available credit in the direction of investment and away from consumer use. This transfer can be accomplished with various consumer credit controls, such as a requirement for greater minimum down payments for car or home loans. Alternatively, lower interest rates can result from a more restrictive fiscal policy with either higher taxes or lower expenditures. Both would produce lower deficits and less competition for investment dollars. Fiscal policy should also be supply-side oriented in another way. Human resource development should continue to be encouraged with job training, education, and health programs whether publicly provided or encouraged with private tax incentives.

This set of policies provides an environment in which households and firms can plan and adapt readily, decreasing the waste of human and physical resources caused by uncertainty and restrictive monetary policy. In that sense the program is not inflationary. But the present inflationary trend is already disruptive, and the short term expansion of employment could add to that trend. While the intent of this set of policies is to reduce upward wage pressures which are caused by concern for minimum economic guarantees, the adjustment period may well require a more ambitious wage and price guidelines policy.

For the longer term, the government could best encourage a stable economy which meets the needs of households by taking an educational and leadership role which involves a de-emphasis of narrow economic issues. A major step in this direction is achieved with the program just described, which provides greater economic security through both social welfare programs and a stable business environment with expanded availability of primary sector employment. Future macroeconomic policy making should also involve a reconsideration of such traditional objectives as "productivity" or the "standard" of living. These traditional data series are measures of material production which perform well only in the context of a growing GNP. But additional GNP growth will curtail freedom in the way we live. The preservation of nature, of quiet, peace, social harmony, and equity, is more important than the production of additional physical output in the promotion of personal and social development. Traditional economic measures of performance encourage both materialistic values and materialistic solutions by focusing attention on quantifiable output. To the extent that quantity and quality are substitutes, the emphasis on productivity runs the danger of decreasing quality: not only the quality of goods and services, but of all aspects of life. The solution does not lie in an expansion of the number of data series maintained by economists and statisticians, although a broadening of the number of measured objectives might serve to promote a more balanced economic development. The danger in quantifying anything, but especially non-material output, is that attention is diverted to that which is being directly measured. Measuring the quality of health care by the mortality rate may be better than looking at the number of dollars spent on health care, but it still leaves little room for evaluation of doctor-patient relationships and questions of ethical choice.

Some of the numbers used in forming economic aggregates manage simultaneously to be both too small or narrowly constructed and too large or broadly constructed. Consumption, the purchases of goods and services by households, is an appropriate measure of economic performance only if we accept the outmoded notion that all such expenditures relieve undifferentiated want. But recognition of positional goods distinguishes ceremonial consumption of such goods from the traditional instrumental consumption. Consumption is in the former case an end in itself; in the latter case it is a means to an end. Similarly, investment in business equipment may either result in useful employment and beneficial output, or it may replace workers and require a great deal of energy consumption to produce items of questionable value. A partial response lies in greater refinements in the measuring process, but it is again true that a numerical solution is antithetical to the development of our spiritual dimension.

What is needed among people in all positions of leadership is a change in attitude and values which recognizes not only the physical limits in the production of output, but also the limits of physical output in meeting human needs. Recognition of these facts would steer us away from demands for more economic growth and from the attempts to achieve personal or national economic advantages through the ceremonial consumption of positional goods. Success in reaching these objectives could result in more stable and sustainable economic relationships. The obvious difficulty in such a strategy is the resistance of individuals to the perceived imposition of values from external sources, particularly governmental sources. However, this difficulty should not be viewed as terminal. Our present economic policies are also inculcated with such implicit values as "more is better." In fact, the source of many of our present difficulties has been the blind acceptance of such statements as matters of fact, rather than of a materialistic and individualistic faith. Surely it is not asking too much to require that the government examine the faith propositions upon which its own objectives are based and refrain from practices which have proven antithetical to the viability of family responsibilities and Christian principles of stewardship and sharing. Such a radical revision of present policies does not amount to a call for greater government activism but, rather, an acknowledgement and respect for the alternative values of interpersonal responsibility, sharing, and stewardship that emanate from the family and the church.

## *Resources*

Blair, J., ed. 1975. *The Roots of Inflation,* NY: Burt Franklin.

Brenner, N. H. 1976. Estimating the Social Costs of National Economic Policy. U.S. Congress, Joint Economic Committee, Washington: Government Printing Office.

Daly, H. 1977. *Steady-State Economics.* San Francisco: Freeman.

Davidson, P. 1980. Post-Keynesian Economics: Solving the Crisis in Economic Theory. *The Public Interest.* 60: 151-73.

Dunlop, J. T. 1979. Wage Contours. in Piore, ed., 1979.

Eichner, A., ed. 1979. *A Guide to Post-Keynesian Economics.* White Plains: M.E. Sharpe.

Galbraith, J. K. 1978. On Post-Keynesian Economics. J. *Post-Keynesian Economics.*

Goldthorpe, J. 1978. The Current Inflation: Towards a Sociological Approach. in F. Hirsch and J. Goldthorpe, eds., *The Political Economy of Inflation.* Cambridge: Harvard U . Press, pp. 186-213.

Goudzwaard, B. 1976. *Aid for the Overdeveloped West.* Toronto: Wedge.

Hirsch, F. 1976. *The Social Limits to Growth.* Cambridge: Harvard U. Press.

Leijonjufvud, A. 1981. *Information and Coordination,* NY. Oxford U. Press.

Lutz, M., and K. Lux. 1979. *The Challenge of Humanistic Economics.* Menlo Park, CA: Benjamin Cummings.

Okun, A. 1979. An Efficient Strategy to Combat Inflation. *Brookings Bulletin.* 15: 1-5.

Okun, A. 1981. *Prices and Quantities.* Washington: Brookings.

Palmer, J., ed. 1978. *Creating Jobs.* Washington: Bookings.

G. L. Perry 1980, Inflation in Theory and Practice. *Brookings Papers on Economic Activity.* 1/80, pp. 207-241.

Piore, M., ed. 1979. *Unemployment and Inflation: Institutionalist and Structuralist Views.* White Plains: M. E. Sharpe.

Schumacher, E. F. 1972. *Small is Beautiful.* NY: Harper & Row.

Scitovsky, T. 1976. *The Joyless Economy.* NY: Oxford U. Press.

Thurow, L. 1980. *The Zero-sum Society.* NY: Basic Books.

Thurow, L. 1983. *Dangerous Currents.* NY: Random House.

Vickers, D. 1976. *Economics and Man.* Philadelphia: Craig Press.

Weintraub, E. R. 1979. *Microfoundations.* Cambridge: Cambridge U. Press.

Wilber, C. K., and K. P. Jameson. 1983. *An Inquiry into the Poverty of Economics.* Notre Dame: U. of Notre Dame Press.

# Chapter XIV
# Economics and Ecclesia

*I knew a man as rich as a king.*
*Still wouldn't give his neighbors a thing.*
*He'll get to Heaven someday I'll bet,*
*He'll get to Heaven, and here's what he'll get:*
*A rusty old halo, a skinny white cloud,*
*Second-hand wings full of patches,*
*A rusty old halo, a skinny white cloud,*
*A robe that's so wooly that it scratches.*
     Bob Merrill (1955)

## Introduction

About a decade ago the author of this chapter lived for half a year in a New Town in Scotland. New Towns are Great Britain's experiment for reducing the density of population in its large cities by locating government services and industries in outlying areas of the country and building cities ("towns") to house the work forces they attract. Such cities, although they have an elected town council, are run by the federal government through an appointive civil service corps. In Glenrothes, County Fife, this stranger became acquainted with three different kinds of what Peter Berger and Richard John Neuhaus call "mediating structures"—organizations or associations that stand between the state bureaucracy and the individual. The churches were there, of course, each church providing somewhat different versions of community. Associations formed around common interests—gunmanship, country-and-western (American) music, art—formed a second type of association. Last were the associations of the elderly, sometimes based on common interest (with lawnbowling a prime attraction), sometimes on neighborhood affinities or church activities. Then there were the rather fluid associations of pub frequenters which will not form part of this study. Although each pub catered to a neighborhood, and within that, to an age and class group, there is probably not enough continuity or cohesiveness to grant a pub the status of a mediating structure.

Marked by uniform disregard were the neighborhood buildings built by the Town as places where people in geographic proximity could come to discuss affairs of mutual interest in those neighborhoods, or to set up cell-like political groups. Those cinder block buildings were outside of anyone's interests except in the one instance where the hall had been built large enough to stage ceilidhs (pronounced kay-lees), musical programs reminiscent of vaudeville except for the native Scots tunes and dances. Although it may be a species of small-sample generalization, we suspect that governments seldom succeed in creating associational units among their citizens.

## The Economics of Altruism

Although our focus in this chapter will be the thorny and many-faceted relationship between the churches and economic life, we want to preface this with a look at a largely undeveloped area of examination by economists—the economics of altruism. The word *altruism* is an odd one. Based on the French *autre*=other, it is usually defined as unselfish concern for the welfare of others. It shows itself within most families, where a measure of altruism is necessary or children would not be tended, and it extends itself through the small friendships and associations of life, where people are willing to give up some measure of acquisitiveness or leisure in order to help others. Altruism was once, writes British economist David Collard [1978 p. 3], a subject studied by the moral philosophers who invented scientific economics, but it is seldom studied today. Adam Smith taught economists that economic life is based on universal selfishness—the antinomy of altruism—and that teaching put closure to scientific investigation. We noted in Chapter II that the economic behavior of neighborly concern is almost totally ignored. Recently, however, some scholarly investigation has taken place, and it provides a good backdrop against which to look at churches and voluntary organizations.

Two separate strands of investigation have brought altruism back into public view. One of these is the question raised by the socio-biologist, E. O. Wilson [1975], as to whether altruism is transmitted in the genetic codes of earthly fauna. He notes that in many species there is a self-sacrificing instinct on the part of individuals that tends toward the preservation of the species. For example, some termites lay down their lives that the colony may survive. The second strand of investigation was picked up by an English economist, Richard Titmuss, in his widely acclaimed book on blood donation, *The Gift Relationship* [1970]. Titmuss tells us that for years he tried to distinguish "economic" from "social" values and finally decided that issues like the morality of society and human regard or disregard for the needs of others could not be ignored. Instead of concentrating on the study of face-to-face economic relationships, he decided to study an area where people give something to strangers: the free donation of blood. We are not interested here in the primal origins of the altruistic urge, nor in the techniques—psychological and mechanical—of giving blood. Instead, we are interested in the prevalence of the need to give to others, an economic fact, and its meaning for churches and voluntary organizations. Titmuss' analysis of the responses given by blood donors about why they give reveals that most of them use what he calls moral vocabulary. Indeed, except for less than two percent who found some personal benefit ("I no longer get nose bleeds"; "I wanted to convince myself I was eighteen"), or responded humorously ("to get a cup of tea"; "to hold my husband's hand"), all the responses Titmuss lists could be interpreted as altruistic, especially if a sense of duty is included under that rubric. (It should be noted that Titmuss' British study does not include the common American practice of donors replacing blood transfused into a relative or friend; his donors are giving to total strangers).

David Collard accepts the validity of Titmuss' study and extends it by more rigorously examining the economics of altruism. He makes several points that are of interest to us and that we shall list: [1978, pp. 147-50]

1. Experience with gaming and gaming theory shows that altruism works best in small groups, where trust can be established and where each person's unselfish acts have a discernable impact upon the outcome of the action. This finding has obvious importance for a study of voluntary associations and is probably related to the phenomenon of the "shrinking dollar for denominational ministry" problem we shall look at a little later.

2. One can distinguish between "meddlesome" and "non-meddlesome" altruism. The former refers to altruism aimed at some particular human problem: jobs, housing, or food, for example. The latter means altruism directed simply at the general betterment of the living conditions of another. For example, to provide money that a poor man might eat is "meddlesome"; to vote for higher welfare benefits is "non-meddlesome." Although we believe this distinction is less clear and less interesting than Collard maintains, it is instructive that Old Testament legislation was generally of the "non-meddlesome" sort. Mosaic law tried to guarantee simply that people were part of the economic life of ancient Israel. People were returned to the land, slaves were freed with goods to allow them to be reproductive, and people could not sell the family's land. As we saw in Chapter V, it was only with the breakdown of the agrarian pattern that specific "meddlesome" laws applied, such as allowing the gleaning of fields by the landless poor.

3. The altruistic giver acts upon the expectation that others will do the same. If presented with evidence that this will not happen, most people will see duty and utility in conflict and will be less likely to give. It goes almost without saying that smaller associations reinforce giving, for the immediate evidence of group cooperation and reinforcement in achieving goals encourages altruistic behavior.

4. The introduction of price into a previously gift-based activity may reduce gifts from altruistically inclined people. It is even more difficult to introduce gift-activity into areas where a cash relationship is already firmly established.

Thus, in the United States the Red Cross has had to wage an uphill battle to establish and expand a free blood donor system, because the practice of paying people to give blood had already been established. The poor quality of the purchased blood, especially the danger of hepatitis infection, has given commercial blood banks a bad reputation. The discovery that it is difficult to decommercialize the economics of blood transfusion underscores the care with which voluntary associations should proceed when they "professionalize" their work. It does not mean that an orphanage run by a church denomination should not hire professionals. It would doubtless be impossible to run an orphanage on volunteer labor alone. But it does mean that a great deal of volunteer activity should be encouraged and rewarded in ways that do not require the exchange of money.

5. Society cannot build a political order on altruism. Roads and bridges, courts, and public welfare, cannot be based on voluntary contribution; at least this seems true in today's large and complex societies. However, there is a significant gift-relationship even here, and that is altruistic voting behavior. Indeed, Collard (in what must be considered a burst of hope and trust considering it comes from an economist!) argues that the wise politician will not try to sneak socially concerned legislation by his constituents, but will build upon the deep fund of altruism that the human race embodies. It will grow, he thinks, by a sort of good infection. But if denied, it will wither and disappear.

6. Finally, Collard finds that trust, duty, and altruism work in dynamic relationship. This simply means that where people trust that their giving is well-used and have been taught or acquired a sense of duty, there you find altruistic behavior. Certainly this is fundamentally biblical. In the scriptures trust describes the relationship of believers to God: "the just shall live by faith (trust)." *Duty* might well be a translation of that pesky Hebrew word for covenant faithfulness, *hesed*. (It is translated several ways: mercy, loyalty, steadfast love, faithfulness.) God shows his people *hesed*, to which they respond in trust (faith), and move out towards others in love. Indeed, altruism seems an awkward and unfortunate euphemism for *agape*-love (giving love) and is probably used only because the English word "love" has so many competing and confusing meanings.

This rapid survey of a small body of literature adds to our understanding of the economic value of human caring. Churches and voluntary associations are a prime conduit for the altruistic behavior of people who are more willing to invest their lives and monies when they can see the goals and participate in reaching them. In addition, we find that giving-economics is probably more useful than exchange-economics for voluntary organizations; that is, many people want to give without being paid for their caring behavior, and churches and voluntary organizations are "better off" in several meanings of that term if they recognize it.

Finally, the reader will remember that in Chapter V on Biblical Principles we said that the Christian should expect that God's will shall be done on earth as well as in heaven. We saw that, biblically, God's activity is in part responsive to the actions of people, that the prophetic call to do justice is accompanied by God's covenant pledge to bless His people. This all means that

God's people ought to expect growth in righteous and just behavior in this world, the diminishing of poverty and extreme hunger, and glimpses of God's peace, *shalom*. God draws us in Christ beyond ourselves through the activity of His Spirit. But this call to action runs counter to a good deal of evangelical Christian passiveness in the face of terrible global conditions, a passiveness that we suggested may have been brought on by disbelief in the biblical pictures of an earthly kingdom of righteousness and peace. If even economists can see evidences of expansive goodwill in human behavior, then surely we should not give up!

## Economic Roles of the Churches

In this major section of the chapter we shall deal with a number of issues: the churches as teachers of economic attitudes, the economic problems of the churches themselves, public disclosure and tax-exemption, and the church as a "mediating structure" between the state and the individual. No other institution in American life has over 500,000 separate organizations with a *weekly* attendance at worship that exceeds the *annual* attendance at professional athletic contests. [Berger & Neuhaus 1977] With such numbers, surely the influence of the churches should be very powerful in the economic aspect of human life. So it is vital to ask some pointed questions about the churches as teachers of economic principles.

If the reader has studied Chapter V, Biblical Principles for Economic Life, and has not read church pronouncements on economic issues, she will assume that the churches often speak about issues from a strongly rooted biblical tradition. There are, we have seen, many texts which give specific teaching in the sphere of economic activity. But the reader would be wrong in her assumption. Most churches do not attempt to teach with authority in economic matters, and when they do, they generally leave the Bible untouched, or, at the most, referred to in passing. This phenomenon was noted by a Presbyterian minister who was assigned to write an adult church school curriculum on poverty. When he checked through the various pronouncements by the General Assemblies of the two largest Presbyterian bodies in the country, he was surprised to find that close to one-half the documents made no appeal to biblical authority, and that of those that do, none chose biblical texts that contain sustained theological justification. During the decade 1964-1974, and in 1978, not one Presbyterian pronouncement on hunger, poverty, welfare, and the like contained a single scriptural allusion. And nowhere among Presbyterians during the period since World War II has there been an appeal to the prophets, to the creation story, to the history of Israel, or to the Zacchaeus account or Jesus' story of the rich man and Lazarus. [Bailey 1981] It is a fairly safe assumption that most denominational records would read like the Presbyterians' save that churches in the Reformed tradition, such as Presbyterians, are more prone to making statements on social issues than are, say, Lutherans.

It is no secret that those two major church bodies are having difficulty holding their people and their congregations, many of whom seem bent upon escaping to more conservative environments, or even upon setting up separate denominations based on Presbyterian polity. It would not be idle, therefore, to ask whether the absence of scriptural warrant for statements that seem "left-wing" issuing from the General Assemblies may not be part of the reason for the uneasiness conservatives feel within those bodies. Most conservative Christians are more willing to listen to arguments based upon scripture than they are to arguments that come from secular analyses of social issues. The scripture speaks again and again to economic affairs. Perhaps it is time for denominations that want to make economic appeals to base them more explicitly upon God's Word.

There is no reason to repeat our earlier chapter. Suffice it to say that Holy Writ contains a great deal about human stewardship of this fair world. The Bible includes heaps of materials about the uses of God's wealth, about what good work means, and about the absolute necessity of Christians to be involved in correcting the injustices and poor stewardship that result from human sin. We suggest that whether it be as local as the deacons of a congregation seeking funds to provide hot meals for the elderly, or as global as the efforts of the Interfaith Center for Corporate Responsibility to influence multi-national corporations in their activities in South Africa, leaders should remember that Christians believe in the authority of the Bible. It is there that we find our warrants for action.

The recent pastoral letter by the U.S. Catholic bishops [Economic Justice 1986] is an excellent example of a denominational statement with firm biblical foundations. Though the bishops draw on traditional Catholic social philosophy, including a number of important papal statements, they also adduce much biblical support for their positions. Because of this attention to the Bible, this pastoral letter has not only stirred up discussion in the Catholic community, but it has also attracted a lot of attention from Protestant Christians. It is significant that the letter is attacked more often for supposedly faulty economic reasoning than for lack of conformity to scripture. Those who place economic theory above the Bible are apt to have problems with the pastoral letter. But for those of us who put things the other way around, the bishops have performed a very useful service. They have brought to the attention of American Christians generally some very important issues in the economic life of our country.

In addition to the churches' inattention to the Bible for specific principles to guide Christians in economic matters, some people have suggested that the voice of religion is muted in America because the churches market themselves exactly as neoclassical economic theory would suggest. We do not accept this argument as a strong one, but we acknowledge its existence and think it deserves some attention. According to this argument American churches simply compete for members and finances like firms that make toothpaste or automobiles. The market has a variety of choices—Roman Catholic, Protestant, and within the latter, Lutheran, Episcopal, Baptist, etc.—and people choose according to certain tastes they have developed or appeals they respond to. Most churches, it is observed in this argument, give "utility" (good things) to people for a modest price.

There is no doubt that the pluralism in religion produces social homogeneity within separate churches and church bodies. Wealthy people are more likely to be Episcopalians and Presbyterians and less likely to belong to the Church of the Nazarene. Blacks are much more likely to attend all-black churches than integrated ones, and the same is true of Hispanics and other ethnic groups. Such analyses are common and accurate. But we believe with most Americans (if not their more ecumenically minded denominational leaders!), that this pluralism has a healthy source and can have healthy consequences. The healthy source is simply that churches have the role of making explicit life's meaning. In a pluralistic society—not a melting pot—people will experience that meaning differently and express it somewhat differently. This does not mean, say, that a theological statement by Roman Catholic bishops and one by the General Synod of the Christian Reformed Church need differ very much in language, nor that they be in conflict. But they will have nuances of difference that have grown from different histories, different pieties, even different experiences of living in America. They will be understood and expressed differently from the pulpit by an Irish priest in Boston than by a Dutch dominie in Iowa. And a schoolteacher of Italian extraction in Boston and a farmer's wife of Frisian extraction in Orange City will apply these statements differently to their own lives. Were the denominational pronouncement made by a church body of the Holiness understanding, the preacher a woman Free Methodist, and the parishioner a Wesleyan grocery worker, then a different set of presuppositions and language would cause the same general teaching to be refracted differently again. So we are not disheartened by the pluralism in American Christianity that is so scandalous to some. In a country made up of people from such varied backgrounds and with such varied experiences, the wonder is that we get along so well together despite our differences.

We note further that just because churches provide private meaning and give social space to those private meanings by their associational or communal character we need not agree that their competition is analogous to that between Ford and General Motors. Neither of the auto companies provides meaning for life; they just make autos, regardless of overblown advertisements. So the competition between churches is really about complementary versions or refractions of life's meaning. Far from being unhealthy, this is what one would expect in a truly pluralistic society. In Europe, where most of the criticism of religious pluralism in America stems from, all nations have had an established church, and other churches have been resisted or grudgingly tolerated. In such a setting people either tended to identify with the state form of religion or to reject it altogether. Active or passive rejection has proceeded apace in all European countries except Romania, Poland, and Ireland, where Eastern or Western Catholicism has been identified with patriotic resistance to outside aggressors. In Europe, then, churches provide meaning, but many people are either not persuaded of that meaning, or else they accept the meaning without bothering themselves much with the institutions that carry it. On the whole, we prefer

American pluralism to the several European models and resist the notion that it is merely a reflection of laissez faire capitalism in religious dress.

But there is an interesting economic problem associated with church choice, growth and decline in the United States. It is sometimes put falsely by averring that in these days of inflation "dollars are giving way to loose change" in the church collection plates. This is simply not true, as per capita giving in all denominations comes pretty close to matching the continuing rise in the cost of living. What is true, however, is that some churches are growing, while others lose members, and the growing ones can survive mediocre per capita giving, while the churches losing members are falling behind. A small simplified table may help. (See Table 14-1).

| Church | Membership Gain or Loss 1974-78 | % Giving Gain 1974-78 | % Benevolence Gain 1974-1978 | Per Capita Giving 1974 | Per Capita Giving 1978 | Per Capita Gain |
|---|---|---|---|---|---|---|
| Southern Baptist | 5.6% | 52% | 43% | $107 | $150 | $43 |
| Nazarene | 7.5% | 48% | 55% | $280 | $386 | $106 |
| American Lutheran | 0.5% | 47% | 43% | $120 | $177 | $57 |
| United Presbyterian | -6.5% | 35% | 21% | $157 | $229 | $72 |
| Presbyterian US | -4.0% | 39% | 40% | $195 | $281 | $86 |
| Episcopal | -5.0% | 41% | 18.5% | $148 | $217 | $69 |
| United Methodist | -3.0% | 35% | 37% | $93 | $130 | $37 |

**Table 14-1.**
Source: *Yearbook of American and Canadian Churches*

It is obvious from the table that Southern Baptists and Nazarenes are growing, as conservative churches have been doing since about 1965. However, it is also obvious that Southern Baptists don't give very much per capita to the work of their churches, and that the increase in per capita giving is very low. Indeed, of all the churches listed, Southern Baptists are the lowest givers save for the Methodists. What those two denominations have in common is that they are the two largest Protestant denominations. One might, indeed, say that conservative churches are growing but are negligent stewards of their money, were it not that the Nazarenes give far and away more than the other denominations listed. Indeed, if one looks up the statistics in *The Yearbook of American and Canadian Churches 1980*, one finds that without exception it is the smaller churches that have the highest per capita giving, whether they are churches thought to have less well-to-do members, like Nazarenes and Free Methodist, or people thought to be somewhat higher on the economic scale, like Orthodox Presbyterians and members of the Evangelical Covenant Church.

So church growth and per capita giving seem to have little correlation—perhaps none at all. What is more noteworthy is that the growing churches manage to sustain a total giving growth that in a four-year period led to a rise of from 47% to 52% overall, and 43% to 55% in benevolence giving. The latter figure is most important, because it represents the dollars not spent to keep the local church operating, but sent out to do some work elsewhere. These figures, one can see at a glance, are somewhat better than the churches that are declining in membership, because their lowered memberships are not able to keep up with the growing churches in total giving and, especially, in giving that reaches beyond the local congregation. This finding is particularly evident in the low benevolence growth for Episcopalians and "Northern" Presbyterians. (However, 1979 figures for the latter church show a growth in benevolence giving in one year that equals the total gain during the four previous years, raising the benevolence giving over a five-year period to forty-five percent. A special major mission fund drive surely accounts for that dramatic increase.)

The possibilities of explaining church growth and decline are many. It does not seem to correlate with intensity of belief, if one can measure that by dollars. But dollars do seem to correlate with smallness, and where one finds smallness and high per capita giving going together, one finds church growth. (The chart does not show that, nor does it show that small churches with small per capita giving are declining. Among such churches are Free Will Baptists and Friends United Meeting). All this leads one to suspect that what is actually being measured in rates of growth and decline is the sense of identity. Small denominations tend to have a strong sense of identity just because they are different from the rest. And among large churches only two are really growing: Southern Baptists and the Churches of Christ (whose financial records are not available). Both these denominations are southern in orientation and have a strong sense of who they are.

So, although it may be true to say that "conservative churches are growing," what is really being said is that people seem to be seeking a church that provides a strong sense of identification; they want their refraction of God's truth in this pluralistic society to have something unique, not the "middle American" fuzziness one associates with, say, Presbyterians and Methodists. It does not appear to be a matter of social actions, as some believe. Indeed, studies of growing congregations indicate that within denominations the growing churches are usually more likely to do social action than their more stagnant sister congregations.

Another economic problem in the churches, particularly the ones not growing, is that while benevolence giving continues to rise (as Table 1 shows), local congregations are choosing more and more to send their monies to locally-determined causes rather than to denomination-wide ones. This means that over-arching needs, such as foreign or home mission agencies, are skimped, while locally designated causes are amply funded. Consider some actual figures: In the United Presbyterian Church, USA, in 1967, giving to general mission causes was $31,200,000, while giving to locally designated causes was only $8,500,000. [Shoemaker 1981] By 1979 a dramatic shift had taken place: general mission is down to 20,800,000, but localized giving has risen to $36,300,000. In real dollars, that is, adjusted for inflation, general mission giving in 1979 was only one-third what it had been a dozen years ago. But by any adjustment specially designated monies had risen dramatically.

We have talked with representatives of denominational boards and agencies, as well as pastors of local churches, and all agree that within this one denomination, at least, there has taken place a radical shift away from trusting denominational officals to handle local benevolence giving. Even giving that reaches overseas is often designated by the local church. One overseas mission board official, now retired, noted that people "who are concerned about the stewardship of their own funds are quite leery of just giving block grants to G(eneral) A(ssembly) to be passed out in ways that aren't of the giver's approval." This means that members of that denomination, at least, now give more money to independent mission groups than they do to those of their own denomination. It means, further, that sons and daughters of the churches are more likely to enlist in these independent or para-church groups (e.g. Sudan Interior Mission, Wycliffe, Navigators), and then local congregations designate funds for their children's support. Thus, increasingly, work in foreign lands done by American missionaries is escaping from the support and supervision of American denominations. In the past decade independent mission agencies have increased eleven-fold, while mainline churches have all cut back. It is no wonder that observers regard the future of mainline denominational support of mission work abroad as "uncertain"!

Is this shrinkage a matter of diminished trust, as we have suggested? Earlier we suggested that trust is more easily maintained in a small association and said that unless there is trust that gifts will be used well, givers will cease giving. It seems clear that in the United Presbyterian Church, and to a slightly lesser extent in other mainline denominations, the trust level has declined in recent years. At least part of the reason for this is that denominational agencies have not securely justified their economic policies on biblical grounds. Suspicious of expenditures that seem "left wing," as for example, the disclosure that World Council of Churches relief funds have been given to revolutionary forces in Africa, and presented with arguments for giving to various good causes that are grounded in humanistic argument instead of the Bible, lay people have backed away and looked for other ways of expressing their stewardship. Thus inadequate argumentation has led to the breakdown in trust and to the impoverishment of once-healthy programs that have done a great amount of good for more than a century.

Decline in lay trust in religious institutions has carried over to the public cry that these institutions be accountable for the way monies are used, and even to calls that tax-exempt status be taken from the churches. While we cannot hope to cover these issues adequately in a short chapter, it is at least worth noting that they are sometimes aroused by poor economic activity on the part of some churches. If the Jonestown suicides raised the issue of trust most sharply, earlier scandals, such as the questionable monetary activities of several Catholic religious orders, and the suspicion that not all monies given to electronic ministries or evangelistic associations among Protestants are being spent carefully, have prompted calls for the government to "do something about it." Since justice issues are clearly within the purview of the state, this plea makes a certain amount of sense; but since the state should be cautious about stepping into the arena of religious activity, it makes sense also to resist the state's intrusion. It appears that the work of the Evangelical Council for Financial Accountability, a coalition of religious groups that do a good deal of fund-raising, may bear good fruit. They have pledged themselves to disclose what monies they have raised and how they have spent them, without granting the state the right to request such disclosure. Because of our general commitment to sphere sovereignty we, of course, support this approach. However, again we point out that it has been careless use of monies entrusted to their care that has brought religious organizations into such disrepute. That Catholic organizations, with their sure sense of hierachy and authority, should be among the worst offenders must make less tightly organized religious bodies doubly careful about the wise use of other people's stewardship.

On the matter of tax exemption, we believe that taxation is not meant to apply to everything that exists in a nation, and that churches as non-profit institutions which contribute significantly to the common weal should be exempt by right, not by privilege. As Dean Kelley [1977] points out, there is a vast array of non-taxable entities in the USA, including social-welfare or action organizations, labor unions and trade associations, clubs, lodges, recreation groups, cooperatives, pension plans and retirement funds, trusts and endowments, private foundations, and political parties. Churches are in the favored group called "public charities" which are not only tax-exempt but can receive contributions whose givers deduct their value before paying income tax. Of all the organizations, only religious ones are specifically mentioned in the First Amendment, where Congress is told that it cannot set up any religious institution, nor hinder the free exercise of religion. Indeed, we believe that the double-taxation upon people who want to send their children to schools with religious teaching is actually a limitation on the free exercise of religion. The courts, however, have not so ruled, and, indeed, have ruled emphatically otherwise. With respect to tax-exemption as an aid to free exercise, the courts have been relatively consistent, and with that we are content. But it has often been bad economic activity by churches that has precipitated calls for an end to tax-exemption. Fortunately, now that churches can no longer own businesses that unfairly compete with private firms because they paid no taxes, much of the occasion for cheating has ended, and the calls for an end to tax-exemption for churches and church-related organizations have been muted.

Finally, we need to say a word about the churches and what Peter Berger and Richard John Neuhaus [1977] called "mediating structures," those voluntary societies which stand between the great power of government or large business corporations and the helplessness of the lone individual. The churches together constitute the largest and most important of the voluntary associations. Such associations necessarily maintain some relationship to the economic and political order because they have resources which are too great and aims which are too broad to escape being economically important and politically sensitive. In 1979, for example, just forty-two Protestant bodies received 7.5 billion dollars from their members; that is economics. In 1980 the so called "moral majority" claimed to have elected Mr. Reagan to the presidency; that is politics.

Like most Americans, we are ambivalent about the role of the churches *vis-a-vis* the economic and political order. On the one hand, as Alexis deTocqueville noted in the 1820's, one of the reasons the churches in young America were more successful than in Europe was that they had not gotten identified with any political movement, save those movements that had as their primary aim the amelioration of human ills. Because they were not so identified in the minds of the people, neither did their fortunes rise and wane with the fortunes of the parties. But on the other hand, churches cannot pretend that political and economic choices have no bearing on human welfare. Indeed, this study is funded by a college that is supported by a denomination, and our initial conclusion—that there is a Christian way of understanding and doing economics that is not identifiable with either ideologies of the left or the right—may appear to be "political" to members of that denomination. Still, we believe that in the U.S. churches qua churches can take part in the humanizing of society in ways that will normally be acceptable to persons with varying views on politics and economics. Indeed, they are already so involved.

Take First Mainline Church in Anytown of Middling Size in the Midwest. Very probably there is a nursery school or day-care center operating in the church plant and under the general direction of the board of elders. Such a school will operate on funds provided by the church, by parents, by scholarships, and by monies provided by both state and federal government under the guise of hot meals, aid to dependent children, and various child-care programs that enable single mothers to work or to be trained for work. The church also conducts a large campaign or two during the year for famine relief and to help people in other lands to rebuild the economic base for their lives. The food may be government-owned surplus grains sitting in bins and elevators waiting for monies, such as First Church's contributions, so that it can be shipped abroad. Overseas missionaries will work closely with AID staff, paid by the U.S. government, to establish new cash or subsistence crops for farmers. Back in the building, the church will be used as a polling place for an election and as a meeting spot for any number of groups, some of which will work with representatives of the state university on pre-natal care, or with farmers on soil erosion. A cadre within the church will be coordinators of the Meals on Wheels program, funded by state and local governments. A once-weekly dinner will be served to community residents who are over sixty-five; local church members will prepare and serve the meal, but the funds will come from the government. Representatives from a nearby college that is associated with Mainline's denomination will visit the church in search of gifts and students. But this college will be recipient of a grant from the state for every citizen of the state that enrolls, and another for each citizen who graduates. In addition, many of the students will be recipients of BEOG funds from the federal treasury or competitive scholarships from the state. A couple in the church will adopt a baby through an adoption agency run by the Catholic or Methodist Church, and that agency, responsive to state legislation regulation adoption agencies, will receive children placed there by state and local agencies. And so it goes, on and on. The church is involved in the practical politics and economics of human welfare, although it is not itself a primary provider of a living to any but its full-time employees.

Where Peter Berger and Richard John Neuhaus are most helpful, we believe, is in their clear call that the government should (1) stop its largely unintended damage to such mediating structures as family, neighborhoods, voluntary associations, and churches, and (2) empower these structures to help realize their helping purposes, wherever possible. On the minimalist side (item 1) they argue that churches should not be cut out of funding for human causes, nor neutered by governmental rules. It is good, they aver, for an elderly Italian Roman Catholic woman to receive care in a nursing home run by Italian Roman Catholics. Why should the state or local government force the woman into a public nursing facility? Similarly, a Black Muslim man is probably best cared for by Black Muslims, who seem pretty proficient at social organization. The so-called Kurland Rule (named after Philip Kurland of the University of Chicago) should hold, namely: that if a policy furthers a legitimate secular purpose, it is a matter of legal indifference whether or not that policy employs religious institutions. Clearly this has far-ranging implications in the areas of education, child care, and social services generally. The "free exercise of religion" clause in the First Amendment simply means that no denomination ought to be favored by the state over any others. It does not mean that churches and church agencies may not be channels for public monies when appropriately located and well-run. Indeed, probably a church-related institution will have a good deal more voluntary help than the public institution, in addition to the professional paid staff. This should make conditions significantly better for patients and clients, other things being equal.

On the maximalist side (item 2) Berger and Neuhaus argue that churches and church-related organizations should be used when possible to carry on the work of human welfare. In some areas this simply means the churches should keep on doing what they are now doing. But if human needs in our society continue to grow—and with increased mobility and a coming jump in the percentage of the elderly, who can doubt it?—the state should turn to religious associations to humanize that network of care that will undoubtedly be necessary. Those who have dealt with government bureaucracies know full well that people whose problems defy general categories find it very difficult to get accurate information or help from public agencies. Such persons need the kind of attention that professional church-related associations can better provide. As Berger and Neuhaus put it: "The Salvation Army needs no lessons from the state on how to be nonsectarian in its compassion for people." (They also point out that the Army is seriously undercut if its workers cannot preach to those to whom they minister). So, in what is sometimes called the eoconmics of welfare, we expect churches in the future to be more involved in these community social concerns, not less so. And social involvement cannot exclude economic activity.

## Voluntary Associations in the United States

When we began our work and contemplated writing this chapter, it seemed to us that we should discuss voluntary associations first and then look at churches as a specific example. However, the now-published work by an earlier group of fellows at the Calvin Center for Christians Studies, *Society, State, and Schools: a Case for Structural and Confessional Pluralism* [McCarthy, et al 1981], makes the case for pluralistic associations in American life in a fuller way than we had thought to do. In addition, the work of Berger and Neuhaus is the proper place to begin such a study. They will send the reader to the early notice that Frenchman Alexis de Tocqueville [1960, v.2, pt.2] gave to the American propensity to form associations for wide ranges of purposes, and then to the efforts of Robert Nisbet [1953] to re-awaken interest in and concern for the pluralism of voluntary associations in a nation where the federal government tends to expand and displace associational effort. Attention should also be drawn to the brief study sponsored by American Enterprise Institute, Michael P. Balzano's *Federalizing Meals-on-Wheels: Private Sector Gain or Loss?* [1979], where the threats to one largely local voluntary kind of association that provides hot meals for elderly shut-ins has been threatened by governmental and professional take-over, however benign.

Because we think of ourselves as neither "right" nor "left" in our political-economic thinking, we believe it unfortunate that encouragement for local, voluntary handling of social needs will probably be dismissed as "right-wing" because of the reputed bias of the American Enterprise Institute. Our concern, however, is to promote neither right nor left, but a biblical perspective on economic activity. Biblically, it appears, everyone is called to stewardly activity with the wealth and work given by God. To do justice in a world where human need is pressing is always the human task. It seems right to us that such work be done as close to the place of need as possible. And in the United States voluntary associations have a long history of providing such care. It is only when local efforts are insufficient, as they often will be, that the state's rightful role of provider of justice should cause it to intervene. If a region of Appalachia cannot meet the human needs of its people (as most cannot), then the state must help. So our principles lead us neither to dismiss the role of the state in such matters, nor to demand that the state evict all local providers and conduits for help in order to get the job done. That the job of justice be done is paramount. But that people play their paramount role in bringing love to bear in person and in association is not a minor consideration for Christian economics. For government directed welfare tends to lose the human touch, and people with wealth become insulated from real human ills, and from the wickedness of injustice, when it is only their money that helps.

## Conclusion

In the earlier part of our study we have focused attention upon the larger economic structures such as the corporation, the state, the labor union. Here we have directed attention to the oft-overlooked infra-structures that buffer the individual from the impersonalities of mega-structures, that promote human association, and that explicate meaning for the deep questions of existence. It is generally assumed that these small associations have no economic utility. We have tried to show that they do. Politically, they make it possible for the individual to own (legitimize) the values of the larger society, resist the onslaughts of anomie, and thus protect social and political order. Economically, they are conduits for altruistic behavior and practical networks for social and welfare services. In a world where the size of government, industry, and labor continue to grow, bureaucratize, and depersonalize human life, we shall find our smaller associations taking on more importance. Every effort should be made to ensure their health.

## Resources

Bailey, W. M. 1981. 'I Was Hungry...' — The Bible and Poverty. *J. Presbyterian History* 59

Balzano, M. P. 1979. *Federalizing Meals-on-Wheels: Private Sector Gain or Loss?* Washington: American Enterprise Institute.

Berger, P. L., and R. J. Neuhaus. 1977. *To Empower People: The Role of Mediating Structures in Public Policy.* Washington: American Enterprise Institute.

Collard, D. 1978. *Altruism and Economy.* Oxford: Martin Robertson.

*Economic Justice for All: Catholic Social Teaching and the U. S. Economy.* 1986. Washington: U. S. Catholic Conference.

Graham, W. F. 1980. Declining Church Membership: Can Anything be Done? *Reformed Journal* 30 (Jan.), pp. 7-13.

Hoge, D. R., and D. A. Roozen. 1979. *Understanding Church Growth and Decline*, NY: Pilgrim Press.

Kelley, D. M. 1977. *Why Churches Should Not Pay Taxes.* NY: Harper & Row.

McCarthy, R. et al. 1981. *Society, State, and Schools.* Grand Rapids: Eerdmans.

Nisbet, R. 1953. *The Quest for Community.* NY: Oxford U. Press.

Shoemaker, D. E. 1981. Good and Bad News about Mission Funding. *Communique/New Times* 8.

Titmuss, R. M. 1970. *The Gift Relationship*. London: George Allen & Unwin.

Tocqueville, Alexis de. 1969. *Democracy in America*. (J. P. Mayer, ed., G. Lawrence, trans.), Garden City: Doubleday.

Tocqueville, Alexis de. 1960. *Democracy in America*. 2 vols. NY: Vintage.

Wilson, E. O. 1975. *Sociobiology*. Cambridge: Harvard U. Press.

*Yearbook of American and Canadian Churches*. 1980. (C. Jacquet, ed.), Nashville: Abingdon.

# Chapter XV
# International Economic Activity

*Oh, Megan, this London's a wonderful sight,*
*There's people here working by day and by night.*
*They don't sow potatoes or barley or wheat,*
*But there's gangs of them digging for gold in the streets.*
*At least, when I asked them, that's what I was told,*
*So I just took a hand in this digging for gold.*
*But, for all that I found there I might as well be*
*Where the mountains of Mourne go down to the sea.*
  *Percy French (c. 1900)*


## International Trade and the Poor Countries

There are several reasons why international economics is usually considered to be a separate branch of the discipline. Economic activity that crosses international boundaries faces some important special problems. The most obvious of these is the difference in money between two countries. Anyone who has done any foreign travel (even to nearby Canada) has experienced some of the frustration that can come when dealing with a strange money. With different money and different governments come disparate macroeconomic policies. The possibility exists that the governments of different countries can unthinkingly or even maliciously influence the level of economic activity or regulations that make it hard to sell abroad, and often governments deliberately erect barriers, like tariffs or quotas, to foreign products. Differences in language and customs make more difficult the movement of people and goods across frontiers.

Christians' interest in international economics rests on other grounds as well as these. We are interested in people living together in some form of community or commonwealth. Since Christianity is a world religion, teaching that we are all brothers and sisters under the parentage of God, we are naturally interested in the international dimensions of this community. Christian mission activity over the centuries has often been an adjunct to or cause of international economic activity. Furthermore, our deep, biblically-based concern about poverty extends beyond the poor of our own country to the far more numerous populations of the poor in countries where poverty is so widespread that domestic solutions to the problem seem to be almost impossible.

### The Purposes and Causes of Trade

The Bible gives us the image of the church as an organism, a body, in which the members have specialized functions according to the gifts each has been given. The same thing is true of an economy, even on an international scale. Each person and each nation has a specialized calling to pursue according to its gifts, and trade permits us to pursue those callings. Trade can lead to the saving of resources by making the most effective use of those special gifts. It can also offer opportunities for the poor to earn a living for themselves. But in order to accomplish these things, trade must be fair; all the parties must have opportunity within the system to benefit from trade. In the international economy poor people and poor countries often do not benefit, because the system is run by the rich for their own benefit. Poor countries can find themselves in a relationship of dependence which is unhealthy in the long run. We believe it is the task of Christians within the rich countries to try to reform the international economic system, so that it operates for the benefit of the whole world community, especially the poor.

Conventional economics offers four explanations for international trade. Though all of them are important in fact, the profession concentrates the most attention on the one that has the most interesting mathematical interpretation, the one concerning differences in factor endowments (known as the Heckscher-Ohlin theory). Students of the subject should bear in mind that this attention is probably unjustified. This theory states that, other things being equal, a country will specialize in producing goods which use intensively in their production the resources that are relatively abundant in that country. So, for example, a country that has a lot of agricultural land and a relatively small working population will export agricultural products like wheat and soybeans and import labor-intensive goods like shoes and textiles (this is the case with the U.S.). This pattern of trade leads to a more efficient use of resources than if each country tried to be self-sufficient (or autarkic), so aggregate income should be higher in both countries (or resource use lower for the same income level).

The mathematical development of this theory has led to an interesting and potentially useful theorem about the distribution of the benefits. This theorem (The Samuelson-Stolper Theorem) states that the owners of the abundant resources in each country end up with larger real incomes as a result of trade, and the owners of the scarce resources get lower real incomes. This does not seem to be terribly significant for the explanation of international poverty until ones realizes that the abundant resources of the poor countries are often owned by individuals or firms from the rich countries. If an underdeveloped country's abundant resource is something like agricultural land (for growing bananas or coffee or cocoa) or mineral deposits (oil wells or copper mines), it is more than likely to be owned by a multinational firm from a developed country which acquired the property under a colonial regime. Thus, the benefits of trade do not accrue to any nationals from the poor country. Economic models that focus on just two production factors, capital and labor, and ignore natural resources, tend to ignore this fact. Yet the poor countries themselves understand these realities, and are beginning to acquire and exert the political power necessary to change the situation. Even if we consider labor to be the poor countries' abundant factor in a two-factor world, traditional patterns of employment, often amounting to a kind of serfdom, limit poor people's opportunities to benefit from trade. Monopoly elements in world markets can also lead to exploitation, which the theorem also ignores, since it rests on the mistaken assumption of perfect competition.

Another approach to the explanation of trade focuses on international differences in technology. The U.S., for example, exports computers, which have reached their highest state of development here, and imports gas-saving automobiles, a technology in which the rest of the world is ahead of us. One version of this hypothesis (the product-diffusion theory, formulated by Raymond Vernon) suggests that countries at first export the products of a new technology and, then, as the technology is learned abroad, lose their advantage. The price of the good comes down, competition opens up, and world trade in the good declines. Multinational firms from the original exporter may diversify their production abroad. Since most research and development activity takes place in the rich countries, poor countries have little opportunity to profit from this kind of trade, since by the time the knowledge reaches them it has also reached everybody else. It also means that new technological developments are usually not directed toward poor country needs. Nevertheless, there may still be some opportunities for the poor to benefit, if the rich countries need products that involve traditional but esoteric skills, like pottery-making or wood carving.

Differences in tastes across national boundaries can also account for some international trade. Two countries that are very similar in their resource endowments and technology might still trade if each country has a very specialized taste for a particular good. Though the U.S. produces many color television sets, and seems well-equipped to do so, we still import sets from the Far East, because there is such a huge demand for them here. This presumably results in some resource saving, since it would be very expensive for us to concentrate so many resources in that one industry. Subtle differences in the quality of different countries' products can have a similar effect; some of us buy British marmalade, because the domestic variety is not sufficiently tart, and the French both import and export wine. This sort of trade does not seem to have any systematic impact on the poor countries.

The fourth reason for trade has to do with economics of scale. If resource savings can be accomplished by producing a good in large quantities of long productions runs, most of the production will end up being concentrated in one or a few countries. This seems to be the reason that most aircraft production is concentrated in the U.S. Though this clearly contributes to efficiency in resource use, it may have a detrimental effect on poor countries. The nations that have the largest domestic markets are the nations that will have the largest share of these kinds of exports, and, for the most part, the largest markets will be in the richer parts of the world. Some smaller countries, both rich and poor, have tried to counteract this tendency by forming regional customs unions. Part of the reasoning behind the European Economic Community is to have a large enough regional market so that large-scale industries can take root there, and Europe can be less dependent on the U.S. for such products as steel or even aircraft. The Latin American Free Trade Association is a group of poorer countries with similar purposes. Companies from rich countries gain scale economics by introducing inappropriate products in poor countries.

Economic relationships between rich and poor countries have also been influenced by a systematic tendency for rich countries to discriminate against poor country manufactured exports. The labor-intensive industries in the rich countries constitute a very powerful political force, and they are the very industries that face the most competition from poor country exports. Hence the rich countries often have high trade barriers erected against such products. The U.S., for example, imposes very low tariffs on imported raw coffee beans, but much higher tariffs on imported processed coffee of all kinds. These tariffs have had an important role in preventing the development of the coffee-processing industry in the coffee-producing countries, which are for the most part poor. International negotiations aimed at reducing trade barriers have usually neglected these industries and products. The rich countries do more trading with each other than with the less-developed world, so when reciprocal reductions of trade barriers are on the agenda, the largest concessions are made on products that are traded among the rich nations. The poor are frozen out, since the volume of business they do is so much less. The international organization that deals with trade barriers, the General Agreement on Tariffs and Trade, has instituted a program called the Generalized System of Preferences, which is designed to deal with this problem. Under the GSP, rich countries can grant unilateral trade concessions to particular groups of poor countries without having to extend them world-wide. The EEC has taken advantage of this program, granting many preferences to former European colonies in Africa and Asia. American participation in the GSP has so far been very limited.

### Primary Commodity Prices

As a result of many of these structural factors, most of the exports of the poor countries to the rich are primary commodities—that is, the products of agriculture and mining. These commodities are often subject to large fluctuations in price over the short run, caused by instability in agricultural production owing to weather, and instability in industrial demand owing to business cycles in the developed countries. In addition, for some commodities over some periods of time, there has been a secular decline in the real price caused by income-inelastic demand and the development of substitutes in the rich countries. The less-developed countries, through the "Group of 70" and the United Nations Conference on Trade and Development (UNCTAD), have proposed an approach to the alleviation of these problems. They have suggested the establishment of a large common fund, supported by the rich nations, which would be used to stabilize, or perhaps even raise, the prices of these primary commodities. The rich nations have been reluctant to agree to this program, partly because of ideological commitments to free markets (combined with deficient concern for the poor), but also because there are some real questions about whether such a plan would work as it is intended to. Let us examine some of those questions.

The support for a commodity fund seems to be based at least in part on the idea that stabilizing prices will stabilize producer (poor country) revenue. This is probably true for industrial minerals, where the major cause of instability comes from the demand side. It is not likely to be the case for agricultural products, where fluctuations in supply are the main cause of price changes. When crops are short, prices tend to rise, which compensates in part for the fall in volume of production. Price stabilization makes the farmers' aggregate income less steady, though there is an offsetting benefit for consumers.

Some countries wish to use the commodity fund to increase the real prices of some goods that have declined in value over the recent past (such as natural rubber, jute, and wheat, which is exported mainly by rich countries). If the common fund attempts to hold these prices above their long-run equilibrium level, it will constantly be buying product, building up huge stockpiles, and it will eventually run out of money. The only way to control the price in the long run is to control the quantity of production. Besides, there is some question about whether raising commodity prices is always a step in the direction of justice for the poor. Things that some poor people sell, other poor people buy. Raising the price helps some of the poor and hurts others. We could perhaps count up how many poor folks are on each side of the market and move the price in the direction that helps the larger group, but then it is not clear that we are talking about justice. We are required to help them all, and moving prices around does not do that. This has become painfully obvious in the case of oil. OPEC has helped the poor of their own countries, but at the expense of the poor in non-oil developing countries, and even poor people within rich countries like the U.S.

Another argument for the commodity program is that it would provide a stock of foodstuffs that could be used to provide emergency aid to famine-struck regions. If a regional famine happens to coincide with a world-wide shortage of food, that might work reasonably well. But if the common fund is trying to buy up food while there is a regional famine going on, the two purposes of the agency would run counter to each other. It is probably better to have a separate emergency food aid program with its own stockpiles and/or funds.

Critics of the commodity program are concerned about the funding features. A fairly limited amount of money is supposed to do the job in stabilizing the prices of at least nine different goods. An underfunded price stabilization agency is worse than none at all, since the prospect of the agency running out of money or goods will cause destabilizing speculation in the market. Since the fund would be in business to buy cheap and sell dear, there is an assumption that after the initial capitalization it would be self-supporting. It is not clear, however, that it would make enough money both to maintain its capital and to pay for its operating expenses. It might, therefore, end up under-capitalized, or else it might demand constant renewal of funds from supporting countries.

In spite of all of these questions and problems, commodity price stabilization is probably a good idea. The usual economist's argument for it suggests that by holding cheap stocks of the good until demand for it rises, the agency is increasing the benefits to both buyers and sellers whose time preferences for the good differ. This argument is based on the assumption that market demand and supply schedules have welfare significance, an assumption that we have questioned throughout this book. A more telling consideration to us is the desirability of maintaining price stability generally. Stable prices enable economic agents to plan their activities in a way that takes into account the true long-run scarcity of the goods. Stability can promote the saving of resources, since it de-emphasizes time-bound artifacts of market conditions. By decreasing the risks to both consumers and producers, it should short-circuit useless speculation and increase the investment in productive capacity. This last consideration is especially important for poor countries with high unemployment.

In conclusion, we believe that a fair, just, and stewardly international trade regime should be founded on a commitment by all countries to a very low level of trade barriers. The reduction of these barriers should focus particularly on barriers to the import of poor country industrial products by rich countries. This regime should be supplemented by a commodity price stabilization program not necessarily based on the common fund proposal. Poor countries should be allowed to benefit from their natural resource endowments by taxation or socialization. Such a package would help to save world resources and also offer opportunities for poor nations to increase their levels of employment and income. This recommendation leaves open the question of the role of multinational corporations to which we now turn our attention.

## Direct Foreign Investment in the Poor Countries

The huge literature about multinational corporations tends to have a very partisan tone. Depending on whom you happen to be reading, MNC's are either the greatest thing that ever happened to the world economic system, rich and poor alike, or else they are evil incarnate and ought to be outlawed. As is usual with such complex social phenomena, the truth is probably somewhere in between. Therefore, policy toward multinationals should no doubt stop short of complete banning, without moving to the other extreme of laissez faire. We will first consider some of the problems caused for poor countries by

MNC's, and then some of the advantages they offer. Then we will move on to policy.

One of the more prominent theories of the existence of MNC's states that they are products of the desire for monopoly power in world markets. Consider an example. If it is expensive for a firm like GM to export cars outside of North America to, say, Latin America, it is more than likely that a new company will be formed to manufacture cars in Latin America to serve that market. This new firm would then become a competitor for GM in the world market for cars. Rather than let such a thing happen, GM will set up a branch plant in Latin America to serve the local market and forestall the appearance of a new competitor. GM thus maintains a high share of the world market and, with it, some power to raise prices above the competitive level. This argument depends on the existence of a moderate but non-trivial level of trade barriers, but mere transportation costs may be a high enough barrier to produce market power. A desire to protect the secrecy of new technology may have similar effects. If this theory is correct, and there is probably some truth in it, MNC's cause high prices, an inefficient allocation of resources, and concentration of wealth in the developed countries.

The other problematical aspects of MNC's do not depend so heavily on a single theory of MNC strategy, but are consistent with a more benign view that such companies diversify abroad simply in order to reduce their production costs. If a firm operates in several countries, it will often be involved in shipping intermediate or unfinished goods around the world among its various subsidiaries. For local tax purposes, it will have to place a value on these goods, even though they may not be traded on any market. The firm can increase its profits by arranging these transfer prices so that most of the firm's profits are earned (or appear to be earned) in countries where the tax rates are the lowest. Similar considerations apply to tariffs and excises, as well as profit taxes. This often means that poor countries, with low tax bases and high revenue demands, and hence high tax rates, are deprived of revenue that they desperately need.

Often the multinationals are accused of transferring inappropriate technology to poor countries where they have operations. A developed-country firm that is looking for a place with abundant cheap labor to locate the more labor-intensive parts of its operations will find poorer countries attractive. Since it is too expensive to draw up a whole new plant design, the new overseas factory will look just like the ones back home. But a process that looks labor-intensive to us is usually much too capital-intensive for a poor country, so that many fewer jobs are created than could be. This could lead to a permanent division in the economy between a modern and a backward sector, with the attendant disparities in incomes and migration problems. The same thing can be true of product technology. Having already spent the money on research and development, a firm will try to spread that cost over a larger market by trying to sell the same thing overseas that it sells back home. So we end up with soft drinks and concentrated baby formula being sold in poor countries where malnutrition is a big problem.

Perhaps the aspect of multinationals that poor countries resent the most is the centralization of economic power that they represent. Countries with deep economic problems find that most of the decisions about the direction of their economies are made in rich countries by people who often have very little understanding of the poor nations' social, cultural, and economic conditions. It is not just that these decisions often will not turn out well for the poor lands, but national and local autonomy and self-determination is compromised. Poor country nationals find that their paths to advancement are blocked. More than that, because the wealthy decision-makers are located abroad, the poor countries do not have the opportunity to develop the kind of cultural infrastructure that comes with being a headquarters location. This can also be a problem for the hinterlands of the rich countries.

Multinationals can also contribute to monetary instability for the poor countries. Many poor lands are small enough and many multinationals large enough that the operations of one company bringing money into and out of a country can cause substantial changes in the balance of payments and/or the exchange rate. It also seems likely that MNC's cause long-term deterioration in the balance of payments of their host countries as they repatriate profits to the homeland, particularly if they have acquired a lot of leverage by borrowing in host country capital markets.

But for all of these problems, the multinationals bring with them some advantages as well. To some extent, at least, it is possible that the international diversification of production and marketing make possible the same kinds of saving of resources that come about through ordinary international trade. If activities are located where they are the least expensive to undertake, that is a rough indication that some real efficiency is being improved. The question then becomes, Why isn't trade itself sufficient to reap these economies? Are these huge organizations necessary to bring efficiency about? Couldn't local firms accomplish the same thing? If modern production and marketing processes are as complex as they seem to be, then there may be some justification for organizing them within the firm rather than through markets. But this question must be explicitly considered when policy toward particular multinationals is being made. If monopoly is the aim of the MNC's rather than efficiency, the case for them is much weaker. Some multinationals go out of their way to investigate technologies that are appropriate to poor country operations. If a firm is interested in a very long term commitment of its resources, the savings from an appropriate technology can justify the increased research expenditure at the beginning. Here, as in so many other cases, the longer the firm's time horizon, the more likely it is to come up with a responsible approach to the problem. The Dutch electronics firm, Philips, has established a research unit at Utrecht for exactly this purpose.

Multinationals do, of course, provide jobs to poor country nationals. While the direct impact of this employment may be relatively small, indirect impacts occur that deserve to be considered. The new employees are often trained in new skills and acquire new attitudes toward work and education. They can take these new skills and attitudes with them to new jobs within their country and convey them, at least in part, to their families and associates. This improves the level of human resources within the country and makes further economic development easier. The money they earn can help them provide for higher levels of education and health for their families.

The challenge in developing policy toward MNC's is to enhance their advantages while controlling their problems. This involves "unbundling the package" of capital, technology, jobs, training, profits, and economic control that the multinationals offer to the poor lands. This usually means that the poor country governments must try to obtain the desirable parts of the package, while retaining some control over the enterprise for their own nationals. In imitation of the rich nations, many poor nations have begun to require that multinationals not establish wholly-owned subsidiaries but, rather, enter into joint ventures with local firms, or at least have a certain degree of local participation in the ownership and management of the firm.

A difficulty that poor countries face in trying to regulate multinationals is the "competition in laxity" among the nations. Other things being equal, an MNC will choose to locate its operations in the country that has the most favorable regulatory environment (the same thing happens within the United States). If the poor countries are interested in attracting a lot of direct investment for the advantages it offers, they will be tempted to relax their regulations about local ownership, taxation, employment practices, environmental controls, and all kinds of other conditions, to those nations' own detriment. The only solution to this problem is to have international agreements about what sort of regulations there will be and how stringently they will be implemented. Once a country is bound, or at least guided, by such an agreement, the temptation to relax local standards at the behest of the multinationals is much less. The United Nations Conference on Trade and Development (UNCTAD), and the Group of 70 within the International Monetary Fund (IMF) have served this purpose to some degree in the last few years.

## The International Monetary Regime

As we said at the beginning of this chapter, one of the most unique, complicated, and esoteric features of international trade is the fact that different countries have different monies. An American cannot just go to a Mexican firm and pay for his or her purchase with U.S. dollars. First, he or she must take the dollars and use them to buy Mexican pesos. So there is a different, separate, set of markets to contend with in discussing international economic affairs, the markets in which the money of one country is exchanged for the money of another. The prices, or exchange rates, that are established in these markets have a very important impact on the pattern of trade. The more expensive the Mexican peso is in U.S. dollar terms, the more expensive Mexican goods will appear to Americans, and the less likely the Americans will be to shop in Mexico. We will not discuss the determinants of exchange rates in great detail here—the textbooks do an adequate job of that. What we will do is discuss the way that foreign exchange markets are structured, paying particular attention to how this structure impedes or facilitates trade, and how it affects the poor countries.

The main argument about the structure of foreign exchange markets has to do with how much flexibility there should be in the prices. Exchange rates that move up and down a lot in somewhat unpredictable fashion can become a barrier to trade and thus take away from the advantages of trade that we set out in the first section of this chapter. Like any other short-term price instability, excessive fluctuations in exchange rates make planning difficult and make the connection between price and real scarcity that much more tenuous. Stewardship of resources, or real care for what we have been given, is made much harder. On top of these considerations, there is the fear that countries will take advantage of the flexibility in exchange rates to improve their own economic conditions at the expense of their trading partners by holding the price of their money below the appropriate level, making their exports artificially cheap. For some of these reasons, the monetary regime established by the Bretton Woods conference in 1947 was built on the commitment by the participating nations to hold their exchange rates very rigidly to fixed levels for long periods of time. The procedure for changing the exchange rate was made very difficult and painful for any country that wished to do so.

It was because of this rigidity that the Bretton Woods system finally collapsed in 1971. It became clear that the U.S. dollar was not properly priced in relation to the other currencies, but that nothing could be done about it without bringing the old system down. Since then, we have operated with a system that provides a great deal more flexibility than the old one did, but still permits, even requires, that countries intervene in the markets to prevent their exchange rates from moving too far too fast. This system has worked rather well overall so far. Flexible rates offer advantages of their own. With flexibility in the market, it is unlikely that rates could remain seriously out of line for very long, so importers and exporters have prices to work with that are closer to reflecting long-run scarcity, even though they are more uncertain over time. Speculation is present, but it is usually stabilizing in nature, at least where markets have some depth. Forward markets have allowed firms to nail down their costs for future transactions and avoid unduly large risks. Large countries have been more free to pursue stabilization policies aimed at domestic economic conditions without being unduly constrained by international considerations, since flexible rates to some extent insulate countries from macroeconomic policies pursued by their trading partners. This is especially true for the U.S. With better understood domestic fiscal and monetary policies, the desire for competitive devaluation has not arisen, and it is no longer necessary to tolerate high unemployment for the sake of exchange stability. There has been enough intervention by central banks to prevent large short-term fluctuations that would disrupt trade. Trade has in fact flourished under this new regime.

The poor countries have not been so happy with the new system, however. Most of them favor a higher degree of stability in exchange rates than the new system provides. Less developed economies often lack the internal flexibility that would allow them to adjust rapidly to changes in the prices of their imports and exports. If their exports are primary commodities whose demand does not respond much to price, and if they have a large need for industrial imports with no domestic substitutes, exchange rates flexibility does not help them. What is more, exchange rate instability will be more of a problem for countries whose primary commodity exports fluctuate a great deal in price. Most of the poor countries also have large external debts, denominated in developed country currencies, which would appreciate in value as the poor country's currency depreciated. Poor countries also believe that they do not benefit from the insulation from foreign income movements that flexible exchange rates provide. Since they would like to see their domestic economies grow faster, they would prefer to have their economies directly linked to those of the rich countries through the monetary system. That way, the rich countries can be the "locomotive" to pull the poor countries to higher income levels. Fixed rates also allow poor country leaders to blame the rich countries and/or the IMF for painful adjustment measures when they must be undertaken.

It should be possible, however, to fashion some sort of hybrid system which would satisfy the needs of all the parties. Even under the current system of managed flexibility, many poor countries maintain a fixed relationship between their own currencies and those of some of the rich countries, usually the former colonial power, with whom they still conduct a high proportion of their trade. This system of fixed rates for the poor countries and flexible rates for the rich countries can help to solve the problems that both face. Furthermore, a flexible rate system may also have some advantages to offer to the poor countries. Flexibility is a better adjustment technique than exchange or import controls: e.g., quotas, to which the poor countries often resort. Many of the more advanced poor countries have higher growth rates than their richer counterparts, so that the "locomotive" effect may actually slow them down. Flexible exchange rates have the potential to free the poor countries from the restrictions imposed on them by rich country bankers or by the IMF which would slow down their growth rates for the sake of maintaining the fixed exchange rate.

Any system that maintains some degree of stability in exchange rates must provide some form of international reserve asset. This international money is the tool used by central bankers to intervene in exchange markets either to slow down changes in the prices or to maintain a fixed price. Under the current system, as under the previous one, the main reserve asset is the U.S. dollar. The U.S. is the largest trading nation, and because of its large economy and stable political environment, one of the safest and easiest places to invest. Therefore, foreigners find the dollar an attractive asset to hold and an easy one to buy and sell. There are, however, some problems with this arrangement. The value of the dollar depends on the strength of the U.S. position in world trade and on the wisdom of American domestic economic policy. Both of these factors have come into question in recent years. The amount of international reserves that are available depends on the willingness of the Federal Reserve to tolerate large dollar balances in the hands of foreigners whose use of that money will follow their own interests and not those of the U.S. The Fed thus may not be willing to provide additional liquidity to the market in the event of a world monetary crisis, and we could conceivably have a replay of the crisis of 1929. Additionally, as the world banker, the U.S. earns the banker's profits, called seigniorage, that comes from providing short-term, liquid assets in exchange for longer term, less liquid ones. That one of the richest countries in the world should earn these profits strikes many nations, particularly the poorest ones, as being unjust.

In the 1970's the U.S. was accused of providing the system with excessive amounts of dollars and thus causing world inflation. Though there may be some truth to this claim, it rests on a couple of assumptions that may not be entirely correct. The first assumption is that the single cause of world-wide inflation is the increase in world liquidity. This monetarist explanation of inflation does not do justice to the complexity of the situation. The tremendous increase in the prices of oil and some other primary goods in the 1970's set off part of the inflation and generated expectations of continuing price increases that are hard to counteract. The result of not ratifying these primary price increases and the subsequent expectations with increases in the world money supply would have been even more serious recessions than the world experienced over this period. The second assumption is that a system with greater flexibility in exchange rates needs less liquidity than one with less flexibility. The shift from fixed to flexible exchange rates may, in fact, have required a higher level of international reserves. Since there is no fixed parity for speculators to rally around, central bankers may well need to intervene more in markets to introduce a limited kind of stability, and thus may need higher reserve balances. This need is probably also increased by the higher level of international capital mobility that has accompanied more flexible exchange rates. It is better to control this mobility by stabilizing interest rates than by reimposing the capital export controls of the old system, but interest rate stability may also involve more intervention in credit markets.

U.S. fiscal policy in the 1980's has created a new set of problems. The huge federal budget deficits, coupled with a concern for controlling inflation, have led to very high interest rates in the U.S. The need to finance the deficits has led to high levels of borrowing by the U.S. in world capital markets and a significant overvaluation of the dollar. This has increased the debt burden of the poor countries who must service debts with high interest rates and denominated in expensive dollars. In addition, it has become very expensive for the poor countries to import the intermediate and capital goods that they need to develop their economies. The large American budget deficits are doing real long-run harm to both the poor countries and to the American economy. Serious efforts should be made to reduce the deficits before the problems get out of hand.

The dangers of relying on a single key country to manage the level of world liquidity have impressed many countries. As a result, many nations have begun to diversify their international reserve balances—adding holdings of German and Japanese money, IMF-provided assets (called Special Drawing Rights or SDR's), and even British pounds and gold, to their dollar reserves. This diversification frees the system somewhat from dependence on the U.S., and thus introduces some additional confidence and stability into the system. However, it makes the management of the system more difficult, because it diffuses responsibility. Which of the key countries should be the lender of last resort in a crisis? Or should the IMF function as a kind of world central bank?

When SDR's (sometimes also called "paper gold") were invented in 1968, the intention was that some day they would take the place of national monies and gold as the principle reserve asset. Reliance on SDR's would have several advantages for both rich countries and poor ones. The rich nations would be freed to concentrate their monetary policies on domestic problems, and the quantity of international liquidity would be tied to the requirements of international transactions rather than the wishes of a single actor in the system. The seigniorage would be earned by the IMF, not by a rich country, and could then be used to provide aid to the poor nations. For this last reason, the poor countries have advocated increased importance for the SDR. The rich countries have not yet been willing to move in this direction for several reasons. Most rich nations are unwilling to cede to the IMF the amount of power necessary for it to function as a central bank. Decisions about world liquidity would have to be made either by some appointed elite of international bureaucrats, or else they would be left at the mercy of the rather cumbersome IMF voting procedure. Voting strength in the IMF is determined by the volume of a country's trade, so that the U.S. and the E.E.C. dominate the proceedings. If the rich countries cannot agree, there could be a political paralysis. There also seems to be some desire among the rich countries to hang on to the benefits of key country status: namely, the seigniorage. The U.S. is frightened at the prospect of a massive attempt to convert dollars into SDR's, and the E.E.C. is trying to develop a European monetary unit that would tie their currencies together and also serve as an alternative to both the dollar and the SDR. In spite of these political problems, however, we hold that the economic advantages of a system based on the SDR are sufficient to justify its adoption.

The growing amounts of debt carried by some of the poorer countries are a matter of great concern under the current system. The increases in energy and other prices in the last decade have come too rapidly for the poorer countries to make an adequate adjustment. Consequently, they have to borrow large amounts just to stay even with their previous levels of imports. Most of this borrowing has been arranged through the private sector, mostly the large American commercial banks, and this development has imposed some discipline on the process. Most of the loans have gone to the larger and faster growing poor countries that have good prospects for increasing their exports enough over the long run to pay back the loans. As a result, it seems unlikely that a major default by any of these nations would trigger a world liquidity crisis. However, this private mechanism also has some disadvantages. The large, private, rich-country lenders can acquire a great deal of influence over poor country domestic economic policy as a result of these loans, and it is more than likely that this influence will be exercised for the benefit of the lender and the lender's country rather than the borrower. The lenders naturally favor stable, market-oriented governments which provide the lenders with security about the loans but may be insensitive to the needs of their poorer citizens and to demands for political and civil rights. This is one of the reasons why the U.S. ends up supporting many right-wing authoritarian governments with poor human rights records in the Third World. Though this is in the short-run interest of the U.S., in the long run it earns us the hatred of the dissident elements who may eventually come to power as they did in Nicaragua and Iran. This private lending system also shuts out of the market the very poorest countries, which also face serious difficulties in making the transition to higher energy prices. Increases in direct foreign aid in the form of grants, preferably by multilateral agencies, are needed to assist the nations that are too poor to get loans and to help the others to limit their outstanding foreign debt. As oil prices assume a more predictable path, this problem should be alleviated.

Before we leave the subject of international monetary affairs, we must address the problems connected with foreign aid. This is a large subject, and we can only offer some principles. The U.S. official development assistance program has many problems. First, the program is not very large in com-parison to the size of the U.S. economy, and under the Reagan administration seems likely to shrink further. The U.S. loses credibility with Third World nations because of the niggardly attitude in this area, as well as foregoing many opportunities to assist the poor meaningfully. The size of the program should be increased. Second, American aid tends to respond to political considerations more than to assessments of true need. Aid is directed in the largest amounts to those countries that we perceive to hold the "correct" ideological positions with respect to U.S. foreign policy. Many very poor nations are thus cut off from our aid. Aid should be based primarily on considerations of need, with the effectiveness of the recipient nations' internal development policies also taken into account. This problem could be dealt with by directing more aid through multilateral and private agencies where political considerations are much less important than they are in the bilateral aid programs. Finally, our aid is usually used to support the urban industrial sector of the recipient's economy. Thus we do not succeed in providing very many jobs for the money that we spend, and the poorest, most traditional sector of the economy receives very little benefit. The problems of an industrial economy, particularly the problems associated with rapid urbanization, are made worse as a result of this strategy. If more of the aid were channeled through private agencies, such as the Church World Service, we would be more effective in reaching the poorest segments of the population without creating many of the problems of modernization.

## Poverty Within Third World Countries

Our discussion thus far has concentrated on changes in the pattern of international economic activity that would make it easier for the underde-veloped countries to increase their aggregate levels of income. It is very important that Christians work for these changes in the world economic order, since they are preconditions for the alleviation of much of the poverty and hunger in the world as well as for improved political and cultural relationships between rich countries and poor. But these changes in the economic order are not sufficient to achieve the reduction in poverty that we seek. Many of the necessary reforms are political and cultural changes that must be undertaken within the poor countries themselves. There are limits to our ability as First World Christians to accomplish these changes. Nevertheless, as responsible members of the world community, we should use whatever influence we have, particularly amongst our Christian brothers and sisters in the Third World, to bring about some of these changes.

But first, a word of caution. Development economists have observed, very perceptively, that no two countries have gone from underdeveloped to developed status in the same way. Each country is unique in terms of its natural endowment, its history, its religion, its customs, and its economic, political, and cultural institutions. We should not expect that newly developing countries will follow our pattern of development in every respect. Nor should we want them to. The style of living that we have evolved calls for such intensive use of natural resources that it cannot be duplicated on a worldwide scale, and, indeed, it will not be possible for us to continue living this way indefinitely. The problems of an industrial society are serious and difficult, and we have not succeeded in solving all of them in a satisfactory manner, so we should be careful about wishing them on others. Furthermore, our pattern of development is probably not appropriate to many countries with different histories and cultures.

What internal policies could help the poor countries to deal with poverty? First, the opportunities for the training and education of the masses of the population should be increased. Knowledge is a resource of great value in increasing productivity and well-being. It also has the advantage of not being exhaustible. Christian missions have been an important tool in spreading education in the poor countries, and there is an obvious connection between the Christian attitude of stewardship of creation and the increase of knowledge about that creation. But the job of educating the masses systematically is probably too big to be undertaken entirely by missionaries, and so Third World governments must also undertake a major portion of the task.

The poverty problem can also be addressed by a wider and more equal distribution of the ownership of natural resources and capital. Concentration of productive wealth too often leads to extravagant consumption by the wealthy elite, and the marshalling of resources in large-scale, capital intensive projects that do not create many jobs for the poor. A wider distribution of wealth will lead to the adoption of smaller-scale, more labor-intensive technology more oriented toward production for local needs. It also would more nearly fulfill the ideal of family stewardship over the productive resources that the family uses to make its own living.

Racial and ethnic discrimination leads to a reduction in the productivity of an economy. The class that is the object of discrimination is cut off from opportunities to develop the talents and gifts of its members. Since they are unable to engage in free economic intercourse with the rest of the community, their ability to provide for themselves and practice stewardship is compromised. We should therefore seek the end of such discrimination as an approach to ending poverty, if for no other reason. The true understanding of Christianity should help to end discrimination, though it is unfortunately the case that in many lands where Christianity is well known, such discrimination continues. Perhaps our witness in this area would be most effective if we begin our attack on racism at home.

One way to assure that the poor are treated fairly by the political system is to see that they are politically enfranchised and organized. If the poor form a coherent political constituency, it is less likely that their needs will be ignored by the government. The difficulty is that political organization requires economic resources, and the poor need their economic resources for more urgent purposes than politics. Yet we must not forget the successes of the civil rights movement here in the U.S., which directed much of its effort toward political activity, with substantial and gratifying results. When the church undertakes to help the poor politically in Third World countries, it sometimes gets into political trouble with the ruling regime or even with its constituency back home. But the church has large resources of good will that it can use towards these ends before real trouble sets in. As First World Christians, we must become more receptive to the idea of the church becoming involved in Third World political struggles.

We have tried to present a realistic picture of international economic relationships, particularly as they affect the stewardship of the earth and the care of the poor. Because we have been realistic, our answers to these problems have often been complex and ambiguous. But we must not allow our frustration with this complexity and ambiguity to stifle our involvement in these affairs. We must, as Christians, see to it that the world economic system becomes more of a global economic community for the good of us all and the glory of God.

## Resources

Balassa, B., ed. 1978. *Changing Patterns in Foreign Trade and Payments*. 3rd ed., NY: Norton.

Barnet, R. J., and R. E. Muller. 1974. *Global Reach*. NY: Simon & Schuster.

Beckmann, D. M. 1981. *Where Faith and Economics Meet*. Minneapolis: Augsburg.

Jegen, M. E., and C. K. Wilber, eds. 1979. *Growth With Equity*. NY: Paulist Press.

*Justice in the International Economic Order*. 1980. Grand Rapids: Calvin College.

Kindleberger, C. P., and B. Herrick. 1977. *Economic Development*. 3rd ed., NY: McGraw-Hill.

Lindert, P. H., and C. P. Kindleberger. 1983. *International Economics.* 7th ed., Homewood: Richard D. Irwin.

Schumacher, E. F. 1973. *Small is Beautiful.* NY: Harper & Row.

Simon, A. 1984. *Bread for the World.* rev. ed., Grand Rapids: Eerdmans.

Wolterstorff, N. 1983. *Until Justice and Peace Embrace.* Grand Rapids: Eerdmans.

# Chapter XVI
# Taking Stock — Again

*In search of a living we've left our poor land,*
*Scattered over the country like seeds in the wind,*
*And I search and I labor, God's purpose to find,*
*And I'm safe in his love all surrounding.*
*But more and more urgent the memories cull,*
*As the years swift and swifter unceasingly roll,*
*And the old songs still offer their wings to my soul,*
*To return to the high hills and mountains.*
　　　　　*Jean Ritchie (c. 1962)*

## Introduction

The reader will recall that we began this volume by taking stock, that is, by describing and analyzing the current state of affairs in economic theory and practice. We observed that economic aspects of human life are caught up in a series of major difficulties, such as the increasing distance between economic theory and economic life, the apparent lack of concern for the way exhaustible resources are being used, the growing disparity between rich and poor peoples, the problems of international trade, inflation, unemployment, economic rigidity, and the like. The election of Margaret Thatcher in Britain and Ronald Reagan in the United States testify not only to the uneasiness of the peoples of these countries with regard to such economic problems, but also to their hope that solutions, or at least a lessening of the severity of the problems, lie in the direction of adopting of different economic policies.

We have emphasized the all-pervasiveness of economic concerns in all of human life. The problems we have described and the analysis which we have suggested lie very close to where most of individual and institutional life takes place. As members of the human community, all of us find it very difficult to pursue any kind of human activity without being confronted, often directly, by immediate and demanding economic concerns. Our discussions of a number of these wide-ranging issues in this book are evidence of our concern for this all-pervasiveness. Now that we have treated these in some detail in the various chapters, it may be well to end our discussion with a few summary remarks, attempting once again to focus attention on the central issues which have been our concern throughout the work. This is the point of this final chapter.

## Normativity

It is apparent by now that the concept of normativity is a central theme in our attempt to sketch the outlines of a distinctively Christian perspective on economic theory, and it is well that we review the concept. We have spoken repeatedly, sometimes explicity and often implicitly, of normative structures and of norms for human activity. We have emphasized that the distinctively Christian perspective which we bring to economic analysis requires the frank and unashamed recognition of these norms and normative structures.

Central to our proposed analysis of economic aspects of human activities is the idea that the analysis must see this activity as being the human response to God's call for obedient living. Thus we are concerned not only with determining, as best we can, the essential characteristics of such an obedient life, but also with recognizing that people are faced with the necessity of choosing between either an obedient and therefore good response, or a disobedient and therefore evil response. It is the possibility of the human response being either good or evil, in the sense just described, which makes the concept of normativity so important.

Such is not the case, by way of contrast, in a situation governed by what may be called physical law. In an informal way, at least, we are all aware of laws of gravitation which govern the way the moon orbits the earth. In following its prescribed course the moon is not acting normatively in that, presumably, it is not being asked to make a choice between being obedient to the law of gravity or ignoring it. Normativity comes in only when such a choice is possible.

The concept of normativity thus is a central issue in our analysis. It is not so much the fact that choices themselves have to be made. After all, the making of choices is an important facet of neoclassical economics as well. Rather, the important idea is the choice between obedience and disobedience to the call of God for right living. Our Christian perspective on economic theory then, comes down to asserting that the root source of economic problems as our society experiences them is the fact that in so many ways the human response has been one of disobedience, while the true understanding of economic harmony and stability, where these are observed, lies in recognizing these to be the result of obedient responses by those involved. If we have done our work well and consistently, this theme has consistently informed our analysis of the family, the firm, the union, the government, and the like. This theme surely is basic to our definition of economics as being a study of the response of people to God's call to be good stewards of the creation.

Two final comments on the idea of normativity are needed. The first is that our basic stance in this regard requires acceptance of God's revelation to the human race, both in the written word and in Jesus Christ as the Incarnate Word, as a true and valid source of knowledge. Any specificity concerning the normative structure of an institution such as the family or concerning norms for individual human behavior to which we have referred is based on this revelation. We hope that our analysis of existing economic theory has persuaded the reader that an analogous stance characterizes the work of all economists, and that in this sense no theorist's work can be value-free. It is important that such basic stances, whether on the part of a neoclassicist or a positive empiricist or anyone else, be exposed for all to see.

The second comment is that this basic stance requires a serious recognition of the presence and the effect of sin in the lives of people. Sin, after all, entered the world as we know it through a very basic act of disobedience, and a true understanding of the human response must recognize this fact. On the other hand, the redemptive sacrifice of Christ Jesus makes possible, already in this earthly life, a beginning of obedient living, and therefore we may expect to see evidence of this fact in the lives of people, including economic aspects. We hope our analysis has pointed out a way to this obedience.

## Stewardship

Beginning already with our attempt to define the proper scope of economic analysis, we have referred often to the concept of stewardship. We have said that economics is the study of the response of people to God's call to be good stewards of the creation, and noted such a call is clearly normative in that the response can be either one of obedience or disobedience. Since this is such an important concept in our work, sometimes explicitly and often implicitly, it is well that we call attention to it once more.

Paul G. Schrotenboer, in an excellent little booklet entitled *Man in God's World* [1967], discusses at some length what it means for man to be God's steward in this world. The central idea, even of the term *steward* itself as used in the Bible, is that of being a manager or an administrator. Schrotenboer says:

> In the broadest sense the idea refers to man's administration of the entire world which God has given him to manage. The creation account in Genesis clearly states that God placed man over the world to rule it in obedience to his Maker. That man as the vice-regent of God is the administrator of the world was not the mere notion of the earliest and most primitive peoples; it was the heartbeat of faith of the Hebrew people of God who got the idea by divine revelation. [1967, p.4]

Again he says:

> In Paradise God said: 'Have dominion.' This command was also
> a benediction. Law and blessing blended in God's first address to
> his creature. Here God put man in his place as ruler under God
> and told him what to do to attain well-being and peace. [p.5]

Much more could be said, of course, but it is plain that many things flow
from such a fundamental starting point. Three things specifically may be mentioned. First, there is no room for autonomous man in such a scheme. Man's
will and actions must reflect those of the One who has assigned him to his office as manager. Second, there is no room for pursuit of self-interest but only
the interest, again, of the One who has made the assignment. Third, there being no room for self-interest, there must be room for the central idea of *service*,
service both to God and to fellow human beings.

The recitation of these three points, which we take to be central to the purpose of man's life on earth, does much to explain why we have written as we
have and why our proposed analysis proceeds as it does. Once again the idea of
normativity is present, inasmuch as man's response to the assignment thus
given to him by God may be either appropriate or inappropriate, obedient or
disobedient, good or evil. This is the organizing principle of our analysis: that
the most effective way to look at human activity, particularly the economic aspects of this activity, is to see it in the light of such a fundamental view of the
purpose of man's existence. This approach explains, too, the grounds on which
we are critical of much of existing economic theory.   More should be said
about the central idea of service. As Schrotenboer points out:

> The office of man is his *position-in-relationship*. His position, as
> it relates to God, constitutes him a *servant* who is called to obedi-
> ence. As it relates to fellow man it makes man a *guardian*, who
> must bring his charge to maturity. As it relates to the world it
> constitutes man a *steward* who must faithfully exercise
> dominion in the name of God. [1967, p. 5]

He continues:

> God intended that man's life in its entirety would be service of
> God. To that service God appointed him, for that service he gave
> him the gifts he needs, and of that service God calls him to ac-
> count [p.6].

Surely part of that service, an aspect of God's call to be a steward, is that of
*developing* the creation. Response to this call can be, once again, either one of
obedience or one of disobedience. The obedient response will take into
account, insofar as possible, the will of God as it was intended to be worked out
through the lives of men. A very clear and necessary component of this
development must be conservation or sustainability. No direction of

development may be allowed which in any way threatens the continued existence of life on earth. Therefore, for the most part, development of the creation must be directed away from satisfaction of sinfully motivated wants and directed toward satisfaction of legitimate needs. Only in this way can we expect to experience the peace and stability in life which God intended. The problems which we experience, including those addressed in this book, stem from the disobedient response to God's call to be servants. That is our claim.

## Free To Serve

Everyone wants freedom. Business men want economic freedom. Citizens want political freedom. Believers want religious freedom. Teachers want academic freedom, and all men want personal freedom.

This is understandable. Man has an essential dignity and a native claim to liberty. He was made in God's image. He was not meant to be a slave, and he can never be happy in bonds.

This the Christian knows better than any man, and that is why he hates all tyranny. It is the reason for his uncompromising opposition to political dictators, economic collectivisms, and coercive religious establishments. It accounts for his resistance to monopolistic education and programs of thought control. It is the reason why he defends human liberty on all fronts. [H. Stob 1954, p. 35]

In many ways, sometimes apparent but mostly subtle, we have been concerned with human freedom in this book. The very phrase *free enterprise* entails some notion of freedom, and depending on what that notion is, a free-enterprise, market-oriented economic system can represent either a misdirected, egocentric, disobedient response to God's call for service, or it can be structured so as to constitute an economic system which not only permits but encourages an appropriately obedient response to this call.

The picture of autonomous, economic, rational man single-mindedly pursuing maximal self-interest, as sketched by the current economic theorists, assumes an individual freedom of the sort that must be rejected. Freedom, as Stob says, is never merely *freedom from* something; it is always *freedom to something*, the freedom to meet one's obligations. The apostle Paul, in Gal. 5:13, clearly and succinctly provides the norm in this regard: "You, my brothers, were called to be free. But do not use your freedom to indulge the sinful nature; rather, serve one another in love." (NIV)

This kind of freedom, in our view, is likely to be stifled by an economic system which features centralized planning and collectivist control. To remove from individuals, and even from institutions such as the family, not only the possibility but also the necessity of freely making decisions which, in obedience to God's command, constitute proper stewardship, is to strike at the heart of the appropriate human response. It effectively destroys the possibility of good stewardship and reduces men to living in the bonds of slavery. For this reason, in spite of our critical analysis of the way in which the market economics of the United States and the United Kingdom operate, we continue to see such economic systems as having the greatest potential for giving people a framework within which to live obediently.

## Judgment and Challenge

There are two matters to which, in this final paragraph, we direct the reader's attention. The first is one of criticism and judgment, while the second is one of challenges and new directions.

We have in these pages leveled heavy criticism against much of present economic theory and current modes of economic living. Our criticism has been substantive in at least two ways. First, we think that present economic theory does *not* present either a clear view or a right understanding of economic aspects of human existence, and does not lay bare the root causes of economic strife and difficulty. It cannot, therefore, point in the direction of a life of obedience as the right way to correct these problems and to experience a life of peace. Our own analysis, by way of contrast, sees these economic difficulties as a judgment of God on a disobedient people. The ignoring of norms and normative structures can, in our view, lead only to continuing judgment in the form of more economic disintegration and chaos. Unless there is a recognition of the root source of the problem, accompanied by a willingness of people to make proper obedience a way of life, only such continued judgment may rightly be expected. The evidence, we think, is clear, and the direction in which a solution is to be found is plain.

Herein lies the challenge of this book and the new directions which it advocates. We have seriously addressed the whole academic community whose life work is the development of economic theory and the making of economic analyses. We challenge all of these practitioners of current theory to examine their own fundamental assumptions and basic premises which lie at the foundations of their work, to assess these in the light of our work, and to consider our stance as a viable alternative, as a new and exciting paradigm for research in the discipline.

For those who agree with the analysis we have made we ask that our study be viewed as laying the groundwork for the development of a genuinely Christian perspective on economic theory. Clearly we have only sketched the rough outlines of such a perspective, with emphasis on the basic principles which will undergird the work. Our hope and expectation is that our work is sufficiently specific and concrete so that it suggests well-defined lines and areas of continued research and development of this perspective.

For students of economics we hope we have provided a challenging and enlightening alternative to much of what the standard elementary economics textbooks provide. We challenge each student to consider carefully his or her own stance relative to the basic questions we have posed and to the answers we have given.

Finally, we challenge the-whole human community to reassess, in the light of what we have written, its response to God's call to obedience and stewardly living. While not everything we have written will be equally accessible to all who are so concerned, surely we have throughout these pages included specific suggestions and hints as to how the economic concerns of our daily lives ought to be addressed. We have considered in some detail what the basic structure of the family is, how the family ought to live, and what its pattern of consumption should be, if it is to experience the shalom of God. We have commented extensively on the importance of work in the lives of people and emphasized that daily work must not be seen, in the language of the economists, as a disutility, but must be viewed as having the potential for being a satisfying component of the obedient life. Likewise, owners of the firm or enterprise must recognize their responsibilities for meaningful work and responsible use of time. Responsible use of resources must be a high priority. It is in these directions that economic peace and stability lie. In the same manner labor organizations can do much to redirect the concerns and interests of their members away from self-centered materialism toward the ideal of service, and thus foster a greater measure of contentment.

Our analysis of the role and significance of voluntary associations, particularly the church, in the economic structure of our society makes possible a critical reassessment of that role, and points out directions for these organizations to follow in order to develop improved channels through which people may serve God and each other. Neglect of such opportunities can only lead to an impoverishment of human relationships.

And, finally, our intensive look at the role of government in the economic aspects of national and international life has made clear what we think that legitimate role is, and what the government rightly must do in order to promote an economic shalom. Here, too, we see a failure to obey as being the root cause of much difficulty, while proper obedience has as its result the economic peace and stability which all seek.

We believe, then, that in these pages we have developed the main lines of a Christian perspective on economic analysis which gives rise to a better understanding of economic aspects of human life, one which identifies the root causes of economic problems, and indicates that only through the avenue of reformation and renewed commitment to a life of obedience can the problems we described at the outset be successfully solved. Our prayer is that the gracious Spirit of the Lord may bring this initial effort to fruition.

# Resources

Schrotenboer, P. G.. 1967. *Man in God's World*. Toronto: Association for the Advancement of Christian Scholarship.

Stob, H. 1954. The Liberty of Man. *La Revue Reformee*. 5.17: 35-47.

# TORONTO STUDIES IN THEOLOGY